World Geography

McDougal Littell
A HOUGHTON MIFFLIN COMPANY

Consultants

Mary Lou McCloskey, 2002–2003 President of TESOL, and President of Educo (Atlanta, Georgia), is an international consultant, adjunct professor at Georgia State University, and author of texts, program materials, and standards in the field of English for Speakers of Other Languages. A former elementary school teacher in multilingual, multicultural classrooms, she has worked with teachers, teacher educators, and departments and ministries of education on five continents and in 31 of the United States. She was awarded the 1999 Moss Chair of Excellence in English at the University of Memphis, the TESOL D. Scott Enright Service Award, and the Georgia TESOL Professional Service Award. Her publications include *Visions: Language, Literature, Content; Voices in Literature; Making Connections; Integrating English;* and *Teaching Language, Literature, and Culture.*

Lydia Stack is currently an Administrator in the San Francisco Unified School District, where she directs ESL professional development, secondary ESL programs, and world languages. From 1992 to 1997, she coordinated the mentor teacher and beginning support and assessment programs. Previously she served as ESL department head at Newcomer High School in San Francisco. She has also taught courses in second language acquisition at San Francisco State University and Stanford University. Ms. Stack helped to write the California English Language Development Standards and was a reviewer for the TESOL K–12 ESL Standards. Currently she is chair of the TESOL Pre-K–12 Teacher Education Standards Committee. Her publications include *Visions; Voices in Literature; Making Connections;* and *WordWays.* In 1991–1992, she was President of TESOL.

Nancy Siddens, McDougal Littell Consulting Editor, English for Speakers of Other Languages, is a native speaker of English, fluent in Spanish, and has dabbled in Portuguese, French, Italian, German, Russian, Japanese, and Guaraní! She studied in Spain, was a member of the Peace Corps in Paraguay, developed language instruction videos in Mexico, and has traveled on five continents. Her credentials include a B.A. in Spanish Literature and an M.A. in ESOL. She has developed educational materials for language learning since 1989 and has worked on programs for foreign language teaching, bilingual education, and ESOL. She consults with all disciplines at McDougal Littell to ensure that materials developed in content areas address the needs of English learners.

Writer

Elizabeth A. Kaplan is a freelance writer and editor with a strong interest in languages and language-learning. She earned her BA in linguistics from Cornell University. Ms. Kaplan has also written chapters for an ESL biology textbook and ESL teacher's materials for various subjects.

ISBN-13: 978-0-618-45491-4   ISBN-10: 0-618-45491-8

Printed in the United States of America.

13 14 15   1410   17 16 15 14

4500493630

Introduction

Social Studies for Learners of English: Teaching Strategies

Lesson Plans and Activity Sheets

Who Needs This Book?

If you have a class that is made up partly or entirely of English learners, this book is for you. If you have little training or experience teaching English learners, this book provides clear and practical techniques for dramatically improving students' comprehension. If you are a trained, experienced teacher of English learners, this book outlines methods and strategies that may be new to you.

Why Use This Book?

Teachers and administrators now agree that instruction methods must be based on solid research. The techniques in this book have been developed by experienced researchers and published in reputable journals. They have also been field-tested in a variety of classrooms.

Publications and seminars on how to teach English learners can be helpful. However, many of them are designed either for the reading classroom or for general "content area" learning, including science and mathematics. Not only does this book provide specific strategies for teaching social studies concepts, it also gives *customized, step-by-step instructions* for teaching every lesson in *World Geography*.

What's in This Book?

Modified Lesson Plans for English Learners has three parts:

- **Introduction** The introduction explains the latest and most important research on teaching English learners in the social studies classroom. The introduction gives you a better understanding of what English learners' specific needs are and how you can help them succeed. (page T1)
- **Teaching Strategies** Dozens of proven strategies for teaching social studies to English learners are provided, along with clear explanations of how to apply them in your classroom. (page T9)
- **Lesson Plans** Section-by-section lesson plans show you how and when to use the teaching strategies when teaching the content in *World Geography*. (page 2)

How Can *World Geography* Be Customized for English Learners?

The authors and editors of *World Geography* have created an array of support materials to help you apply the Three Principles for Success when teaching your English learners. See the next page for more information.

Three Principles for Success

1. Increase comprehensibility
2. Increase interaction
3. Increase thinking/study skills

World Geography: Components that increase . . .	
1. Comprehensibility: improve understanding through language scaffolding and through verbal and nonverbal support	
Print Support	Audiovisual Support
• *Multilanguage Glossary* **English** • *Reading Study Guide Workbook* • *In-Depth Resources: Building Vocabulary* • *Reading Toolkit* • *eEdition Plus Online:* hypertext vocabulary support • *ClassZone:* chapter summary transcripts **Spanish** • *Reading Study Guide Workbook* • *Access for Students Acquiring English: Spanish Translations* • *eEdition Plus Online:* hypertext vocabulary support • *ClassZone:* chapter summary transcripts	**English Audio** • *Reading Study Guide Audio CDs* • *eEdition Plus Online:* vocabulary pronunciation, chapter summaries **Spanish Audio** • *Reading Study Guide Audio CDs* • *eEdition Plus Online:* vocabulary definitions, chapter summaries **Visuals** • *World Geography Posters* • *Reading Toolkit* • *Transparencies: Map, Cultures Around the World* • Video Series: *Geographic Voyageur* • *Power Presentations CD-ROM* • *eEdition CD-ROM:* visual animations
2. Interaction: promote communication with pair and group cooperative activities	**3. Thinking and/or Study Skills**
• *Teacher's Edition* • *Modified Lesson Plans for English Learners* • *In-Depth Resources: GeoWorkshops* • *Integrated Assessment*	• *Critical Thinking Transparencies* • *Strategies for Test Preparation* • *Test Practice Transparencies* • *Writing for Social Studies*

Adapted from Number 6, From Theory to Practice, 1999. The Region XIV
Comprehensive Center at Educational Testing Service and used with permission.

Social Studies and English Learners

Secondary learners of English are faced with a great challenge. In a few short years, they must learn both academic English and the challenging content of their academic curriculum. The McDougal Littell *Modified Lesson Plans for English Learners* help teachers with that challenge, both because learning the concepts of social studies is essential for success and because, when effective approaches are used, teaching language through content is effective for development in both areas.

Researchers estimate that it will take five to seven years of high-quality instruction for English learners to perform, on average, at the level of native speakers (Thompson & Collier, 2003). English learners in secondary schools obviously do not have five to seven years until they reach that level of English proficiency to learn essential social studies concepts! Nor would waiting for English proficiency provide the most efficient language learning, as most experts agree that the best way to learn academic English is by using it to learn. To do this, teachers must provide an academic environment that makes the language comprehensible to learners through careful application of scaffolding strategies to support learning.

Importance of Scaffolding What is scaffolding? When workers construct a tall building, they often erect scaffolding—supportive structures around the building—to enable them to do their construction work. As the building progresses, scaffolding that is no longer needed is removed. Likewise, teachers provide useful tools and strategies to support learners in developing new language and concepts. And as students become proficient and independent, they begin to use tools and strategies for learning on their own as teachers guide them toward even higher achievement.

Teaching language through social studies content is important and effective because the content provides language that is academic, age-appropriate, relevant, necessary, and (with appropriate support) accessible for English learners. The meaningful content of the high school curriculum makes language learning more interesting, motivating, and communicative for secondary learners of English (Cantoni-Harvey, 1987; Crandall, 1993; Mohan, 1986; Short, 1994).

Audience for Modified Lesson Plans
These Modified Lesson Plans are designed for two groups:

1. social studies teachers whose classes include learners of English at the early intermediate level and above, and

2. social studies teachers of special classes designed for learners of English at the intermediate level and above.

Description of Secondary Early Intermediate English Learners

This description of early intermediate English learners was developed by the San Francisco Unified School District.

Listening & Speaking

English learners are understood when speaking, but may have some inconsistent use of standard English grammatical forms and sounds. They can ask and answer questions using phrases or simple sentences. They retell familiar stories and short conversations by using appropriate gestures, expressions, and illustrative objects. They recite familiar poems, songs, and simple stories. They can restate and execute multi-step oral directions. They restate in simple sentences the main idea of oral presentations of subject matter content. They can prepare and deliver short oral presentations.

Reading

English learners produce English phonemes [the smallest phonetic unit that can convey a distinction in meaning], including long and short vowels and initial and final consonants. They can read simple vocabulary, phrases, and sentences independently. While orally reading their own writing or simple content-area material, English learners demonstrate their knowledge of English grammar, usage, and word choice by recognizing and correcting some errors they make when speaking or reading aloud. Students recognize obvious cognates in phrases, simple sentences, literature, and content area. They use their knowledge of English morphemes [a word or word element that cannot be divided into smaller meaningful parts], phonics, and syntax to decode and interpret the meaning of some unfamiliar words. They read simple paragraphs and passages independently. They recognize simple idioms, analogies, and figures of speech in literature and realize that words sometimes have multiple meanings. They read their own writing of narrative and expository text aloud with appropriate pacing, intonation, and expression. They use a dictionary to find the meaning of unknown vocabulary.

Writing

After listening to text read by the teacher, English learners can write simple sentences about these historical events or characters. They can follow a model given by the teacher to independently write short paragraphs of at least four sentences. English learners consistently use common verbs, nouns, and high-frequency modifiers when writing simple sentences. They can write brief responses to selected readings, and they are able to use the writing process to produce independent writing that is understood when read, but may include an inconsistent use of standard grammatical forms. (San Francisco Unified School District, 2000)

The Modified Lesson Plans will help teachers make the textbook accessible to English learners at the intermediate and advanced levels. They include many kinds of scaffolding.

For English learners at beginner and advanced beginner levels, we recommend that teachers of those students use materials at a lower reading level. An appropriate component of McDougal Littell's social studies programs is the *Reading Study Guide,* which is available in English and Spanish.

Basic Principles

Below are basic principles for teaching language through content upon which the strategies and activities in this book are based. Teachers are encouraged always to keep these principles in mind in classroom planning, instruction, and interactions.

1. **What happens in the classroom must be *comprehensible* to learners of English.** Assess your learners' language levels (and ask assistance from ESOL specialists in assessments and expectations of learners in your classroom), and adapt your language input to your learners' levels. Ideally, your language should be at the "learning zone" where it is both understandable by your learners and is gauged to add to their knowledge by introducing new terms and concepts in ways that learners can come to understand them. How will you know when you are in this zone? You should frequently check your learners' comprehension as you teach, use the strategies provided in this book, and adjust your language and content input to keep it at a level where learners can stay with you.

   With multi-level classes, you will find that you need to provide input at several levels to keep all the students with you. In order to be comprehensible, you must know when your learners understand and when they don't. Your classes must be highly interactive. The interactive strategies and activities provided in this book have been chosen for their effectiveness in eliciting feedback from learners.

2. **Learning should be interesting, meaningful, relevant, and purposeful.** Effective learning always starts *where learners are.* Introduce new concepts by making connections between what learners are learning and experiences in their own lives. Though they are learning the English language, and may also be new to the content, English learners have rich cultural and life experience that they bring to the classroom.

   Find out what English learners already know that is related to what they are learning and use this knowledge to build bridges to the unknown. This will both assist learning and build learners' confidence in themselves. Building confidence is perhaps even more important than the specific learning in encouraging learners to stay in school and keep trying. Point out the relevance of the content to their lives in the present and in the future. Communicate your own apparent and infectious interest in and enthusiasm for the content you are helping students learn.

3. **Learning must be both active and interactive.** Learners acquire language most effectively when they need to use it. Make sure that in your classroom, learners play active roles and *use* the language and content that is being presented. Provide exercises, games, role-plays, projects, and hands-on map work that require students to use the language of the content.

4. **Build background.** Sometimes learners may not have important background information to understand concepts you are developing. They may not know basic facts of U.S. history or where countries are in the world. When beginning a new topic, carefully check what learners know. If background knowledge is missing, you need to stop and help them build that background.

5. **Teach strategies for learner independence.** Researchers have found that effective learning of language through content involves developing metacognitive strategies to foster independent learning. To help learners develop independence, this book will help you model, teach, monitor, and review learners' use of effective learning strategies.

6. **Increase thinking/study skills.** Many English learners need explicit teaching to develop thinking skills and "thinking language." Chamot and O'Malley developed a method to focus instruction on higher order thinking tasks (discovery, synthesis, evaluation). You can encourage high-order thinking by asking open-ended questions (e.g., What would happen if . . . ?), modeling "thinking language" by thinking aloud, assessing learning in a manner/language consistent with instruction, explicitly teaching and reinforcing study skills and test-taking skills, and holding high expectations for learning for English learners.

7. **Teach both needed language and needed content.** When working with English learners, social studies teachers must be both language teachers and content teachers. Snow, Met, & Genesee (1989) describe a distinction between two types of language:

   - Content-obligatory language is the new social studies terms and structures needed for reading, writing, listening, and speaking about the content.

   - Content-compatible language is general language needed for communication about the content that can be taught naturally within the context of a particular subject matter.

   It is important for social studies teachers to "think language"—to look carefully at the language of the text and of discussions of the text and analyze what language learners need to think and talk and write about the content. At the same time, it is also important to "think content"—look carefully at the content and at learner performance, develop ways to present (and have learners apply) the most important concepts of the content that are comprehensible to learners. Keep in mind that English learners have all the same intellectual capabilities as their English-proficient peers, but they don't know the language yet. Find ways to keep cognitive content demanding while not going beyond learners' language capabilities.

Providing Comprehensible Input

In second-language learning, the role of comprehensible input is crucial (Krashen). This means linking language that is new with clues to its meaning that make the language (input) understandable (comprehensible). The following suggestions are provided to help social studies teachers make new content comprehensible to English learners.

1. **Face students.** Students need all the cues you can provide, including those from your mouth positions and facial expressions. Therefore, you should face students when you speak. You might choose, when possible, to switch from the board to the overhead projector to make it easier to face learners when writing and using visuals.

2. **Use gestures and realia.** Make rich use of gestures to add contextual information as you speak. Make conscious efforts to increase and exaggerate your use of gestures to communicate meaning. Whenever possible, use pictures or maps or objects that will help students be very clear on what you are talking about. Though your English learners are learning language, they can understand nonlinguistic representations as well as any student in the class, so their use helps them stay with you.

3. **Increase wait time.** Learners of a language need more time to process information than proficient speakers. Most teachers wait only about one second after a question (Rowe, 1969). Long et al. (1984) found that increasing wait time after questions

resulted in more complete answers by learners. In addition, increased wait time helps more learners stay in the conversation, even if they are not the ones to respond.

When you interact with learners of English, increase wait time and pause frequently to give learners time to process the language. When you ask questions in classes with English learners, wait a little longer before asking anyone to respond. Count slowly, 1, 2, 3, 4, 5 (adjust count to your students' language levels). This will ensure that everyone has time to think about what you have asked and to construct a response. Calling on a student too quickly can deny many students an opportunity to participate.

In addition, avoid overuse of the "ping pong" participant structure in which the teacher asks one student a question, that student responds, and then the teacher asks another student a question, and so forth. This structure provides individual learners with very few opportunities to actually use the language in interaction. Instead, use the many active learning and cooperative learning strategies included in this book to increase engagement and opportunity for English learners to acquire the language by using it.

4. **Stop to paraphrase often.** If, when you check comprehension, students don't understand what you are saying when you explain things one way, they may understand the second or third way. Include nonlinguistic information in your explanations whenever possible.

5. **Adapt your language as needed.** Explain or rephrase idioms and figurative language. Use fewer idioms with learners of English, and explain the idioms you use whenever needed. Don't assume that students understand figurative language; stop to explain it.

Use direct sentence structure. Active voice is easier to understand than passive voice.

Articulate carefully. Speakers of English in the United States generally blend many words together (e.g., we might say, "Jeet yet?" when inviting someone to join us for lunch). Speak naturally, but try to separate words so they can clearly be understood by English learners.

Adjust vocabulary. Though we encourage our students to use many synonyms when they write or speak for class, using too many different words with the same meaning may lead to overload for language learners. At first, stick with one term for a concept. Add synonyms slowly, when learners seem ready, and explain new terms when introducing them.

Paraphrase, demonstrate, act out, translate. When learners don't understand, don't hesitate to explain something in another way. Use different words, pictures, miming, gesturing—whatever it takes. And keep in mind that sometimes the fastest way to learn a new term is to get a translation. Don't hesitate to use your translation possibilities as available. Use a bilingual staff member, another student who can translate the term, a translation dictionary, or an online dictionary.

Point out key ideas and vocabulary in the content you cover. Help students choose the most important terms. These include key *content-obligatory* terms—terms students need to understand the content. They also include key *content-compatible* terms—English terms students need to understand the content, such as transition terms like *because, therefore, including,* or sequencing terms like *first, second, third.*)

Check comprehension frequently. Your comprehension-checking questions need not be answered by one student at a time. You might check comprehension by asking students to repeat your instructions, by asking students to clarify a concept with partners and listening in on a few, or by using one of the signaling techniques included in the strategies below.

Learning Strategies

Learning strategies are specific actions, behaviors, or steps taken by an English learner to enhance his or her own learning (Scarcella and Oxford, 1992). Rebecca Oxford (2001) has identified six major groups of learning strategies that help English learners acquire language.

1. **Cognitive strategies** help students manipulate the language through reasoning, analysis, note taking, summarizing, and synthesizing to develop stronger knowledge structures and to formally practice English structures and sounds.

2. **Metacognitive strategies** are used by English learners to identify their own learning preferences and needs, to plan tasks, to gather and organize materials, to arrange space to study, to monitor mistakes, and to evaluate both task success and learning strategy success.

3. **Memory-related strategies** help English learners link one concept or language item with another. Some memory-related strategies enable learners to learn and retrieve information in an orderly way, while others help with the retrieval of sounds (e.g., rhyming words), images (e.g., pictures), body movements, (e.g., nonverbal gestures) or location (e.g., part of a page).

4. **Compensatory strategies** help English learners fill in the gaps in their knowledge. These strategies include guessing from context in listening and reading, "talking around" a missing word, using a synonym, and using gestures to imply meaning.

5. **Affective strategies** such as identifying one's mood or anxiety level, talking about feelings, and rewarding oneself for good performance help English learners lower anxiety so that learning can take place.

6. **Social strategies** help English learners work with others and understand American culture as well as the English language. These strategies include asking questions to get information and verification, asking for clarification of confusing points, asking for help in doing a language task, and talking with native speakers of English.

Teaching the Text Backwards

One strategy to help English learners learn information from textbooks is **Teaching the Text Backwards.** The traditional teaching sequence is:

1. Read the text.

2. Answer the study questions at the end of the chapter.

3. Discuss the material in class.

4. Do selected applications based on the material.

This sequence is very difficult for many English learner students, who often read English with difficulty and may not have cultural or background knowledge necessary to completely understand the text. Instead, try this approach.

1. Do selected applications based on the material.

2. Discuss the material in class.

Adapted from Number 7, From Theory to Practice, 1999. The Region XIV Comprehensive Center at Educational Testing Service and used with permission.

3. Answer the study questions at the end of the chapter.

4. Read the text.

1st. Start by doing something that applies the material to be learned in a concrete, real-life way. The "applications and extensions" at the end of the chapter or in the teacher's guide are a good source of ideas. For English learners, this hands-on application puts the new material in context and increases comprehensibility. For example, in science, take a field trip to the planetarium early in the unit, not at the end; in social studies, interview families about what countries their ancestors came from before starting units on geography or immigration; in math, read opposing articles citing similar statistics before studying formulas; in computer literacy, struggle with preparing a simple document before learning terminology or practicing keyboarding skills.

2nd. Discuss the application and the related concepts in class. Ask students *what happened, why, what would happen if,* and so forth. Use the key vocabulary in the discussion, pointing to objects or demonstrating relationships to connect the new words and sentences to their meaning. Oral language is usually easier than textbook language for English learners to understand, and the discussion of a concrete activity teaches key vocabulary and concepts, activates prior knowledge, provides schema (the "big picture"), and models thinking skills.

3rd. Ask students to review the study questions at the end of the chapter to identify main ideas and to set a purpose for reading. Preview the chapter by looking at pictures and diagrams. Read the subheadings to show students how the chapter is organized and where they can expect to find specific information. These strategies increase comprehensibility and teach thinking and study skills.

4th. Lastly, have students read the text to find the answers to the most important study questions. Teachers can divide the chapter to reduce the amount of text each student reads and to increase understanding for key sections and model study skills. Graphic organizers and visuals can demonstrate key relationships in the content and increase comprehensibility and thinking skills.

The **Teach the Text Backwards** sequence also aids other students who are less skilled readers or who learn best through less traditional learning styles. It is a practical, consistent framework for teaching and learning into which additional ESOL strategies can be integrated.

The McDougal Littell *Modified Lesson Plans for English Learners* will help you address the challenge of teaching both the concepts of social studies and the language needed to discuss these concepts. With these materials, students will learn both academic English and the challenging content of the social studies curriculum.

References

Cantoni-Harvey, G. (1987). *Content-area language instruction: Approaches and strategies.* Reading, MA: Addison-Wesley.

Chamot, A. U., & O'Malley, J. M. (1991). *The CALLA handbook.* Reading, MA: Addison-Wesley.

Crandall, J. A. (1993). Content-centered learning in the United States. *Annual Review of Applied Linguistics,* 13, 111–126.

Cummins, J. (1986). Empowering minority students: A framework for intervention. *Harvard Educational Review, 56* (1), pp. 18–36.

Krashen, Stephen D. *Second Language Acquisition and Second Language Learning,* Prentice-Hall International, 1988.

Mohan, B. A. (1986). *Language and Content.* Reading MA: Addison-Wesley.

Long, M. H., Brock, C., Crookes, G., Deicke, C., Potter, L., & Zhang, S. (1984). *The effect of teachers' questioning patterns and wait-time on pupil participation patterns in public high school classes in Hawaii for students of limited English proficiency.* (Technical Report No. 1.) Honolulu, HI: University of Hawaii, Center for Second Language Classroom Research, Social Science Research Institute.

Oxford, R. (2001). *Language Learning Styles and Strategies.* In Celce-Murcia, M. (Ed.), *Teaching English as a Second or Foreign Language,* 3rd ed. Boston, MA: Heinle & Heinle.

Scarcella, R. and Oxford, R. (1992). *The tapestry of language learning: the individual in the communicative classroom.* Boston, MA: Heinle & Heinle.

Short, D. J. (1993). Assessing Integrated Language and Content Instruction. *TESOL Quarterly,* 27 (4).

Thomas, W. P., & Collier, V. P. (2003). *A national study of school effectiveness for language minority students' long-term academic achievement.* Santa Cruz, CA: Center for Research on Education, Diversity and Excellence, University of California-Santa Cruz.

Tobin, K. (1987). The role of wait-time in high cognitive level learning. Review of Educational Research 57 (1): 69–95.

— (2000). *Summary of SFUSD Core Programs.* San Francisco, CA: San Francisco Unified School District.

① Anticipation Guide

Purpose

An Anticipation Guide (Herber, 1978) lets students think about the topic they will study and express opinions about main ideas. In this strategy, English learners read debatable statements and decide if they agree or disagree with them.

Target learning strategies

- Planning
- Predicting
- Making inferences
- Using background knowledge
- Self-evaluation

Procedure

1. Read the section. Determine main ideas by checking the objectives in the Pupil Edition and the Teacher's Edition.

2. Create an Anticipation Guide. An example is shown below. Write three to six short, declarative, "yes or no" statements about the main ideas. Statements should activate students' prior knowledge if possible.

3. Distribute your Anticipation Guide and have individual students complete the "You" section, writing *T* for true or *F* for false.

4. Ask students to discuss their answers in small groups. They should be ready to explain why they answered as they did.

5. After reading, ask students to rethink their answers and write *T* or *F* in the second column, answering according to information from the text.

6. Discuss the answers. Students should use the text to support their opinions.

Example

Read the statements below. If you believe the statement is true, put a T in the first column. If you disagree, put an F in the first column.

You	Text	Topic: Westward Expansion
		The Homestead Act brought more settlers to the West.
		Increasing numbers of settlers caused many Native Americans to change their way of life.
		The railroad did not affect the way Native Americans and settlers lived in the West.
		Native Americans accepted the changes without protest.
		There were conflicts between soldiers, cattle ranchers, and prairie farmers.
		Fenced prairies solved all the conflicts in the West.

② Brainstorming

(includes Concept Map, Cluster Map, and Semantic Map)

Purpose

Brainstorming (or semantic mapping) helps learners visualize the content they are learning and remember the "schema"—the organization of information and the relationships among concepts and terms. This strategy improves oral communication, comprehension, problem-solving skills, and memory. Teachers can use it to introduce or review a topic. Learners can use it as a note-taking strategy or a prewriting strategy. (Marzano, Pickering, & Pollock, 2001; Armbruster, Anderson, & Meyer, 1992)

Target learning strategies

- Selective attention
- Using images
- Using background knowledge
- Taking notes

Procedure

1. Select a main idea or topic. Write it in a circle on the center of the board or on a transparency. An example is shown. Ask students for terms related to the main idea. Offer your own input as well. Write these ideas off to the side.

2. Ask students to help you sort the words into clusters of related terms. Choose a key word or phrase from each cluster.

3. Write these key words around your main idea. Draw one line from the main topic to each subtopic.

4. Write the words related to the key words around those key words and connect them with lines. Usually, the general ideas are in the center and the more specific ones are at the edges. Continue until all relevant ideas have been categorized.

5. Encourage students to make statements about the relationships between the subtopics and the main topic. For the example below, such a statement might be, "Monet's paintings used bright colors to show the impression of a moment."

Example

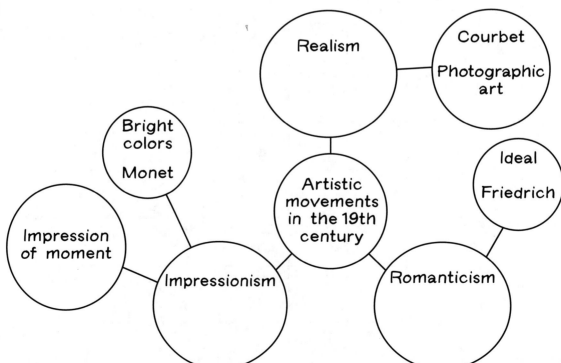

③ Card Responses

Purpose

Getting feedback on comprehension helps teachers and students track progress (Walberg, 1999; Bangert-Downs, Kulik, Kulik, & Morgan, 1991; Daniels & Bizar, 1998). Through card responses, students can check their own comprehension and give you feedback on how they are learning.

Target learning strategy
- Self-evaluating

Procedure

1. Have students make answer cards for questions you will ask. Cards can be true/false, yes/no/maybe, multiple choice A/B/C/D, or whatever fits your content. Create or find comprehension questions on the topic being studied.

2. Ask the question. At a signal from you, learners hold up their cards. To help students answer individually, be very clear about the signal and have everyone give it at the same time, for example, "Ready, one, two, three, cards up!"

3. Every ten minutes or so, ask a few recall questions about the lessons and have students answer the questions by holding up a card. If the class's accuracy rate is less than 90 percent, it might be time to reteach another way. This technique also helps you pinpoint those who need individual help.

Variation: Have students hold up the cards with their eyes closed, so no one can see anyone else's response.

Example

④ Carousel Review
(includes Carousel Preview and Carousel Reports)

Purpose

Learners need to be active in the language learning process and to use the language as they learn (Lindfors, 1987). In this strategy, learners listen and speak as the group works together to answer a set of questions.

Target learning strategies

- Selective attention
- Taking notes
- Cooperating with peers
- Summarizing

Procedure

1. Arrange chart paper in different parts of the room. (This strategy can be done on notebook paper if that is all that is available.) On each paper, write a question to preview or review content.

2. Divide students into small groups and assign each group a chart. Give each group a different colored marker.

3. Groups review their question, discuss their answer, and write a response.

4. After five to ten minutes, each group rotates to the next station. Groups put a check by each answer they agree with, comment on answers they don't agree with, and add their own answers. Continue until all groups have reviewed all charts.

5. Invite each group to share information with the class.

Variations:

This is an efficient way to do oral reports. Students have a chance to present and discuss their work with you and their peers in a short time.

1. Each student places his or her report (or poster, or map) on the wall of the classroom or hallway.

2. Authors of every third (or every other, or every fourth) product stand by their products.

3. The rest of the class rotates in small groups from poster to poster while the authors explain about their work. Encourage viewers to ask questions and offer positive feedback.

4. Provide viewers with a focus for their attention, such as content questions or an assessment rubric.

⑤ Cause-Effect Chart

Purpose

Graphic representation has been shown to improve comprehension of content-area reading (Armbruster, Anderson, & Meyer, 1992). Teachers can use cause-effect charts to preview or review material. Students can use them to take notes or to organize their thoughts before writing.

Target learning strategies

- Planning
- Selective attention
- Making inferences
- Using background knowledge
- Using images
- Taking notes
- Summarizing

Procedure

1. Help students find a cause-effect relationship in their reading.
2. Discuss the relationship between the cause(s) and the effect(s).
3. Write the cause in a box across the top of the chart. An example is shown.
4. Write the effects in boxes beneath that are linked to the cause.
5. Help learners make a concluding statement about the cause and effects and write it in a box across the bottom. Encourage students to use information in the chart to make statements about relationships between the causes and the effects. For example, "Alexander's conquests led to a blending of cultures."

Example

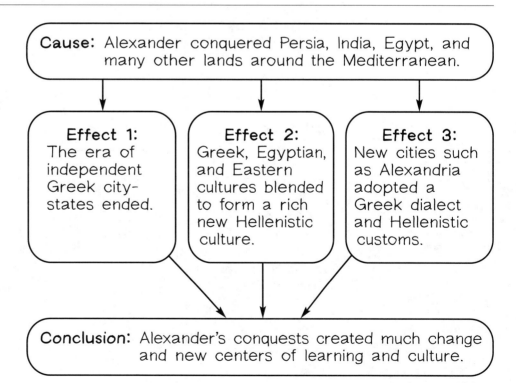

Cause: Alexander conquered Persia, India, Egypt, and many other lands around the Mediterranean.

Effect 1: The era of independent Greek city-states ended.

Effect 2: Greek, Egyptian, and Eastern cultures blended to form a rich new Hellenistic culture.

Effect 3: New cities such as Alexandria adopted a Greek dialect and Hellenistic customs.

Conclusion: Alexander's conquests created much change and new centers of learning and culture.

⑥ Chain of Events Chart

Purpose

Many psychologists describe storage of knowledge in two forms: linguistic and imagery (Marzano, Pickering, & Pollock, 2001). Creating a chain of events chart helps link and reinforce these two forms. Use this type of chart for previewing, reviewing, taking notes, or organizing students' thoughts before writing.

Target learning strategies

- Planning
- Selective attention
- Making inferences
- Using background knowledge
- Using images
- Taking notes
- Summarizing

Procedure

1. Help students find a chain of events in their readings.

2. Discuss the chain of events. Have students tell you the order of the events as you fill in boxes on a chain of events chart, with arrows showing the direction of causality from one event to the next. An example is shown.

3. Help learners use the information on the chart to make statements about the chain of events. In the example shown below, such a statement might be, "In the late 16th and early 17th centuries, just about everyone in Europe wanted tulips."

Example

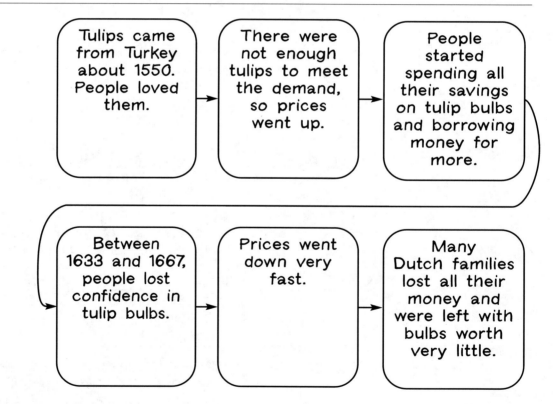

(7) Circle/Cycle Diagram

Purpose

Graphic representations help students understand content-area reading (Armbruster, Anderson, & Meyer, 1992). The circle/cycle diagram shows a series of events in which one event leads to another but eventually returns to the first event. This graphic is useful for whole-class activities (previewing and reviewing) and for individual students (taking notes or preparing to write).

Target learning strategies

- Planning
- Selective attention
- Making inferences
- Using background knowledge
- Using images
- Taking notes
- Summarizing

Procedure

1. Help students find a cyclical event or phenomenon in their readings.

2. Have students tell you the order of the events as you fill in a circle/cycle diagram, with arrows showing the direction of causality from one event to the next. An example is shown.

3. Help learners use information from the diagram to make statements about the chain of events. For the example shown below, such a statement might be, "Farmers in Egypt harvested their crops every spring."

Example

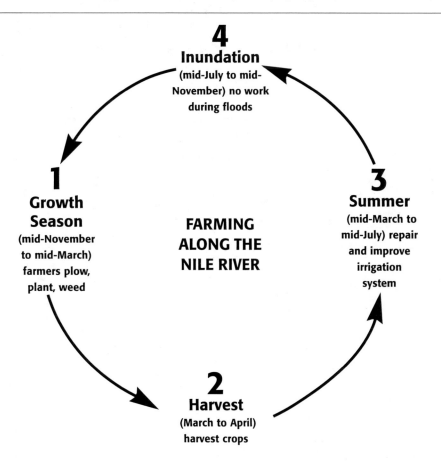

4
Inundation
(mid-July to mid-November) no work during floods

1
Growth Season
(mid-November to mid-March) farmers plow, plant, weed

FARMING ALONG THE NILE RIVER

3
Summer
(mid-March to mid-July) repair and improve irrigation system

2
Harvest
(March to April) harvest crops

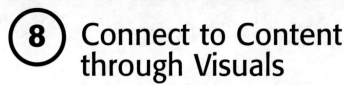

⑧ Connect to Content through Visuals

(includes Picture Imaging, Word Imaging, and Sentence-by-Sentence Imaging)

Purpose

Imagery is particularly important for English learners. Imaging (Chamot & O'Malley, 1994) is a strategy that effective readers use to make sense from a text. Readers create a picture in their minds to support their understanding. Though learners of English may be at a disadvantage in comprehending the language of a text, they are on more equal ground in being able to make sense of the images. It is wise to help them to create images as much as they can when they read.

Target learning strategies

- Selective attention
- Summarizing
- Using images

Procedure

Picture imaging: Have students look at a picture and describe what they see. Keep asking questions as you help them see more and more detail. Use words such as *what, size, color, number, shape, where, movement, background, perspective, when, sound, pattern,* and *direction.* Clarify the meanings of these words as needed.

Word imaging: Choose an important term, such as *imperialism.* Share with students what you visualize when you see the term—for example, a chessboard where one person moves all the pieces. Ask the students to tell you what they "see" connected to a certain word they are learning. Use the description words above in framing your questions.

Sentence-by-sentence imaging: Use different-colored squares of paper to represent each sentence of a paragraph of text. Have students read a sentence and describe what they "see." Ask for more detail. When that student is finished, repeat what he or she "sees" and put one square of paper on the wall or board to represent that sentence. When the paragraph is completed, students give a picture summary, telling what each square (or sentence) is about. Eventually, with practice, students can learn to visualize an entire paragraph with one square and can answer higher-level thinking questions related to that paragraph.

(9) Debate

Purpose

Research on second language acquisition suggests that interaction is important to language development (Ellis, 1994; Swain, 1995; van Lier, 1996). In particular, students need opportunities to negotiate and reword what they want to say (Gibbons, 2002; Pica, Young, and Doughty, 1987; Pica, 1994). Debate offers English learners the opportunity to formulate and negotiate language.

Target learning strategies

- Researching issues
- Taking notes
- Focusing on important points

- Analyzing and organizing information logically
- Learning to argue a point in English
- Speaking to an audience

Procedure

1. Divide the class into opposing teams. Give each team one side of an issue related to the text they have read. For example, they might debate the statement "Napoleon should have conquered Russia."

2. If possible, show the students a video clip of a debate. Provide students with the debate format you want them to follow. (One possible format: Each team member prepares an opening statement. The moderator asks questions and gives each side time to respond. Then the captain of the team summarizes.)

3. Teams study the topic and agree on at least three points that the team will make. Coach each side carefully, helping them develop arguments for their position and facts to support those arguments.

4. Provide the language structures students will need, such as: *Based on _____ (author's name), Napoleon should have_____; and Napoleon should (not) have invaded Russia because_____.*

5. Give the teams time to discuss the issues. Have them decide who will present each point.

6. Have each member of each team present ideas on the topic for a timed period of one or two minutes. The first time, students might want to read written statements; later, they can use note cards with key points.

7. Have each team prepare questions for the other team to answer. Depending on the debate format, either the students or the moderator will ask the questions.

8. Have debate captains summarize each team's arguments for two to three minutes each. Then offer your own constructive feedback on content, format, and language.

(10) Directed Reading-Thinking Activity (DRTA)

Purpose

A directed reading-thinking activity (Stauffer, 1968; Vacca & Vacca, 1989) lets students use strategies of proficient readers: asking questions of the text and predicting what will happen next. It helps English learners understand why the information they are reading is important and what they are expected to learn.

Target learning strategies

- Making predictions
- Summarizing
- Focusing on the main ideas

Procedure

1. Establish the reasons students are reading this text and why they are learning this material (for example, to design a poster on the topic, take a test, compare the topic to another in a discussion, or debate the issue). When possible, choose topics that are somewhat familiar to students. This will improve comprehension and ability to make predictions.

2. Present the topic and title of the selection and ask students to predict what the selection will be about. Provide sentence structures such as *I predict . . .; I think . . .; and I believe. . . .*

3. Introduce key vocabulary. This includes content-specific vocabulary (terms to understand the content) and content-compatible vocabulary (general academic terms that may be more important for comprehension).

4. Read aloud a portion of the selection, stop at predetermined points, and ask students to summarize what they heard. Ask students to check their previous predictions and provide support for their decisions by finding and citing evidence from the text.

5. Continue asking students to predict and confirm their predictions as they read.

6. Check for comprehension by asking students to summarize the reading.

7. Ask students to complete the purpose for the reading (poster, test, discussion, or debate).

⑪ Draw It Out

Purpose

Effective readers use imaging (Chamot & O'Malley, 1994) to make sense of a text. It is wise to help English learners to create images as often as they can when they listen, read, and write. This strategy helps students visualize what they are learning and then apply the new language to the concepts.

Target learning strategies

- Predicting
- Making inferences
- Using background knowledge
- Using images
- Taking notes
- Summarizing

Procedure

1. As students watch, draw a picture that illustrates a main event or concept in the reading. Don't worry about your level of talent—stick figures and shapes will do. Talk aloud as you draw. For example, this commentary might accompany your drawing of a map of the Nile River: *I'm going to draw a map. Here's a long river. These arrows show how the river flows north. People here call the south of the country "up" because it's upstream toward the beginning of the river. The river is going to a big sea. It makes a fan when it gets near the sea. Here's the sea. I'm going to draw people and houses and farms along the river, because almost everyone in the country lives near the river.*

2. Have students open their books to the relevant pages and help you label all the important parts of the picture: Egypt, the Nile, the Cataract, the Delta, Upper Egypt, Lower Egypt, and the Mediterranean.

3. Pair students. Have each partner draw a picture about a section of the book. Then they trade pictures and try to find the labels for everything that the partner drew. Partners and the teacher then check the labels for accuracy. If students have text summaries in their home languages, they can use those texts, along with graphic information in the text, to help them make the drawings. Then they use the English-language text to add labels in English.

(12) Frayer Method

Purpose

The Frayer method (Frayer, Frederick, & Klausmeier, 1969) is a strategy to teach new, challenging concepts and words. Gibbons (2002) points out that English learners should be allowed to develop an understanding of a concept before they use more complex discourse to discuss it. The Frayer method helps to develop the understanding of a challenging concept and the words to explain that concept.

Target learning strategies

- Comparing and contrasting
- Introducing key vocabulary
- Developing listening comprehension

Procedure

1. Define a new term or concept. Whenever possible, show an example and use visuals or drawings. For example: *A time line is a list of events placed on a line in the order in which they happened. Look at the time line on pages 130–131.*

2. Distinguish between the new concept and a similar but different concept: *How is a time line different from a list? Right, the items are organized and placed on the line based on the date they happened. Usually they go from left (earlier time) to right (later time).*

3. Show examples of the concept and explain why they are examples: *Time lines usually show the chronological order of historical events by date. For example, you could make a time line of the Civil War or a time line of the Mexican Revolution.*

4. Give non-examples of the concept and explain why they are non-examples: *Look at the list on the top of page 137. Is this a time line? No, it is not a list of events in chronological (time) order.*

5. Give students both examples and non-examples and have them distinguish between the two: *Now look at the charts on page 62 and page 150. Which one is a time line?*

6. Ask students or pairs to look for examples and non-examples in their texts: *Now look in your book for lists that are time lines and lists that are not. Be prepared to give the page number, the name of the list, and your reasons why it is or is not a time line.* Offer constructive feedback on learners' responses.

⑬ Inside-Outside Circles

Purpose

Inside-outside circles provide English learners with real opportunities to give and get information from other students (High, 1993). Research on second-language acquisition suggests that interaction is important to language development (Ellis, 1994; Swain, 1995; van Lier, 1996). The repetition of vocabulary and concepts in English lets students rehearse and master new information (Kagan, 1994).

Target learning strategies

- Asking and answering questions
- Giving information
- Learning new terms

Procedure

1. After students have read a selection, give each an index card with a question from the text. Students write their answers on the back of the index cards. Check the answers or provide a key to make sure they are correct. Have students adjust incorrect answers.

2. Students pair up and form two circles. One partner is in an inside circle; the other is in an outside circle. The students in the inside circle face out, and the students in the outside circle face in.

3. Each student in the inside circle asks his or her partner the question on the index cards. The partner answers. If the answer is incorrect, the student in the inside circle teaches the other student the correct answer. Repeat this step with the outside-circle students asking the questions.

4. Have each student on the outside circle rotate one person to the right. He or she faces a new partner and gets a new question. Students rotate after each pair of questions. (You can vary the rotation by moving more than one person, moving to the left, and so on, but try to make sure that partners are always new.)

Variations:

1. The teacher asks a question and the students tell their partners the answer.

2. The students hold flash cards with the questions to be asked. Each student shows his or her flash card and gets a response before rotating.

3. The activity can be used for vocabulary review: each card has a word on one side and a definition on the other.

(14) Interactive Writing

Purpose

In interactive writing (Herrell, 2000), teacher and students create a text together. This strategy provides effective modeling and scaffolding as students learn about the writing process. Students learn to brainstorm ideas, plan writing, draft, revise, edit, and produce a final version. They can also learn to distinguish the "schema" or plan of various types of writing and to assess their writing as they create it.

Target learning strategies

- Writing processes
- Planning
- Self-evaluation

Procedure

1. Have students read and study quality models of the genre in which they are asked to write. Provide language for describing elements of quality, perhaps reviewing rubrics or other assessment tools for this type of writing. Help learners recognize the elements of quality writing and of quality writing in this genre.

2. Discuss and plan a topic for the class's interactive writing.

3. Create a cluster map to assemble the vocabulary needed for the writing. Use brainstorming, graphic organizers, or writing frames to develop the content to be included and the organization of the piece. (Look in the table of contents in this book for more on brainstorming, cluster maps, and writing frames.)

4. Have students dictate sentences to you as you draft the piece on a chart, transparency, or blackboard. Or learners can draft assigned sentences or paragraphs in small groups, and then the piece can be assembled and revised in the large group.

5. Have students reread the piece to check that it is complete, clear, and in a logical order.

6. Revise the piece as needed and check it against a rubric. *Integrated Assessment* has rubrics for a variety of forms and genres.

7. Celebrate the final text with many oral readings and publication as a poster or classroom paper. This work can serve as a model as students write independently.

(15) Jigsaw Reading

Purpose

Considerable evidence shows the positive effects of tutoring interactions in pairs (Samway, et al, 1995) and of small cooperative learning task interactions (Slavin, 1983; Kagan, 1994). Jigsaw reading is a technique first researched by Arronson (1978). It lets students cover more material in less time.

Target learning strategies

- Cooperating with peers
- Summarizing
- Self-assessment

Procedure

1. Divide participants into "home groups" of about four. Have each group number off, one through four. (If a group has five students, two of them should share a number.)

2. Divide the reading into four numbered sections. Group 1 will study section 1, group 2 will study section 2, and so on.

3. Students reassemble into "expert groups"—all the Group 1 students get together, all the Group 2 students get together, and so on. Each group reads and studies its section and develops a "lesson plan" for summarizing and teaching the concepts.

4. When the material has been mastered, experts return to their home groups, where each expert teaches the group about his or her part.

5. Use an informal assessment (such as Numbered Heads Together, described elsewhere in this book) to check comprehension.

(16) KWL Chart: Know, Want to Know, Learned

Purpose

The KWL chart (Ogle, 1986) is a three-column graphic that can be used as a pre-assessment tool for the teacher and as a study guide as students read and review. This process acknowledges the language structures and vocabulary the students already know (Echevarria, Vogt, & Short, 2000). It also prepares them with questions for checking their predictions and for learning new information about a topic.

Target learning strategies

- Activating prior knowledge
- Generating questions
- Predicting
- Organizing learned material

Procedure

1. Give students a prepared KWL chart or have them draw three columns and write the following headings at the top of each column: What I Know; What I Want to Know; What I Learned.

2. Ask students to list what they already know about the theme or topic in the "Know" column of their papers. Provide learners with needed language structures, such as *The causes of . . . are . . .; There are . . . in . . .; The people from . . . are . . .; They live. . .; and They have. . . .* After two to five minutes of independent thinking and writing, ask students to share what they know with the class. List what they say in the "Know" column of a class chart. Have students add new information from their peers to their own charts.

3. Ask students what they want to know about the topic. Write their questions in the second column, the "Want to Know" column of the chart. Help learners use language structures such as *What are . . .?; Are all . . .?; When did . . .?; and Why did . . .?* Assign individuals or pairs specific questions to answer.

4. After the reading or unit of study has been completed, ask students to tell you what they have learned. Students might use language structures such as *I learned that . . .; Often . . .; Most . . .; and Some. . . .* List what students learned on the class chart. Correct misinformation that they "knew" before their study. An example of a KWL chart is shown below.

Example

What I **K**now	What I **W**ant to Know	What I **L**earned
• Mount Saint Helens is a volcano.	• Where are most volcanoes located?	• Most volcanoes are in the "Ring of Fire," the edges of the Pacific Ocean. • Mount Fuji in Japan is an active volcano.

(17) Learning Log/Double-Column Note-Taking

Purpose

Learning logs (Fulwiler, 1980) are informal reflective writing by students as they learn new information. This technique lets students think about what they have learned and allows them to reformulate and express that knowledge in their own words (Buehl, 2001). English learners can give a personal response to information they are learning and can summarize important points (Peyton, 1990).

Target learning strategies

- Activating knowledge
- Building writing and study skills
- Integrating and applying knowledge
- Summarizing

Procedure

1. Instruct students to fold their paper vertically into two sections. Have students label the left column "Note Taking" and the right column "Note Making."

2. Before asking students to take notes, use the think-aloud strategy (described elsewhere in this book) and modeling to demonstrate good note-taking on a transparency divided into two columns.

3. The left column is used for traditional note-taking: direct quotations, outlines, or summaries from the text.

4. The right column is used for analyzing and commenting on the left column's notes.

5. Model how as students take new notes, they should reread their previous pages of notes, making new connections in the right column before starting another page.

6. Show examples of anonymous learners' notes and have students identify features of good note-taking, such as organization, inclusion of important information or terms, not too many details, and thoughtful analysis in the right column.

7. Have learners read one another's notes, giving feedback using the criteria above.

Example

Note Taking	Note Making
Mohandas Gandhi • leader of India • wanted people to protest without violence • wanted women and men to have the same rights	 • How can you protest without violence? • Did he succeed getting equal rights?

18 Matrix

Purpose

Using graphic representations improves comprehension of content-area reading (Armbruster, Anderson, & Meyer, 1992). A matrix helps learners visualize a system for classifying information. Matrices are useful for previewing or reviewing material. English learners can use them to take notes or to organize their thoughts before writing.

Target learning strategies

- Planning
- Making inferences
- Using background knowledge
- Taking notes
- Selective attention
- Comparing and contrasting information
- Using images
- Summarizing

Procedure

1. Choose the information to be organized, or help learners choose the information they wish to organize. An example is shown below.

2. Decide how many rows and columns your matrix will need to be. Label them.

3. Do a think-aloud (described elsewhere in this book) in which you find information and decide how to categorize it.

4. Have a student model how to categorize additional information.

5. Encourage learners to complete the chart independently.

6. Review and discuss students' work. Help learners make statements about the information on the chart. In the example below, such a statement might be, "Four of the worst earthquakes of the 20th century happened in China." Then have students work in small groups or as individuals to make matrices of their own.

Example

Ten Most Deadly Earthquakes of the 20th Century			
Date	Location	Deaths	Magnitude
1976, July 27	Tangshan, China	255,000	8.0
1920, Dec. 16	Gansu, China	200,000	8.6
1927, May. 22	Nan-Shan, China	200,000	8.3
1923, Sept. 1	Yokohama, Japan	143,000	8.3
1908, Dec. 28	Messina, Italy	83,000	7.5
1932, Dec. 25	Gansu, China	70,000	7.6
1970, May 31	Northern Peru	66,000	7.8
1935, May 30	Quetta, India	50,000	7.5
1990, June 20	Western Iran	40,000	7.7
1988, Dec. 7	Armenia	25,000	7.0

⑲ New Word Analysis

Purpose

New word analysis (Routman, 1991) is a sequence of strategies for analyzing and decoding new words in context. For English learners, vocabulary competence is the key to communicating successfully and appropriately (Coady and Huckins, 1997). English learners need multiple ways to attack new words, and word-association techniques have proved successful (Nation, 1990).

Target learning strategies

- Using context clues
- Predicting
- Word analysis
- Letter/sound correspondence

Procedure

Point out a challenging word in the text and give the following instructions:

1. Look at the word carefully—beginning, middle, and end.

2. Read on to try to find the meaning in the context—the words and phrases around the word. Then try to read the word again.

3. Stretch out the letters and say the word slowly. Then put the word back together again.

4. Try some words that you know would make sense in the place of the unknown word.

5. Try some words you know that "sound right" where the unknown word is.

6. Look at the parts of the word. Think of words you know that have pieces of the word or that look like the word. Use these parts to figure out what the unknown word might mean.

7. Divide the word into parts or syllables by how you say the word. Think: "What do these parts mean? How do you say them?" Then put the word back together and try to read it.

8. Skip the word and go on. If you still can't make sense of the word, ask someone what the word means, look it up in the glossary, or check an English-English dictionary or a translation dictionary.

(20) Numbered Heads Together

Copyright © McDougal Littell/Houghton Mifflin Company.

Purpose

Numbered heads together (Kagan, 1994) is especially effective in "decreasing the learning gap" for English learners because all learners in a group are held equally responsible and have motivation to support one another's learning (High, 1993).

Target learning strategies

- Summarizing
- Synthesizing
- Reviewing
- Retelling
- Negotiating meaning
- Problem-solving

Procedure

1. Have students work in groups of about four. Students in each group number off, one to four. (If groups have five, two students take turns as one number. If groups have three, one student has two numbers.)

2. Ask questions about the reading and give a time limit. After students have learned the strategy well, a student can ask a question instead.

3. Students take a few minutes to "put their heads together" to find and agree on an answer. This may include looking in the text.

4. Give a number to designate which student will answer for the team.

5. Students with that number give their group's answer verbally, on paper, or on the board.

6. Give feedback as appropriate. Teams may receive points for correct answers, creative answers, correct spelling, and so on.

Variations: This activity is extremely versatile and can be used with higher-order thinking activities. Instead of answering questions, students can brainstorm ideas, solve a problem, draw a diagram, or even invent a product.

(21) Pair-Share
(includes Think-Pair-Share and Think-Quickwrite-Pair-Share)

Purpose

Pair-share structures (Kagan, 1994) let English learners listen and respond appropriately to their peers. Students think about the theme or topic of the lesson and make a connection to their own experience. Reading and listening are closely related language processes (Gibbons, 1991). Both require the students to question their peers as well as the text.

Target learning strategies

- Active listening
- Asking questions
- Activating prior knowledge
- Summarizing

Procedure

1. Pair students, or allow them to choose a partner. Invite pairs to think about a topic and to relate it to their own experience. For example, you might ask them to describe a time when they were separated from someone or from something.

2. Each student describes the experience to their partner and listens to the partner's description. Students may take notes and ask questions to remember details.

3. Have each pair get together with another pair of students. Each person in this foursome takes a turn retelling his or her *partner's* story. The group can then select one or two stories to share with the class.

Variations: To use the Think-Pair-Share strategy, introduce the topic and have students reflect on it before they pair up. To use the Think-Quickwrite-Pair-Share strategy, have individual students write about an assigned topic for five minutes without stopping. During quickwriting, students should not worry about grammar, spelling, or punctuation. They should try to get as many ideas as possible on paper. A student who runs out of ideas can write his or her name over and over until a new idea emerges. Then each student should read his or her writing to a partner, listen to the partner's ideas, and proceed as described above.

(22) Peer Tutoring

Purpose

Peer tutoring is an effective way to promote language learning (Labbo & Teale, 1990; Samway, Whang, & Pippitt, 1995). Peers can help one another by providing comprehensible input and purpose for conversations. While the tutor develops confidence, self-esteem, and the ability to articulate learning strategies, the student being tutored gains practice and confidence in using English both orally and in writing.

Target learning strategies

- Cooperating with peers
- Promoting active involvement

Procedure

1. Identify students who need help in specific academic areas.

2. Identify students with strengths in these areas to be peer tutors.

3. Train tutors in how to ask questions to support thinking; how to break learning tasks into smaller, more manageable sections; how to determine when first-language support is helpful; and how to support vocabulary development.

4. Match students, considering such factors as gender, home language, and personality. When possible and appropriate, match by language background so that the pair can use both languages to negotiate meaning.

5. Structure times for pairs to work together. Monitor their work and meet with them to celebrate successes, address problems, and answer questions. If teams work well together, have them continue as partners. Consider changing partners as needed for better matches or for different skills and purposes.

(23) Peer Vocabulary Teaching and Review

(includes Flash Card Game)

Purpose

This type of interaction improves how well students provide and receive comprehensible input, assess their own comprehension and learning, ask questions, analyze words, and know when to use first- and second-language resources (Kulik & Kulik, 1982; Johnson, Johnson, & Holubec, 1994; Kagan, 1992).

Target learning strategies

- Planning
- Making inferences
- Using background knowledge
- Taking notes
- Cooperating with peers
- Using images
- Self-evaluating

Procedure

1. Teach students strategies that can help them study and learn new terms, such as analyzing similarities and differences, grouping and classifying terms, studying common word parts, creating analogies (relating new words to other words with the same structure or pattern), visualizing, using word squares (described elsewhere in this book), and keeping personal dictionaries.

2. Pair students and have them select a set of key words to study. Have pairs select a strategy to use and then teach one another the terms.

3. Show students how to assess one another by holding up cards with terms on them and sorting the cards into "know" and "don't know" piles. Pairs can focus on the words they don't know with a new strategy until they have mastered them all.

Sample assessment activity: Flash Card Game (High, 1993)

1. Show students how to make flash cards with words they are learning on one side and pictures or phrases showing the meanings on the reverse. Choosing a group of related words will help students learn them more quickly.

2. Pair students. Have one student from each pair ask a partner to name the words from the pictures or phrases. To make early rounds easier, allow students to give hints such as *It starts with . . .; It has . . . in the middle;* and *It rhymes with. . . .*

3. Tell the student doing the asking to give praise after correct answers. He or she puts aside all the cards answered correctly and retests on the rest until they are mastered.

4. Have pairs swap roles and repeat.

Card front   Card back

(24) QAR: Question-Answer Relationships

Purpose

This strategy is designed to help students classify questions and locate answers in a text (Raphael, 1985). English learners need to know how to answer and write different levels of questions in English (Gibbons, 1993). In QAR, there are four levels of questions: Right There, Think and Search, Author and You, and On Your Own. Students need to know how to ask and answer all four types of questions.

Target learning strategies

• Asking and answering questions

Procedure

1. Explain the four levels of questions to the class:

   • Right There: The answer is stated in the text. The question asks for facts from the text. For example, *What is an immigrant? When did most immigrants come to the United States?*

   • Think and Search: The question asks the reader to bring together information from different parts of the text. For example, *How does European immigration of the 1900s compare to Chinese immigration of the 1860s?*

   • Author and You: The answer is a combination of information from what the reader knows and what the author has written. The question asks for information from both the reader and the text. For example, *Are there migrant workers in your country?*

   • On Your Own: The answer comes from the reader's knowledge and experience. The question asks for an opinion from the reader. For example, *In what ways is United States culture an immigrant culture?*

2. Prepare a list of questions in the four areas for the students to answer.

3. In small groups of three to four, have students read the text and answer the questions. They should indicate the QAR category for each question and justify their decisions.

4. Have the students read another selection from the text and write their own QAR questions. Groups should then exchange their questions with other groups, answer them, and categorize them into QAR levels.

(25) Questions to Guide Reading

Purpose

Effective questioning (Walberg, 1999) can help learners achieve deeper levels of thought and process their own reading strategies while discussing a text. It can help learners recognize their own questions regarding the language and meaning of the text and work to find strategies for solving them.

Target learning strategies

- Selective attention
- Predicting
- Making inferences
- Using background knowledge
- Using images
- Summarizing
- Self-evaluating

Procedure

1. Think of key questions to ask before, during, and after a reading session to show students how to go beyond the surface level and to take control of considering, evaluating, and understanding what they read.

2. Questions for before the reading:
   - How will the author treat this topic?
   - What do you already know about the topic? What do you want to know?
   - What kind of writing is this? What do you expect from this kind of writing?

3. Questions for during the reading or rereading:
   - Read until _____ (a term or topic). What have you learned? What do you expect to learn next?
   - Raise your hand when you come to a troublesome word. Let's do a think-aloud about how to solve this word.
   - What is the significance of _____ (key term or concept)?

4. Questions for after the reading:
   - What is the most important part of the reading?
   - How well did you answer what you wanted to know before you started reading?
   - What question do you have to ask others about the reading?

5. Encourage students to ask one another questions and to listen actively to the responses of their peers.

(26) Ranking Ladder

Purpose

Many psychologists believe that knowledge can be stored as language or as images (Marzano, Pickering, & Pollock, 2001). Using graphic representations improves understanding of content-area reading (Armbruster, Anderson, & Meyer, 1992). A ranking ladder helps learners to make judgments about importance and to rank concepts in order of importance. Use this strategy when previewing or reviewing material. Encourage your students to use it when taking notes or when organizing thoughts before writing.

Target learning strategies

- Planning
- Making inferences
- Using background knowledge
- Taking notes
- Making judgments
- Selective attention
- Comparing and contrasting information
- Using images
- Summarizing

Procedure

1. Choose, or help students choose, a series of concepts, events, or people to rank. List them on the board or on an overhead projector.

2. Do a think-aloud (described elsewhere in this book) in which you decide which of two items is more important.

3. Draw a ladder as shown in the example below. Discuss the order in which to rank the items. Encourage students to explain their choices. Then write the items on the rungs of the ladder in order, from least important on the bottom to most important on the top.

4. Have learners use information from the ladder to make statements about the importance of different items. In the example shown below, such a statement might be, "History is probably the most important part of creating a nation-state, because the people in that state need to feel that they have a shared past."

5. Have a student model how to categorize additional information. Encourage learners to complete the chart independently and to create their own ranking ladders for other topics.

Example

Ranking Ladder: Bonds that Create a Nation-State

What is the order of importance? Items to rank: territory, religion, history, culture, language, nationality.

Most important

Least important

Copyright © McDougal Littell/Houghton Mifflin Company.

(27) Reciprocal Teaching

Purpose

Palincsar and Brown (1986) found that when reciprocal teaching was used with learners for just 15 to 20 days, students' reading comprehension assessment increased from 30 percent to 80 percent. Follow-up research on the strategy (reported in Oczkus, 2003) has shown it to be effective in many situations. This technique teaches students to focus intently on what they are reading by using four key strategies. Consciously asking questions and summarizing content helps readers understand and remember what is read. English learners must listen to one another's questions and comments and teach each other the material.

Target learning strategies

- Predicting
- Clarifying
- Questioning
- Summarizing

Procedure

1. Introduce the reading strategies one at a time in whole-class sessions:

   - **Predicting:** This involves previewing the text to make logical predictions about what will come next. It may involve previewing text structure, headings, illustrations, and other features. Language needed: *I think . . ., I bet . . ., I predict . . ., I suppose . . ., I imagine . . ., and I wonder if. . . .*

   - **Questioning:** Effective readers ask themselves questions about main ideas, important details, and textual inferences as they read. Language needed: questions with *who, what, when, where, why, how,* and *what if.*

   - **Clarifying:** Clarifying is problem solving during reading that helps learners monitor their own comprehension and solve the meanings of new words as they read. They learn strategies such as rereading, looking at word parts, looking at the context, thinking about other words that are like the word, and trying another word that makes sense. Language needed: *This is not clear. I can't figure out . . .,* or *This word is tricky because. . . .*

   - **Summarizing:** Summarizing involves using many skills and strategies at once to remember and rearrange the most important information in a text. Language needed: *The most important ideas were . . .; First, . . ., Next, . . ., Then . . ., Finally. . . .*

   Provide common language and terms for using these strategies and show how they are often used to understand social studies content. Frequently model each strategy with a student. Then have students model the strategies.

2. Assign students to work in small groups of two to five. One student assumes the role of leader. He or she reads a paragraph aloud, asks questions about events in the text, asks another group member to summarize, asks members if they need clarification of meaning and then works to clarify, and has group members predict what will happen next.

3. Have the next student in the group become the leader for the next section or paragraph, and so on.

28 Round Robin
(includes Roundtable)

Purpose

English learners need good language models to improve their spoken and written language (Gibbons, 1993). Providing comprehensible input is essential for language-learning classrooms (Larsen-Freeman & Long, 1991; Krashen, 1987), and native-English-speaking peers can be excellent models for English learners. Interaction improves student understanding (Long, 1980; Pica, 1994). These strategies encourage students to generate as many facts and ideas about a topic as they can (Kagan, 1994). Then you can assess which terms or concepts English learners already know and which need to be taught.

Target learning strategies

- Active listening
- Categorizing
- Activating prior knowledge

Procedure

Round Robin (oral version)

1. Divide the class into groups of three or four.

2. Write the topic, such as "Religions of the World," on the board.

3. Ask a student to give an example of that topic.

4. Have another student give a different example. Explain that students cannot repeat something that has already been said. Have students continue to add responses until you call time, after three to five minutes.

5. Ask one student from each group to give as many answers as he or she can remember. Ask students not to repeat an answer already stated by another group. Chart each group's answers on the board or chart paper.

Roundtable (written version)

1. Divide the class into groups of three or four. Give each group one sheet of paper.

2. Write the topic on the board. For example, you might write "List the causes of World War II."

3. The first student writes something she knows about the topic on the paper and passes it to the next student. That student writes something different about the topic, and so on.

4. After five or ten minutes, ask one student from each group to read what is on the group list. Compile a class list from student responses.

Roundtable Variation

Rather than having the papers rotate among students, rotate the groups of students. Set out papers with questions or prompts on them and have groups of students move from station to station writing answers.

(29) Semantic Feature Analysis

Purpose

Semantic feature analysis (Johnson & Pearson, 1984) helps English learners identify important characteristics of related concepts, compare features of those concepts, and distinguish between the concepts. It helps students understand confusing terms by showing them similarities and differences between concepts. English learners need vocabulary instruction that helps them extend their understanding of concepts and differentiate between related or similar words (Buehl, 2001).

Target learning strategies

- Making connections between texts
- Confirming and revising hypotheses and inferences
- Expanding vocabulary

Procedure

1. Identify a category or concept from your text, such as wars of the 20th century. Select terms and features that they share, as shown in the example below.

2. Use the board or an overhead projector to create a matrix of the terms and features you selected. List the terms in the left column and the features across the top.

3. Model how to fill in the matrix. Use a plus sign if the feature applies to the term and a minus sign if it does not.

4. Distribute copies of the matrix to the students and brainstorm additional terms and features for it. Ask students to fill these in as you add them to the overhead transparency.

5. Ask students to work in pairs to complete the matrix, using the textbook to verify their answers. They should be ready to discuss their decisions with the class. Help students use the information on the chart to develop statements about the subject matter. In the example below, such a statement might be, "All these wars caused innocent people to be displaced or killed."

Example

Some Wars of the 20th Century			
Name of war	Began as civil war	Atomic weapons used	Many innocent people displaced or killed
World War I	–	–	+
World War II	–	+	+
Korean War	+	–	+
Vietnam War	+	–	+
1991 Gulf War	–	–	+

(30) Signals

Purpose

Setting goals provides clear direction and makes learning easier. Getting feedback helps teachers and students track progress toward those goals (Walberg, 1999; Bangert-Downs, Kulik, Kulik, & Morgan, 1991; Daniels & Bizar, 1998). Providing oral and written language that learners can make sense of is essential (Larsen-Freeman & Long, 1992; Krashen, 1987), and interaction makes input easier to understand (Long, 1980; Pica, 1994). Signals allow students to check comprehension, monitor their use of learning, and give teachers much-needed feedback.

Target learning strategies

- Summarizing
- Self-evaluating
- Checking comprehension

Procedure

1. Teach students signals to show you how well they are understanding the topic. Here are some examples.

   - Thumbs up: I get it. Thumbs down: I don't get it. Thumbs sideways: I sort of get it.
   - Hand behind ear: I can't hear what you are saying very well.
   - Hand held flat from low to high: I understand this (a little, most of it, all of it).
   - Holding up one, two, three, or four fingers: answers to multiple-choice questions.

2. Periodically during lessons, have students give you feedback on how well they understand the content. Your instructions for this activity might be something like this: *Now I'd like to check whether you understand this section and are ready to go on. I'm going to make true-false statements. If you think the statement is true, hold your thumb up like this. If you think it's false, hold your thumb down like this. If you don't know, hold your thumb sideways like this. Close your eyes before you respond so you won't be influenced by others' answers. Question 1: The Second Estate was made up of the priests and bishops of the Catholic Church. [pause] Okay, show me your thumbs.*

3. Scan the group and estimate the percentage of correct answers. If you see several errors, it's time to review or to reteach another way. Use this strategy to pinpoint individuals who need more help.

 **Slates**

Purpose

It is essential to provide oral and written language that learners can make sense of (Larsen-Freeman & Long, 1992; Krashen, 1987). Interaction has been demonstrated to make information more comprehensible (Long, 1980; Pica, 1994). Using slates, students can check their own comprehension, monitor their use of learning, and give you feedback on how they are learning. Slates have an advantage over signals (which are discussed elsewhere in this book) because they allow you to ask higher-order questions that can't be answered with numbers or symbols.

Target learning strategies

• Summarizing

• Self-evaluating

• Checking comprehension

Procedure

1. Have students make dry-marker slates by clipping a blank transparency to a piece of white paper or a notepad. (Students can also write with marker or crayon on the back of used paper.)

2. Teach students to use the slates to give short answers to questions you ask. At a signal, they hold up the slates to show you their answers. Students can write answers on the slates individually or as pairs or small groups. Scan the answers and gauge the proportion of correct answers. If there are several wrong answers, consider reviewing or reteaching the materials another way. Be explicit about the signal and have everyone hold up answers at the same time. For example, you might say, "Ready, one, two, three, slates up!"

3. Every ten minutes or so during a lesson, ask a question or pose a problem about the lesson and have students respond on their slates. Scan the answers and use them for clarification, expansion, and discussion. Slates also help you pinpoint individuals who need more help.

(32) SQ3R: Survey, Question, Read, Recite, Review

Purpose

SQ3R (Vacca & Vacca, 1989) is a study system to help English learners manage and monitor their own learning as they read. Grade-level textbooks are usually very difficult for English learners. By focusing on the structure of the text and the headings, visuals, and study questions, students can organize their thoughts to better understand what they are reading. By using metacognitive strategies such as SQ3R, English learners plan, monitor, and evaluate their own learning (Chamot & O'Malley, 1994).

Target learning strategies

- Asking and answering questions
- Reading for information
- Using text visuals and format to aid learning

---

1. Introduce and model the steps in SQ3R. You might introduce one at a time and practice each for a day or two before moving on to the next.

2. Have students model the process in front of the class using a think-aloud (described elsewhere in this book).

3. Have students use the process in class and check on how it is working.

4. Once the strategy has been mastered, remind students to use it in their studies outside of class.

The Steps:

SURVEY: Gather information you need to set your reading goals.

- Read the title. Prepare your mind to receive the information.

- Read the introduction and/or summary. Think about the author's purpose in writing and what you hope to get from reading.

- Note all headings and subheadings in bold type. Bold words usually mean something is important.

- Look at the graphics. Charts, maps, photographs, and diagrams are there to make a point.

- Look at all the reading aids. Italics, bold print, chapter or section objectives, and end-of-chapter questions help you sort, comprehend, and remember.

QUESTION: Help your mind focus on what is important by asking questions.

- Use the boldface headings to form questions you think will be answered in the section. Good questions help you read with a purpose and will improve your comprehension.

- After you have formed your own questions, read the questions at the end of the chapter. They will focus on information you should learn. You will learn better when your mind is actively searching for answers. Using a two-column chart, write your questions in the first column and the answers in the second.

READ: Fill in the information.

- Read one section at a time with your questions in mind. Look for the answers, and notice if you need to make up some new questions. Add them to your two-column chart.

RECITE: Stop to help your mind to concentrate and learn.

- After each section, stop, recall your questions, and see if you can answer them. If not, look back again (as often as necessary) but don't go on to the next section until you can answer all the questions.

REVIEW: Refine your organization and memory of the reading.

- When you've finished the entire chapter using these steps, go back over the questions you created. Fold your chart so that you can't read the answers. See if you can still answer the questions. If not, look back and refresh your memory.

(33) Sunshine Outline

Purpose

A sunshine outline is a graphic organizer that asks all the "reporter's questions" about a reading. Graphic organizers are visual aids that help learners to use visual cues to define relationships among concepts (Dunston, 1992). They can help English learners identify main ideas, focus attention on key vocabulary, paraphrase to recall information, use context to construct meaning, and make predictions. Hudelson (1986) points out that language develops best when the language learner focuses on accomplishing something with others rather than on the language itself. Group activities such as developing a sunshine outline are ideal for language learning.

Target learning strategies

• Asking factual questions   • Answering questions   • Summarizing

Procedure

1. Discuss how someone who is writing nonfiction must be careful to get all the facts straight. The questions *who, what, when, where, why,* and *how* help us to find the most important information.

2. Draw a sunshine outline on the board or an overhead projector. Demonstrate its use by having students ask you the questions on the organizer about an event that happened to them, such as an event at school. Write brief answers on the outline. Explain that you are using the past tense of verbs to tell about something that already happened.

3. Have students copy the sunshine outline onto their papers. Ask students to complete the outline by describing an interesting event from their past. Have pairs or small groups share and discuss their answers.

4. Demonstrate using the organizer to outline the narrative of a section of their textbook. For example, you might answer these questions: *Who helped build the railroad in the west? When was it built? Where did it begin and end?* Show learners anonymous student outlines and have them discriminate between complete ones and incomplete or inaccurate ones.

5. Have students use the sunshine outline to take notes on a chapter section. Have students share their outlines. Offer constructive feedback and encouragement.

Example

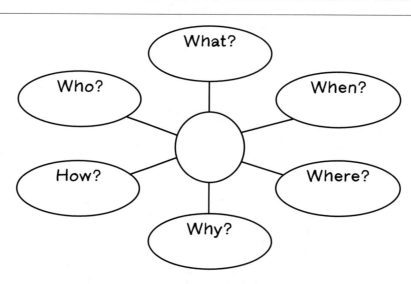

(34) T-Chart

Purpose

A T-chart is a graphic organizer that asks students to focus attention on key issues or items in a reading and to record important details about them. Language develops best when English learners focus on accomplishing something with others rather than on the language itself (Rigg & Hudelson, 1986). As a result, group activities such as T-charts are ideal for learning a language.

Target learning strategies

- Classifying
- Comparing
- Developing key vocabulary
- Taking notes to record important information

Procedure

1. Have students draw a T on their papers. Help them label the two columns with two classes or categories, as shown in the example below.

2. Model finding items to categorize under one of the two labels.

3. Encourage students to work together to complete the chart. Review and assess their work. Then encourage them to use T-charts when taking notes or reviewing for a test.

Example

Reformers	Ideas
John Calvin	People are sinful by nature. The ideal government is a theocracy (a religious state).
Anabaptists	Only adults should be baptized. Church and state should be separate.

(35) Think-Aloud

Purpose	A think-aloud (Dave, 1983) is a teacher modeling strategy that lets students observe learning strategies in action. The goal is to move from demonstration to supported practice to independent performance of the strategies by English learners.

Target learning strategies

- Drawing on prior knowledge to make hypotheses
- Making connections between texts
- Using text format, sequence, and features to decide what is important

Procedure

1. Decide on the learning strategy to be taught and the content you will use. For example, you might use predicting when teaching about the colonization of Africa.

2. Determine what you really want students to know about the strategy, what you want the outcome to be, and how you will assess comprehension.

3. Plan your think-aloud carefully.
   - Think about the strategy to be taught.
   - Identify the central concept and key themes of the text you have selected.
   - Think about your own experiences related to the themes.
   - Put self-stick notes in your text at points where you might pause and think aloud.

4. Introduce the lesson. Explain what a think-aloud is.

5. Demonstrate the think-aloud as you read the text. Stop and look at the ceiling or otherwise show when you're stopping to think as you read. Use language such as "I predict that . . ." and " I am using this predicting strategy because . . .". It may take many repetitions before students understand the technique thoroughly.

6. Ask students to try a think-aloud on their own.

7. Assess the think-aloud, perhaps having individuals think aloud themselves as they use the new strategy.

(36) Time Line

Purpose

A time line is a graphic organizer that asks students to focus attention on key dates and to record important information that happened on those dates. A graphic organizer is a visual aid that defines relationships among concepts (Dunston, 1992). Graphic organizers can help English learners identify and classify information into categories, visualize a classification system, compare information, focus attention on key information, and take notes to record important information. Rigg and Hudelson (1986) point out that language develops when the English learner focuses on accomplishing something with others rather than focusing on the language itself. So group activities to fill in graphic organizers such as time lines are ideal for language learning.

Target learning strategies

- Classifying
- Comparing
- Developing key vocabulary
- Analyzing

Procedure

1. Provide students with a time line or ask students to draw a line on a piece of notebook paper. Explain that time lines can be vertical or horizontal.

2. Have students mark off points in the time line and label them with key years or points in time. An example is shown below.

3. Model labeling important events that happened during that time period. Encourage students to work together to complete the chart.

4. Review and assess students' work, perhaps creating a time line on the board and filling in with answers from students in the class.

Example

The Breakup of the Soviet Union

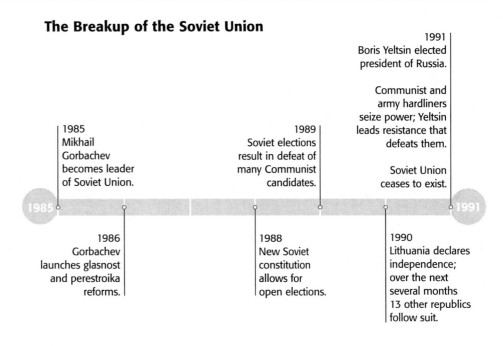

(37) Tree Diagram

Purpose

A tree diagram is a graphic organizer that asks students to focus attention on details that support a main idea. It illustrates superordinate and subordinate relationships. A graphic organizer is a visual aid that defines relationships among concepts (Dunston, 1992). It can be used to help English learners identify and classify information, visualize a classification system, compare information, focus on key information, and take notes. Hudelson (1986) points out that language develops when the English learner focuses on accomplishing something with others rather than focusing on the language itself. Therefore, group activities such as filling in a tree diagram are ideal for language learning.

Target learning strategies

- Classifying
- Comparing
- Developing key vocabulary
- Analyzing

Procedure

1. Provide students with a tree diagram, or have each student draw one.

2. Provide students with the main statement for the organizer. An example is shown below.

3. Model adding important concepts that support the main idea. Encourage students to work together to complete the chart.

4. Review and assess students' work, perhaps creating a tree diagram on the board and filling it in with answers from students.

Example

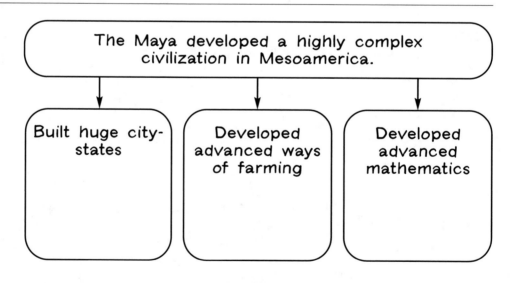

(38) Venn Diagram

Purpose

A Venn diagram charts comparisons and contrasts between two concepts. Venn diagrams help students understand similarities and differences. A graphic organizer is a visual aid that defines relationships among concepts (Dunston, 1992). As explained in other sections of this book, graphic organizers can help English learners identify and classify information, visualize a classification system, compare information, focus attention on key information, and take notes to record important information. Hudelson (1986) explains that language develops when the English learner focuses on accomplishing something with others rather than concentrating on the language itself. Group activities that use graphic organizers such as Venn diagrams are ideal for language learning.

Target learning strategies

- Analyzing
- Comparing
- Contrasting

Procedure

1. Provide students with a Venn diagram or ask them to draw two overlapping circles on a piece of paper.

2. Explain that each circle represents one of the concepts being compared, and that the overlapping area represents what these two concepts have in common. Demonstrate with a simple comparison, such as cats and dogs.

3. Help students label the sections of the diagram for the comparison they will make. An example is shown below.

4. Support students as they brainstorm a few items that might go in each section of the diagram.

5. Help students use the information from the diagram to make comparisons and contrasts. For the example below, such a statement might be, "People in Athens moved from farming to trade, while people in Sparta remained a farming community. In both Athens and Sparta, people spoke Greek." Encourage students to use Venn diagrams as they take notes or review for a test.

Example

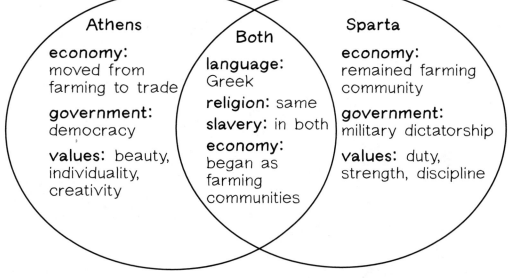

(39) Viewing Videos with Language Learners

Purpose

Videos are very helpful to language learners because they can comprehend images though their language is still developing. With videos, they also have opportunities to connect the images to the language of the videos and use both to develop mental images (Stempleski & Arcario, 1992). Students may need help in developing the supporting language with which to discuss the videos and clips you watch together. The following suggestions are meant to help you use video materials effectively with learners of English to teach language, culture, and content.

Target learning strategies

- Using images
- Selective attention
- Summarizing
- Making inferences

Procedure

1. Use short sequences to promote active viewing. The best sequences for language learners are those in which words and pictures are closely parallel.

2. Provide repeated viewings. Treat the video sequence as a two-level text of a) words and b) pictures.

3. Provide support for active viewing before, during, and after the video.

   Previewing

   - Use preparation and prediction to help students understand topic, background, context, and expectations.
   - Give students a specific focus on what to look and listen for.

   Viewing and re-viewing

   - Show the video with the sound off; use the freeze frame to stop and discuss what students see. Or show the video with the picture off. (Cover the screen or turn the color contrast to black.) Stop frequently to discuss what students think they would be seeing if they could see the pictures.
   - At first, focus on specific information: names, numbers, places, characteristics, events. Then move on to higher-order analysis. (See the QAR strategy elsewhere in this book.)
   - Check understanding frequently—for key ideas, situations, activities, connections, and who said what. Use question types such as true-false, matching, cloze passages (passages with words missing, usually every fifth or tenth word), scrambled order of events, lists of terms, or partial dictation.

   Language analysis

   - Recall key terms, phrases, expressions, and language structures.
   - Discuss how specific lines were said (pronunciation, intonation, fluency) and practice saying them the same way.

   Content and culture

   - Ask questions and offer insights about culture represented in the video. Focus on perspectives and issues; look for causes and effects without assigning judgment.

(40) Word Squares

Purpose

A word square graphic organizer (McCloskey & Stack, 1996) is a tool for multidimensional vocabulary development. Students use a variety of ways to study a new term.

Target learning strategies

- Planning
- Selective attention
- Using images
- Cooperating with peers
- Taking notes
- Self-evaluating

Procedure

1. Have students help you create a word square for an unfamiliar word in the chapter you are studying. Help them provide a translation, a symbol or picture for the word, the meaning in their own words and in the words of a dictionary or glossary, and a sentence that demonstrates the meaning of the word (not just one that uses the word). An example is shown below.

2. Help students each select an important word to study with a word square.

3. Have students create their word squares. Circulate and offer feedback and suggestions.

4. Have students pair up and teach one another the words. Remind students that they can use this tool on their own with challenging words.

Example

Word: Imperialism Translation: imperialismo	Symbol or Picture:
My meaning: Imperialism is when one country is in charge of another country. Dictionary definition: imperialism (noun) 1. rule of a country, territory, or nation by an emperor or empress; 2. one nation extending control over the political or economic life of other nations; 3. the system or practices of an imperialist government	Sentence: European imperialism meant that most African colonies could not control their own politics or economics.

(41) Writing Frames

Purpose

A writing frame is a pattern or template (Buehl, 2001) that students may use as a model in learning to write specific genres. Teachers use writing frames to help English learners develop their own mental structures for various kinds of writing, such as cause-effect, compare-contrast, problem-solution, or letter writing. Writing frames contain key necessary vocabulary and structures—for example, words for transition such as *first, next,* and *then*—to support students in their first attempts at writing in a particular genre (Wood & Harmon, 2001).

Target learning strategies

- Using context clues
- Analyzing words
- Predicting
- Writing using a text format
- Understanding features of various text structures

Procedure

1. Share models of the type of writing students will be asked to do. An example is shown below. Show the template on a transparency and point out the structure by highlighting key elements of the writing such as the topic sentence, transitions, and the summary or conclusion.

2. Have learners listen as you read aloud a quality example of the target writing type, such as an answer to an essay question.

3. Put the frame transparency back on the screen and have learners help you use the frame to create an example. Read the result together. Then have learners help you make a list of the features of a quality performance of this type of writing.

4. Assign the writing task to the students. Encourage them to use the frame to structure their writing.

5. Have learners evaluate their own writing by looking at the list the class created in step 3.

Example

Essay Question: What effects did the development of farming have in Native American societies?

The change from hunting and gathering to farming had many important effects on Native American societies. First,

_____

_____. Also,

_____

_____. Both of these

changes led to _____

_____.

In conclusion, _____

_____

_____.

References and Resources

Agor, B. (ed.). (2000). *Integrating the ESL standards into classroom practice: Grades 9–12.* Alexandria, VA: TESOL.

Anderson, N.J. (1999). *Exploring second language reading: Issues and strategies.* Boston, MA: Heinle.

Armbruster, B. B., Anderson, T. H. & Meyer, J. L. (1992). Improving content-area reading using instructional graphics. *Reading Research Quarterly, 26*(4), 393–416.

Bangert-Downs, R. L., Kulik, C. C., Kulik, J. A., & Morgan, M. (1991). The instructional effects of feedback in test-like events. *Review of Educational Research, 61*(2), 212–238.

Bryant, D. P., Ugel, N., Thompson, S., & Hamff, A. (1999). Instructional strategies for content-area reading instruction. *Intervention in School and Clinic, 34*(5), 293–302.

Buehl, D. (2001). *Classroom strategies for interactive learning.* Newark, DE: International Reading Association.

Building comprehension skills by teaching imaging. *The ESOL Multicultural Newsletter, Fort Hays State University.* (2003). Retrieved September 18, 2003: http://www.fhsu.edu/~rbscott/news/apr/story8.htm

California Department of Education. (2000). *Strategic teaching and learning: Standards-based instruction to promote content literacy in grades four through twelve.* Sacramento, CA: CDE Press.

Cary, S. (1997). *Second language learners.* York, ME: Stenhouse.

Chamot, A., & O'Malley, M. (1994). *The CALLA handbook: Implementing the cognitive academic language learning approach.* Reading, MA: Addison Wesley.

Chamot, A., & O'Malley, M. (1989). "The Cognitive Academic Language Learning Approach." In *When They Don't all Speak English: Integrating the ESL student into the regular classroom,* edited by P. Rigg and V. Allen. Urbana, Illinois: NCTE

Christison, M.A., & Bassano, S. (1987). *Purple cows and potato chips: Multi-sensory language acquisition activities.* Burlingame, CA: Alta Book Center.

Coady, J. & T. Huckin, eds. (1997). Second language vocabulary acquisition. Cambridge: Cambridge University Press.

Daniels, H. & Bizar, M. (1998). *Methods that matter: Six structures for best practice classrooms.* York, ME: Stenhouse.

Davey, B. (1983) Think-Aloud—Modeling the Cognitive Process of Reading Comprehension. *Journal of Reading, 10,* 44–47.

Dunston, P.J. (1992). "A critique of graphic organizer research." *Reading Research and Instruction, 31,* (2), 57–65. (ERIC document Reproduction Service No. 441 050)

Echevarria, J. & Graves, A. (2003). *Sheltered content instruction: Teaching English-language learners with diverse abilities, 2nd Ed.* New York: Allyn & Bacon.

Echevarria, J., Vogt, M., & Short, D.J. (2000). *Making content comprehensible for English language learners: The SIOP model.* Needham Heights, MA: Allyn & Bacon.

Ellis, R. (1994). *The Study of Second Language Acquisition.* Oxford, UK: Oxford University Press.

ESL standards for pre–K-12 students. (1997). Alexandria, VA: TESOL.

Frayer, D., Frederick, W. C., and Klausmeier, H. J. (1969). *A Schema for Testing the Level of Cognitive Mastery.* Madison, WI: Wisconsin Center for Education Research.

Fulwiler, T. (1980). Journals across the disciplines. *The English Journal, 69*(9), 14–19.

Gibbons, P. (1993). *Learning to learn in a second language.* Portsmouth, NH: Heinemann.

Gibbons, P. (2002). *Scaffolding Language, Scaffolding Learning: Teaching Second Language Learners in the Mainstream Classroom.* Portsmouth, NH: Heinemann.

Halliday, M. (1985). "Three aspects of Children's Language Development: Learning language, learning through language, and learning about language." In *Oral and Written Language Development Research: Impact on the Schools.* Y. Goodman, M. Haussler, and D. Strickland (eds.). Urbana, IL: NCTE.

Harvey, S., & Goudvis, A. (2000). *Strategies that work: Teaching comprehension to enhance understanding.* York, ME: Stenhouse.

Herber, H. (1978). *Teaching reading in content areas (2nd Ed.)* Englewood Cliffs, NJ: Prentice-Hall.

Herrell, A.L. (2000). *Fifty strategies for teaching English language learners.* Upper Saddle River, NJ: Merrill.

High, J. (1993). *Second Language Learning Through Cooperative Learning in the Classroom.* Riverside, CA: Kagan.

Hudelson, S. (1986). "ESL Children's Writing: What We've Learned, What We're Learning." In Children and ESL: Integrating Perspectives. P. Rigg & D. S. Enright, (eds). Alexandria, VA: TESOL.

Johnson, D. W., Johnson, R. T., & Holubec, E. J. (1998). *Cooperation in the classroom.* Edina, MN: Interaction Book Company.

Johnson, D. & Pearson, P. D. (1984). *Teaching reading vocabulary (2nd Ed.).* New York: Holt, Rinehart & Winston.

Kagan, S. (1994). *Cooperative learning.* Riverside, CA: Kagan.

Kinsella, K. (1998). Strategies for promotion of active and effective reading to learn for English language learners. Handout for San Francisco Unified School District Language Academy workshop, March 5, 1998.

Krashen, S. (1987). *Principles and practices in second language acquisition.* New York: Prentice-Hall.

Kulik, C. L. C. & Kulik, J.A. (1982). Effects of ability grouping on secondary school students: A meta-analysis of evaluation findings. *American Educational Research Journal, 19*(3), 415–428.

Labbo, L.D. & Teale, W.H. (1990). Cross-age reading: A strategy for helping poor readers. *The Reading Teacher, 43*:6, 362–369.

Larsen-Freeman, D. & Long, M. H. (1991). *An introduction to second language acquisition research.* New York, NY: Longman Inc.

Lindfors, J. (1987). *Children's language and learning.* Pearson.

Long, M. (1980). Inside the "black box": Methodological issues in research on Language teaching and learning. *Language Learning, 30,* 1, 1–42.

Marzano. R. J., Pickering, D. J., & Pollock, J. E. (2001). *Classroom instruction that works: Research-based strategies for increasing student achievement.* Alexandria VA: Association for Supervision and Curriculum Development.

Mason, P. A., & Schumm, J. S. (eds.). (2003). *Promising practices for urban reading instruction*. Newark, DE: International Reading Association.

McCloskey, M. L. & Stack, L. (1996). *Voices in Literature*. Boston: Heinle & Heinle.

Nation, P. (1990). *Teaching and learning vocabulary*. Heinle & Heinle, Boston, MA, 1990.

Oczkus, L. D. (2003). *Reciprocal teaching at work: Strategies for improving comprehension*. Newark, DE: International Reading Association.

Ogle, Donna M. (1986). "K-W-L: A Teaching Model That Develops Active Reading of Expository Text." *Reading Teacher,* 39, 564–570.

Palinscar, A.S. & Brown, A.L. (1986). Interactive teaching to promote independent learning from text. *The Reading Teacher, 39,* 771–777.

Peyton, J. & Reed, L (1990). *Dialogue Journal Writing with Nonnative English Speakers: A Handbook for Teachers*. Alexandria, VA: TESOL.

Pica, T., R. Young, and C. Doughty (1987). "The Impact of Interaction on Comprehension." *TESOL Quarterly 21* (4): 737–58.

Pica, T. (1994). "Research on Negotiations: What Does It Reveal About Second Language Learning Conditions, Processes and Outcomes?" Language Learning 44: 493–527.

Raphael, T. E. & C. Wonnacott. (1985) Heightening Fourth-grade Students' Comprehension: Sources of Information for Answering Comprehension Questions. *Reading Research Quarterly, 20*(10), 282–96.

Routman, R. (1991). *Invitations: Changing as teachers and learners K-12*. Portsmouth, NH: Heinemann.

Sadler, R. S. (2001). *Comprehension Strategies for Middle Grade Learners*. Newark, DE: International Reading Association.

Samway, K. D., Whang, G., & Pippitt, M. (1995). *Buddy reading: Cross-age tutoring in a multicultural school*. Portsmouth, NH: Heinemann.

Slaven, R. E. (1983). *Cooperative learning*. New York: Longman.

Stauffer, R. (1968). *Directing reading maturity as a cognitive process*. New York: Harper & Row.

Stempleski, S., & Arcario, P. (1992). *Video in second language teaching: Using, selecting, and producing video for the classroom*. Alexandria, VA: TESOL.

Swain, M. (1995). "Three Functions of Output in Second Language Learning." In *Principle and Practice in Applied Linguistics: Studies in Honour of H. G. Widdowson,* ed. G. Cook and B. Seidlehofer. Oxford, UK: Oxford University Press.

Vacca, R. T., & Vacca, J. L. (1998). Content Area Reading (3rd ed.). New York: HarperCollins.

Van Lier, L. (1996). *Interaction in the Language Curriculum: Awareness, Autonomy and Authenticity*. London: Longman.

Walberg, H. J. (1999). Productive teaching. In H. C. Waxman & H. J. Walberg (eds.) *New directions for teaching practice and research,* 75–104. Berkeley, CA: McCutchen Publishing Corporation.

Wilhelm, J. D., Baker, T. N., & Dube, J. (2001). *Strategic reading: Guiding students to lifelong literacy, 6–12*. Portsmouth, NH: Heinemann.

Wood, K., & Harmon J. (2001). *Strategies for integrating reading & writing in middle and high school classrooms*. Westerville, OH: National Middle School Association.

Wood, K. (1988). Guiding students through informational text. *The Reading Teacher, 41*(9), 912–920.

Introduction to Lesson Plan Structure

These lesson plans have been designed to implement proven strategies for teaching content to English learners (ELs). **It is important that *all* steps be done.** Those without training in techniques for teaching English to speakers of other languages (ESOL) may want to skip steps or pick and choose the activities they prefer. However, it is the cumulative process that makes the lesson effective. Teachers who persist should find the investment of time worthwhile, and students should retain the material. Those who take short cuts may not experience such success.

The lesson plan for Chapter 1, Section 1, has been laid out in detail, with explanations of the steps, and suggestions for how to approach them. The remaining lesson plans are abbreviated, but they should be approached in a similar manner.

Using the English Language Strategies

As you read the lesson plans, you will see references to EL strategies in **boldface type.** You may refer to the front of the book, on pages 00–00, to find an in-depth explanation of how to use each strategy. All of the strategies are arranged in alphabetical order for ease of reference.

Key to Text and Ancillary References

CT	Critical Thinking Transparencies	**RSG**	Reading Study Guide (English and Spanish)
FA	Formal Assessment	**RSG Audio**	Reading Study Guide Audio CDs (English and Spanish)
IA	Integrated Assessment		
IDR	In-Depth Resources	**SAE**	Access for Students Acquiring English: Spanish Translations
MLG	Multi-Language Glossary of Social Studies Terms		
MT	Map Transparencies	**TE**	Teacher's Edition
OMA	Outline Maps with Activities	**TT**	Test Practice Transparencies
PE	Pupil's Edition	**Video**	*The Voyageur Experience in World Geography* Video Series

Suggestions for Providing Comprehensible Input

1. Face students when speaking.

2. Speak clearly and a little slowly as needed.

3. Use gestures and facial expressions to enhance meaning.

4. Increase wait time. Pause after asking questions.

5. Paraphrase often.

6. Be aware of use of idioms and figurative language. Explain or paraphrase as needed.

7. Frequently ask questions to check comprehension.

8. Reteach as needed.

Chapter 1 Section 1

Resources for English Learners		
TE pp. 6, 9	TT 1	OMA p. 2
RSG pp. 5–6	RSG Audio	IA p. 8
IDR1 p. 10	FA p. 4	MLG

The Five Themes of Geography

Step 1 Activate Prior Knowledge

This step lets students contribute information about something in their own lives that can be related to the lesson. Teachers should isolate and emphasize student contributions that most closely parallel concepts in the lesson and explain their relationship to what students are about to learn. Engaging students by beginning with what they know helps them in learning new material.

Do a **Round Robin** activity to have students activate their experience with and prior knowledge of world geography. Place a globe in the center of the room. Ask students what the object in the center of the room is called (globe). Ask them what it shows (scale model of Earth that shows places and geographical features). Ask several students to come up to point out where they have been on the globe. Divide students into groups of three or four. Ask students to go around the group and name things that will be labeled on the globe. The first student might name an ocean, the second student might name a mountain range. Other students might mention continents, rivers, countries, cities, and so forth. Then ask students to name places and things that they have direct experience with that are labeled on the globe. Point out and describe the following elements of a globe to students: equator, longitude, latitude. Describe several students' birth places using these terms.

Step 2 Preview Main Ideas and Language

Connect Visually Using visuals to preview the content of text material is important for English learners.

Have students look at the diagram of the Geographic Grid on PE p. 6 of their text. Have them trace with their fingers the lines of latitude and longitude on the top two diagrams. Indicate that lines of longitude run up and down, meeting at the poles. Indicate that lines of latitude run parallel to the equator. Then ask students how the latitude and longitude lines might be used to identify where they were born. Use thumbs up/thumbs down to check student comprehension. Record students' answers on the board or the overhead for later use.

Build Vocabulary This activity clarifies student understanding of essential vocabulary. The key term or terms that explain the main concepts of the lesson must be defined and discussed. Check for accurate understanding of terms, paraphrasing or giving examples as needed.

Go over the definitions of the social studies terms defined in the gray box in Part A of Activity Sheet 1.1. Use **Peer Vocabulary Teaching** to check if students have understood the definitions and the hints that appear with some of them. Reexplain any terms students find difficult to understand. Once students indicate they are comfortable with the definitions, have them write the terms that complete the statements on the Activity Sheet.

Continued

Step 3
Make Objectives Explicit

It is important to clarify objectives before having students read a section so that they understand why they are reading. Making objectives clear helps students focus on what is most important in the section. There is one objective given for each major heading in a section of the textbook.

Explain that students will be using **Signals** to tell how well they understand each objective for this lesson. Read each objective aloud and write it on the board or on an overhead projector.

- Describe the ways that geographers study the world.
- Tell what *location* means and the two different ways geographers describe it.
- Tell how geographers define *place*.
- Explain what a *region* is.
- Tell what is meant by *human-environment interaction*.
- Explain what geographers mean by *movement*.

Repeat and paraphrase objectives that students signal are confusing. If possible, ask students to translate difficult words for their classmates. If students' first language is Spanish, have them read the lesson summary in the *Reading Study Guide* (English or Spanish).

Step 4
Support Student Reading

Cooperative Work Cooperative learning is especially important for English learners. A key principle for making information comprehensible is increasing interaction in the classroom. Increased interaction promotes communication, which in turn provides more practice with language skills. It has been shown that this cooperative work helps students retain new language as well as new content knowledge.

Use Part B of Activity Sheet 1.1 to complete a **Jigsaw Reading** activity, as described in detail on page 00. Divide students into groups of four to six, including students who are good at explaining abstract concepts in each group. Assign each of the "expert groups" one of the themes of geography to study, dividing the theme of location into two sub-themes: absolute location and relative location. Students should complete the chart on the Activity Sheet together when they get back to their "home groups." After students have completed the chart, go over the definitions and examples of each theme, to make sure that students have understood the concepts and vocabulary.

On One's Own These questions check student comprehension. To guide students, the page and paragraph indicating the location of the answer is provided.

Preview the following questions by asking students what they understand them to mean and providing clarification, as needed. Have them use the questions as a guide for reading the section. Once students have finished reading, help them create complete sentences to reflect their answers.

1. What are the five themes of geography? (p. 5, par. 6 and graphic organizer)

2. How do you determine absolute location? (p. 6, pars. 2–4)

3. What is the difference between a place and a location? (p. 6, par. 1; p. 7 par. 1)

4. What are three types of regions? (p. 7, pars. 2–3; p. 8, pars. 1–2)

5. What kinds of things do people do when they interact with their environment? (p. 8, par. 1)

6. What kinds of things do geographers studying movement pay attention to? (p. 9, par. 1)

Step 5
Prepare for
Assessment

Alternative Assessment This activity allows English learners to demonstrate understanding without formal testing.

Have students complete the Reteaching Activity from TE p. 9. Share with students the Standards for Evaluating a Group Discussion on p. 8 of *Integrated Assessment* and have them use this form as a guide for running a good discussion. Then assign students to complete the worksheet on p. 10 of *Unit 1 In-Depth Resources* to consolidate their understanding of important concepts of Chapter 1, Section 1. You can collect and grade this worksheet for your assessment.

Formal Assessment These activities provide preparation, practice, and options for formal testing.

Review the test-taking strategies that go with Transparency TT1 or use Transparency TT1 as a formal assessment. In addition, you may wish to assign the Section Quiz for Chapter 1, Section 1, found on page 4 of the *Formal Assessment* book.

ACTIVITY SHEET 1.1

Part A. Build Vocabulary

Key Terms Write the term in each blank that best completes the statement.

> **absolute location:** the exact place where a geographic feature is found
>
> **relative location:** a place described in relation to other places around it
>
> **equator:** the imaginary line that divides the northern half of the earth from the southern half
>
> **latitude:** imaginary lines that circle the earth and are parallel to the equator
>
> **longitude:** imaginary lines that go around the earth meeting at the poles

1. The imaginary line that circles the earth dividing the earth exactly in half is called the _____.

2. If you describe a place by explaining how far it is from your home you are describing the _____ of the place.

3. The imaginary lines that run north and south around the earth and all meet at the poles are called _____ lines.

4. The imaginary lines that run east and west around the earth and are parallel to the equator are called _____ lines.

5. If you describe a place using latitude and longitude to say exactly where it is, you are describing the _____ of the place.

Part B. Cooperative Work

Complete the chart by working with your group to define each term and list examples.

Theme	Definition/description	Examples
Location: Absolute Location (p. 6, pars. 1–4)		
Location: Relative Location (p. 6, pars. 1, 5)		
Place (p. 7, par. 1 and photograph)		
Region (p. 7, pars. 2–3; p. 8, pars. 1–2)		
Human-Environment Interaction (p. 8, pars. 3–4)		
Movement (p. 9)		

Resources for English Learners
TE p. 12   OMWA   RSG pp. 7–8, 11–12
RSG Audio   IA p. 28   TT 2
FA pp. 5, 7–10   MLG

The Geographer's Tools

**Step 1
Activate Prior
Knowledge**

Have students draw a map of their neighborhood, a mall, or some other favorite place. Then do a **Brainstorming** activity to share what tools they would use to make a map. During discussion, reinforce the idea that students would need not only tools for drawing but also their own knowledge of locations and distances.

**Step 2
Preview Main
Ideas and
Language**

Connect Visually Ask students to turn to the diagram on PE p. 11. Define the term *data* in context and explain that the plural of *data* is data ("these data"). Direct students to point to the numbered steps in order on the diagram and then to match the steps with the numbers in the picture.

Build Vocabulary Go over the definitions of the terms defined in Part A of Activity Sheet 1.2. Point to the globe on p. 10, the satellite on p. 11, and relevant pages of the Geography Skills Handbook (pp. 14–23) to explain the terms. Check to see whether students understood the definitions, using any of the **Signals** activities. Have them work in pairs to complete the graphic organizer on the Activity Sheet.

**Step 3
Make Objectives
Explicit**

Write the following objectives on the board. Ask students to work in pairs to look through Chapter 1, Section 2, to find text or illustrations that will help them fulfill each objective. If students' first language is Spanish, have them read the lesson summary in the *Reading Study Guide* (English or Spanish).

- Compare advantages and disadvantages of maps and globes.
- Identify three types of maps.
- Tell how mapmakers use satellites and other tools.

**Step 4
Support Student
Reading**

Cooperative Work Divide students into groups of six; in each group, the students should divide the reading into the chunks indicated in the chart on Activity Sheet 1.2, Part B. Have students do a **Draw It Out** activity to visualize what they are learning as they read their assigned chunks. Once drawings have been labeled, the group should complete the chart.

On One's Own Preview the following questions by asking students what they understand them to mean and by providing clarification as needed. Have students use the questions as a guide for reading the section. Once students have finished reading, help them create complete sentences for their answers.

1. How would a globe show a region differently than a map? (p. 10, pars. 3–4)

2. What does a topographic map show? (p. 11, par. 1)

3. What do surveyors do and how is most surveying done today? (p. 11, par. 3)

4. What is GIS and how does it work? (p. 12, diagram; p. 13 pars. 1–2)

**Step 5
Prepare for
Assessment**

Alternative Assessment Assign students to create a sketch map, as described in the Skillbuilder Lesson on TE p. 12. Go over the general guidelines for Information Assessing Activities and the specific guidelines for evaluating maps on p. 28 of the *Integrated Assessment* book. Use this form when evaluating students' maps.

Formal Assessment Review the test-taking strategy for TT 2 prior to testing. You may want to use *Formal Assessment* Form A, the less-challenging assessment, or administer it as a practice test prior to formal testing with Forms B or C.

ACTIVITY SHEET 1.2

Part A. Build Vocabulary

Key Terms Use the graphic organizer to show the relationships among the
key terms. Note that you will need to use plurals of some or all of the words.

> **globe:** a three-dimensional representation of the earth
>
> **map:** a flat, graphic representation of certain parts of the earth's surface
>
> **cartographer:** a mapmaker
>
> **satellite:** an information-gathering device that people have put into orbit around the earth or another planet
>
> **database:** a large collection of information, organized, stored, and made available by one or more computers

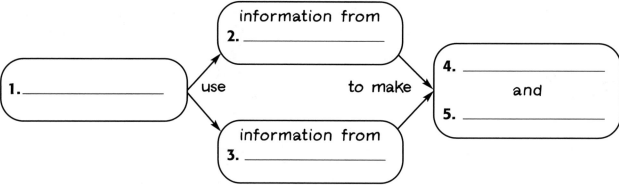

Part B. Cooperative Work

Complete the chart by working with your group to figure out the answers.

1. List 2 advantages a globe has over a map. (p. 10, pars. 3–4)	
2. List 2 advantages a map has over a globe. (p. 10, par. 4)	
3. Name 3 basic types of maps and tell the purpose of each. (p. 11, par. 1)	
4. What is the first step in making a map? What are 2 ways this can be done? (p. 11, par. 3; p. 12, par. 1)	
5. What is Geographic Information Systems (GIS) and how is it used? (p. 12 diagram, p. 13 pars. 1 and 2)	
6. How do geographers use Global Positioning System (GPS)? (p. 13, pars. 3)	

Resources for English Learners
TE p. 29   RSG pp. 13–14   RSG Audio
IA pp. 7, 28   TT 3   FA p. 19
MLG

The Earth Inside and Out

**Step 1
Activate Prior Knowledge**

Bring an apple, a peach, an avocado, and a hard-boiled egg to school. Show the food items to students and ask what the inside of each is like. Elicit the idea that each has different layers. Divide the class into small groups and give each group one of the items to examine. Use a **Draw It Out** activity and have students diagram and label the different layers. Point out that the earth has layers similar to those of the food items they examined.

**Step 2
Preview Main Ideas and Language**

Connect Visually Ask students to look at the diagram of the solar system on PE p. 27. Have students point to each planet in order from the sun outward. Let students share what they know about the planets. Write students' responses on the board, returning to them after the class finishes the section.

Build Vocabulary Go over the key terms for this lesson. Make sure that students understand all of the terms by giving a right/wrong definition for each term and having them show answers with **Signals.** Point to illustrations in the lesson to explain some of the terms. Use Part A of Activity Sheet 2.1 to organize vocabulary terms under one of three headings.

**Step 3
Make Objectives Explicit**

Write the objectives on the the board and read them to the class. Have each student work with a partner to restate the objectives. If students' first language is Spanish, have them read the lesson summary in the *Reading Study Guide* (English or Spanish).

- Describe the solar system and the earth's location in the solar system.
- Describe the structure of the earth, both inside and outside the planet.
- Explain the theory of continental drift and describe the evidence for it.

**Step 4
Support Student Reading**

Cooperative Work Pair students up to complete Part B of Activity Sheet 2.1. Once you have gone over the answers and students have made corrections to their graphic organizers, use **Inside-Outside Circles** to review the information. Have students use their Activity Sheets to ask and answer questions 1–10.

On One's Own Preview the following questions by asking students what they mean. Then have students search for their answers while reading. Once students have finished, help them create complete sentences to reflect their answers.

1. What are the three basic layers or shells that form the earth? (p. 28, par. 2)

2. What are the four spheres found above the earth's surface? (p. 28, par. 3)

3. What is the inside of the earth like? (p. 28, par. 2 and diagram)

4. What three spheres form the biosphere? (p. 28, par. 3)

**Step 5
Prepare for Assessment**

Alternative Assessment Have students complete the Reteaching Activity from TE p. 29, which has groups create diagrams. Share with students the Standards for Evaluating a Cooperative Activity on p. 7 of *Integrated Assessment* and the Specific Guidelines for Evaluating a Chart/Table/List on p. 28 of *Integrated Assessment*. Use both of these forms when evaluating their diagrams.

Formal Assessment Review the test-taking strategies for TT3 prior to testing. Then assign the Section Quiz for Chapter 2, Section 1, found on p. 19 of the *Formal Assessment* book.

ACTIVITY SHEET 2.1

Part A. Build Vocabulary

Key Terms Organize the key terms under one of the three headings in the chart.

continent   solar system   continental drift   magma   crust
atmosphere   lithosphere   hydrosphere   biosphere   core   mantle

Earth in outer space	Earth's landmasses	Structure of Earth	
		(Inside the Earth)	(At or above Earth's surface)

Part B. Cooperative Work

Complete the graphic organizer with your partner and then review answers in a class activity.

Solar System

1. The solar system consists of (p. 27, par. 2) _____
2. The number of known planets in the solar system is (p. 27, par. 2) _____
3. The earth's location is (p. 27, par. 2) _____

Earth Inside

What are the three main layers of the earth? (p. 28, par. 2)
4. _____
5. _____
6. _____

Earth Inside and Out

Earth Outside

What are the four main layers on or above the earth? (p. 28, par. 3)
7. _____
8. _____
9. _____
10. _____

Resources for English Learners

TE p. 35	RSG pp. 15–16	RSG Audio
IA p. 25	TT 4	FA p. 20
MLG		

Bodies of Water and Landforms

**Step 1
Activate Prior
Knowledge**

Do a **Think-Pair-Share** activity to have students describe to each other the most beautiful place they have either visited or imagined visiting. What is the general landscape like? What makes the place especially beautiful? Explain that this lesson will introduce students to different landforms and bodies of water.

**Step 2
Preview Main
Ideas and
Language**

Connect Visually Bring photographs or illustrations of some of the different types of landforms and the bodies of water illustrated on PE pp. 34–35. Direct students to turn to this two-page illustration. One at a time, read aloud the description of each landform and show the photograph or illustration you have of it.

Build Vocabulary Go over the definitions of the social studies terms defined in the gray box in Part A of Activity Sheet 2.2. Use **Numbered Heads Together** to check student comprehension of definitions. Have students write the terms that complete the sentences in the paragraph on the Activity Sheet.

**Step 3
Make Objectives
Explicit**

Write the objectives on the board and read them aloud to the class. After you've read the objective ask students to indicate their level of understanding by holding up two fingers if they understand it completely, one finger if they partially understand it, and zero fingers if they do not understand it at all. Have students holding up two fingers explain the objective to the other students. If students' first language is Spanish, have them read the lesson summary in the *Reading Study Guide* (English or Spanish).

- Describe what the earth's oceans are like.
- Describe the structure of the earth's lakes and rivers.
- Explain what ground water is and how it is related to the water table.
- Describe the landforms that appear on the continents and the ocean floor.

**Step 4
Support Student
Reading**

Cooperative Work Divide students into groups of eight and divide the section into four parts: first, the oceans; second, the hydrologic cycle; third, lakes, rivers, and ground water; fourth, landforms. Within each group, students should pair up and do a **Draw It Out** activity using the section of Activity Sheet 2.2, Part B that corresponds to their topic.

On One's Own Preview the following questions by asking students what they understand them to mean. Then have students search for the answers while reading. Help them write their answers in complete sentences.

1. How does ocean water circulate, or move, from place to place? (p. 32, par. 4)

2. How does the hydrologic cycle circulate water? (pp. 32–33 and diagram)

3. How does water collect in drainage basins? (p. 33, par. 1–2)

4. Name four kinds of landforms. (p. 34–35 and p. 36, par. 1)

**Step 5
Prepare for
Assessment**

Alternative Assessment Assign the Activity Option: Exploring Local Geography from TE p. 35. Share with students the General Guidelines for Evaluating Art Type Activities and Specific Guidelines for Evaluating an Illustration/Diagram both on p. 25 of *Integrated Assessment*.

Formal Assessment Review the test-taking strategies for TT4. Assign the Section Quiz for Chapter 2, Section 2, on p. 20 of the *Formal Assessment* book.

ACTIVITY SHEET 2.2

Part A. Build Vocabulary

Key Terms Write the term in each blank that best completes the sentences
in this paragraph.

> **drainage basin:** an area that includes a large river and all of its smaller
> branches (called tributaries) and the land that is nearby; all of the rain and
> snow that falls on this land eventually flows into the river
>
> **ground water:** water in the rocks below the surface of the earth
>
> **hydrologic cycle:** the continuous movement of water from the air, the
> oceans, the earth's surface, and back again
>
> **water table:** the highest level that ground water fills up, or saturates

The **1.** _____ is the continuous cycling of water between
the air, the oceans, and the earth. Part of this cycle includes the falling of
rain and snow, which flows into rivers. An area that is drained by a large
river and all of its tributaries is called a **2.** _____. Some
water on the surface of the earth does not flow in rivers, but is held by the
soil. Some water is held in the pores of rock below the soil. This is called
3. _____. The level in the rock that the ground water
saturates, or fills up, is called the **4.** _____. This level may
change, depending on the amount of rain or snow in a region or the amount
of water that is pumped out of the ground.

Part B. Cooperative Work

Work in pairs and then together with your entire group to complete the chart.

Oceans	Hydrologic Cycle	Lakes, Rivers, and Ground Water	Landforms

Resources for English Learners
TE p. 41	RSG pp. 17–18	RSG Audio
IA p. 7	TT 5	FA p. 21
MLG		

Internal Forces Shaping the Earth

Step 1 **Activate Prior Knowledge**	Do a **Think-Quickwrite-Pair-Share** activity to have students share what they know about earthquakes. Give students three minutes to write, asking them to explain how they came by their information. Explain that these natural phenomena all give evidence of the powerful forces inside the earth that shape its surface.
Step 2 **Preview Main Ideas and Language**	**Connect Visually** Bring two wooden or plastic-foam blocks to class to demonstrate the different types of plate movements that occur at plate boundaries, illustrated at the bottom of PE pp. 38–39. Have students look at each illustration, while you read the name of the plate movement shown. Then do your demonstrations. After each demonstration, ask students which type of plate movement they think you've shown. **Build Vocabulary** Create a **Word Square** for the word *magma,* with students making suggestions for the definition, a symbol, translations into other languages, and a sample sentence. Then, assign each student to make a Word Square for one of the five words listed in Part A of Activity Sheet 2.3. Refer students to the Glossary at the back of the book to find the definition. Then have them complete the sentences on the Activity Sheet.
Step 3 **Make Objectives Explicit**	Write the objectives on the board. Then read them one at a time and have students indicate their level of understanding with thumbs up, down, or sideways. Encourage a student who has his or her thumb up to restate the objective. If students' first language is Spanish, have them read the lesson summary in the *Reading Study Guide* (English or Spanish). • Define tectonic plates and describe the different ways that they can move. • Explain the causes and effects of earthquakes. • Tell about the location and actions of volcanoes.
Step 4 **Support Student Reading**	**Cooperative Work** Pair students for a **Peer Tutoring** activity. Have them work together to complete the chart in Activity Sheet 2.3, Part B. Review answers with the entire class. **On One's Own** Preview the following questions by asking students what they understand them to mean. Then have students search for their answers while reading. Once students have finished, help them create complete sentences to reflect their answers. **1.** What is a tectonic plate and why are tectonic plates important? (p. 37, par. 2 and p. 38, par. 1) **2.** What are earthquakes and what kind of damage can they cause? (p. 39, par. 2–3, p. 40, par. 1–4) **3.** What are volcanoes and where do they occur? (p. 40, par. 5 and p. 41, par. 2)
Step 5 **Prepare for Assessment**	**Alternative Assessment** Assign the Reteaching Activity on TE p. **41.** Share with students the Standards for Evaluating a Cooperative Activity on p. 7 of *Integrated Assessment.* Use these criteria when evaluating their work. **Formal Assessment** Review the test-taking strategies for TT5 prior to testing. Then assign the Section Quiz for Chapter 2, Section 3, found on p. 21 of the *Formal Assessment* book.

ACTIVITY SHEET 2.3

Part A. Build Vocabulary

Key Terms Write the term in each blank that best each sentence. You may need to make some terms plural.

| tectonic plate | fault | earthquake | tsunami | volcano |

1. An opening in the earth's surface where melted rock can pour out is called a _____.

2. The earth's crust is made of very large moving pieces. These pieces are called _____.

3. _____ occur when the earth shakes or trembles because of movement of the tectonic plates.

4. A crack or break in the earth's crust is called a _____.

5. Earthquakes can cause a huge, fast-moving ocean wave to form. Such waves are called _____.

Part B. Cooperative Work

Work with a partner to complete the chart. Define all key terms and use complete sentences.

Cause	Effect
1.	Tectonic plates move. (p. 37, par. 2)
2.	The Red Sea widened. (p. 38, par. 2–3)
3.	The Himalayas are created. (p. 38, par. 2, 4; p. 39)
4.	Earthquakes occur. (p. 39, par. 2)
5.	Tsunamis form. (p. 40, par. 4)

Resources for English Learners
RSG pp. 19–20   RSG Audio
IA p. 7   FA pp. 22, 23–26
TT 6   MLG

External Forces Shaping the Earth

Step 1 Activate Prior Knowledge	Sand a piece of wood with sandpaper. Point out the sawdust that results as well as changes in the surface of the wood. Then do a **Brainstorming** activity, asking students if they can think of other similar actions (scouring a pan, cleaning a sink with abrasive cleanser). Explain that similar actions also happen on the earth's surface. These shape the landscape and cause soil to form.

**Step 2
Preview Main
Ideas and
Language**

Connect Visually Show students illustrations of landforms, such as the dramatic photograph on PE p. 42. Encourage students to describe how the landform might have come to be. Record student answers on the board, returning to them when students have completed the section so that they can confirm or revise.

Build Vocabulary Tell students how to use the **Anticipation Guide** in Part A of Activity Sheet 2.4, first filling in their individual responses, next filling in a second set of responses after they discuss each statement with their group. Allow time after students have read the section to fill in the "Textbook" column and to correct answers.

**Step 3
Make Objectives
Explicit**

Write the objectives on the board. Have students pair up and, referring to their textbook, take turns identifying the objective that will be covered in each section. If students' first language is Spanish, have them read the lesson summary in the *Reading Study Guide* (English or Spanish).

• Describe mechanical weathering and chemical weathering.

• Explain how erosion (water, wind, glacial) helps to create landforms.

• Identify the materials that are mixed together in the soil.

**Step 4
Support Student
Reading**

Cooperative Work Group students for a **Numbered Heads Together** activity to answer the questions on the chart in Activity Sheet 2.4, Part B. Allow time for students to write the answers on their charts before going on.

On One's Own Preview the following questions by asking students what they understand them to mean. Then have students search for their answers while reading. Once students have finished, help them answer in complete sentences.

1. What is the difference between mechanical weathering and chemical weathering? (p. 42, par. 3 and p. 43, par. 1-)

2. What is erosion and how does water contribute to erosion? (p. 43, par. 3–6)

3. Describe the five main factors that affect the soil in a place. (p. 45, par. 2)

**Step 5
Prepare for
Assessment**

Alternative Assessment Assign the GeoActivity on PE p. 45 as a group project. Share with students the Standards for Evaluating a Cooperative Activity on p. 7 of *Integrated Assessment*. Use these criteria when evaluating their work.

Formal Assessment Assign the Section Quiz for Chapter 2, Section 4, found on p. 22 of the *Formal Assessment* book. Then prepare students for the Chapter Test by going over the test-taking strategies for TT6. Then give a Chapter Test from the *Formal Assessment* book. Note that Form A of the Chapter Test is less challenging than Forms B and C.

ACTIVITY SHEET 2.4

Part A. Build Vocabulary

Key Terms Work individually and then with your group to fill in the first two columns of the Anticipation Guide. Marking *T* for true or *F* for false. Fill in the third column after you have read the entire section. Correct any false answers.

You	Group	Textbook	Topic—External Forces Shaping the Earth
			1. Weathering refers to the changes in weather that occur on the earth's surface.
			2. Tiny pieces of rock are called **sediment.**
			3. Erosion occurs when blowing wind or moving water pushes sediment from one place to another.
			4. A large, long-lasting mass of ice that moves downhill due to gravity is called a **glacier.**
			5. Humus includes the minerals and ground-up rock that form part of the soil.

Part B. Cooperative Work

Work with your group to learn about external factors shaping the earth.

Tell how these external forces shape the earth.
1. Mechanical and chemical weathering (p. 42, par. 2–3, p. 43, par. 1–2)
2. Water erosion (p. 43, par. 4–6)
3. Wind erosion (p. 44, par.1–2)
4. Glacial erosion (p. 44, par. 3–5)
5. Soil formation (p. 45, par. 1, 3)

Resources for English Learners
TE p. 52   RSG pp. 23–24   RSG Audio
IA pp. 7, 28   TT 7   FA p. 35
MLG

Seasons and Weather

**Step 1
Activate Prior
Knowledge**

Group students so that in each group there is one student who moved to your state from a different place. Have students work together to make a **Venn Diagram** comparing the weather in your local area to the weather where the student came from. Elicit the idea that wide variations in weather occur on the earth's surface.

**Step 2
Preview Main
Ideas and
Language**

Connect Visually Do a demonstration with a globe and a flashlight to show how the earth's tilt affects the angle at which the sun's rays hit the Northern Hemisphere at different times of year. Then refer students to the diagram on p. 49. Repeat the demonstration, asking students to identify which part of the diagram you are showing at each of the four stages of your demonstration.

Build Vocabulary Go over the definitions of the vocabulary words listed in the chart in Part A of Activity Sheet 3.1. (You can find these definitions in the Glossary at the back of the textbook.) Then have students draw a picture to illustrate the definition of each word. Students can share their pictures in small- or large-group discussion.

**Step 3
Make Objectives
Explicit**

Write the objectives on the board. For each objective, ask students to find the picture or paragraph in the section that they think will be most helpful to study while they work on the objective. Let students pair up to share their ideas. If students' first language is Spanish, have them read the lesson summary in the *Reading Study Guide* (English or Spanish).

- Explain how the yearly changes in the earth's position as it goes around the sun cause the seasons.

- Identify different factors that affect the weather in a place.

- Describe the four main types of very severe, or extreme, weather.

**Step 4
Support Student
Reading**

Cooperative Work Divide students into groups of six and have them do **Jigsaw Reading** to fill in the chart in Part B of Activity Sheet 3.2. Review answers with the entire class.

On One's Own Preview the following questions by asking students what they understand them to mean. Then have students search for answers while reading. Once students have finished, help them answer in complete sentences.

1. How do the earth's revolution and tilt cause the seasons? (p. 49, par. 3–5)

2. What is the difference between weather and climate? (p. 50, par. 1)

3. What causes the three types of precipitation? (p. 50, diagram; p. 51, par. 1)

4. What are five types of weather extremes? Describe their effects. (pp. 51–53)

**Step 5
Prepare for
Assessment**

Alternative Assessment Assign the Cooperative Learning Activity on TE p. 52, which asks students to create a map. Share with students the Standards for Evaluating a Cooperative Activity on p. 7 of *Integrated Assessment* and General Guidelines for Evaluating Information Assessing Activities and Specific Guidelines for Evaluating a Map, both on p. 28 of *Integrated Assessment*.

Formal Assessment Review the test-taking strategies for TT7 prior to testing. Then assign the Section Quiz for Chapter 3, Section 1 found on p. 35 of the *Formal Assessment* book.

ACTIVITY SHEET 3.1

Part A. Build Vocabulary

Key Terms Draw a picture to help you remember the definition of each key term.

solstice	equinox
climate	**weather**
precipitation	

Part B. Cooperative Work

Work with your group to complete the chart.

Cause of the seasons (p. 49, par. 2–5)			
Causes of weather patterns (p. 50, par. 2–3)			
General cause of precipitation (p. 50, par. 4)			
Causes of the three types of precipitation (p. 50, diagram; p. 51, par. 1)			
Causes and effects of hurricanes (p. 51, par. 3–4)			
Causes and effects of tornadoes (p. 51, par. 5; p. 52, par. 1)	Causes and effects of blizzards (p. 52, par. 2–3)		
Effects of droughts (p. 53, par. 1	Effects of floods (p. 53, par. 2–3)		

Resources for English Learners
OMA p. 4   RSG pp. 25–26   RSG Audio
IDR1 p. 32   TT 8a, 8b   FA p. 36
MLG

Climate

Step 1 Activate Prior Knowledge	Write the terms *tropics, polar zone,* and *temperate zone* on the board. Then define the terms. You may wish to bring in props, such as pineapples, coconuts, mangos, or other tropical fruit to represent the tropics; a stuffed polar bear, a heavy parka, or other items could represent polar zones. Then have students categorize the objects by climate zone. Write down their answers under the appropriate term.

Step 2 Preview Main Ideas and Language

Connect Visually Hand out copies of the World Map on page 4 of *Outline Maps with Activities* or any outline map of the world. Ask students to use a red pencil to color the tropic region, a green pencil to color the temperate regions, and a blue pencil to color the polar regions. Let students look at their maps after they read the section to make corrections, as necessary.

Build Vocabulary Help students figure out the meaning of the key terms in Part A of Activity Sheet 3.2. Once students are sure that they understand the meanings of the words, have them complete the vocabulary exercise. Go over the correct answers with the class.

Step 3 Make Objectives Explicit

Write these objectives on the overhead or on the board. Read the objectives aloud, and ask students to indicate their level of understanding. Have students who indicate they understand the objectives reexplain them to others. If students' first language is Spanish, have them read the lesson summary in the *Reading Study Guide* (English or Spanish).

- Discuss the five main factors that influence the climate of a region
- Tell how El Niño, La Niña, and the greenhouse effect change the climate

Step 4 Support Student Reading

Cooperative Work Divide students into groups of four to complete the spider diagram in Part B of Activity Sheet 3.2. Do a **Carousel Review** and help students correct any incorrect answers.

On One's Own Preview the following questions by asking students what they understand them to mean. Then have students search for their answers while reading. Once students have finished, help them answer in complete sentences.

1. How do wind and ocean currents affect climate? (p. 54, par. 3–5; p. 55 par. 1–2)

2. How do latitude and elevation affect climate? (p. 55, par. 3, p. 56, par. 1–3)

3. What is El Niño and how does it affect climate? (p. 57, par. 1, diagram)

Step 5 Prepare for Assessment

Alternative Assessment Have students work in pairs to complete the worksheet on p. 32 of the *In-Depth Resources* for Unit 1, which involves filling in blanks with a missing word or phrase. Review any of the concepts students seem to be having difficulty understanding.

Formal Assessment Review the test-taking strategies for TT8a and TT8b prior to testing. Then assign the Section Quiz for Chapter 3, Section 2 found on p. 36 of the *Formal Assessment* book.

ACTIVITY SHEET 3.2

Part A. Build Vocabulary

Key Terms Fill in the blanks with the correct terms to complete the
sentences in the paragraph.

convection	elevation	greenhouse effect	topography

Several different factors affect the climate a region has. One factor
is **1.** _____, which is the shape and surface of the land
and the location of different kinds of landforms. Another factor is
2. _____, which is the height of the land above sea level.
A third factor is **3.**_____, which is movement of heat in
the atmosphere due to the upward motion of the air. Ocean currents and
a region's latitude also affect the climate. The earth's climate has been
warming up since the late 1800s. Some scientists think that this global
warming is caused by **4.** _____, which is the trapping of
heat close to the earth because of an increase of certain gases in the
atmosphere that hold in heat.

Part B. Cooperative Work

Work with your group to describe how the factors listed affect climate.

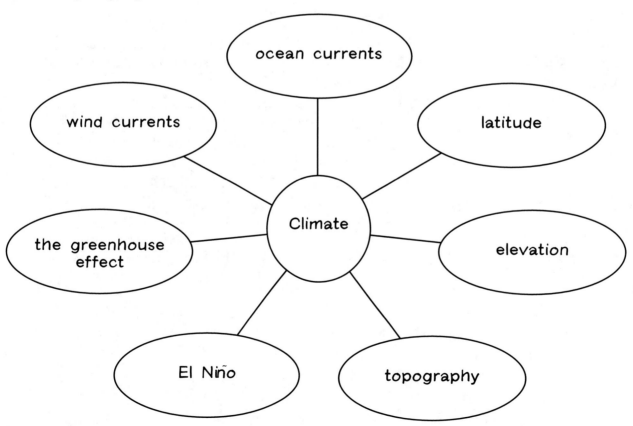

Resources for English Learners
RSG pp. 27–28   RSG Audio
IA pp. 7, 28   TT 9a, 9b
FA p. 37   MLG

World Climate Regions

Step 1 **Activate Prior Knowledge**	Do a **Think-Pair-Share** activity to have students describe their ideal climate. Encourage them to give details on the relative amounts of sunshine and rainfall, temperature range, and seasons they think they would most enjoy. Explain that in this section they will learn about the 12 different types of climate.
Step 2 **Preview Main Ideas and Language**	**Connect Visually** Use the map on PE pp. 60–61 to list the names of the 12 different kinds of climate on the board or the overhead. Then have students take out their corrected maps from the Connect Visually activity done to introduce Chapter 3, Section 2. Have students work in pairs to predict which part of the world will have each type of climate. They should write their predictions on their map.
	Build Vocabulary Go over the definitions of the terms in the gray box in Part A of Activity Sheet 3.3. Once students are sure that they understand the meanings of the words, have them pair up to complete the vocabulary exercise. Go over the correct answers and reasons for them with the class.
Step 3 **Make Objectives Explicit**	Write these objectives on the board and read them aloud to students. Pair students up and have them explain the objectives to each other in their own words. If students' first language is Spanish, have them read the lesson summary in the *Reading Study Guide* (English or Spanish).
	• Identify five factors that define climate regions.
	• Describe the temperature and precipitation patterns of each of the world's major climate regions.
Step 4 **Support Student Reading**	**Cooperative Work** Divide students into groups of four to record information about types of climates on the map in Part B of Activity Sheet 3.3. Suggest that each student be in charge of describing 3 of the 12 climate types to the others in the group. Go over the climate types on a large map with the entire class.
	On One's Own Preview the following questions by asking students what they understand them to mean. Then have students search for their answers while reading. Once students have finished, help them answer in complete sentences.
	1. What are five factors that determine climate type? (p. 59, par. 3–4)
	2. How do tropical climates differ from each other? (p. 60, par. 1; p. 61, par. 1)
	3. How do the two types of dry climates differ from each other? (p. 61, par. 2; p. 62, par. 1–2)
	4. How do humid subtropical and Mediterranean climates differ from each other? (p. 62, par. 3, 5)
Step 5 **Prepare for Assessment**	**Alternative Assessment** Do a **Roundtable** activity, dividing the class into six groups. Give each group an outline map for a different continent from *Outline Maps with Activities* and have them label the different climate regions. Share with students the Specific Guidelines for Evaluating a Map on p. 28 of *Integrated Assessment*.
	Formal Assessment Review the test-taking strategies for TT9a and TT9b prior to testing. Then assign the Section Quiz for Chapter 3, Section 3 found on p. 37 of the *Formal Assessment* book.

ACTIVITY SHEET 3.3

Part A. Build Vocabulary

Key Terms For each group of words, identify the word that does not belong with the other two and tell how the other two words are related.

> **humid:** moist
>
> **permafrost:** lower layer of soil that is always frozen
>
> **semiarid:** receiving only a small amount of rainfall; *semi-* means partly; *arid* means dry
>
> **temperature:** degree of heat or cold; temperature is measured with a thermometer in units called degrees
>
> **tundra:** the flat, treeless land that is found near the Arctic Ocean

1. tundra   temperature   permafrost   Word that doesn't belong _____

How the two words are related _____

2. humid   semiarid   temperature   Word that doesn't belong _____

How the two words are related _____

Part B. Cooperative Work

Work with your group to locate the different climate regions on the map.

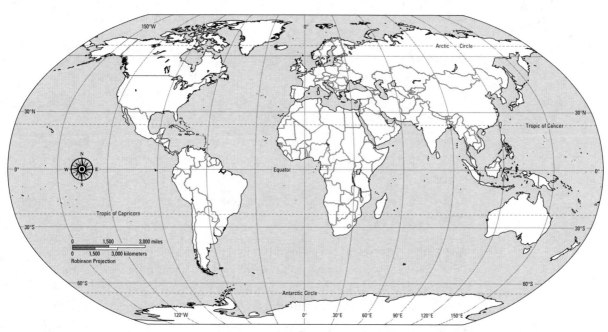

Chapter (3) Section 4

Resources for English Learners		
TE p. 67	RSG pp. 29–32	RSG Audio
IA p. 25	FA pp. 33, 39–42,	TT 10
MGT	43–46, 47–50	

Soils and Vegetation

**Step 1
Activate Prior
Knowledge**

Bring in pictures of the ten different biomes (world vegetation regions) listed in the map key on PE p. 66. Write the names of the biomes on the board. Divide students in groups of three and have them write down the names of the biomes in a list. Show students the pictures, identifying them by number, and have students work together to classify the pictures by biome.

**Step 2
Preview Main
Ideas and
Language**

Connect Visually Have students study the map on PE p. 66 and then compare it with the map on pp. 60–61. Talk about the main topic of each map. Then ask students to tell similarities they see between the maps. Write their responses on the board.

Build Vocabulary Go over the definitions of the terms in Part A of Activity Sheet 3.4, using the Glossaries at the back of the book. Once students are sure that they understand the meanings of the words, have them pair up to categorize the terms in the **T-Chart.** Go over the correct answers with the class.

**Step 3
Make Objectives
Explicit**

Write these objectives on the board and read them aloud to students. Have students identify and discuss the most important word or phrase in each of the objectives. If students' first language is Spanish, have them read the lesson summary in the *Reading Study Guide* (English or Spanish).

- List the important characteristics of soils.
- Identify and describe the world's main vegetation regions.
- Describe ways in which people have changed the environment.

**Step 4
Support Student
Reading**

Cooperative Work Divide students into groups of three to complete the matrix in Part B of Activity Sheet 3.4. Students will need to use the map and the text on p. 66 to complete the chart. When groups are done, go over the answers in a **Numbered Heads Together** activity.

On One's Own Preview the following questions by asking students what they understand them to mean. Then have students search for their answers while reading. Once students have finished, help them answer in complete sentences.

1. How does soil affect the vegetation in a region? (p. 65, par. 2–3)

2. What are the four main types of biomes? (p. 65, par. 3)

3. What are some differences between deciduous and coniferous forests? (p. 66, par. 1)

4. How are plants that live in the tundra and the desert adapted to harsh conditions? (p. 66, par. 3)

**Step 5
Prepare for
Assessment**

Alternative Assessment Have students complete the Reteaching Activity from TE p. 67, which involves their creating illustrations of the four main biomes. Share with students the General Guidelines for Evaluating Art Type Activities and Specific Guidelines for Evaluating Illustrations both on p. 25 of *Integrated Assessment*. Use these criteria when evaluating their illustrations.

Formal Assessment Assign the Section Quiz for Chapter 3, Section 4, found on p. 38 of the *Formal Assessment* book. Then prepare students for the Chapter Test by going over the test-taking strategies for TT10. Then give a Chapter Test from the *Formal Assessment* book.

ACTIVITY SHEET 3.4

Part A. Build Vocabulary

Key Terms

| biome | coniferous | deciduous | savanna | steppe |

Title: Two types of 1. _____

Category 2. _____ | Category 3. _____

Part B. Cooperative Work

Work with your group to fill in this matrix chart.

Biome	Trees	Grass	Moss	Cacti or shrubs	Hot	Temperate	Polar	Wet	Semi-arid	Dry
Rain Forest										
Deciduous Forest										
Coniferous Forest										
Savanna										
Steppes/ pampas										
Desert										
Tundra										

Resources for English Learners

TE p. 77	RSG pp. 33–34	RSG Audio
IA p. 8	TT 11	FA p. 51
MGT		

The Elements of Culture

**Step 1
Activate Prior Knowledge**

Ask students to bring in symbols of their family culture to share with the class. Students can bring in samples of food or objects related to daily life, art, handicraft, music, language, or religion. Define *culture* and talk about different aspects of culture, categorizing with students the examples they brought.

**Step 2
Preview Main Ideas and Language**

Connect Visually Pair students and direct them to use the map on p. 74 to figure out the language family that their first language(s) most likely belong(s) to. If their first language is an Indo-European language, students should locate it on the tree diagram and note the other languages closely related to it. Students should trace the origins of any other Indo-European languages they are learning.

Build Vocabulary Have students work in small groups to learn the meaning of each word in Part A of Activity Sheet 4.1. Assign students to work individually to complete Part A, going over the answers in class.

**Step 3
Make Objectives Explicit**

Write the objectives on the overhead or on the board and read them aloud to students. Have students indicate their degree of understanding by holding up zero, one, or two fingers. If necessary, let students who understand the objectives reexplain them to the class. If students' first language is Spanish, have them read the lesson summary in the *Reading Study Guide* (English or Spanish).

- Define culture and explain its importance.
- Discuss how culture changes and spreads.
- Describe how language unites and divides people and how it changes and spreads.
- Describe and categorize the world's major religions.
- Tell about ways cultures express themselves creatively.

**Step 4
Support Student Reading**

Cooperative Work To help students learn about different aspects of culture, divide them into groups of four and have them do **Jigsaw Reading** to complete the diagram in Part B of Activity Sheet 4.1. Go over answers in class.

On One's Own Preview the following questions by asking students what they understand them to mean. Then have students search for the answers while reading. Once students have finished, help them answer in complete sentences.

1. What factors make up culture? (p. 71, par. 2)

2. How does language diffuse, or spread? (p. 73, par. 5–6)

3. What are the world's major religions? (p. 75, par. 3–6, p. 76, p. 77. par. 1)

4. Give the three main ways cultures express themselves (p. 77, par. 2)

**Step 5
Prepare for Assessment**

Alternative Assessment Have students complete the Reteaching Activity from TE p. 77, which asks students to cite examples of cultural diffusion. Share with students the Standards for Evaluating a Group Discussion on p. 8 of *Integrated Assessment*. Use these criteria when evaluating the discussion.

Formal Assessment Go over the test-taking strategies for TT11. Then assign the Section Quiz for Chapter 4, Section 1, found on p. 51 of the *Formal Assessment* book.

ACTIVITY SHEET 4.1

Part A. Build Vocabulary

Key Terms Write the word described by each sentence.

acculturation   culture   diffusion   innovation

1. _____ This ties people to one group and separates them from other groups. It includes the knowledge, attitudes, and behaviors people of the group share and pass on.

2. _____ This occurs when a society changes because it adopts a new way of doing something.

3. _____ This occurs when ideas, patterns of behavior, or inventions spread from one society to another.

4. _____ This occurs when people create something new using a resource or a technology that that is not new to them.

Part B. Cooperative Work

Work with your group to learn about culture and its different aspects and to complete the spider diagram.

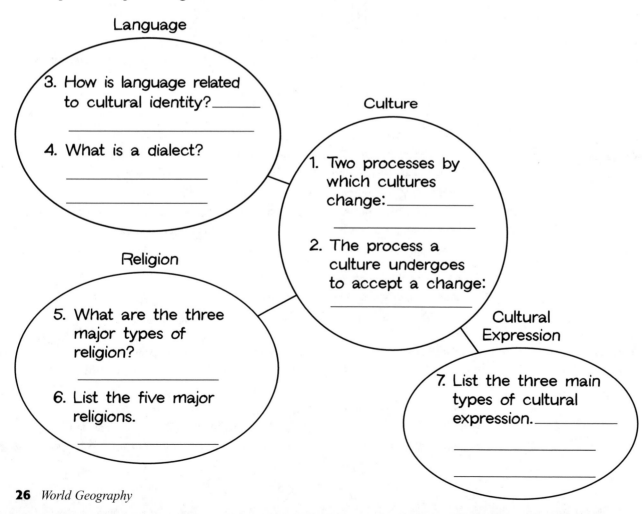

Language
3. How is language related to cultural identity?_____
_____
4. What is a dialect?
_____
_____

Culture
1. Two processes by which cultures change:_____
_____
2. The process a culture undergoes to accept a change:
_____

Religion
5. What are the three major types of religion?
_____
6. List the five major religions.
_____

Cultural Expression
7. List the three main types of cultural expression._____
_____
_____

Resources for English Learners
TE pp. 60–61	OMA p. 2	RSG pp. 35–36
RSG Audio	IDR1 p. 40	IA p. 7
TT 12	FA p. 52	MLG

Population Geography

**Step 1
Activate Prior
Knowledge**

Divide students into pairs and have them do a **Think-Pair-Share Activity** addressing the question: Does the world already have too many people, or can it support many more? In discussion, formally define *world population*. Explain that the section covers how geographers study and analyze world population.

**Step 2
Preview Main
Ideas and
Language**

Connect Visually Divide students into small groups and hand out copies of the World Map on p. 2 of *Outline Maps with Activities*. Refer students to the Climate Regions map on PE pp. 60–61; have students use this map and prior knowledge to predict places where many people live and few people live. Students should review their predictions after completing the section.

Build Vocabulary Go over the definitions of the terms in the gray box in Part A of Activity Sheet 4.2. When all students indicate that they understand the terms, let students work together to fill in the blanks to show their understanding of the concepts. Go over the correct answers with the class.

**Step 3
Make Objectives
Explicit**

Write these objectives on the overhead or on the board and read them aloud to students. Have students turn to a partner and explain, in their own words, what they will be learning in the section, based on the objectives. If students' first language is Spanish, have them read the lesson summary in the *Reading Study Guide* (English or Spanish).

- List the different factors that affect world population growth.
- Describe how the world's population is distributed, or spread out.
- Describe some things that influence the population density of a place and the carrying capacity of the place.

**Step 4
Support Student
Reading**

Cooperative Work Divide students into groups of three and have them do **Reciprocal Teaching** to read the section. Encourage students to rotate the role of leader. When they have finished the section, they should work together to complete the graphic organizer in Part B of Activity Sheet 4.2.

On One's Own Preview the following questions by asking students what they understand them to mean. Then have students search for the answers while reading. Once students have finished, help them answer in complete sentences.

1. How do you figure out the rate of natural increase for a population? Why is this rate important? (p. 79, par. 2)

2. Where does the majority of the world's population live? (p. 80, par. 3)

3. How does population density affect a nation or a region? (p. 81, par. 2–3)

**Step 5
Prepare for
Assessment**

Alternative Assessment Have students work together to complete the worksheet on p. 40 of *In-Depth Resources,* Unit 1. Adapt the Standards for Evaluating a Cooperative Activity (*Integrated Assessment,* p. 7) to this assignment, share your standards with students, and use them for evaluating each group's work.

Formal Assessment Go over the test-taking strategies for TT12. Then assign the Section Quiz for Chapter 4, Section 2, found on p. 52 of the *Formal Assessment* book.

ACTIVITY SHEET 4.2

Part A. Build Vocabulary

Key Terms Fill in the blanks to indicate how these key terms are related.

> **carrying capacity:** the number of people a particular area of land can support
>
> **mortality rate:** the number of deaths per thousand people; also called the death rate
>
> **population:** the number of people that live in a place
>
> **population density:** the average number of people who live in a measurable area

1. _____ is one of the factors that affects how fast a
2. _____ grows. The **3.** _____ of a place can
help determine the upper limit of the **4.** _____ of the place.

Part B. Cooperative Work

Read the section with your group to learn about population geography.
Then work together to complete the graphic organizer. Define each term
and explain the relationship between the terms, based on the arrows.

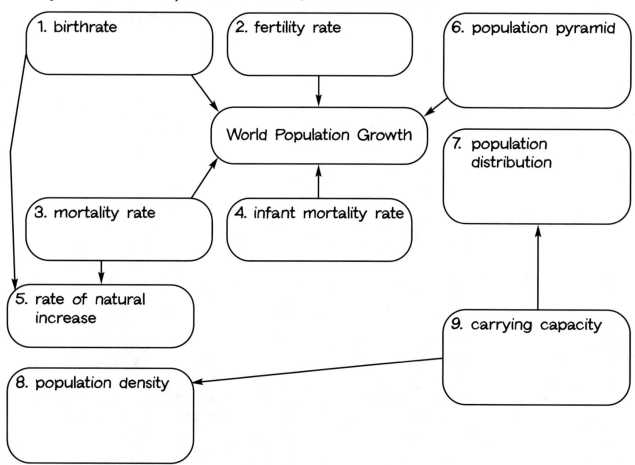

Resources for English Learners
TE p. 86   RSG pp. 37–38   RSG Audio
IA p. 7   TT 13a, TT 13b   FA p. 53
MLG

Political Geography

Step 1 **Activate Prior Knowledge**	In a class discussion, ask students to describe countries they or their family members have lived in or visited. In their descriptions, students should tell about the location, size, and political system of the country. If possible, have a world map and print or Internet resources available for students to quickly look up information. At the end of the discussion, explain that *nation* is another word for *country,* and that this section covers general characteristics of nations.
Step 2 **Preview Main Ideas and Language**	**Connect Visually** Group students in pairs and direct them to look at the world map on PE p. 74. Have them work together to identify all of the nations that they can. Let students check their answers against a classroom map or a globe. **Build Vocabulary** Pair students for **Peer Vocabulary Teaching** and suggest they use the flashcard game to practice the key terms in Part A of Activity Sheet 4.3. When both students have mastered all four words, have them complete Part A individually. Go over the answers with the class.
Step 3 **Make Objectives Explicit**	Write the objectives on the overhead or on the board. Then ask students to write a personal learning goal based on each objective. Let students share their goals with a partner. If students' first language is Spanish, have them read the lesson summary in the *Reading Study Guide* (English or Spanish). • Describe the different types of government. • List the three most important geographic characteristics used in describing a country. • Tell the difference between a natural boundary and an artificial boundary.
Step 4 **Support Student Reading**	**Cooperative Work** To help students understand what nations are, pair them up to complete Part B of Activity Sheet 4.3. Be sure to review student answers as a class. Once you have gone over the answers and students have made any necessary corrections to their charts, review the information using **Inside-Outside Circles.** Students can make up questions based on the information asked for in each part of the chart. **On One's Own** Preview the following questions by asking students what they understand them to mean. Then have students search for the answers while reading. Once students have finished, help them answer in complete sentences. **1.** What are the types of governments? (p. 83, par. 4) **2.** What are three geographic characteristics of countries? (p. 84) **3.** How do natural and artificial boundaries differ? (p. 85, par. 2–3) **4.** Why are local political systems useful? (p. 86, par. 1–2) **5.** Why are international political systems useful? (p. 86, par. 3–4)
Step 5 **Prepare for Assessment**	**Alternative Assessment** Assign the Reteaching Activity from TE p. 86, in which students summarize section objectives. Share the Standards for Evaluating a Cooperative Activity (*Integrated Assessment,* p. 7) and use them for evaluating each group's work. **Formal Assessment** Go over the test-taking strategies for TT13a and TT13b. Then assign the Section Quiz for Chapter 4, Section 3, found on p. 53 of the *Formal Assessment* book.

ACTIVITY SHEET 4.3

Part A. Build Vocabulary

Key Terms Fill in the blanks with the correct terms to complete the sentences in the paragraph.

| communism | democracy | dictatorship | monarchy |

In a **1.** _____, citizens hold political power either directly or through elected representatives. In a **2.** _____, a king, queen, or ruling family holds political power and may or may not share the power with citizens. In a **3.** _____, an individual or a group holds complete political power. With **4.** _____, nearly all political power and means of production (economic resources) are held by the government.

Part B. Cooperative Work

Work with your partner to read the section and complete the chart.

Nation/State: Define the following terms.	Types of Government: Describe the four main types.	Geographic Characteristics of Nations: Discuss the three most important.	National Boundaries: Define the two types and give an example for each.	Regional Political Systems: Give examples of the following.
1. state	**4.**	**8.**	**11.**	**13.** smaller than a state
	5.	**9.**		
2. nation			**12.**	**14.** larger than a state
	6.			
3. nation-state	**7.**	**10.**		

Resources for English Learners

TE p. 90   RSG pp. 39–40   RSG Audio
IA p. 8   TT 14   FA p. 54
MLG

Urban Geography

Step 1 **Activate Prior Knowledge**	Divide students in small groups and give them chart paper they can use to draw pictures of what they think are the good points and bad points of city life. Let groups share their drawings and ideas with the class. Explain that cities, called *urban areas,* have important functions.
Step 2 **Preview Main Ideas and Language**	**Connect Visually** Have students look at the map of Chicago on PE p. 90. Have them trace with their fingers how they might walk from LaSalle and Madison to the theater district. Ask students to list what they know about cities and how they know it. Record student input on the board. **Build Vocabulary** Divide students into groups of three. In each group, students should select a different key term from Part A of Activity Sheet 4.4. Have them use a **Word Square** to define the term and then teach it to the group. Let students share their Word Squares with the class.
Step 3 **Make Objectives Explicit**	Write these objectives on the overhead or on the board and read them aloud to students. Through class discussion, ask students to identify the most important word or phrase in each objective. If students' first language is Spanish, have them read the lesson summary in the *Reading Study Guide* (English or Spanish). • Explain how urban areas grow. • Give reasons why cities tend to be located in particular types of places. • List the three basic land-use patterns found in all cities. • Describe the functions of cities and tell why good transportation is essential.
Step 4 **Support Student Reading**	**Cooperative Work** Have students complete Part B of Activity Sheet 4.4, working in pairs. Let students share their answers with the class and discuss the variety of correct answers for each instruction. **On One's Own** Preview the following questions by asking students what they understand them to mean. Then have students search for the answers while reading. Once students have finished, help them answer in complete sentences. 1. What are the different parts that form a metropolitan area? (p. 87, par. 4–5) 2. What is urbanization and why is it important? (p. 88, par. 1) 3. What are the three basic land-use patterns found in all cities? (p. 89, par. 1) 4. Why is good transportation important in cities? (p. 90, par. 1–3)
Step 5 **Prepare for Assessment**	**Alternative Assessment** Assign the Reteaching Activity from TE p. 90, which has students draw a "Cities" word web. Share the Standards for Evaluating a Group Discussion on p. 8 of *Integrated Assessment* and use them for evaluating the participation and contributions of students. **Formal Assessment** Go over the test-taking strategies for TT14. Then assign the Section Quiz for Chapter 4, Section 4, found on p. 54 of the *Formal Assessment* book.

ACTIVITY SHEET 4.4

Part A. Build Vocabulary

Key Terms Use the Word Square to help you define one of the terms below. Share your Word Square with your group.

| suburb |
| metropolitan area |
| urbanization |

Word: Translation:	Symbol or Picture:
My meaning: Dictionary definition	Sentence:

Part B. Cooperative Work

Work with your partner to read the section. As you read the text under each heading, follow the instructions to draw and label a map of an urban area.

1. Draw an urban area, labeling the central city and suburbs.
2. Add small cities and towns to make a metropolitan area.
3. Show two geographic characteristics that explain why your city is where it is.
4. Use colored pencils and a key to indicate a land use pattern for your city.
5. Indicate places important to your city's functions; show transportation routes within the city.

Resources for English Learners
TE p. 94   RSG pp. 41–44   RSG Audio
IA p. 7   FA pp. 55, 56–59,   TT 15a, TT 15b
MLG   60–63, 64–67

Economic Geography

**Step 1
Activate Prior
Knowledge**

Write the word *economy* on the overhead or the board and lead students in a **Brainstorming** Activity related to the word. Once students have generated all the ideas they can, work together to categorize the ideas in a cluster diagram. Point out that the economy of a place is an important feature of the place.

**Step 2
Preview Main
Ideas and
Language**

Connect Visually Direct students to turn to the illustration showing the economics of pencil production on PE pp. 92–93. Have them divide into groups of three and refer to the illustration to make paper labels for a pencil identifying the materials the pencil is made of and indicating where each material might have come from.

Build Vocabulary Go over the key terms listed in Part A of Activity Sheet 4.5. Make sure students understand all the terms by using Thumbs Up/Thumbs Down or another **Signals** strategy. Then have students work in pairs to complete Part A.

**Step 3
Make Objectives
Explicit**

Write these objectives on the overhead or the board and read them aloud to the class. Have students look through the section to locate the information related to each objective. If students' first language is Spanish, have them read the lesson summary in the *Reading Study Guide* (English or Spanish).

- Identify the four basic types of economic systems.
- Define the four levels of economic activity.
- Explain renewable, non-renewable, and inexhaustible resources.
- Tell what makes up a nation's infrastructure, its GNP, and its GDP.
- Discuss the difference between developing and developed nations.

**Step 4
Support Student
Reading**

Cooperative Work To help students understand economic systems, divide them into groups of eight to do **Semantic Feature Analysis** of the sets of related terms from this section. The entire group should work together to complete the sample chart on the types of economic systems in Part B of Activity Sheet 4.5.

On One's Own Preview the following questions by asking students what they understand them to mean. Then have students search for the answers while reading. Once students have finished, help them answer in complete sentences.

1. What are the four basic economic systems? (p. 91, par. 3–5)

2. Describe the four levels of economic activity. (p. 92, par. 3–4)

3. What are natural resources, how are they classified, and why are they important? p. 93, par. 1–3)

4. What systems are part of a country's infrastructure? (p. 94, par. 1–3)

**Step 5
Prepare for
Assessment**

Alternative Assessment Assign the Cooperative Learning Activity from TE p. 94. Share the Standards for Evaluating a Cooperative Activity, p. 7 of *Integrated Assessment* and use them for evaluating students' work.

Formal Assessment Assign the Section Quiz for Chapter 4, Section 5, found on p. 55 of the *Formal Assessment* book. Prepare students for the Chapter Test by going over the test-taking strategies for TT15a and TT15b. Then give a Chapter Test from the *Formal Assessment* book.

CURRICULUM MATERIALS
BALDWIN WALLACE UNIVERSITY

ACTIVITY SHEET 4.5

Part A. Build Vocabulary

Key Terms Write the term in each blank that best completes the statement.

| economy   infrastructure   per capita income |

1. Geographers study the _____ of a nation by finding out how the people in that nation support themselves.

2. The average amount of money each person in a nation earns is the nation's _____.

3. Support systems including communications, transportation, water, electrical power, and sanitation are needed to keep a nation's economic system running. These support systems form the nation's _____.

Part B. Cooperative Work

Work with the entire group to complete the first chart. Then work with your partner to make your own chart on the set of terms from the section you've selected or been assigned.

Types of Economic Systems

	Production of goods and services is determined by a central government	Production of goods and services is determined by consumer demand
command economy	+	−
market economy		
mixed economy		

Landforms and Resources

Step 1 **Activate Prior Knowledge**	Review different landforms and then use a **Round Robin** activity to encourage students to name the landforms in the United States and Canada. Explain that all of the major types of landforms are found in the United States and Canada.
Step 2 **Preview Main Ideas and Language**	**Connect Visually** Hand out copies of the United States and Canada Physical Map on p. 10 of *Outline Maps with Activities* and ask students to work in pairs to draw or locate and label all of the landforms that they can on think of on the map. Students can refer to the list from the previous class discussion. **Build Vocabulary** Use a large map of North America to locate the places listed in Part A of Activity Sheet 5.1. Once students can identify each of the landforms, divide the class in small groups and ask each group to come up with three different ways of categorizing the places listed. Have each group share its methods of categorization.
Step 3 **Make Objectives Explicit**	Write these objectives on the overhead or on the board and read them aloud to students. Through class discussion, ask students to identify the most important word or phrase in each objective. If students' first language is Spanish, have them read the lesson summary in the *Reading Study Guide* (English or Spanish). • Tell about the location, size, and natural resources of the United States and Canada. • Describe five or more major landforms in the United States and Canada. • Explain how the region's resources shape life in the United States and Canada.
Step 4 **Support Student Reading**	**Cooperative Work** Divide the class into groups of five and have students complete the chart in Part B of Activity Sheet 5.1. Assign students who need extra help a **Peer Tutor** from among the group. Let students review and correct answers using a **Numbered Heads Together** Activity. **On One's Own** Preview the following questions by asking students what they understand them to mean. Then have students search for the answers while reading. Once students have finished, help them answer in complete sentences. **1.** How would you describe the size and resources of the United States and Canada? (p. 117, par. 3–4) **2.** Name seven landforms found in both the United States and Canada. (p. 118, map) **3.** Why are the Great Lakes important to both the United States and Canada? (p. 121, par. 4–5)
Step 5 **Prepare for Assessment**	**Alternative Assessment** Assign the Reteaching Activity from TE p. 122, which has students write brief summaries of objectives. Share the Standards for Evaluating a Cooperative Activity on p. 7 of *Integrated Assessment* and use them for evaluating the participation and contributions of students. **Formal Assessment** Go over the test-taking strategies for TT16. Then assign the Section Quiz for Chapter 5, Section 1, found on p. 68 of the *Formal Assessment* book.

ACTIVITY SHEET 5.1

Part A. Build Vocabulary

Key Places Work with your group to categorize the places listed below. One way of categorizing is already shown by the labels at the top of each column. Another way might be East, Central, and West. You can use the chart or draw your own graphic organizers on a separate sheet of paper.

| Appalachian Mountains | Great Plains | Canadian Shield |
| Rocky Mountains | Great Lakes | Mackenzie River |

Mountains	Flat Areas	Bodies of Water

Part B. Cooperative Work

Work on your own or with your group to complete the chart. As a group, go over your answers together.

Canadian and U.S. Landforms

	Eastern Lowlands	Appalachian Mountains	Great Plains	Canadian Shield	Rocky Mountains	Canadian Islands
Description						
General Location						
Size/variety						
Age/other						
Way shapes life						

Chapter 5 Section 2

Resources for English Learners
TE p. 125	RSG pp. 47–48	RSG Audio
IA p. 7	TT 17	FA p. 69
MLG		

Climate and Vegetation

**Step 1
Activate Prior
Knowledge**

Do a **Think-Quickwrite-Pair-Share** activity, with students describing local climate and vegetation. What are the different seasons like in terms of temperature and precipitation? What kinds of plants grow in the area? Explain that the United States and Canada have a variety of climates and vegetation.

**Step 2
Preview Main
Ideas and
Language**

Connect Visually Divide the class into small groups. Have students compare the two maps on p. 125 and come up with three questions based on the maps. As students share their questions, write them on the board. Encourage them to try to find the answers as they read; also, have resources available for students to look up information about vegetation and climate zones.

Build Vocabulary Use **New Word Analysis** to help students understand the meaning of the two words listed in Part A of Activity Sheet 5.2. Then have them complete Part A and share their drawings with a partner.

**Step 3
Make Objectives
Explicit**

Write the objectives on the board and read them to students. Check students' understanding using thumbs up/thumbs down. Let students who understand the objectives explain them to those who do not. If students' first language is Spanish, have them read the lesson summary in the *Reading Study Guide* (English or Spanish).

- Identify climate and vegetation types that the United States and Canada share.
- Identify differences in climate and vegetation between the United States and Canada.
- Discuss the effects of extreme weather in the United States and Canada.

**Step 4
Support Student
Reading**

Cooperative Work Divide the class into groups of three to complete the **Venn Diagrams** in Part B of Activity Sheet 5.2. When students have completed the activity, make a set of class diagrams that incorporate the correct answers.

On One's Own Preview the following questions by asking students what they understand them to mean. Then have students search for the answers while reading. Once students have finished, help them answer in complete sentences.

1. In which two types of climate might you find permafrost? (p. 123, par. 4–5)

2. What are four vegetation zones found in the United States but not in Canada? Give a reason for this. (p. 124, par. 4–6)

3. Why are some effects of extreme weather in the United States and Canada? (p. 126, par. 1–4)

**Step 5
Prepare for
Assessment**

Alternative Assessment Have students work in groups to complete the activity on TE p. 125, on severe weather events. Share the Standards for Evaluating a Cooperative Activity on p. 7 of *Integrated Assessment* and use them for evaluating the participation and contributions of students.

Formal Assessment Go over the test-taking strategies for TT17. Then assign the Section Quiz for Chapter 5, Section 2, found on p. 69 of the *Formal Assessment* book.

ACTIVITY SHEET 5.2

Part A. Build Vocabulary

Use the spaces below to make a drawing that helps you remember the
meaning of each of the two key terms.

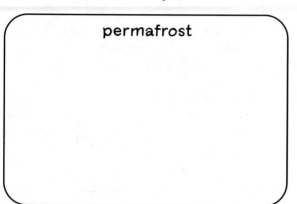

permafrost

prevailing westerlies

Part B. Cooperative Work

Work with your group to complete the Venn Diagrams.

Climate Zones of the United States and Canada

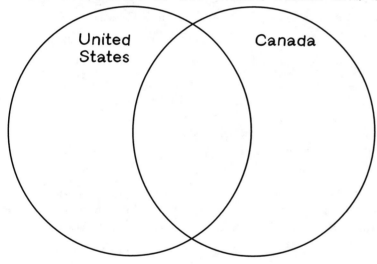

United
States

Canada

Vegetation of the United States and Canada

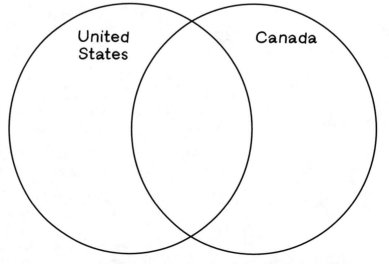

United
States

Canada

Resources for English Learners
RSG pp. 49–52   RSG Audio   IA p. 7
TT 18a, TT 18b   FA pp. 70, 71–74,   MLG
75–78, 79–82

Human-Environment Interaction

Step 1 Activate Prior Knowledge	Write the title of the section on the board and ask students what the term means. If necessary, have students discuss and define each of the words that make up the term. Then do a **Brainstorming** Activity to elicit examples of human-environment interaction in the United States and Canada.
Step 2 Preview Main Ideas and Language	**Connect Visually** Pair students and refer them to the photographs in this and previous sections of the chapter, on pp. 117, 123, 127, and 128. Encourage students to select three of the photographs to discuss what each shows about human-environment interaction in the United States and Canada. Put pairs together in groups and ask each pair to share ideas with the group.
	Build Vocabulary Have students work in groups to learn the meaning of each word in Part A of Activity Sheet 5.3. Then have them complete Part A and go over the correct answers with the class.
Step 3 Make Objectives Explicit	Write the objectives on the board and read them to students. For each objective, have students write a learning goal. If students' first language is Spanish, have them read the lesson summary in the *Reading Study Guide* (English or Spanish).
	• Tell how settlement and agriculture have changed the land in Canada and the United States.
	• Explain what makes some places good sites for the location of cities.
	• Describe ways people have worked to overcome distances in the United States and Canada.
Step 4 Support Student Reading	**Cooperative Work** Divide the class into groups of six and have them do a **Jigsaw Reading** Activity to complete the chart in Part B of Activity Sheet 5.3. Review answers with the class.
	On One's Own Preview the following questions by asking students what they understand them to mean. Then have students search for the answers while reading. Once students have finished, help them answer in complete sentences.
	1. How did the first people who lived in the United States and Canada alter the land? (p. 127, par. 1–4)
	2. What are some factors that influence where a city is built? (p. 128, par. 1)
	3. What are four ways settlers of the United States and Canada overcame distances across the continent? (pp. 128–130)
Step 5 Prepare for Assessment	**Alternative Assessment** Have students work in cooperative groups to complete the Geoactivity on PE p. 130. Share the Standards for Evaluating a Cooperative Activity on p. 7 of *Integrated Assessment* and use them for evaluating the participation and contributions of students.
	Formal Assessment Assign the Section Quiz for Chapter 5, Section 3, found on p. 70 of the *Formal Assessment* book. Then prepare students for the Chapter Test by going over the test-taking strategies for TT18a and TT18b. Then give a Chapter Test from the *Formal Assessment* book. Form A of the Chapter Test is less challenging than Forms B and C.

ACTIVITY SHEET 5.3

Part A. Build Vocabulary

Key Terms Fill in the blanks with the correct terms to complete the sentences in the paragraph. You may have to make some terms plural.

highway	lock	nomad	urban sprawl	transcontinental

The first inhabitants of what is now the United States and Canada were

1. _____, people who moved from place to place. Around 3,000 years ago, they began to settle down in farming communities. Some of these became cities. Cities can cause great changes in the environment. For example, sometimes a city grows and spreads over a wide area, causing loss of natural vegetation, air pollution, and other problems. Rapid, unplanned growth of a city is called **2.** _____. People in the United States and Canada have changed the environment in other ways, as well. They built **3.** _____ railroads, all the way across both countries; they built waterways with

4. _____, sections where the water level is raised and lowered, to move ships from one body of water to another; they built vast

5. _____ systems that allow drivers to travel throughout the land.

Part B. Cooperative Work

Work with your group to complete the chart. Include the purpose of the activity and how people interacted with and changed the environment.

Building agricultural settlements (p. 127, par. 4–5)	
Building Montreal (p. 128, par. 2)	
Building Los Angeles (p. 128, par. 3–4)	
Building trails and inland waterways (p. 129, par. 1–3)	
Building transcontinental railroads (p. 130, par. 1–2)	
Building national highway systems (p. 120, par. 2–3)	

Resources for English Learners

TE p. 139   RSG pp. 53–54   RSG Audio
IA p. 8   TT 19   FA p. 83
MLG

History and Government of the United States

**Step 1
Activate Prior Knowledge**

Do a **K-W-L** Activity with the class on the subject of the history of the United States, from prehistoric times to the present. Explain that this section summarizes U.S. history, focusing on topics of interest to geographers. Fill in the L section of the class chart when students complete the section.

**Step 2
Preview Main Ideas and Language**

Connect Visually Pair students and refer them to the infographic (map with arrows and small drawings) on PE p. 136. Ask students to study the infographic. Then have them make a two-column chart that lists the items brought from the Eastern Hemisphere to the Western Hemisphere and vice versa.

Build Vocabulary Help students learn the definitions of the four key terms listed in Part A of Activity Sheet 6.1. Then have them complete Part A and go over the correct answers with the class.

**Step 3
Make Objectives Explicit**

Write these objectives on the overhead or on the board and read them aloud to students. Have students work in pairs to identify the paragraph or paragraphs that will help them meet each objective. If students' first language is Spanish, have them read the lesson summary in the *Reading Study Guide* (English or Spanish).

• Explain how the United States was formed.

• Tell how migration and industrialization caused changes in the United States.

• Describe how the United States has changed since the early 1900s.

• Describe the U.S. system of government.

**Step 4
Support Student Reading**

Cooperative Work Have students work in groups of three to complete the time line in Part B of Activity Sheet 6.1. Then make a class time line with input from all of the groups. Let students vote on the events they think are most important.

On One's Own Preview the following questions by asking students what they understand them to mean. Then have students search for the answers while reading. Once students have finished, help them answer in complete sentences.

1. Why is the United States sometimes called "a nation of immigrants"? (p. 135, par. 2–4, p. 136, par. 1)

2. What drew immigrants to the United States in the 1800s? (p. 137, par.1–4)

3. During the 1900s, how did the United States become a world power? (p. 137, par. 6–7)

4. What are the branches of the U.S. federal government? (p. 139, par. 2)

**Step 5
Prepare for Assessment**

Alternative Assessment Have students complete the Reteaching Activity on TE p. 139, which has them identify main ideas. Share the Standards for Evaluating a Group Discussion on p. 8 of *Integrated Assessment* and use them for evaluating the participation and contributions of students.

Formal Assessment Go over the test-taking strategies for TT19. Then assign the Section Quiz for Chapter 6, Section 1, found on p. 83 of the *Formal Assessment* book.

ACTIVITY SHEET 6.1

Part A. Build Vocabulary

Key Terms Write the term in each blank that best answers the question.

> frontier   immigration   migration   representative democracy

1. What do we call the movement of people from their native country to a new country? _____

2. What do we call a political system in which citizens elect officials who act as their representatives in the government? _____

3. What do we call the open land in the American West that was available for people to settle on in the 1800s? _____

4. What do we call the movement of people within a single country?

_____

Part B. Cooperative Work

As you study the section, work with your group to add six entries to the time line, related to important events in U.S. history.

Some Important Events in U.S. History

11,000 B.C.   A.D. 1500   1600   1700   1800   1900   2000

Nomads come from Asia to North America

The United States today

Chapter (6) **Section 2**

Resources for English Learners		
TE p. 143	RSG pp. 55–56	RSG Audio
IA p. 7	TT 20a, TT 20b	FA p. 84
MLG		

Economy and Culture of the United States

**Step 1
Activate Prior Knowledge**

Do a written **Roundtable** Activity, having students list contributions that people of their family background have made to U.S. culture. You might give a few examples from PE p. 143 or from your own background before starting the activity. After the lists have been read, explain that people from many cultures have contributed to the culture of this country.

**Step 2
Preview Main Ideas and Language**

Connect Visually Divide the class in groups of three and have them study the circle graphs on PE p. 140. For each of the general job categories in the key, ask students to list specific jobs that fall into that category. Let groups share their examples with the class. Talk about how the shift in job types over the last century might have changed the United States and its culture.

Build Vocabulary Pair students for **Peer Vocabulary Teaching** to help students learn the definitions of the words in Part A of Activity Sheet 6.2. Ask students to complete Part A on their own. Go over the correct answers with the class.

**Step 3
Make Objectives Explicit**

Write these objectives on the overhead or on the board. Have students identify the single most important word or phrase in each objective, sharing their ideas and the reasons for them. If students' first language is Spanish, have them read the lesson summary in the *Reading Study Guide* (English or Spanish).

• List some of the reasons the United States is a great economic power.

• Describe the ways in which the United States is culturally diverse.

• Give some statistics that show what life in the United States is like today.

**Step 4
Support Student Reading**

Cooperative Work Pair students to read the section and complete the chart in Part B of Activity Sheet 6.2. Go over the correct answers with the class and then have students use their corrected charts in an **Inside-Outside Circles** Activity.

On One's Own Preview the following questions by asking students what they understand them to mean. Then have students search for the answers while reading. Once students have finished, help them answer in complete sentences.

1. What are three reasons the United States is a leader in agriculture? (p. 141, par. 1)

2. Which general industry drives the American economy? (p. 142, top)

3. Why is the United States so culturally diverse? (p. 142, par. 3)

4. What invention made the shift to the suburbs possible? (p. 143, par. 6)

**Step 5
Prepare for Assessment**

Alternative Assessment Have students complete the Cooperative Learning Activity on TE p. 143. Share the Standards for Evaluating a Cooperative Learning Activity on p. 7 of *Integrated Assessment* and use them for evaluating the participation and contributions of students.

Formal Assessment Go over the test-taking strategies for TT20a and TT20b. Then assign the Section Quiz for Chapter 6, Section 2, found on p. 84 of the *Formal Assessment* book.

ACTIVITY SHEET 6.2

Part A. Build Vocabulary

Key Terms Fill in the blanks with the correct terms to complete the sentences in the paragraph.

| services | postindustrial | multinational | free enterprise | exports |

The United States has one of the world's strongest economies. In global trade, it accounts for ten percent of the world's **1.** _____, which are goods sold to another country. In fact, many large U.S. companies do business throughout the world. These companies are called **2.** _____ companies. Manufacturing no longer accounts for most of the economic activity in the United States. Instead most economic activity in this country involves providing **3.** _____, rather than goods. This kind of economy is called a **4.** _____ economy. In the United States, private individuals and companies own most of the resources, technology, and businesses, which they run without much government control. This type of economic system is called **5.** _____.

Part B. Cooperative Work

Work with your partner to answer the questions. Review the answers with your class.

1. Name three factors that have contributed to the success of the U.S. economy. (p. 140, par. 4)	
2. How does American agriculture benefit the rest of the world? (p. 141, par. 1)	
3. What are some important jobs in the postindustrial economy? (p. 142, top)	
4. What are the percentages of major religions in the United States? (p. 143, par. 2)	
5. List the origins of some of America's musical styles. (p. 143, par. 4)	
6. Where do most Americans live? (p. 143, par. 6)	

Resources for English Learners
TE p. 146   OMA p. 14   RSG pp. 57–60
RSG Audio   TT 21a, TT 21b   FA pp. 85, 86–89,
MLG   90–93, 94–97

Subregions of the United States

Step 1
Activate Prior Knowledge

Do an oral **Round Robin** Activity, with students identifying all of the states they can on an overhead transparency map, such as TT21a. Explain that groupings of states form subregions.

Step 2
Preview Main Ideas and Language

Connect Visually Hold a class discussion on what different states near one another have in common. Then divide students into groups of three and give each group a copy of the U.S. map on p. 14 of *Outline Maps with Activities*. Direct students to work together to divide the states into five subregions. Tell students to check their answers against the map on PE p. 134.

Build Vocabulary Use the **Frayer Method** to teach the two terms *(megalopis, metropolitan area)* listed in Part A of Activity Sheet 6.3. Then have students work in pairs to complete Part A. Go over the answer with the class.

Step 3
Make Objectives Explicit

Write these objectives on the overhead or on the board. Ask students to read the objectives aloud and then to write individual learning goals, giving details for each objective. If students' first language is Spanish, have them read the lesson summary in the *Reading Study Guide* (English or Spanish).

• Describe the U.S. subregion called the Northeast.

• Describe the U.S. subregion called the Midwest.

• Describe the U.S. subregion called the South.

• Describe the U.S. subregion called the West.

Step 4
Support Student Reading

Cooperative Work Divide students in groups for a **Jigsaw Reading** Activity during which they complete the chart in Part B of Activity Sheet 6.3. Review student answers in class.

On One's Own Preview the following questions by asking students what they understand them to mean. Then have students search for the answers while reading. Once students have finished, help them answer in complete sentences.

1. Why is the Northeast one of the most heavily industrialized and urbanized areas in the United States? (p. 145, par. 3; p. 146, top)

2. How is the economy of the Midwest changing? (p. 147, par. 4)

3. What gave a boost to industry in the South and is also a factor in the growth of the West? (p. 148, par. 3; p. 149, par. 1)

Step 5
Prepare for Assessment

Alternative Assessment Have students work in pairs to complete the Skillbuilder Lesson on TE p. 146. Assess their work by evaluating the answers to the Using the Bar Graph questions at the bottom of the worksheet.

Formal Assessment Assign the Section Quiz for Chapter 6 Section 3, on p. 85 of the *Formal Assessment* book. Then prepare students for the Chapter Test by going over the test-taking strategies for TT21a and TT21b. Then give a Chapter Test from the *Formal Assessment* book. Note that Form A of the Chapter Test is less challenging than Forms B and C.

ACTIVITY SHEET 6.3

Part A. Build Vocabulary

Key Terms Make a Venn Diagram to show the relationship between the metropolitan areas listed and the megalopolis.

Boston, MA	**Hartford, CT**	**Providence, RI**
New York City, NY	**Philadelphia, PA**	**Newark, NJ**
Baltimore, MD	**Washington, DC**	**BosWash**

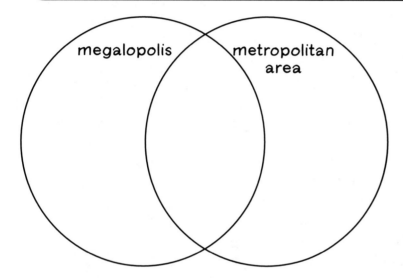

megalopolis   metropolitan area

Part B. Cooperative Work

Work with your group to complete the chart. Go over the answers with the class.

Subregion	Land (States/Areas)	Economic Activities/ Resources	Current Trends/ Issues
Northeast	1.	2.	3.
Midwest	4.	5.	6.
South	7.	8.	9.
West	10.	11.	12.

Resources for English Learners
TE p. 158   RSG pp. 61–62   RSG Audio
IA p. 7   TT 22a, TT 22b   FA p. 98
MLG

History and Government of Canada

**Step 1
Activate Prior
Knowledge**

As a class, make a **T-Chart** to note similarities and differences between Canadian and U.S. history and government. Run this as a **Brainstorming** Activity and accept all ideas. Return to the chart when students have completed the section to make additions, deletions, and corrections.

**Step 2
Preview Main
Ideas and
Language**

Connect Visually Divide the class in groups of three and have them compare the three maps on PE p. 157. Each group should generate three questions related to the maps that they think the section will answer. Collect the questions, select one question from each group, and distribute them to other groups to answer after students finish reading the section.

Build Vocabulary Preview the key terms in Part A of Activity Sheet 7.1. Use **Card Responses** or another Signals activity to make sure students understand the terms. Then have students work in pairs to complete Part A.

**Step 3
Make Objectives
Explicit**

Write these objectives on the board. Have students read the objectives and write a question they will answer related to each objective. Ask students to share their questions with the class. If students' first language is Spanish, have them read the lesson summary in the *Reading Study Guide* (English or Spanish).

- Explain how Canada was settled.
- Tell how Canada became one unified nation.
- Examine Canadian expansion and development.
- Describe the Canadian government.

**Step 4
Support Student
Reading**

Cooperative Work Divide the class into groups of four or five to complete the chart in Part B of Activity Sheet 7.1. Use a **Carousel Review** to go over the material.

On One's Own Preview the following questions by asking students what they understand them to mean. Then have students search for the answers while reading. Once students have finished, help them answer in complete sentences.

1. Why were the British and the French both interested in colonizing Canada? (p. 156, par. 1)
2. What was the main difference between Upper Canada and Lower Canada? (p. 156, par. 2)
3. What two things spurred the development of the Canadian west? (p. 157, par. 3)
4. What is Canada's government like? (p. 158, par. 2)

**Step 5
Prepare for
Assessment**

Alternative Assessment Have students complete the Reteaching Activity on TE p. 158. Share the Standards for Evaluating a Cooperative Learning Activity on p. 7 of *Integrated Assessment* and use them for evaluating the participation and contributions of students.

Formal Assessment Go over the test-taking strategies for TT22a and TT22b. Then assign the Section Quiz for Chapter 7, Section 1, found on p. 98 of the *Formal Assessment* book.

ACTIVITY SHEET 7.1

Part A. Build Vocabulary

Key Terms For each key term listed, write the other key term that you
think belongs with it. Explain your reasoning on the line provided.

> **confederation:** political union
>
> **parliament:** legislature
>
> **prime minister:** head of a parliamentary government
>
> **province:** political unit of a country

province   **1.** _____

Reason for pairing: **2.** _____

parliament   **3.** _____

Reason for pairing: **4.** _____

Part B. Cooperative Work

Work with your group to fill in the chart. Review the answers with the class.

Factors Influencing the Development of Canada
1. early peoples
2. colonization by France and Britain
3. establishing the Dominion of Canada
4. settlement of the West
5. urban and industrial growth

Chapter **(7)** **Section 2**

Resources for English Learners		
TE p. 160	RSG pp. 63–64	RSG Audio
IA p. 7	TT 23	FA p. 99
MLG		

Economy and Culture of Canada

Step 1 **Activate Prior Knowledge**	Ask students to define *diversity* and write a definition on the board. Then do a **Think-Quickwrite-Pair-Share** Activity for students to focus on what they think of when they hear or read the word *diversity*. Explain that, Canada, like the United States, also has a very diverse economy and culture.
Step 2 **Preview Main Ideas and Language**	**Connect Visually** Have the class divide into small groups and turn to the graphic at the bottom of PE p. 161. Ask them to look at the graphic and to talk about the main idea it presents. Students should work together to write a group summary. As a class, discuss how this graphic addresses the idea of diversity. **Build Vocabulary** Present definitions of the key terms in Part A of Activity Sheet 7.2. Then have students work in pairs to complete Part A. They can share their drawings with the class.
Step 3 **Make Objectives Explicit**	Write these objectives on the overhead or on the board and read them aloud to students. Ask students for thumbs up/down to indicate their comprehension of each objective. Let students who understand the objectives reexplain them to other students. If students' first language is Spanish, have them read the lesson summary in the *Reading Study Guide* (English or Spanish). • List some of the reasons Canada is a great economic power. • Describe the ways in which Canada is culturally diverse. • Give some statistics that show what life in Canada is like today.
Step 4 **Support Student Reading**	**Cooperative Work** Divide the class into groups of three to complete the graphic organizer in Part B of Activity Sheet 7.2. Correct answers using a **Numbered Heads Together** Activity. **On One's Own** Preview the following questions by asking students what they understand them to mean. Then have students search for the answers while reading. Once students have finished, help them answer in complete sentences. **1.** Which type of industry dominates Canada's economy? (p. 160, par. 1) **2.** Which two languages and religions dominate Canadian culture? (p. 161, par. 4) **3.** How have Canada's urban areas changed in the past 100 years? (p. 162, par. 1) **4.** What is Inuit art like? (p. 163, par. 2)
Step 5 **Prepare for Assessment**	**Alternative Assessment** Have students work in a group to complete the Activity on TE p. 160. Share the Standards for Evaluating a Cooperative Learning Activity on p. 7 of *Integrated Assessment* and use them for evaluating the participation and contributions of students. **Formal Assessment** Go over the test-taking strategies for TT23. Then assign the Section Quiz for Chapter 7, Section 2, found on p. 99 of the *Formal Assessment* book.

ACTIVITY SHEET 7.2

Part A. Build Vocabulary

Use the spaces below to make a drawing that helps you remember the meaning of each of the key terms.

First Nations	métis	reserve

Part B. Cooperative Work

Work with your group to fill in the graphic organizer. Go over the answers with the class.

1. Fishing
_____
_____
_____

2. Forestry
_____
_____
_____

3. Services
_____
_____
_____

4. First Nations
_____
_____
_____

5. English
_____
_____
_____

6. French
_____
_____
_____

7. metis
_____
_____
_____

Diverse Economy

Diverse Society

Resources for English Learners
OMA p. 16   RSG pp. 65–68   RSG Audio
IA p. 7   FA pp. 100, 101–104,   TT 24a, TT 24b
105–108, 109–112   MLG

Subregions of Canada

Step 1
Activate Prior Knowledge

Divide students in groups of three and give each group an outline map of Canada, such as the map on p. 16 of *Outline Maps with Activities*. Ask students to work together to label as many Canadian provinces as they can. Explain that Canadian provinces can be grouped into subregions.

Step 2
Preview Main Ideas and Language

Connect Visually While students are still in their same groups of three, direct them to turn to the map on PE p. 157 and to correct and complete their map of the Canadian provinces. Then ask the class how they would divide the provinces into subregions. Refer to a large map and ask students to explain their ideas.

Build Vocabulary Write the key places from Part A of Activity Sheet 7.3 on the board. Use a map to point to the three Canadian provinces and the territory in the list and have students name what you are pointing to. Then tell them to label the map on Activity Sheet 7.3. Then have them turn to p. 154 and identify, label, and color the Atlantic Provinces and the Prairie Provinces. Go over the answers with the class.

Step 3
Make Objectives Explicit

Write these objectives on the board. Ask students to read the objectives aloud and then predict what the provinces in each subregion will have in common, based on the names. Write the predictions on the board and return to them after students complete the section. If students' first language is Spanish, have them read the lesson summary in the *Reading Study Guide* (English or Spanish).

- Describe the Canadian subregion known as the Atlantic Provinces.
- Describe the Canadian subregion known as the Core Provinces.
- Describe the Canadian subregion known as the Prairie Provinces.
- Describe the Canadian subregion known as the Pacific Provinces and the Territories.

Step 4
Support Student Reading

Cooperative Work Assign students in groups for **Peer Tutoring** and have them work together to complete the chart in Part B of Activity Sheet 7.3.

On One's Own Preview the following questions by asking students what they understand them to mean. Then have students search for the answers while reading. Once students have finished, help them answer in complete sentences.

1. Why is the population of the Atlantic Provinces small? (p. 166, par. 3)

2. Why are Ontario and Quebec called the heartland of Canada? (p. 167, par. 4–6)

3. What economic activities take place in British Columbia? (p. 169, par. 1)

Step 5
Prepare for Assessment

Alternative Assessment Have students work in small groups to complete the GeoActivity on PE p. 171. Share the Standards for Evaluating a Cooperative Learning Activity on p. 7 of *Integrated Assessment* and use them for evaluating the participation and contributions of students.

Formal Assessment Assign the Section Quiz for Chapter 7 Section 3, on p. 100 of the *Formal Assessment* book. Then prepare students for the Chapter Test by going over the test-taking strategies for TT24a and TT24b. Then give a Chapter Test from the *Formal Assessment* book. Note that Form A of the Chapter Test is less challenging than Forms B and C.

ACTIVITY SHEET 7.3

Part A. Build Vocabulary

Key Places Label all of the key places on the map below.

> **Atlantic Provinces**
>
> **Quebec**
>
> **Ontario**
>
> **Prairie Provinces**
>
> **British Columbia**
>
> **Nunavut**

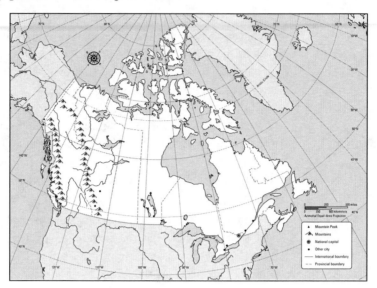

Part B. Cooperative Work

Work with your group to complete the chart. Go over the answers with the class.

Provinces	Land/Political Units	Economic Activities/ Resources	People/Issues
Atlantic	1.	2.	3.
Core	4.	5.	6.
Prairie	7.	8.	9.
Pacific and Territories	10.	11.	12.

Resources for English Learners
TE p. 175   RSG pp. 69–70   RSG Audio
IA p. 7   TT 25   FA p. 113
MLG

The Fight Against Terrorism

Step 1 Activate Prior Knowledge	Bring in a news magazine or the front page or front section of a newspaper from September 2001, focusing on the terrorist attacks in New York City and Washington, D.C. Show these to students and hold a class **Brainstorming** session to talk about students' memories from the time.
Step 2 Preview Main Ideas and Language	**Connect Visually** Have students work with a partner to study the map on PE p. 174. Encourage students to make a time line to record the terrorist attacks. After students complete their time line, let them discuss the different patterns they notice when the information is on a time line versus a map. **Build Vocabulary** Review the strategy **New Word Analysis,** using one of the key terms from Part A of Activity Sheet 8.1. Have students work with a partner and use New Word Analysis to figure out the meaning of the other key terms. Students can work individually to complete the rest of Part A.
Step 3 Make Objectives Explicit	Write these objectives on the board. Have students read the objectives and identify what they think is the single most important phrase in each. Hold a brief class discussion in which students can explain their choices. If students' first language is Spanish, have them read the lesson summary in the *Reading Study Guide* (English or Spanish). • Describe how the United States responded to the events of September 11, 2001. • Discuss the difficulties the United States and its allies, including Canada, face in fighting terrorism.
Step 4 Support Student Reading	**Cooperative Work** Divide the class into groups of three to complete the Problems/Solutions chart in Part B of Activity Sheet 8.1. Go over the answers with the class. Then ask each group to make up a 5-question quiz on the section. Groups should trade quizzes and answer the questions for review. **On One's Own** Preview the following questions by asking students what they understand them to mean. Then have students search for the answers while reading. Once students have finished, help them answer in complete sentences. **1.** What happened in the terrorist attacks on the United States on September 11, 2001, and who was believed to be responsible? (p. 173, pars. 3–6) **2.** How did the United States respond to the attacks? (p. 174, pars. 1–2; p. 175, par. 1) **3.** What might become problems for democratic governments waging war against terrorism? (p. 175. par. 5)
Step 5 Prepare for Assessment	**Alternative Assessment** Have students work in pairs to complete the Reteaching Activity on TE p. 175. Share the Standards for Evaluating a Cooperative Learning Activity on p. 7 of *Integrated Assessment* and use them for evaluating the participation and contributions of students. **Formal Assessment** Go over the test-taking strategies for TT25. Then assign the Section Quiz for Chapter 8, Section 1, found on p. 113 of the *Formal Assessment* book.

ACTIVITY SHEET 8.1

Part A. Build Vocabulary

Key Terms Work with a partner to figure out the meaning of the key terms. Then complete the vocabulary exercise on your own. You may need to make some of the words plural.

| biological weapon | coalition | global network | terrorism |

The unlawful use or threatened use of violence as a form of intimidation to achieve social or political ends is called **1.** _____.
It may include the release of disease-causing bacteria or viruses via
2. _____. After the September 11 attacks, the United
States organized a **3.** _____ of nations working together
to fight against terrorism. They were hoping to stop additional acts of
violence planned by a **4.** _____, or an interconnected
group spread throughout the world.

Part B. Cooperative Work

Work with your group to fill in the chart. Review the answers with the class.

Problems	
1. damage and destruction	**2.** threat of further attack
3. finding those responsible	**4.** safeguarding rights
Solutions	
5. coalition against terrorism	**6.** improved homeland security

Resources for English Learners
TE p. 177   RSG pp. 71–72, 75   RSG Audio
IA p. 7   TT 26   FA p. 114
MGL

Urban Sprawl

Step 1
Activate Prior Knowledge

Do a **K-W-L activity** so students can tap into their prior knowledge about urban sprawl. (If necessary, have students look back at PE pp. 123, 127, and 128, where the term *urban sprawl* is used.) Explain that this section goes into detail about urban sprawl, which is a problem in both the United States and Canada. Return to the chart to fill in the L column after students have completed the section.

Step 2
Preview Main Ideas and Language

Connect Visually Divide students in groups of three and ask each group to come up with a drawing to illustrate the term *urban sprawl.* The drawing could be realistic, schematic, or even a cartoon related to the connotations of the term. Post the drawings or give groups time to share them with the class.

Build Vocabulary Do a quick review on how to use a **Word Square.** Then divide students into groups of three. In each group, every student should choose a different key term from Part A of Activity Sheet 8.2, using the Word Square to define the term. Direct students to take turns teaching their terms to the group.

Step 3
Make Objectives Explicit

Write these objectives on the overhead or on the board and read them aloud to the class. Check students' comprehension using Number of Fingers or another **Signals** Activity. Let students who understand the objectives explain them to students who do not understand them. If students' first language is Spanish, have them read the lesson summary in the *Reading Study Guide* (English or Spanish).

- Explain how cities have tended to grow when there is no plan for their growth.
- List some negative effects of urban sprawl.
- Identify some solutions to urban sprawl.

Step 4
Support Student Reading

Cooperative Work Divide the class into groups of three and have them do **Jigsaw Reading** to complete the two charts in Part B of Activity Sheet 8.2. Review answers with the entire class.

On One's Own Preview the following questions by asking students what they understand them to mean. Then have students search for the answers while reading. Once students have finished, help them answer in complete sentences.

1. What are some of the causes of urban sprawl? (p. 177, par. 1)
2. What are some effects of urban sprawl? (p. 177, pars. 3--4)
3. What are some ways cities are solving the problem of urban sprawl? (p. 178, pars. 1-3)

Step 5
Prepare for Assessment

Alternative Assessment Have students work in small groups to complete the Skillbuilder Lesson on TE p. 177. Share the Standards for Evaluating a Cooperative Learning Activity on p. 7 of *Integrated Assessment* and use them for evaluating the participation and contributions of students.

Formal Assessment Go over the test-taking strategies for TT26. Then assign the Section Quiz for Chapter 8, Section 2, found on p. 114 of the *Formal Assessment* book.

ACTIVITY SHEET 8.2

Part A. Build Vocabulary

Key Terms Use the Word Square to help you define one of the terms below. Share your Word Square with your group.

| infrastructure |
| smart growth |
| sustainable community |

Word:	Symbol or Picture:
Translation:	
My meaning:	Sentence:
Dictionary definition:	

Part B. Cooperative Work

Work with your group to fill in the charts. Review the answers with the class.

Causes and Effects of Urban Sprawl

1. What is urban sprawl?	2. Causes of urban sprawl	3. Effects of urban sprawl

Solutions to Urban Sprawl

4. Portland's plan	5. Vancouver's plan	6. Grassroots opposition

Chapter ⑧ Case Study

Resources for English Learners		
TE p. 183	RSG pp. 73–74	RSG Audio
FA pp. 114, 116–120,		TT 27
121–125, 126–130		MLG

Diverse Societies Face Change

**Step 1
Activate Prior
Knowledge**

Do a **Think-Pair-Share** activity to have students discuss where their families originally came from and when they came to the United States. Native Americans should talk about their tribal heritage.

**Step 2
Preview Main
Ideas and
Language**

Connect Visually Ask students to look through the unit and find three photos, maps, or other graphics that relate to the idea of cultural diversity. For each illustration, students should write down one piece of information. Let students share the information in a **Round Robin** discussion.

Build Vocabulary Divide students into groups of three and have them use this method to learn the meaning of each key term listed in Part A of Activity Sheet 8.3. Students should complete Part A on their own. Go over the answers with the class.

**Step 3
Make Objectives
Explicit**

Write these objectives on the board and read them aloud to the class. Check students' comprehension using thumbs up/thumbs down. Students who understand the objectives can explain them to students who do not. If students' first language is Spanish, have them read the lesson summary in the *Reading Study Guide* (English or Spanish).

- Explain why Canada is a cultural "mosaic."
- Explain why the United States is a "melting pot."
- Discuss recent cultural issues that the United States and Canada face.
- Analyze primary sources for different views on multiculturalism.

**Step 4
Support Student
Reading**

Cooperative Work Divide the class into groups of five and direct them do a **Reciprocal Teaching** activity to read the primary sources on pp. 182–183. Students should use Part B of Activity Sheet 8.3 to summarize the primary sources. Then encourage students to find other sources of information as they work on the Case Study Project.

On One's Own Preview the following questions by asking students what they understand them to mean. Then have students search for the answers while reading.

1. Why are the United States and Canada so culturally diverse? (p. 180, par. 2)
2. What is the official Canadian policy toward cultural diversity? (p. 180, par. 5)
3. How have Americans traditionally expected new immigrants to change on coming to this country? (p. 181, pars. 1–2)
4. Summarize the divided opinion on policies toward America's new immigrants. (p. 181, pars. 4–5)

**Step 5
Prepare for
Assessment**

Alternative Assessment Have students work in groups of five to complete the Case Study Project. Share the Grading Rubric on TE p. 183 with students and use it to evaluate their project.

Formal Assessment Assign the Section Quiz for Chapter 8 Section 3, on p. 115 of the *Formal Assessment* book. Then prepare students for the Chapter Test by going over the test-taking strategies for TT27. Then give a Chapter Test from the *Formal Assessment* book. Note that Form A of the Chapter Test is less challenging than Forms B and C.

ACTIVITY SHEET 8.3

Part A. Build Vocabulary

Key Terms For each clue, write the word in the blank that best fits it.

> **assimilation   ethnic   mosaic   multicultural**

1. Canada's policy toward immigrants of different cultures has been compared with this art form, because each group has been encouraged to hold on to its own identity. _____

2. We use this word when we are talking about something that relates to many cultures. _____

3. We use this word when we are talking about something related to a particular cultural or racial group. _____

4. This process occurs when people from a minority culture adopt the language, customs, and lifestyle of the people of the main or dominant culture. _____

Part B. Cooperative Work

Work with your group to read and summarize the primary sources on pp. 182–183. Go over the answers with the class.

Main Idea or Summary of Primary Sources
Newspaper article by William Booth:
Social commentary by Michelle Young:
Political commentary by Patrick Buchanan:
Excerpt from the Canadian Multiculturalism Act:
Excerpt from the U.S. 2000 census:

Resources for English Learners
RSG pp. 77–78   RSG Audio
IA p. 28   TT 28
FA p. 131   MLG

Landforms and Resources

Step 1 **Activate Prior Knowledge**	Review the concept of landforms. Then ask students if they can name any landforms in Latin America. Write students' responses on the board or the overhead, and let students tell what they know about these landforms. If students have little familiarity with landforms in Latin America, name some of the more famous landforms, and ask students what they know.
Step 2 **Preview Main Ideas and Language**	**Connect Visually** Have students pair up and use the map on PE p. 191 to locate the landforms you discussed above. Then have students locate these and other landforms on a large wall map. **Build Vocabulary** Divide students in small groups and encourage any Spanish-speakers in your class to lead their group in a **Peer Vocabulary Teaching** Activity for the key terms in Part A of Activity Sheet 9.1. Have students complete Part A on their own and go over the answers in class.
Step 3 **Make Objectives Explicit**	Write these objectives on the overhead or on the board and read them aloud to the class. Have students turn to a partner and explain in their own words what they will be learning in the section, based on the objectives. If their first language is Spanish, have them read the lesson summary in the *Reading Study Guide* (English or Spanish). • Name and locate Latin America's mountains and highlands. • Name and locate Latin America's three main plains and major rivers. • Identify the major islands of the Caribbean. • Describe Latin America's important resources.
Step 4 **Support Student Reading**	**Cooperative Work** Divide the class into groups of three to complete the chart in Part B of Activity Sheet 9.1. Combine groups to make groups of six and run a written **Roundtable** Activity to go over the material. During the last part of the activity, make sure to clarify and reinforce correct answers. **On One's Own** Preview the following questions by asking students what they understand them to mean. Then have students search for the answers while reading. Once students have finished, help them answer in complete sentences. **1.** How have the Andes Mountains affected people's movement in South America? (p. 201, par. 3) **2.** What are the main economic activities on the plains of South America? (p. 202, pars. 2–5) **3.** What the three major groups of Caribbean Islands? (p. 203, par. 3) **4.** What is the main resource found on Trinidad and how has this affected the island? (p. 205, par. 3)
Step 5 **Prepare for Assessment**	**Alternative Assessment** Have students complete the GeoActivity on p. 205. Share the Rubric for Information Assessing Activities on p. 28 of *Integrated Assessment* and use it for evaluating students' sketch maps. **Formal Assessment** Go over the test-taking strategies for TT28. Then assign the Section Quiz for Chapter 9 Section 1, found on p. 131 of the *Formal Assessment* book.

ACTIVITY SHEET 9.1

Part A. Build Vocabulary

Key Terms For the key terms listed, show what they have in common through words, a diagram, or a drawing. Then match each term to the correct location(s).

1. _____ cerrado

2. _____ llanos

3. _____ pampas

a. Argentina

b. Brazil

c. Colombia

d. Uruguay

e. Venezuela

What the terms have in common

Part B. Cooperative Work

Work with your group to fill in the chart to describe Latin America's landforms and resources. Review the answers with the class.

Landforms of Latin America	
1. mountains	**2.** highlands
3. llanos	**4.** cerrado
5. pampas	**6.** Amazon
7. Other rivers	**8.** Major islands
Resources of Latin America	
9. mineral resources	**10.** energy resources

Resources for English Learners
TE p. 209   RSG pp. 79–80   RSG Audio
IA p. 7   TT 29   FA p. 132
MLG

Climate and Vegetation

**Step 1
Activate Prior
Knowledge**

In a class discussion, ask students to share what they know about rain forests. Write down their answers on the board or the overhead, and keep them for students to revise or to make additions to after they finish the section. Explain that tropical rain forests are an important vegetation zone (biome) in Latin America.

**Step 2
Preview Main
Ideas and
Language**

Connect Visually Direct students to work in groups of three and study the map on PE p. 207. Display a large class map of Central and South America that students can refer to for names of countries. Ask students to name all of the countries in Latin America where rain forests are found. In a **Round Robin** activity, let groups list the countries. Referring to the map on p. 207, have students name all of the other types of vegetation Latin America has.

Build Vocabulary Use the Frayer Method to teach the two key terms in Part A of Activity Sheet 9.2. When you are sure that all students understand these terms, divide the class in small groups and have them complete Part A. Go over the answers in class.

**Step 3
Make Objectives
Explicit**

Write these objectives on the overhead or on the board and read them aloud to the class. Direct students to look through the section and find a map or graphic that will help them learn about each objective. If students' first language is Spanish, have them read the lesson summary in the *Reading Study Guide* (English or Spanish).

- Describe the climate and vegetation of Latin America.
- Name and locate the tropical climate zones of Latin America.
- Name and locate the dry climate zones of Latin America.
- Name and locate the mid-latitude climate zones of Latin America.

**Step 4
Support Student
Reading**

Cooperative Work Divide the class into groups of three to complete the chart in Part B of Activity Sheet 9.2. Go over the answers with the class. Then do an **Inside-Outside Circles** Activity to review and reinforce the information.

On One's Own Preview the following questions by asking students what they understand them to mean. Then have students search for the answers while reading. Once students have finished, help them answer in complete sentences.

1. What are three reasons that Latin America has a variety of climate and vegetation zones? (p. 207, par. 4)

2. What kind of vegetation grows in Latin America's tropical wet and dry climate? (p. 156, par. 2)

3. Which mid-latitude climate zone varies depending on elevation? (p. 209)

**Step 5
Prepare for
Assessment**

Alternative Assessment Have students complete the Reteaching Activity on TE p. 209. Share the Standards for Evaluating a Cooperative Activity on p. 7 of *Integrated Assessment* and use it for evaluating students' performance.

Formal Assessment Go over the test-taking strategies for TT29. Then assign the Section Quiz for Chapter 9 Section 2 found on p. 132 of the *Formal Assessment* book.

ACTIVITY SHEET 9.2

Part A. Build Vocabulary

Key Terms Work with your group to answer the questions.

> **vegetation**
> **rain forest**

A word analogy implies a relationship between two words. For example, **United States: Canada** is a word analogy; it gives a relationship between two equals—two nations.

1. Explain the relationship between the two words in the analogy below.

vegetation: rain forest

_____

2. Complete the analogies below so that each set of words has the same relationship as the words in the analogy in question 1.

a. Latin America: _____   **b.** South American mountain ranges: _____

c. Amazon River: _____   **d.** Mineral resources: _____

Part B. Cooperative Work

Work with your group to fill in the chart to describe Latin America's climate zones. Review the answers with the class.

Zone	Zone Type	Where Found	Characteristics of Climates
Tropical	1. 4.	2. 5.	3. 6
Dry	7. 10.	8. 11.	9. 12.
Mid-Latitude	13. 16. 19. 22.	14. 17. 20. 23.	15. 18. 21. 24.

Resources for English Learners
RSG pp. 81–82   RSG Audio
IA p. 25   TT 30
FA pp. 133–145   MLG

Human-Environment Interaction

**Step 1
Activate Prior
Knowledge**

Ask volunteers to define the terms *urbanization* and *tourism*. Then ask students to pair up. Have half the groups discuss the pros and the cons of urbanization and half the groups discuss the pros and cons of tourism. After a brief discussion, let the groups share their ideas. Make one class **T-Chart** on the pros and cons of urbanization and one on the pros and cons of tourism.

**Step 2
Preview Main
Ideas and
Language**

Connect Visually Divide students into small groups and have them study the illustration on PE pp. 210–211. Then direct them to draw their own diagram of the slash-and-burn process as a cycle. Let groups share their diagrams and refer to them as they read the section.

Build Vocabulary Go over the definitions of the two boldfaced terms in the chart in Part A of Activity Sheet 9.3. Once you are sure that students understand these terms, ask them to work with a partner to complete the **Semantic Feature Analysis.** Fill in the first column with the class, as a demonstration.

**Step 3
Make Objectives
Explicit**

Write these objectives on the overhead or on the board and read them aloud to the class. Check students' comprehension using Number of Fingers or another **Signals** Activity. Students who understand the objectives can explain them to students who do not understand them. If students' first language is Spanish, have them read the lesson summary in the *Reading Study Guide* (English or Spanish).

- Describe how agriculture has changed the environment in Latin America.

- Discuss the effects of urbanization on Latin America.

- List the positive and negative effects of tourism.

**Step 4
Support Student
Reading**

Cooperative Work Divide the class into groups of four and have students work together to read the section and to fill out the **T-Charts** in Part B of Activity Sheet 9.3 on the pros and cons of Latin American urbanization and the pros and cons of Latin American tourism. When students have finished their charts, post the class charts, made in Step 1.

On One's Own Preview the following questions by asking students what they understand them to mean. Then have students search for the answers while reading. Once students have finished, help them answer in complete sentences.

1. What are the steps in slash-and-burn farming? (p. 213, photos)

2. What factors draw people from rural parts of Latin America to the cities? (p. 211, pars. 4–5)

3. What are some of the advantages of tourism in the Caribbean? (p. 212, pars. 3–4)

**Step 5
Prepare for
Assessment**

Alternative Assessment Assign students to work on the GeoActivity on p. 213. Share the guidelines for evaluating a poster and an illustration, on p. 25 of *Integrated Assessment*, and use these guidelines for evaluating students' work.

Formal Assessment Assign the Section Quiz for Chapter 9 Section 3, on p. 133 of the *Formal Assessment* book. Then prepare students for the Chapter Test by going over the test-taking strategies for TT30. Then give a Chapter Test from the *Formal Assessment* book. Note that Form A of the Chapter Test is less challenging than Forms B and C.

ACTIVITY SHEET 9.3

Part A. Build Vocabulary

Work with your group to complete the **Semantic Feature Analysis Charts** for the key terms, in **boldfaced** type.

Two Agricultural Methods Used in Latin America					
	Ancient technique	Used in tropical, humid areas	Used in mountainous areas	Requires farmers to move frequently to new land	Reduces soil erosion
Slash-and-burn					
Terraced farming					

Part B. Cooperative Work

Work with your group to read the section and fill in the charts. Go over your answers with the class.

Urbanization in Latin America

pros	cons
1. _____	4. _____
2. _____	5. _____
3. _____	6. _____
	7. _____
	8. _____

Tourism in Latin America

pros	cons
10. _____	14. _____
11. _____	15. _____
12. _____	16. _____
13. _____	17. _____
	18. _____
	19. _____
	20. _____

Resources for English Learners
TE pp. 218, 219 OMA p. 22   RSG pp. 85–86
RSG Audio   IA pp. 30, 32 TT 31
FA p. 146   MLG

Mexico

**Step 1
Activate Prior
Knowledge**

Ask students to bring in items from or about Mexico. Students might bring in produce, manufactured items, prepared food, cultural items, postcards, books, or brochures. Divide students into groups of five or six and direct them to discuss the items they brought in. Then the class can work together to categorize the items.

**Step 2
Preview Main
Ideas and
Language**

Connect Visually Have students draw a map of Mexico or give them a copy of the map on p. 22 of *Outline Maps with Activities*. Direct students to work in pairs and label cities, mountains, other landforms, rivers, bodies of water, and states or other subregions of Mexico. In a class discussion, let students talk about what they know about Mexico and how they know it.

Build Vocabulary Demonstrate how to do a **Think-Aloud** to figure out the meaning of the key term *Spanish conquest*. Once students understand the technique, have them choose two of the key terms in Part A of Activity Sheet 10.1 and do a Think-Aloud on each of the terms, using the textbook and other resources. Then ask students to work in groups of three or four to share what they learned and to complete Part A. Go over the answers in class.

**Step 3
Make Objectives
Explicit**

Write these objectives on the overhead or on the board and read them aloud to the class. Have students work with a partner to write a question based on each of the objectives. If students' first language is Spanish, have them read the lesson summary in the *Reading Study Guide* (English or Spanish).

• Discuss colonialism and independence in Mexico.

• Describe how Mexican culture blends native and Spanish influences.

• Explain the economics of cities and factories in Mexico.

• Describe issues related to life in Mexico today.

**Step 4
Support Student
Reading**

Cooperative Work Divide the class into groups of three and direct students to work together to complete the chart in Part B of Activity Sheet 10.1. Go over the answers with the class and then do a **Carousel Review** to reinforce the material.

On One's Own Preview the following questions by asking students what they understand them to mean. Then have students search for the answers while reading. Once students have finished, help them answer in complete sentences.

1. What was the Aztec culture like? (p. 217, par. 1; p. 218, par. 6)

2. Describe the Spanish conquest. (p. 217, par. 4; p. 219, par. 1)

3. What are maquiladoras? (p. 220, par. 3)

4. How does emigration affect Mexican families? (p. 221, par. 2)

**Step 5
Prepare for
Assessment**

Alternative Assessment Assign students to do either of the family history projects at the bottom of TE pp. 218 or 219. Share the guidelines for evaluating an oral presentation on p. 30 or the guidelines for evaluating an essay on p. 32 of *Integrated Assessment* and use them for evaluating students' projects.

Formal Assessment Go over the test-taking strategies for TT31. Then assign the Section Quiz for Chapter 10 Section 1, found on p. 146 of the *Formal Assessment* book.

ACTIVITY SHEET 10.1

Part A. Build Vocabulary

For each key term, fill in the chart based on your work with your group.

Key Term	1. mestizo	2. maquiladora	3. NAFTA
Defining sentence in textbook	a.	a.	a.
Pronunciation	b.	b.	b.
My questions or ideas about the word	c.	c.	c.

Part B. Cooperative Work

Work with your group to fill in the chart. Go over the answers with the class.

Effects on Mexico's Development
1. Spanish conquest (p. 217, pars. 1–4)
2. independence from Spain (p. 217, par. 5; p. 218, pars. 1–2)
3. one-party rule (p. 218, par. 3)
4. native influences on culture (p. 218, par. 6; p. 219, pars. 1–4)
5. Spanish influences on culture (p. 219, pars. 2, 4)
6. urbanization (p. 220, par. 1)
7. oil industry (p. 220, par. 2)
8. manufacturing (p. 220, par. 3)

Resources for English Learners
TE p. 224   OMA p. 24   RSG pp. 87–88
RSG Audio   IA p. 29   TT 32a, TT 32b
FA p. 147   MLG

Central America and the Caribbean

Step 1
Activate Prior Knowledge

Bring in recordings of reggae and/or calypso music and play for students. Direct students to do a **Think-Quickwrite-Pair-Share** activity to record their responses to the music. Ask students to also write down what experience they've had with this type of music and what they know about it. Explain that reggae and calypso originated in the Caribbean and show the blending of cultures that has occurred in this subregion.

Step 2
Preview Main Ideas and Language

Connect Visually Divide students in groups of three and give each group an outline map of the Caribbean and Central America, such as the map on p. 24 of *Outline Maps with Activities*. Ask students to work together to label as many countries and bodies of water as they can.

Build Vocabulary Help students learn the definitions of the two key terms listed in Part A of Activity Sheet 10.2. Then have students complete Part A and share their drawings with the class.

Step 3
Make Objectives Explicit

Write these objectives on the overhead or on the board and read them aloud to the class. Ask students to identify the most important phrase in each objective. If students' first language is Spanish, have them read the lesson summary in the *Reading Study Guide* (English or Spanish).

• Summarize the history of Central America and of the Caribbean.

• Describe ways that different cultures have blended in Central America and the Caribbean.

• Discuss economic conditions and popular culture in the subregion.

Step 4
Support Student Reading

Cooperative Work Have students work in groups of four, doing a **Jigsaw Reading** activity to complete the chart in Part B of Activity Sheet 10.2. One pair of students should find the information on Central America and the other pair of students should find the information the Caribbean. Go over the answers with the class.

On One's Own Preview the following questions by asking students what they understand them to mean. Then have students search for the answers while reading. Once students have finished, help them answer in complete sentences.

1. Which European country settled most of Central America? (p. 223, par. 2)

2. Which European countries had colonies in the Caribbean? (p. 224, chart)

3. What are some major sources of income in the economies of Central America and the Caribbean? (p. 225, par. 4; p. 226, pars. 1–2; p. 227, pars. 3–5)

4. What forms of music started in the Caribbean? (p. 227, par. 1)

Step 5
Prepare for Assessment

Alternative Assessment Assign students to do the Skillbuilder Lesson on TE p. 224. Share the guidelines for evaluating a Venn Diagram on p. 29 of *Integrated Assessment* and use them for evaluating students' work.

Formal Assessment Go over the test-taking strategies for TT32a and TT32b. Then assign the Section Quiz for Chapter 10 Section 2, found on p. 147 of the *Formal Assessment* book.

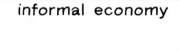

ACTIVITY SHEET 10.2

Part A. Build Vocabulary

Use the spaces below to make a drawing that helps you remember the meaning of each of the key terms.

cultural hearth	informal economy

Part B. Cooperative Work

Work with your group to fill in the chart. Correct the chart in class.

Region	History	Culture
Central America	**1.** native peoples	**2.** colonial powers
	3. groups who have influenced the culture	**4.** religion
		5. language
Caribbean	**6.** native peoples	**7.** colonial powers
	8. groups who have influenced the culture	**9.** religions
		10. languages

Resources for English Learners
TE p. 232   RSG pp. 89–90   RSG Audio
IA p. 7   TT 33a, TT 33b   FA p. 148
MLG

Spanish-Speaking South America

Step 1 **Activate Prior** **Knowledge**	Do a **K-W-L** activity with the class on South America. Encourage students to tell what they know and what they'd like to learn about South American history, economics, and cultures. Fill in the L section of the class chart when students complete the section.
Step 2 **Preview Main** **Ideas and** **Language**	**Connect Visually** Display a wall map of South America. Ask students to identify and locate the countries that speak Spanish. Use a **Round Robin** format, with each participant naming one country at a time. Write students' responses on the board. **Build Vocabulary** Have students work in pairs to find the definitions of the key terms listed in Part A of Activity Sheet 10.3. Students should use the textbook, referring to pp. 230–231, 234, 195, and 210. Then have students complete Part A on their own. Go over the answers in class.
Step 3 **Make Objectives** **Explicit**	Write these objectives on the overhead or on the board and read them aloud to the class. Have students write a personal goal for studying each objective. If students' first language is Spanish, have them read the lesson summary in the *Reading Study Guide* (English or Spanish). • Describe the Spanish conquest and independence movements in South America. • Explain why South America is said to form a cultural mosaic and explain why literature, music, and arts and crafts are important in the subregion. • Discuss economic resources and trade in South America. • Tell why education is important for South America's future.
Step 4 **Support Student** **Reading**	**Cooperative Work** Divide the class into groups of four or five and have them work on the **Anticipation Guide** in Part B of Activity Sheet 10.3. Go over the answers with the class, including the text students found to support their answers and the corrections they wrote to make false statements true. **On One's Own** Preview the following questions by asking students what they understand them to mean. Then have students search for the answers while reading. Once students have finished, help them answer in complete sentences. 1. What was the extent of the Incan empire in South America? (p. 231, par. 2) 2. Who were two great leaders of South American independence? (p. 231, par. 7) 3. How has authoritarian rule affected South America? (p. 232, par. 3) 4. What has made Chile an economic success? (p. 234, par. 1) 5. How do literacy rates in South America compare with those of Central America? (p. 234, par. 3)
Step 5 **Prepare for** **Assessment**	**Alternative Assessment** Assign students to do the Activity Option on TE p. 232. Share the Standards for Evaluating a Cooperative Activity on p. 7 of *Integrated Assessment* and use them for evaluating students' work. **Formal Assessment** Go over the test-taking strategies for TT33a and TT33b. Then assign the Section Quiz for Chapter 10 Section 3, found on p. 148 of the *Formal Assessment* book.

ACTIVITY SHEET 10.3

Part A. Build Vocabulary

Key Terms Find the definitions of the key terms with your group. Then work on your own to match each term with its description.

1. _____ Inca

2. _____ Mercosur

3. _____ Quechua

a. main language spoken in the Andes Mountains of Peru before the Spanish conquest

b. advanced civilization of South America, with imperial capital at Cuzco

c. association of countries in South America which have agreed to allow the free flow of trade among group members

Part B. Cooperative Work

Work individually and then with your group to fill in the first two columns of the Anticipation Guide. Fill in the third column after you have read the entire section. Correct any false answers.

You	Group	Textbook	Topic—Spanish-Speaking South America
			1. The Incas established a large and advanced empire in the Andes Mountains of South America.
			2. The Spanish conquered the Incas in the 1500s through a combination of force and trickery.
			3. After 1500, Spanish became the sole language of South America and Catholicism, the sole religion.
			4. Most countries in South America gained independence from Spain peacefully in the early- to mid-1800s.
			5. South America's rugged geography made it difficult for people in different parts of the continent to pursue common goals.
			6. Most South American nations became democracies that quickly erased traces of colonial culture.
			7. South America is a complex cultural region, with many different cultures near one another but not mixing with each other.
			8. Agriculture and mining are the main economic activities in many South American countries.

Resources for English Learners
TE p. 239   RSG pp. 91–92   RSG Audio
IA p. 32   TT 34a, TT 34b   FA pp. 149, 150–153
MLG

Brazil

**Step 1
Activate Prior
Knowledge**

Divide the class into groups of three and have each group make a **T-Chart** to compare how colonialism helped European countries and hurt native groups in those countries. Make a class T-Chart using ideas contributed by the different groups. Explain that Brazil was a Portuguese colony.

**Step 2
Preview Main
Ideas and
Language**

Connect Visually Ask students to turn to the map of Latin America on p. 193 and the regional data file on pp. 196–199. Based on the data file, have students write down the most obvious thing they notice about Brazil compared with the other Latin American nations. Let students share what they wrote with a partner.

Build Vocabulary Go over the definitions of the terms defined in Part A of Activity Sheet 10.4. Check students' comprehension with any of the **Signals** activities and redefine terms if needed. Let students work in pairs to put these terms in two broad categories. Students can share categorizations with the class.

**Step 3
Make Objectives
Explicit**

Write these objectives on the board and read them aloud to the class. Then have students write a question based on each objective that they will answer after they have studied the section. If students' first language is Spanish, have them read the lesson summary in the *Reading Study Guide* (English or Spanish).

• Explain why South America was divided during the era of colonization.

• Describe the culture of Brazil.

• Summarize why Brazil has a strong economy.

• Explain why Brazilians are moving to cities and discuss some problems in Brazil's largest cities.

**Step 4
Support Student
Reading**

Cooperative Work Have students work in pairs to complete the graphic organizer in Part B of Activity Sheet 10.4. Go over the answers with the class and ask students to correct any incorrect or incomplete information in their graphic organizers. Then organize a review using **Inside-Outside Circles.**

On One's Own Preview the following questions by asking students what they understand them to mean. Then have students search for the answers while reading. Once students have finished, help them answer in complete sentences.

1. Who lived in Brazil before European settlers arrived? (p. 236, par. 3)

2. Which European country sent the most settlers to Brazil? (p. 236, par. 5)

3. How do Brazil's rivers contribute to its wealth? (p. 238, par. 3)

4. What are some aspects of Brazilian culture that show an African influence? (p. 237, par. 5; p. 239, pars. 1–2)

**Step 5
Prepare for
Assessment**

Alternative Assessment Assign students to do the Reteaching Activity on TE p. 239. Share the general criteria for evaluating writing activities on p. 32 of *Integrated Assessment* and use them for evaluating students' writing.

Formal Assessment Go over the test-taking strategies for TT34a and TT34b. You may want to use *Formal Assessment* Form A, the less-challenging assessment, or administer it as a practice test prior to formal testing with Form B or Form C.

ACTIVITY SHEET 10.4

Part A. Build Vocabulary

Read the definitions of the key terms. Then work with your partner to categorize the terms in two groups.

Treaty of Tordesillas: agreement between Spain and Portugal that gave Portugal control over the land that became Brazil

capoeira: Brazilian martial art and dance form that has African origins

Carnival: the most colorful feast day in Brazil

samba: a Brazilian dance with African influences

Part B. Cooperative Work

Work with your partner to complete the graphic organizer. Go over your answers with the class and correct and complete the information.

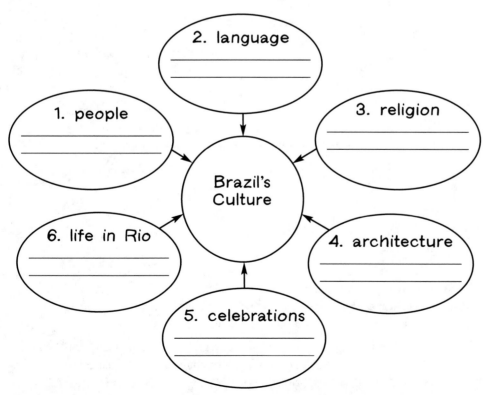

Resources for English Learners

Video: *Costa Rica:*   RSG pp. 95–96   TT 35
Ecotourism and Economic   RSG Audio   FA p. 162
Development   IDR3 p. 28   MLG

Rain Forest Resources

Step 1 Activate Prior Knowledge	Open a class discussion about what students already know about rain forests in Latin America, their destruction, and the effects of this destruction on the world's climate. Write students' answers on the board or on an overhead. Then have students divide into groups of two to four and let them discuss what right they think outsiders have to tell a country how to manage its land, such as rain forest land. Allow students to share their ideas with the entire class.

Step 2 Preview Main Ideas and Language

Connect Visually Show students part of the video *Costa Rica: Ecotourism and Economic Development.* Refer to the Teacher's Resource Book for *The Voyageur Experience in World Geography,* p. 15, and show the sequence that includes the visit to La Selva Biological Station. Follow the suggestions for **Viewing Videos with Language Learners.**

Build Vocabulary Encourage students to work in small groups to figure out the meaning of the key terms in Part A of Activity Sheet 11.1. Students should work in pairs to complete Part A. Go over the answers in class.

Step 3 Make Objectives Explicit

Write these objectives on the overhead or on the board and read them aloud to the class. Check students' comprehension using Thumbs Up/Down or another **Signals** activity. Encourage students who understand the objectives to explain them to students who do not. If students' first language is Spanish, have them read the lesson summary in the *Reading Study Guide* (English or Spanish).

- Discuss ways people use rain forest land.
- Describe problems that result from the destruction of the rain forest.
- Tell some of the ways people are working to prevent rain forest destruction.

Step 4 Support Student Reading

Cooperative Work Pair students up for **Peer Tutoring** and have them work together to read the section and complete the Cause/Effect graphic organizer in Part B of Activity Sheet 11.1. Go over the answers with the class.

On One's Own Preview the following questions by asking students what they understand them to mean. Then have students search for the answers while reading. Once students have finished, help them answer in complete sentences.

1. What are some ways people use rain forest land? (p. 245, pars. 3–5; p. 246, par. 1)

2. What effect might the destruction of the rain forest have on the planet? (p. 246, par. 4)

3. What is the debt-for-nature swap plan? (p. 247, pars. 4–5)

Step 5 Prepare for Assessment

Alternative Assessment Have students work in pairs to complete the Skillbuilder Practice on p. 28 of Unit 3 *In-Depth Resources.* Combine groups and do a **Numbered Heads Together** activity to assess their learning.

Formal Assessment Go over the test-taking strategies for TT35. Then assign the Section Quiz for Chapter 11 Section 1, found on p. 162 of the *Formal Assessment* book.

ACTIVITY SHEET 11.1

Part A. Build Vocabulary

Key Terms Fill in the blank with the best key term to complete each sentence.

> **biodiversity**   **debt**   **deforestation**   **global warming**

1. When a country borrows money, the government of that country must pay back the _____.

2. The rise in the temperature of the atmosphere around the world is referred to as _____.

3. Some places have a wide range of different kinds of plants and animals. This variety in life forms is known as _____.

4. When people cut down and clear away trees, they are engaging in a process called _____, which may harm the earth, in the long run.

Part B. Cooperative Work

Work with your partner to fill in the Cause/Effect graphic organizer. Go over the answers with the class.

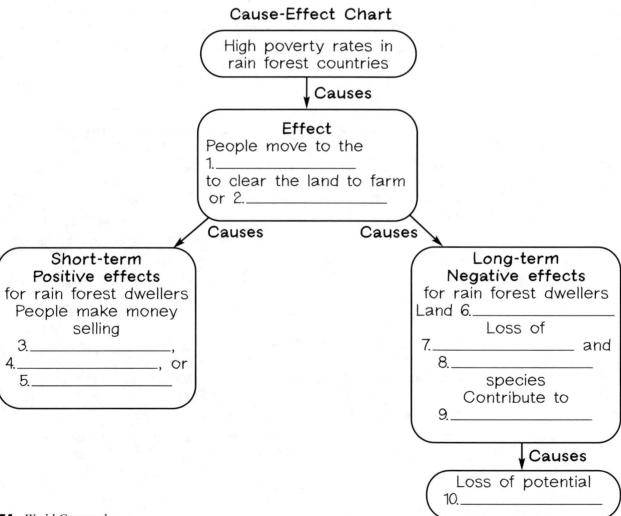

Cause-Effect Chart

Resources for English Learners
RSG pp. 97–98   RSG Audio
IA pp. 7, 28, 29   TT 36
FA p. 163   MLG

Giving Citizens a Voice

Step 1 Activate Prior Knowledge	Review what a democracy is and what a democratic government involves. Use a **Signals** activity to check that all students understand the concepts. Then run a **Brainstorming** activity to discuss the pros and cons of democracy. Explain that few Latin American countries have had democratic governments in the past. Let students return to the pro/con list, to add to it, after they complete the section.
Step 2 Preview Main Ideas and Language	**Connect Visually** Divide the class into groups of three and have students to study the political cartoon on PE p. 249. Pose the questions: What does the man represent? What does the crowd represent? What does the caption indicate about the crowd? What is funny about this cartoon? What is the cartoonist trying to say? Have groups share their responses to these questions in a class discussion. **Build Vocabulary** Pair students for **Peer Vocabulary Teaching** to learn the definitions of the key terms in Part A of Activity Sheet 11.2. Encourage Spanish speakers to teach the words that come from Spanish and English speakers to teach the other two terms. Refer students to the textbook when they start working on their categorization. Go over the answers and reasons for them with the class.
Step 3 Make Objectives Explicit	Write these objectives on the overhead or on the board and read them aloud to the class. Have students turn to a partner in the classroom and explain in their own words what they will be learning in the section, based on the objectives. If students' first language is Spanish, have them read the lesson summary in the *Reading Study Guide* (English or Spanish). • Describe the struggle for democratic government in Latin America. • List some conditions helpful for the establishment of stable democracies.
Step 4 Support Student Reading	**Cooperative Work** Ask students to work in groups of three or four to read the section, using the **SQ3R** method. They should also work together to fill in the graphic organizer in Part B of Activity Sheet 11.2. Go over answers in class. **On One's Own** Preview the following questions by asking students what they understand them to mean. Then have students search for the answers while reading. Once students have finished, help them answer in complete sentences. **1.** How did colonialism affect the development of democracy in Latin America? (p. 249, pars. 3–4) **2.** What is a caudillo? (p. 249, par. 5; p. 250, pars. 1–2) **3.** Why is economic stability important for the establishment of democracy? (p. 251, par. 5)
Step 5 Prepare for Assessment	**Alternative Assessment** Have students work in small groups to complete the GeoActivity on p. 251. Share the Standards for Evaluating a Cooperative Activity on p. 7 of *Integrated Assessment*, the general criteria for information assessing activities on p. 28, and the specific criteria for a report on p. 29. **Formal Assessment** Go over the test-taking strategies for TT36. Then assign the Section Quiz for Chapter 11 Section 2, found on p. 163 of the *Formal Assessment* book.

ACTIVITY SHEET 11.2

Part A. Build Vocabulary

Key Terms Use the chart to categorize the key terms.

caudillo	junta	land reform	oligarchy

Supported by Latin America's wealthy	To spread wealth in Latin America more fairly

Part B. Cooperative Work

Work with your group to read the section and fill in the graphic organizer. Go over the answers with the class.

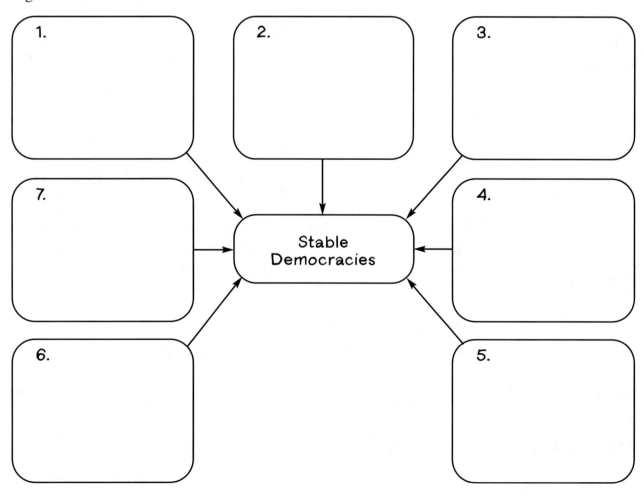

Resources for English Learners
TE p. 255   TT 37a, TT 37b   RSG pp. 99–100, 101
RSG Audio   MLG   FA pp. 164, 165–169,
170–174, 175–179

The Income Gap

Step 1 **Activate Prior Knowledge**	Discuss the idea of an income gap, referring students to pp. 188, 189, 210, 222, and 230, where the term is used. Then do a **Think-Draw-Pair-Share** activity to have students make a drawing or a cartoon that illustrates the income gap. Explain the section covers problems and solutions for the income gap in Latin America.
Step 2 **Preview Main Ideas and Language**	**Connect Visually** Show students the circle graphs from TT37a in *Test Practice Transparencies*. Have them rank the four Latin American countries shown, based on the percentage of the population living in poverty. Explain that according to the U.S. Census Bureau, just over 12% of the U.S. population lives in poverty. **Build Vocabulary** Review the **New Word Analysis** strategy for learning vocabulary. Then divide students into groups of three and have them use this method to learn the meaning of each key term listed in Part A of Activity Sheet 11.3. Students should complete Part A on their own. Go over the answers with the class.
Step 3 **Make Objectives Explicit**	Write these objectives on the overhead or on the board and read them aloud to the class. Check students' comprehension using Number of Fingers or another **Signals** Activity. Students who understand the objectives can explain them to students who do not understand them. If students' first language is Spanish, have them read the lesson summary in the *Reading Study Guide* (English or Spanish). • Explain the problem of the income gap in Latin America. • Describe possible solutions to the income gap. • Analyze primary sources for different views on the income gap in Latin America.
Step 4 **Support Student Reading**	**Cooperative Work** Divide the class into groups of four and direct them pair up, one pair taking the primary source readings on p. 254 and the other pair taking the primary source readings on p. 255. Students pairs should work together on a **Double-Column Note-Taking** activity on their two primary sources, using Part B of Activity Sheet 11.3. When students are done taking notes on their readings, the pairs should come together to share their notes and ideas about the readings. **On One's Own** Preview the following questions by asking students what they understand them to mean. Then have students search for the answers while reading. Once students have finished, help them answer in complete sentences. **1.** What ethical questions does Latin America's income gap raise? (p. 252, par. 5) **2.** Why is the income gap a political issue? (p. 252, par. 8; p. 253, par. 1) **3.** What are some possible solution for Latin America's income gap? (p. 253, pars. 4–6)
Step 5 **Prepare for Assessment**	**Alternative Assessment** Have students work in groups of five to complete the Case Study Project. Share the Grading Rubric on TE p. 255 with students and use it to evaluate their project. **Formal Assessment** Go over the test-taking strategies for TT37a and TT37a. You may want to use *Formal Assessment* Form A, the less-challenging assessment, or administer it as a practice test prior to formal testing with Form B or Form C.

ACTIVITY SHEET 11.3

Part A. Build Vocabulary

Key Terms Match each key term with its definition.

1. _____ **distribution**

2. _____ **elite**

3. _____ **ethical**

4. _____ **income gap**

5. _____ **poverty**

a. the difference in the quality of life enjoyed by the rich and the poor

b. the condition of being poor, of being unable to provide for one's material needs

c. belonging to a group that considers itself superior

d. the way something is divided in portions

e. having to do with moral duty and what is good and bad

Part B. Cooperative Work

Work with your group to read and take notes on the primary sources on pp. 254–255. Go over the answers with the class.

Notes on Primary Sources		
Primary Source	Note Taking	Note Making
Income Distribution Graph		
Cable News story by Marina Marabella		
Newspaper story by Steven Gutkin		
Magazine article from *The Economist*		

Resources for English Learners
TE p. 274   RSG pp. 103–104   RSG Audio
IA p. 7   TT 38   FA p. 180
MLG

Landforms and Resources

**Step 1
Activate Prior
Knowledge**

Write the word *peninsula* on the board and ask the class for a definition. If students do not know, have a volunteer look the word up in a dictionary or other reference and read the definition aloud. Write the definition on the board. Then ask students to draw and label a peninsula, checking their comprehension with a **Slates** activity. Explain that the continent of Europe is a peninsula.

**Step 2
Preview Main
Ideas and
Language**

Connect Visually Have students pair up and use the map on pp. A14–A15 to see why the continent of Europe is called a peninsula. Then ask them to trace five smaller peninsulas in Europe. Direct them to turn to p. 273 and identify the names of the different peninsulas. Students can locate and name these on a wall map in a Round Robin activity.

Build Vocabulary As a demonstration, work with a student to make a **Word Square** using the word *peninsula*. Then divide students into groups of six. Within each group, students should pair up and choose a different key term from Part A of Activity Sheet 12.1. Have them use the Word Square and work together to define the term.

**Step 3
Make Objectives
Explicit**

Write these objectives on the overhead or on the board and read them aloud to the class. For each objective, tell students to look through the section or the Unit Opener pages and identify a map or photo that might help them learn about that objective. If students' first language is Spanish, have them read the lesson summary in the *Reading Study Guide* (English or Spanish).

- Name and locate Europe's main peninsulas and islands.
- Tell how mountains, uplands, and rivers have affected life in Europe.
- Discuss the importance of plains in Europe.
- Identify Europe's key natural resources and explain how they shape Europe's economy and daily life.

**Step 4
Support Student
Reading**

Cooperative Work Divide the class into groups of three and direct students to work together to complete the chart in Part B of Activity Sheet 12.1. Go over the answers with the class and then do a **Carousel Review** to reinforce the material.

On One's Own Preview the following questions by asking students what they understand them to mean. Then have students search for the answers while reading. Once students have finished, help them answer in complete sentences.

1. Why is Europe called a "peninsula of peninsulas"? (p. 273, par. 2, map)

2. How have Europe's mountain ranges affected life there? (p. 275, pars. 3–5)

3. Why are the rivers of Europe very important? (p. 275, pars. 2–4)

4. How did natural resources help Europe become industrialized? (p. 276, par. 1)

**Step 5
Prepare for
Assessment**

Alternative Assessment Have students work in pairs to complete the web diagram activity on TE p. 274. Share the Standards for Evaluating a Cooperative Activity on p. 7 of *Integrated Assessment* and use it for evaluating students' graphic organizers.

Formal Assessment Go over the test-taking strategies for TT38. Then assign the Section Quiz for Chapter 12 Section 1, on p. 180 of the *Formal Assessment* book.

World Geography **79**

ACTIVITY SHEET 12.1

Part A. Build Vocabulary

Key Terms Working with a partner, use the Word Square to help you define one of the terms below. Share your Word Square with your larger group.

fjord uplands peat

Word: Translation:	Symbol or Picture:
My meaning: Dictionary definition:	Sentence:

Part B. Cooperative Work

Work with your group to fill in the chart. Review the answers with the class.

How Landforms Shape Life in Europe		
Landform	Location	How Shapes Life
fjords		
Alps		
Pyrenees Mountains		
Apennines Mountains		
Balkan Mountains		
Danube River		
Rhine River		
Northern European Plain		

Resources for English Learners
RSG pp. 105–106   RSG Audio
IA p. 28   TT 39
FA p. 181   MLG

Climate and Vegetation

Step 1 **Activate Prior Knowledge**	Divide the class into groups of four or five. Pose the question: Which do you think has warmer winters, Fargo, North Dakota, or Paris, France? Encourage students to look at a globe or a world map that has latitude marked on it to come up with a prediction. Use the board to record all groups' predictions.
Step 2 **Preview Main Ideas and Language**	**Connect Visually** Keeping students in their groups, direct them to turn to p. 278 and to study the climographs. Point out that the climographs show two things: average monthly rainfall and average monthly temperature. Circulate among students and help them read the two climographs. Then return to the predictions students made in Step 1. Let them revise their predictions as needed. **Build Vocabulary** Go over the definitions of the two boldfaced terms in the chart in Part A of Activity Sheet 12.2. Once you are sure that students understand these terms, ask them to work with a partner to complete the **Semantic Feature Analysis.**
Step 3 **Make Objectives Explicit**	Write these objectives on the overhead or on the board and read them aloud to the class. Check students' comprehension using Thumbs Up/Thumbs Down **Signals** activity. Students who understand the objectives can explain them to students who do not understand them. If students' first language is Spanish, have them read the lesson summary in the *Reading Study Guide* (English or Spanish). • Explain how and why winds warm much of Europe. • Describe the climate of inland Europe. • Describe the climate of Mediterranean Europe. • Tell how climate affects vegetation in far northern Scandinavia.
Step 4 **Support Student Reading**	**Cooperative Work** Have students work with a partner to complete the chart in Part B of Activity Sheet 12.2. Go over the answers with the class. Then do a written **Roundtable** activity to review and reinforce the information. **On One's Own** Preview the following questions by asking students what they understand them to mean. Then have students search for the answers while reading. Once students have finished, help them answer in complete sentences. **1.** How do the North Atlantic Drift and the prevailing westerlies affect Europe's climate? (p. 278, par. 3) **2.** How are a mistral and a sirocco different? (p. 279, pars. 6–7) **3.** Why is northern Scandinavia sometimes called the Land of the Midnight Sun? (p. 280, par. 3)
Step 5 **Prepare for Assessment**	**Alternative Assessment** Have students work in pairs to complete the GeoActivity on PE p. 280. Share the general guidelines for evaluating information assessing activities and for evaluating charts on p. 28 of *Integrated Assessment* and use these for evaluating students' work. **Formal Assessment** Go over the test-taking strategies for TT39. Then assign the Section Quiz for Chapter 12 Section 2 found on p. 181 of the *Formal Assessment* book.

ACTIVITY SHEET 12.2

Part A. Build Vocabulary

Work with your partner to complete the **Semantic Feature Analysis** for
the key terms, in boldfaced type.

Type of wind	Blows from the north	Blows from the south	Hot	Cold	Dry	May bring rain	May bring desert sand or dust
mistral							
sirocco							

Part B. Cooperative Work

Work with your group to fill in the chart to describe Europe's climate,
winds, and vegetation. Review the answers with the class.

Region	Climate	Current/Winds	Crops/Vegetation
northern Spain, France, Germany, British Isles, western Poland	1.	2.	3.
Sweden, Finland, Romania, much of Poland, Hungary, and Slovakia	4.		5.
southern Spain and France, Italy, Greece, parts of the Balkan Peninsula	6.	7.	8.
northern Scandinavia	9.		10.

Human-Environment Interaction

Step 1
Activate Prior Knowledge

Do a **Think-Pair-Share** activity to have students list specific examples of ways people have changed your local environment from its natural state. As an example, you might mention the city planting grass in a park. Explain that Europe has been densely populated for many centuries and that over this time, Europeans have changed their environment in numerous ways.

Step 2
Preview Main Ideas and Language

Connect Visually Direct students to work in groups of five to study the diagram on p. 282. With each student taking a step, they should take turns explaining the process to each other and asking questions about it.

Build Vocabulary Go over the definitions of the boldfaced terms in Part A of Activity Sheet 12.3. Once you are sure that students understand these terms, ask them to work with a partner to complete Part A.

Step 3
Make Objectives Explicit

Write these objectives on the board. Ask students to identify what they think is the single most important word or phrase in each objective and have them explain their selections to the class. If students' first language is Spanish, have them read the lesson summary in the *Reading Study Guide* (English or Spanish).

- Describe how land is reclaimed in the Netherlands.
- Tell how the city of Venice, Italy, was built and what it is like.
- Define deforestation and discuss how it has affected Europe.

Step 4
Support Student Reading

Cooperative Work Divide the class into groups of six. Within each group, students should pair up and fill out a **Sunshine Outline** as shown in Part B of Activity Sheet 12.3, explaining how Europeans have changed their environment: one group should cover the Dutch; another group should cover Venice; and another group should cover deforestation. The pairs should share their outlines with the larger group. Go over the answers in class.

On One's Own Preview the following questions by asking students what they understand them to mean. Then have students search for the answers while reading. Once students have finished, help them answer in complete sentences.

1. How have the Dutch created more land for their country? (p. 282, par. 2 and diagram; p. 283, pars. 2–3)

2. How has pollution affected the city of Venice? (p. 283, par. 8)

3. Why did Europeans clear their forests? (p. 284, par. 1)

Step 5
Prepare for Assessment

Alternative Assessment Assign students to work in pairs on the Activity on TE p. 283. Share the Standards for Evaluating a Cooperative Activity on p. 7 of *Integrated Assessments*, and use these guidelines for evaluating students' work.

Formal Assessment Go over the test-taking strategies for TT40. You may want to use *Formal Assessment* Form A, the less-challenging assessment, or administer it as a practice test prior to formal testing with Form B or Form C.

ACTIVITY SHEET 12.3

Part A. Build Vocabulary

Fill in the blanks with the correct terms to complete the sentences in the paragraph. You may need to make nouns plural.

> **dike:** banks of earth built to hold back water
>
> **polder:** land that used to be under water but that becomes usable because people drain the water
>
> **reclaim:** to make land usable for living on or for farming
>
> **terpen:** high earthen platform built to provide a place of safety during high tides or floods

    In the country of the Netherlands, the people who lived there, called the Dutch, needed more land for their growing population. So, hundreds of years ago, they began to **1.** _____ land from the sea. To do this, they built **2.** _____ around shallow areas of water and slowly drained or pumped the water off the land. The land that results is called a **3.** _____. This land is below sea level. During especially high tides or floods, the land will be underwater. The Dutch have built high earthen platforms called **4.** _____ that they can go to to stay safe.

Part B. Cooperative Work

Work with your partner to fill in the **Sunshine Outline.** Share your outline with your group and go over your answers with the class.

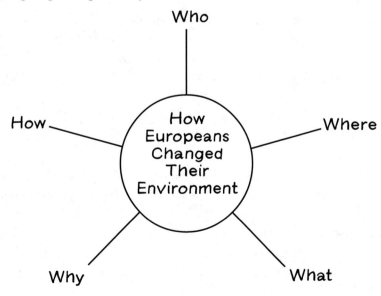

Resources for English Learners
RSG pp. 111–112   IA p. 7   TT 41
FA p. 195   MLG
RSG Audio; Video: *Italy: Natural Hazards and Disasters*

Mediterranean Europe

**Step 1
Activate Prior
Knowledge**

Do a **K-W-L** activity with the class on ancient Greece and Rome. Encourage students to tell what they know and what they'd like to learn about these two influential cultures. Fill in the L section of the class chart when students complete the section.

**Step 2
Preview Main
Ideas and
Language**

Connect Visually Have students pair up and turn to the map on pp. 264–265. Ask them to identify the Mediterranean Sea and locate the European countries that border the Mediterranean. List the countries that make up Mediterranean Europe on the overhead or the board and pose the question: Based on the map, what do these countries have in common that they would form the subregion of Mediterranean Europe? Let pairs share their ideas.

Build Vocabulary Use the **Frayer Method** to teach the key terms in Part A of Activity Sheet 13.1. When you are sure that all students understand these terms, divide the class in small groups and have them complete Part A. Go over the answers in class.

**Step 3
Make Objectives
Explicit**

Write these objectives on the overhead or on the board and read them aloud to the class. Check students' comprehension using Number of Fingers or another **Signals** activity. Students who understand the objectives can explain them to students who do not understand them. If students' first language is Spanish, have them read the lesson summary in the *Reading Study Guide* (English or Spanish).

- Describe the two great civilizations of ancient Europe.
- Discuss historic events in the Mediterranean subregion.
- Discuss the culture, the economy, and modern life in Mediterranean Europe.

**Step 4
Support Student
Reading**

Cooperative Work Divide the class into groups of three and ask them to work together to complete the timeline in Part B of Activity Sheet 13.1. Then make a class time line with input from all of the groups.

On One's Own Preview the following questions by asking students what they understand them to mean. Then have students search for the answers while reading. Once students have finished, help them answer in complete sentences.

1. What legacy did ancient Greece leave for modern government? (p. 289, par. 4)

2. What is Rome's cultural legacy in Mediterranean Europe today? (p. 291, pars. 8–10)

3. How has the Mediterranean Europe's economy changed since World War II? (p. 292, pars. 2–5)

4. What are some problems caused by urban growth in Mediterranean Europe? (p. 293, par. 2)

**Step 5
Prepare for
Assessment**

Alternative Assessment Show students the part of the video *Italy: Natural Hazards and Disasters* that includes the scenes from the ruins at Pompeii. Direct students to work in small groups to write a report about Pompeii. Share the Standards for Evaluating a Cooperative Activity on p. 7 of *Integrated Assessments*, and use these guidelines for evaluating students' work.

Formal Assessment Go over the test-taking strategies for TT41. Then assign the Section Quiz for Chapter 13 Section 1, found on p. 195 of the *Formal Assessment* book.

ACTIVITY SHEET 13.1

Part A. Build Vocabulary

Key Terms Write the term in each blank that best answers the question.

> **city-state**   **democracy**   **republic**   **classical**

1. What do we call a government in which citizens elect representatives to govern in their name? _____

2. What do we call a political unit made up of a city and its surrounding land? _____

3. What do we call something that relates to ancient Greece or Rome? _____

4. What do we call a government in which citizens hold political power directly or through elected representatives? _____

Part B. Cooperative Work

As you study the section, work with your group to add eight entries to the time line, related to important events in Mediterranean history.

Some Important Events in the history of Mediterranean Europe

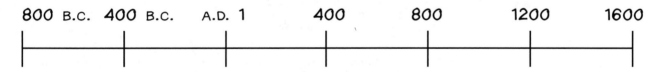

800 B.C.   400 B.C.   A.D. 1   400   800   1200   1600

Resources for English Learners
RSG pp. 113–114   RSG Audio
IA pp. 28, 29   TT 42a, TT 42b
FA p. 196   MLG

Western Europe

Step 1 Activate Prior Knowledge	Let students work in pairs to list cultural differences among different groups of people in your town, city, or local region. Ask students to discuss the problems and benefits of different cultural groups being in close contact. Explain that cultural differences in Western Europe have shaped the subregion's history.
Step 2 Preview Main Ideas and Language	**Connect Visually** Direct students' attention to the time line on pp. 296–297. Through class discussion, ask students to share what they already know about events on the time line and how they learned these things. Point out the colored bars that indicate different eras on the time line. **Build Vocabulary** Go over the key terms in Part A of Activity Sheet 13.2. Use **Word Imaging** to help students understand the definitions. Then assign students to complete Part A. Let students share their drawings in groups.
Step 3 Make Objectives Explicit	Write these objectives on the overhead or on the board and read them aloud to the class. Have students work in pairs to identify the paragraph or paragraphs that will help them meet each objective. If students' first language is Spanish, have them read the lesson summary in the *Reading Study Guide* (English or Spanish). • Identify the cultural divisions in Western Europe. • Describe the rise of nation-states. • Analyze the economies of different countries in Western Europe. • Describe artistic achievements and modern life in Western Europe.
Step 4 Support Student Reading	**Cooperative Work** Divide students into groups of three and have them do **Jigsaw Reading** to fill in the chart in Part B of Activity Sheet 13.2. Each group should take the items under one of the heads in the chart. Review answers with the class. **On One's Own** Preview the following questions by asking students what they understand them to mean. Then have students search for the answers while reading. Once students have finished, help them answer in complete sentences. **1.** Which two countries dominate Western Europe and why? (p. 296, par. 2) **2.** How did the Reformation create new divisions in Western Europe? (p. 297, pars. 2–3) **3.** How has nationalism led to conflicts? (p. 297, par. 6; p. 298, pars. 1–3) **4.** How is Western Europe's economy diverse? (p. 298, par. 6) **5.** What have been some sources of recent conflicts in Western Europe? (p. 301, pars. 5–6)
Step 5 Prepare for Assessment	**Alternative Assessment** Have students complete the GeoActivity on p. 301. Share the guidelines for evaluating Information Assessing Activities and for a Venn Diagram on pp. 28–29 of *Integrated Assessment* and use them for assessing students' work. **Formal Assessment** Go over the test-taking strategies for TT42a and TT42b. Then assign the Section Quiz for Chapter 13 Section 2, found on p. 196 of the *Formal Assessment* book.

ACTIVITY SHEET 13.2

Part A. Build Vocabulary

Use each box below to make a drawing that helps you remember the meaning of the following two key terms. Write the meaning at the bottom of the drawing.

feudalism	nationalism

Part B. Cooperative Work

Complete the chart by working with your group. Go over the answers with your class.

A History of Cultural Divisions	
1. the two dominant countries in Western Europe	**a.** **b.** Conquered by Rome: **c.** Not conquered by Rome:
2. period when many Christians broke away from Catholicism and formed own churches	**a.** **b.** Catholic countries: **c.** countries divided between Catholics and Protestants:
The Rise of Nation-States	
3. political system that developed after fall of Rome	
4. how nation-states evolved in Western Europe	
5. when and why the French Revolution occurred	
6. general causes of World War I	
7. general causes of World War II	
8. what happened to Germany after World War II	
9. what happened to Germany after 1990	
Economics: Diversity and Luxury	
10. Western European countries that export dairy products	
11. three of Europe's top manufacturing nations	
12. why Western Europe is popular with tourists	

Resources for English Learners
RSG pp. 115–116   RSG Audio
IA p. 8   TT 43
FA p. 197   MLG

Northern Europe

Step 1 **Activate Prior Knowledge**	Display a wall map of Europe and ask students to do a **Round Robin** activity to name the countries that form the subregion of Northern Europe. List these countries on the board. Have students turn to p. 288 to check their list against the map.
Step 2 **Preview Main Ideas and Language**	**Connect Visually** Students can remain in their pairs and turn to the Regional Data File on pp. 268–271. Direct them to look at the flags of the countries that make up Northern Europe. Based on these flags, ask students to identify countries that form a subregion of Northern Europe. Point out the similarity in the flags of Denmark, Finland, Iceland, Norway, and Sweden. Explain that these Nordic countries have a common cultural heritage and form a subregion of Northern Europe. **Build Vocabulary** Review how to use an **Anticipation Guide** for Part A of Activity Sheet 13.3. Students should first fill in their individual responses and, after discussion, fill in group responses. Allow time after students have read the section to fill in the "Textbook" column and to correct answers.
Step 3 **Make Objectives Explicit**	Write these objectives on the board and read them to the class. Have students work with a partner to identify one or more paragraphs in the section that they will need to read to meet each objective. If students' first language is Spanish, have them read the lesson summary in the *Reading Study Guide* (English or Spanish). • Identify Northern Europe's seafaring conquerors and describe the formation of Great Britain's local and global empires. • Describe how representative government and the industrial revolution developed in Great Britain, spreading from there to other parts of the world. • Discuss Northern Europe's economy and tell how it is changing. • Describe the culture and daily life of people in Northern Europe.
Step 4 **Support Student Reading**	**Cooperative Work** Ask students to work in groups of three or four to read the section, using the **SQ3R** method. They should also work together to fill in the chart in Part B of Activity Sheet 13.3. Go over answers in class. **On One's Own** Preview the following questions by asking students what they understand them to mean. Then have students search for the answers while reading. **1.** Who were the Vikings and what did they do? (p. 302, par. 5) **2.** What are some characteristics of governments in Northern Europe? (p. 303, par. 6; p. 304, par. 1) **3.** How did the Reformation affect Northern Europe? (p. 306, par. 3) **4.** How did the industrial revolution spur the growth of Britain's empire? (p. 304, par. 2)
Step 5 **Prepare for Assessment**	**Alternative Assessment** Assign students to work in groups to answer Assessment question 4 on p. 307. Share the Standards for Evaluating a Group Discussion on p. 8 of *Integrated Assessments* and use them to evaluate students' answers. **Formal Assessment** Go over the test-taking strategies for TT43. Then assign the Section Quiz for Chapter 13 Section 3, found on p. 197 of the *Formal Assessment* book.

ACTIVITY SHEET 13.3

Part A. Build Vocabulary

Key Terms Work individually and then with your group to fill in the first two columns of the Anticipation Guide. Fill in the third column after you have read the entire section. Correct any false answers.

You	Group	Textbook	Topic—Northern Europe
			1. Northern Europe has a seafaring culture and a history of **conquest,** especially of invasions by sea.
			2. Representative government, such as that of Britain, always includes a king to represent the nation in meetings with foreign rulers.
			3. Northern Europe's first representative lawmaking body, a **parliament,** met in Iceland in 930.
			4. The **euro** is a popular car, made in Sweden.

Part B. Cooperative Work

Work with your group to read the section and fill in the chart. Go over the answers with the class.

	Nordic Countries	Other Countries of Northern Europe
Name of Countries	**1.**	**2.**
Ancient Inhabitants	**3.**	**4.**
Empire Building	**5.**	**6.**
Languages/Religions	**7.**	**8.**
Cultural Figures	**9.**	**10.**
Customs/Leisure	**11.**	**12.**
Social Welfare Today	**13.**	**14.**

Resources for English Learners
TE p. 314   RSG pp. 117–118, 119–120
RSG Audio   IA pp. 7, 28   TT 44a, TT 44b
FA pp. 198, 199–202, 203–206, 207–210   MLG

Eastern Europe

Step 1 **Activate Prior Knowledge**	Lead a **Brainstorming** session in which students share what they know about Communism and the Cold-War era. Jot down students' answers on the board. Point out that Eastern Europe was under Communist rule during the Cold War and that this has strongly affected the subregion.
Step 2 **Preview Main Ideas and Language**	**Connect Visually** Let students pair up and turn to the maps on p. 312. Have them study the key and then discuss how Eastern Europe changed between 1949 and 2000. Ask students to compose a sentence that describes the change and let each group share the sentence they wrote with the class. **Build Vocabulary** Ask a volunteer to go over the **New Word Analysis** strategy for analyzing and decoding vocabulary words. Then have students work in groups of three and use New Word Analysis to understand the key terms in Part A of Activity Sheet 13.4. Students should complete Part A on their own. Go over the answers with the class.
Step 3 **Make Objectives Explicit**	Write these objectives on the board and read them to the class. Have students turn to a partner and explain in their own words what they will be learning in the section, based on the objectives. If students' first language is Spanish, have them read the lesson summary in the *Reading Study Guide* (English or Spanish). • Tell why Eastern Europe is considered a cultural crossroads. • Describe the turmoil in Eastern Europe in the 20th century. • Explain how the economy of Eastern Europe has developed. • Discuss the challenges Eastern Europe faces in terms of culture, economic growth, and politics.
Step 4 **Support Student Reading**	**Cooperative Work** Divide the class into groups of four and have them do **Reciprocal Teaching** to read and study the section. Direct them to work together to fill in the chart in Part B of Activity Sheet 13.4. Use a **Numbered Heads Together** activity to go over and correct the answers. **On One's Own** Preview the following questions by asking students what they understand them to mean. Then have students search for the answers while reading. **1.** Why is Eastern Europe considered a cultural crossroads? (p. 310, par. 3) **2.** Why did independent nation-states develop later in Eastern Europe than in Western Europe? (p. 310, par. 2; p. 311, pars. 1–2) **3.** Which country dominated Easter Europe after World War II? (p. 312, par. 1) **4.** What problems has the move toward a market economy caused? (p. 313, pars. 2–5)
Step 5 **Prepare for Assessment**	**Alternative Assessment** Assign students to work in small groups on the Activity on TE p. 314. Share the three sets of guidelines for evaluating a cooperative activity, information assessing activities, and a chart on pp. 7 and 28 of *Integrated Assessment* and use them to evaluate students' work. **Formal Assessment** Go over the test-taking strategies for TT44a and TT44b. You may want to use *Formal Assessment* Form A, the less-challenging assessment, or administer it as a practice test prior to formal testing with Form B or Form C.

ACTIVITY SHEET 13.4

Part A. Build Vocabulary

Key Terms Work with a partner to figure out the meaning of the key terms. Then complete the vocabulary exercise on your own. You may need to make some of the words plural.

> **anti-Semitism   balkanization   cultural crossroads   satellite nation**

Various cultures cross paths in Eastern Europe. That is why this subregion is considered a **1.** _____. In the early 1900s, some parts of the Balkan region formed independent nations. However, the small, new nations were hostile to one another. The process by which a region breaks into smaller units that fight against each other is now called **2.** _____. At the end of World War II, the Soviet army occupied Eastern Europe. The Soviet Union set up Communist governments in the region, making the Balkan countries **3.** _____ of the Soviet Union. Throughout history, many minority groups in the Balkans have faced discrimination. For example, there frequently has been **4.** _____ against the Jews in the region.

Part B. Cooperative Work

Work with your group to read the section and fill in the spider diagram.

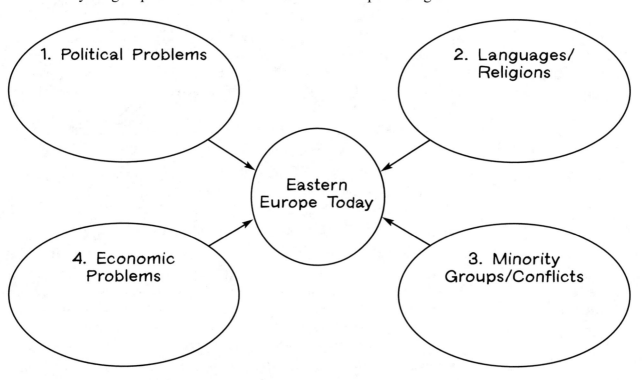

Resources for English Learners
TE p. 321   RSG pp. 121–122   RSG Audio
IA p. 8   TT 45   FA p. 211
MLG

Turmoil in the Balkans

**Step 1
Activate Prior Knowledge**

Tell students that thirty years ago Yugoslavia was made up of six republics and two self-governing provinces. Today Yugoslavia is made up of two republics and two provinces. Using this information, ask students to make a prediction about Yugoslavia in the future. Students should think about what they've already learned about the Balkans from the previous chapter and share any knowledge they have from other sources. Record students' predictions on the board or the overhead for future revision.

**Step 2
Preview Main Ideas and Language**

Connect Visually Divide the class into groups of three. Direct students to turn to the map on p. 322 and cover up the bottom of the page where the assessment questions are given. Each group should make up three questions that the map answers; have the groups pair up, ask each other their questions, and share answers. Circulate among students to help clarify information.

Build Vocabulary Help students understand the key terms in Part A of Activity Sheet 14.1. For *Bosnia and Herzegovina,* read p. 320, par. 3. For *ethnic cleansing,* read p. 320, par. 7. Students can complete Part A in pairs. Go over the answers with the class to clarify understanding.

**Step 3
Make Objectives Explicit**

Write these objectives on the overhead or on the board. Have students read the objectives and then write a question they will answer based on each objective. Go over the questions to clarify students' understanding. If students' first language is Spanish, have them read the lesson summary in the *Reading Study Guide* (English or Spanish).

- Analyze the roots of the Balkan conflict.
- identify causes of fighting in the Balkans near the end of the 20th century.

**Step 4
Support Student Reading**

Cooperative Work Divide the class into groups of three and ask them to work together to complete the chart in Part B of Activity Sheet 14.1. Go over the answers with students and then organize a review using **Inside-Outside Circles.**

On One's Own Preview the following questions by asking students what they understand them to mean. Then have students search for the answers while reading. Once students have finished, help them answer in complete sentences.

1. Why did centuries of foreign rule help lead to ethnic conflict in the Balkans? (p. 319, pars. 4--5)

2. Why have a number of Yugoslav republics declared independence? (p. 320, pars. 5–7; p. 321, par. 2)

3. What has been the effect of decades of war in the Balkans? (p. 321, par. 5)

**Step 5
Prepare for Assessment**

Alternative Assessment Have students read the Geography Today feature on p. 321. Pose the questions about that feature on TE p. 321 and have students discuss in small groups. Share the Standards for Evaluating a Group Discussion on p. 8 of *Integrated Assessments,* and use these guidelines for evaluation.

Formal Assessment Go over the test-taking strategies for TT45. Then assign the Section Quiz for Chapter 14 Section 1, found on p. 211 of the *Formal Assessment* book.

World Geography **93**

ACTIVITY SHEET 14.1

Part A. Build Vocabulary

Key Terms Work with your partner to answer the questions.

> **Bosnia and Herzegovina**   **ethnic cleansing**

1. a. Based on the 1946 constitution, how many republics were included in Bosnia and Herzegovina? _____

    b. How do you know? _____

    c. Turn to the map on p. 265. How many independent nations are included in Bosnia and Herzegovina today? _____

    d. How do you know? _____

2. a. Which of the following terms is most closely related to the term *ethnic cleansing?* (1) feudalism   (2) Holocaust   (3) balkanization

    b. How are these terms related? _____

    c. A euphemism is an expression that uses agreeable words to represent something that may be disagreeable or offensive. In what way is the term *ethnic cleansing* a euphemism? _____

Part B. Cooperative Work

As you study the section, work with your group to fill in the cause/effect chart.

Cause	Effect
Different Slavic groups migrate from Poland and Russia into the Balkan region; they came to be called the South Slavs.	**1.**
2.	Foreign rule led to the development of cultural differences among the South Slavs.
3.	Ethnic rivalries of different Balkan groups remained submerged for many decades.
Tito died in 1981; presidency rotated among Yugoslavia's six republics and two provinces.	**4.**
5.	Slovenia and Croatia declared independence.
Slovenia and Croatia declared independence.	**6.**
Thousands of people died.	**7.**
Bosnia and Herzegovina declared independence.	**8.**

Resources for English Learners
Video: *Greece: Urbanization and the Environment*
RSG pp. 123–124   RSG Audio   IA pp. 28–29
TT 46a, TT 46b   FA p. 212   MLG

Cleaning Up Europe

Step 1 **Activate Prior Knowledge**	Take a class poll on whether students think that their local region suffers from serious air pollution, water pollution, or both. After the vote, lead a discussion on how students made their decisions and what they have noticed about pollution in the local region. Students should share knowledge of pollution sources, effects of pollution, and clean-up attempts. Explain that parts of Europe suffer from serious air and water pollution problems.
Step 2 **Preview Main Ideas and Language**	**Connect Visually** Show students part of the video *Greece: Urbanization and the Environment*. Refer to the TRB for The Voyageur Experience in World Geography, p. 35, and show the sequence that discusses pollution in Athens. Follow the suggestions for **Viewing Videos with Language Learners.** **Build Vocabulary** Have students work in groups of two for **Peer Vocabulary Teaching** to learn the definitions of the key terms in Part A of Activity Sheet 14.2. Students should complete Part A on their own. Go over the answers with the class to clarify understanding.
Step 3 **Make Objectives Explicit**	Write these objectives on the overhead or on the board and read them aloud to the class. Check students' comprehension using Thumbs Up/Down or another **Signals** activity. Students who understand the objectives can explain them to students who do not understand them. If students' first language is Spanish, have them read the lesson summary in the *Reading Study Guide* (English or Spanish). • Identify causes of water pollution in Europe and some ways Europeans are trying to clean up water pollution. • Identify causes of air pollution in Europe and some ways Europeans are trying to clean up air pollution.
Step 4 **Support Student Reading**	**Cooperative Work** Have students divide into groups of three and work together to complete the chart in Part B of Activity Sheet 14.2. Students can share their answers in a written **Round Table** activity. **On One's Own** Preview the following questions by asking students what they understand them to mean. Then have students search for the answers while reading. Once students have finished, help them answer in complete sentences. **1.** What dilemma do countries that are developing industries face? (p. 323, par. 5) **2.** What are two harmful effects of burning fossil fuels? (p. 323, par. 4; p. 324, par. 9) **3.** What diseases are linked to air pollution? (p. 325, par. 4)
Step 5 **Prepare for Assessment**	**Alternative Assessment** Have students work in pairs to make a diagram or flow chart that shows the sequence of problems that occurs with chemical fertilizers. Share the guidelines for information assessing activities on pp. 28–29 of *Integrated Assessments*, and use these guidelines for evaluating students' work. **Formal Assessment** Go over the test-taking strategies for TT46a and TT46b. Then assign the Section Quiz for Chapter 14 Section 2, found on p. 212 of the *Formal Assessment* book.

ACTIVITY SHEET 14.2

Part A. Build Vocabulary

Key Terms Match each key term with its definition.

1. _____ ozone

2. _____ particulate

3. _____ smog

a. a brown haze that occurs when the gases released from burning fossil fuels react with sunlight, creating harmful chemicals

b. a form of oxygen that causes health problems

c. a very small particle of liquid or solid matter; some particulates pollute air and water

Part B. Cooperative Work

As you study the section, work with your group to fill in the chart.

	Water Pollution	Air Pollution
Sources	**1.** industry	**5.** fossil fuels
	2. sewage	**6.** fires
	3. chemical fertilizers	**7.** chemical use
	4. oil spills	**8.** industry
Solutions	**9.**	**10.**

Resources for English Learners
TE p. 329   RSG pp. 125–126, 127–128
RSG Audio   TT 47a, TT 47b   MLG
FA pp. 213, 214–217, 218–221, 222–225

Unification: The European Union

Step 1
Activate Prior Knowledge

Write the phrase the *United States of Europe* on the board and ask students what they think this phrase suggests. Record students' responses. Then ask students to discuss how a United States of Europe would be different from the United States of America. Encourage students to think of historical, political, cultural, and economic differences between Europe and our nation.

Step 2
Preview Main Ideas and Language

Connect Visually Have students pair up and turn to p. 327. Using information from the map, they should work together to make a chart or a time line that tells when the different countries joined the European Union.

Build Vocabulary Divide students into groups of four and have them learn the meaning of each key term listed in Part A of Activity Sheet 14.3. Students can complete Part A in pairs.

Step 3
Make Objectives Explicit

Write these objectives on the board and read them to the class. Have students identify the most important word in each objective. Have a brief class discussion of their reasons for their key words. If students' first language is Spanish, have them read the lesson summary in the *Reading Study Guide* (English or Spanish).

• Describe Europe's first steps toward unification.

• Examine issues facing the European Union by analyzing primary sources.

Step 4
Support Student Reading

Cooperative Work Divide the class into groups of five and have them do a **Jigsaw Reading** activity to summarize the primary sources on pp. 328–329 and complete the chart in Part B of Activity Sheet 14.3. Go over answers with the entire class. Then encourage students to find other sources of information as they work on the Case Study Project.

On One's Own Preview the following questions by asking students what they understand them to mean. Then have students search for the answers while reading. Once students have finished, help them answer in complete sentences.

1. Why did European leaders believe that an economic alliance would help prevent war in Europe? (p. 326, par. 2)

2. Which organizations did Europeans form as they took steps toward unity? (p. 326, pars. 2–4)

3. What are some possible problems associated with admitting former Communist countries to the EU? (p. 327, par. 5)

Step 5
Prepare for Assessment

Alternative Assessment Have students work in groups of five to complete the Case Study Project. Share the Grading Rubric on TE p. 329 with students and use it to evaluate their project.

Formal Assessment Go over the test-taking strategies for TT47a and TT47b. You may want to use *Formal Assessment* Form A, the less-challenging assessment, or administer it as a practice test prior to formal testing with Form B or Form C.

ACTIVITY SHEET 14.3

Part A. Build Vocabulary

Key Terms Write the term in each blank that best completes the statement.
Use each term only once.

> alliance   currency   stability   unification

1. After World War II, some European countries signed treaties to give them joint control of certain resources, beginning a process of _____.

2. European nations hoped by forming a single political and economic unit, the continent would achieve _____, and destructive wars would be prevented.

3. Soon some European nations formed a(n) _____ to lower trade barriers and set common economic goals.

4. Eventually, some European nations adopted a common _____ to increase business efficiency and trade.

Part B. Cooperative Work

Work with your group to read and summarize the primary sources on pp. 328–329. Go over the answers with the class.

Main Idea or Summary of Primary Sources
Political commentary from Global Britain:
Speech by Günter Veheugen:
Data related to EU Support levels:
Political analysis by Edmund C. Andrews:
Political cartoon by Pat Oliphant:

Chapter 15 Section 1

Resources for English Learners
TE p. 347   RSG pp. 129–130   RSG Audio
IA p. 7   TT 48   FA p. 226
MLG

Landforms and Resources

**Step 1
Activate Prior
Knowledge**

Display a wall map of the world and point to Russia and the Republics on this map, identifying it as the topic of the World Geography unit. Ask students which two continents this region is in. Then write the word *Eurasia* on the board or the overhead and ask students what they think this name refers to. Explain that Russia and the Republics make up a large part of Eurasia.

**Step 2
Preview Main
Ideas and
Language**

Connect Visually Use the physical geography map of Eurasia on pp. 336–337. Point to each of the landforms given in capital letters on the map and say the landform names aloud for students. Have students repeat them after you. Do this again several more times, with different students leading. This will aid students' reading comprehension of the section.

Build Vocabulary Go over the definitions of the terms defined in Part A of Activity Sheet 15.1. Check to see whether students understood the definitions, using any of the **Signals** activities. Have students work in pairs to answer the questions. Go over the answers with the class to clarify understanding.

**Step 3
Make Objectives
Explicit**

Write these objectives on the overhead or on the board and read them aloud to the class. For each objective, have students write a personal goal for studying the section. Go over students' goals to clarify understanding. If students' first language is Spanish, have them read the lesson summary in the *Reading Study Guide* (English or Spanish).

- Describe the landforms of the northern two thirds of Russia and the Republics.
- Describe the landforms of the southern third of Russia and the Republics.
- Name two main drainage basins and three main lakes of the region.
- Identify the region's resources and explain why many are difficult to develop.

**Step 4
Support Student
Reading**

Cooperative Work Let students pair up to work on Part B of Activity Sheet 15.1. Go over the answers with the class and then do an oral **Round Robin** activity to reinforce the material.

On One's Own Preview the following questions by asking students what they understand them to mean. Then have students search for the answers while reading. Once students have finished, help them answer in complete sentences.

1. Why might a large part of the region's population live on the Northern European Plain? (p. 345, pars. 3–4)
2. Why does Central Asia tend to be very dry? (p. 346, par. 7; p. 347, top)
3. Which two of the region's lakes are remarkable for their size? (p. 348, pars. 3–4)
4. How is the region's use of its resources affected by climate? (p. 349, pars. 2–3)

**Step 5
Prepare for
Assessment**

Alternative Assessment Have students work in groups of four to complete the Activity Option on TE p. 347. Share the Standards for Evaluating a Cooperative Activity on p. 7 of *Integrated Assessment* and use them for evaluating students' brochures.

Formal Assessment Go over the test-taking strategies for TT48. Then assign the Section Quiz for Chapter 15 Section 1, found on p. 226 of the *Formal Assessment* book.

ACTIVITY SHEET 15.1

Part A. Build Vocabulary

Key Terms Work with your partner to solve the riddles.

> **chernozem:** the fertile soil found on the Northern European Plain; means "black earth"
>
> **Eurasia:** the name for the combined continents of Europe and Asia
>
> **Transcaucasia:** the subregion across, or south of, the Caucasus Mountains, that consists of the republics of Armenia, Azerbaijan, and Georgia

1. This is the name for two continents that combined, form a huge landmass.

_____

2. Agriculture thrives in parts of Russia and the western Republics because of this. _____

3. Three republics make up this subregion that has a mountainous border to its north. _____

Part B. Cooperative Work

Work with your partner to label the map with landforms, rivers, and lakes. Use the map located on PE pages 336–337 to locate the physical features. List one or two key facts under each label. Review the answers with the class.

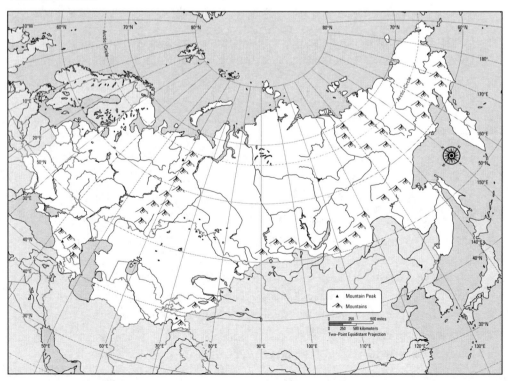

Mountain Peak
Mountains

250   500 miles
0   250   500 kilometers
Two-Point Equidistant Projection

Resources for English Learners
OMA p. 42   RSG pp. 131–132   RSG Audio
IA p. 28   TT 49a, TT 49b   FA p. 227
MLG

Climate and Vegetation

Step 1
Activate Prior Knowledge

Let students review what they already know about climates in far northern regions. Write their responses on the board and let students correct information by referring them to Chapter 3, Section 3 (pp. 59–63). Then hand out copies of an outline map of the region of Russia and the Republics, such as the one on p. 42 of *Outline Maps with Activities*. Ask students to work in pairs to draw their prediction of the region's climate zones.

Step 2
Preview Main Ideas and Language

Connect Visually Keep students paired up and direct them to p. 351 to study the vegetation map. Remind students that climate and vegetation are often closely related. Encourage them to revise the climate map of the region that they made in the above activity, based on new things they learn from looking at this map. Then they should turn to p. 340 and make final corrections of their climate map.

Build Vocabulary Go over the definitions of the three key terms in Part A of Activity Sheet 15.2 and read the paragraphs that introduce these terms. Then have students work individually to draw a climate/vegetation map that shows the terms. Let students share their maps and explain how they labeled them so you can clarify any misunderstandings of the vocabulary and concepts.

Step 3
Make Objectives Explicit

Write these objectives on the board and read them aloud to the class. Have students turn to a partner in the classroom and explain what they will be learning in the section, based on the objectives. Circulate throughout the class to clarify any misunderstandings. If students' first language is Spanish, have them read the lesson summary in the *Reading Study Guide* (English or Spanish).

- Identify the main climates of Russia and the Republics.
- Describe four major vegetation regions of Russia and the Republics.

Step 4
Support Student Reading

Cooperative Work Have students work with a partner to complete the chart in Part B of Activity Sheet 15.2. Go over the answers with the class. Then do a **Carousel Review** to reinforce the information.

On One's Own Preview the following questions by asking students what they understand them to mean. Then have students search for the answers while reading. Once students have finished, help them answer in complete sentences.

1. How does distance from the sea affect the region's climate? (p. 350, pars. 3–4)
2. What are the major vegetation regions in Russia and the Republics? (pp. 351–352)
3. How does latitude affect the type of vegetation found in Russia's forests? (p. 352, par. 1)

Step 5
Prepare for Assessment

Alternative Assessment Have students work in pairs to complete the GeoActivity on p. 352. Share the general guidelines for evaluating information assessing activities and for evaluating graphs on p. 28 of *Integrated Assessment* and use these for evaluating students' work.

Formal Assessment Go over the test-taking strategies for TT49a and TT49b. Then assign the Section Quiz for Chapter 15 Section 2, found on p. 227 of the *Formal Assessment* book.

ACTIVITY SHEET 15.2

Part A. Build Vocabulary

Key Terms Go over the key terms with the class. Then work on your own to draw a map in the empty box that illustrates all three terms.

continentality: the influence on climate of being far from moderating (temperate) influences of the sea

taiga: world's largest forest, consisting mainly of coniferous trees, that lies south of the Russian tundra

steppe: temperate grassland

Part B. Cooperative Work

Work with your partner to fill in the chart to describe the vegetation of Russia and the Republics. Review the answers with the class.

Vegetation Regions of Russia and the Republics	
1. tundra	**2.** forest
3. steppe	**4.** desert

Resources for English Learners
TE p. 356   RSG pp. 133–134, 135–136   RSG Audio
IA p. 7   TT 50   MLG
FA pp. 228, 229–232, 233–236, 237–240

Human-Environment Interaction

**Step 1
Activate Prior
Knowledge**

Explain to students that Russia and the Republics were once united as one nation, the Soviet Union, under Communist rule. Divide the class into small groups and have the groups predict types of human-environment interactions in Russia and the Republics, based on what they already know about the region and their knowledge of human-environment interactions in Eastern Europe.

**Step 2
Preview Main
Ideas and
Language**

Connect Visually Have students pair up and study the photographs of the Aral Sea on pp. 353 and 354. Pose this question, writing it on the board or the overhead: What do the photographs indicate about the Aral Sea? Have students share their answers.

Build Vocabulary Write the word *runoff* on the board or the overhead and ask students what they think it means. Then go over the definition and talk about why the word is a good one for what it describes. Have students pair up and read about runoff into the Aral Sea on pp. 353–354. They can use Part A of Activity Sheet 15.3 to take notes. Do a **Roundtable** activity with the sheet to fill in the chart and go over the answers. Clarify understanding as needed.

**Step 3
Make Objectives
Explicit**

Write these objectives on the overhead or on the board. Check students' comprehension using Number of Fingers or another **Signals** activity. Students who understand the objectives can explain them to students who do not understand them. If students' first language is Spanish, have them read the lesson summary in the *Reading Study Guide* (English or Spanish).

- Identify the causes and effects of the shrinkage of the Aral Sea.

- Describe how Russia's harsh winter has been both an obstacle and an advantage to the country.

- Tell why the Trans-Siberian Railroad has been important to Russia.

**Step 4
Support Student
Reading**

Cooperative Work Divide the class into groups of four. Within each group, students should pair up and fill out one part of the chart in Part B of Activity Sheet 15.3. The pairs should share their charts with the larger group. Go over the answers in class.

On One's Own Preview the following questions by asking students what they understand them to mean. Then have students search for the answers while reading. Once students have finished, help them answer in complete sentences.

1. Why is the Aral Sea shrinking? (p. 353, pars. 2–3)

2. Why do swamps form in Siberia in the spring and what effect do swamps have on the people living in Siberia? (p. 354, par. 7; p. 355, top)

3. What were the main reasons for the construction of the Trans-Siberia Railroad? (p. 355, par. 7; p. 356, pars. 2–4)

**Step 5
Prepare for
Assessment**

Alternative Assessment Assign students to work in pairs on the Reteaching Activity on TE p. 356. Share the Standards for Evaluating a Cooperative Activity on p. 7 of *Integrated Assessments*, and use these guidelines for evaluating students' work.

Formal Assessment Go over the test-taking strategies for TT50. You may want to use *Formal Assessment* Form A, the less-challenging assessment, or administer it as a practice test prior to formal testing with Form B or Form C.

World Geography **103**

ACTIVITY SHEET 15.3

Part A. Build Vocabulary

Complete the cause/effect chart based on your work with your partner
and your class discussion.

```
┌─────────────────────────┐        ┌─────────────────────────────────┐
│  Cause of polluted runoff│        │      Effect on Aral Sea         │
│                          │        │ 2. _____ │
│ 1. _____ │   ┌──▶ │    _____ │
│                          │───┤    └─────────────────────────────────┘
│    _____ │   │    ┌─────────────────────────────────┐
│                          │   └──▶ │ Effects on region when seabed   │
└─────────────────────────┘        │ dried up                        │
                                    │ 3. _____ │
                                    │    _____ │
                                    │    _____ │
                                    │ 4. _____ │
                                    │    _____ │
                                    │    _____ │
                                    └─────────────────────────────────┘
```

Part B. Cooperative Work

Work with your partner to fill in part of the chart. Share your chart with
your group and go over your answers with the class.

	Obstacles for inhabitants	Benefits for inhabitants
Winter	1. 2.	3.
Huge Distances	4. 5.	6. 7.

Resources for English Learners
RSG pp. 137–138   RSG Audio
TT 51   IA pp. 7, 35, 36
FA p. 241   MLG

Russia and the Western Republics

Step 1 **Activate Prior Knowledge**	Direct students to turn to the map on p. 360 and compare the size of the different subregions. Then lead students in a **Brainstorming** activity discussing how Russia might have become so large. Write down student answers on the board.
Step 2 **Preview Main Ideas and Language**	**Connect Visually** Tell students to pair up and to turn to the map on p. 362. Students should study the map and figure out what it shows about Russia. Then let students return to the list of ideas they had about how Russia became so large and eliminate ideas based on what they learned from the map. Guide students to realize that Russia started as a small state that expanded and took control of vast areas of land over time. **Build Vocabulary** Review the **Frayer Method** and use it to teach the key term *czar*. Then divide students into groups of three. Each student should take one of the other terms in Part A of Activity Sheet 16.1 and use the Frayer Method to teach it to the other group members. Then the group should work together to complete Part A. Go over the answers to clarify misunderstandings.
Step 3 **Make Objectives Explicit**	Write these objectives on the board and read them to the class. Have students identify the single most important word or phrase in each objective. Ask students to explain their choices. If students' first language is Spanish, have them read the lesson summary in the *Reading Study Guide* (English or Spanish). • Summarize the history of Russia. • Explain how the command economy of the Soviet Union worked. • Describe the cultural background, achievements, and modern life in Russia and the Western Republics.
Step 4 **Support Student Reading**	**Cooperative Work** Split the class into groups of four and have them do a **Jigsaw Reading** activity to complete Part B of Activity Sheet 16.1. The groups should divide up the questions. Go over the answers with the class. **On One's Own** Preview the following questions by asking students what they understand them to mean. Then have students search for the answers while reading. Once students have finished, help them answer in complete sentences. **1.** Which former Soviet republics are located west of Russian (p. 361, par. 2) **2.** How did the Russian Empire lag behind Western Europe? (p. 362, pars. 1–2) **3.** Tell what the Soviet Union was and what life was like there. (p. 363, pars. 1–2; p. 364 pars. 3–6; p. 366, par. 3) **4.** How did the Soviet Union come to an end? (p. 363, p. 5)
Step 5 **Prepare for Assessment**	**Alternative Assessment** Assign students to read the feature on Chernobyl on p. 368–369 and to do the GeoActivity on p. 369. Share the Standards for Evaluating a Cooperative Activity and the guidelines for technology activities and multimedia presentations on pp. 7, 35, and 36 of *Integrated Assessment*s. Use these guidelines for evaluating students' presentations. **Formal Assessment** Go over the test-taking strategies for TT51. Assign the Section Quiz for Chapter 16 Section 1, on p. 241 of the *Formal Assessment* book.

ACTIVITY SHEET 16.1

Part A. Build Vocabulary

Key Terms Work with your group to go over the meaning of each key term. Then work together to answer the true/false questions. Correct any false answers.

> **czar** **Cold War** **collective farm** **command economy**

1. _____ Small groups of people worked together and prospered on Soviet collective farms.

2. _____ Russia used to be a huge empire that was ruled by an emperor, who was called a czar.

3. _____ In a command economy, consumers make the major economic decisions and so are in command.

4. _____ Millions of soldiers died fighting in the Cold War between Soviet Union and the United States.

Part B. Cooperative Work

Work with your group to complete the chart. Go over the answers with the class.

1. Name two different groups who invaded the region between the Baltic and Black seas and took control of this area.
2. Who put an end to the rule of the second group?
3. Why did Peter the Great move his capital to St. Petersburg?
4. When and why did the Russian Revolution occur?
5. What happened during the Cold War and why did it end?
6. What was the ideal behind communism?
7. What were two goals of the Soviet command economy?
8. What are three ways in which this economy failed?
9. Why do Russia and the Western Republics have many different ethnic groups and religions?
10. Who are some famous Russian writers and composers?

Chapter 16 Section 2

Resources for English Learners
TE p. 372   RSG pp. 139–140   RSG Audio
IA pp. 8   TT 52a, TT 52b   FA p. 242
MLG

Transcaucasia

Step 1
Activate Prior Knowledge

Review the meaning of the word *Transcaucasia* from Chapter 15, Section 1. Then display a wall map of Russia and the Republics and have students locate the subregion on the map. Ask different students to locate the three different republics that make up the region: Armenia, Azerbaijan, and Georgia. Explain that the central location of the subregion has made Transcaucasia a meeting place.

Step 2
Preview Main Ideas and Language

Connect Visually Have students pair up and to turn to the map on p. 370. Ask students what they notice about the map and if the situation in Transcaucasia reminds them of situations in any other regions they have studied. Have them turn to the language map on p. 267 and compare it to the language map on p. 370. Students should notice that this map is even more complex than the map of languages in Eastern Europe. Discuss what this might imply about the region.

Build Vocabulary Present definitions of the key terms in Part A of Activity Sheet 16.2. Use visual cues, such as a map of Transcaucasia for *gateway,* pictures showing the use of the color red in the Soviet and Chinese flags for *Red Army,* and the photo on p. 374 for *supra.* Then have students work in pairs to complete Part A.

Step 3
Make Objectives Explicit

Write these objectives on the board and read them to the class. Ask students for thumbs up/thumbs down or another signal to indicate their comprehension of each objective. If students' first language is Spanish, have them read the lesson summary in the *Reading Study Guide* (English or Spanish).

- Identify some effects of the use of Transcaucasia as a migration route.
- Summarize some things that have influenced the history of Transcaucasia.
- Describe the economy of Transcaucasia and explain some conflicts related to it.
- Describe the culture of Transcaucasia.

Step 4
Support Student Reading

Cooperative Work Have students work in groups of three to read the section, using the **SQ3R** method. They should also work together to fill in the chart in Part B of Activity Sheet 16.2. Go over answers in class.

On One's Own Preview the following questions by asking students what they understand them to mean. Then have students search for the answers while reading. Once students have finished, help them answer in complete sentences.

1. Which republics are included in Transcaucasia and what are they like, culturally? (p. 370, pars. 1, 3–5; p. 371, pars. 1–3)

2. What roles did imperial Russia and the Soviet Union play in Transcaucasia? (p. 371, pars. 5–8)

3. How has the oil industry affected Transcaucasia? (p. 373, pars. 1–4)

Step 5
Prepare for Assessment

Alternative Assessment Ask the question on TE p. 372 for the 5 Themes. Share the Standards for Evaluating a Group Discussion on p. 8 of *Integrated Assessment*s. Use the guidelines for evaluating students' participation.

Formal Assessment Go over the test-taking strategies for TT52a and TT52b. Then assign the Section Quiz for Chapter 16 Section 2, found on p. 242 of the *Formal Assessment* book.

ACTIVITY SHEET 16.2

Part A. Build Vocabulary

Use the spaces below to make a drawing that helps you remember the meaning of each of the key terms.

gateway	Red Army	supra

Part B. Cooperative Work

Work with your group to read the section and complete the chart. Go over the answers with the class.

Influences on Life in Transcaucasia	
Migration	**1.** cultures
	2. religions
Outside Control	**3.** czarist rule
	4. Soviet rule
Economic Potential	**5.** agriculture and economy
	6. oil

Resources for English Learners
TE p. 378 MLG   RSG Audio
IA p. 32   TT 53a, TT 53b FA pp. 243, 244–247,
RSG pp. 141–142, 143–144   248–251, 252–255

Central Asia

Step 1
Activate Prior Knowledge

Ask students to share anything that they know about Central Asia. Write down their responses on the board or the overhead. Keep the class list so students can correct it and add to it after they finish the section.

Step 2
Preview Main Ideas and Language

Connect Visually Have students form groups of three, turn to p. 376, and look at the graphic at the top of the page. In each group, one student should read the captions while the other students point to the numbered pictures in their books. Then students should switch until all students get a turn to be readers.

Build Vocabulary To review how to define terms using a **Word Square,** draw a Word Square on the board and ask a volunteer to define the word *stability* by using this graphic. Then divide students into groups of four. Within each group, students should pair up and choose two different key terms from Part A of Activity Sheet 16.3. Have them use the Word Square and work together to define their key term. Circulate among the groups to clarify understanding.

Step 3
Make Objectives Explicit

Write these objectives on the board. For each objective, have students look through the section and identify a map, chart, or paragraph that might help them learn about that objective. If students' first language is Spanish, have them read the lesson summary in the *Reading Study Guide* (English or Spanish).

- Explain the historical importance of Central Asia.
- Describe environmental problems and important resources of the region.
- Explain how Soviet policies caused problems in the region.
- Describe unifying cultural forces and the lifestyle of nomads in Central Asia.

Step 4
Support Student Reading

Cooperative Work Pair students up for **Peer Tutoring** and have them work together to read the section and complete the chart in Part B of Activity Sheet 16.3. Go over the answers with the class.

On One's Own Preview the following questions by asking students what they understand them to mean. Then have students search for the answers while reading.

1. What were some of the objects traded or transported over the Silk Road? (p. 375, par. 3)
2. How has Soviet nuclear testing caused problems in Central Asia? (p. 377, pars. 2-3)
3. How did the Soviet Union divide Central Asian ethnic groups among different republics and why did the Soviet government do this? (p. 377, pars. 7–9)
4. What are two important unifying forces in Central Asia? (p. 378, par. 1)

Step 5
Prepare for Assessment

Alternative Assessment Have students work in groups of three on the Activity Option on TE p. 378. After students discuss the questions, they should write their answers in a three-paragraph essay. Share the guidelines for evaluating an essay on p. 32 of *Integrated Assessment*s, and use these guidelines for evaluating students' writing.

Formal Assessment Go over the test-taking strategies for TT53a and TT53b. You may want to use *Formal Assessment* Form A, the less-challenging assessment, or administer it as a practice test prior to formal testing with Form B or Form C.

ACTIVITY SHEET 16.3

Part A. Build Vocabulary

Key Terms Working with a partner, use the Word Square to help you define two of the terms below. Share your completed Word Squares with your larger group.

Silk Road border nomad yurt	Word: Translation:	Symbol or Picture:
	My meaning: Dictionary definition:	Sentence:

Part B. Cooperative Work

Work with your partner to fill in the chart. For each entry, briefly describe what it is and tell why it has been or is important in Central Asia. Go over your answers with the class.

Central Asia: Past and Future	
History	**1.** Silk Road **2.** Great Game **3.** Soviet rule
Economics	**4.** nuclear testing **5.** petroleum
Cultures	**6.** forming nations **7.** language/religion **8.** traditions

Resources for English Learners
RSG pp. 145–146 RSG Audio FA p. 256
IA pp. 7, 35, 36 TT 54a, TT 54b MLG
IDR5 pp. 28–29

Regional Conflict

**Step 1
Activate Prior
Knowledge**

Ask students to discuss the causes and effects of regional conflicts, based on what they've read about Eastern Europe and what they know from other sources or even from personal experience. Make a **T-Chart** on the board or the overhead for recording their answers. Keep the T-Chart so students can correct and add to it during the next activity and when they complete the section.

**Step 2
Preview Main
Ideas and
Language**

Connect Visually Divide the class into groups of three and have students look through the unit to identify photos that show regional conflict. Students should briefly discuss what the photos show about regional conflict in their groups; then let students share their ideas with the class and add to the **T-Chart.**

Build Vocabulary Review the meaning of the word Transcaucasia from Chapter 15, Section 1. Then refer students to the map on p. 385. Have students use the map to locate the three places listed as key terms in Part A of Activity Sheet 17.1. Then have them work in groups of three to complete Part A. Go over the answers with the class to clarify any misunderstandings.

**Step 3
Make Objectives
Explicit**

Write these objectives on the board. Tell students to read the objectives and then write a question based on each objective that they will answer after they have studied the section. Have students share their questions, so you can help clarify any misunderstandings. If students' first language is Spanish, have them read the lesson summary in the *Reading Study Guide* (English or Spanish).

- Explain reasons why conflict broke out in the Caucasus after the Soviet Union collapsed in 1991.

- Identify factors that may help resolve the conflicts in the Caucasus.

**Step 4
Support Student
Reading**

Cooperative Work Divide the class into groups of five and have them do **Reciprocal Teaching** to read and study the section. Direct them to work together to fill in the chart in Part B of Activity Sheet 17.1. Go over the answers with the class.

On One's Own Preview the following questions by asking students what they understand them to mean. Then have students search for the answers while reading. Once students have finished, help them answer in complete sentences.

1. Why did ethnic tensions in Russia and the Republics seldom result in armed conflict before the 1990s? (p. 385, par. 1)

2. Why did Russian troops invade Chechnya in the 1990s? (p. 386, pars. 2–4)

3. Which groups of people have come into conflict in Georgia? (p. 386, pars. 5–6)

4. What led to the conflict between Armenia and Azerbaijan? (p. 386, par. 7)

**Step 5
Prepare for
Assessment**

Alternative Assessment Assign the case study project on Chechnya on pp. 28–29 of Unit 5, *In Depth Resources.* Share the Standards for Evaluating a Cooperative Activity and the guidelines for technology activities and documentaries on pp. 7, 35, and 36 of *Integrated Assessments.* Use these guidelines for evaluating students' presentations.

Formal Assessment Go over the test-taking strategies for TT54a and TT54b. Then assign the Section Quiz for Chapter 17 Section 1, found on p. 256 of the *Formal Assessment* book.

ACTIVITY SHEET 17.1

Part A. Build Vocabulary

Key Terms Use a map to locate the places listed as key terms. Then work with your group to complete the statements.

Transcaucasia	Caucasus	Chechnya	Nagorno-Karabakh

1. The Caucasus Mountains run through the _____ region, which includes dozens of different ethnic groups.

2. _____ is a republic of Russia in central Caucasia that includes many people who would like their republic to be an independent country.

3. _____ is a mountainous region totally within the country of Azerbaijan that is controlled by the country of Armenia.

4. _____ is across the Caucasus Mountains from Russia and consists of Georgia, Armenia, and Azerbaijan—three independent nations that each includes ethnic groups in conflict.

Part B. Cooperative Work

Work with your group to complete the Cause/Effect chart. Go over the answers with the class.

Regional Conflict in Russia and the Republics		
	Causes	Effects
General conflict in former Soviet Union		
Chechnya		
Georgia		
Armenia and Azerbaijan		

Resources for English Learners
TE p. 388   Video: *Russia: Rebuilding a Nation*
RSG pp. 147–148   RSG Audio   IA p. 8
TT 55   FA p. 256   MLG

The Struggle for Economic Reform

**Step 1
Activate Prior Knowledge**

Do a **Round Robin** activity to have students tell what they know about Russia's size. List students' answers on the board or the overhead. Explain that Russia's immense size has caused some economic difficulties.

**Step 2
Preview Main Ideas and Language**

Connect Visually Show students part of the video *Russia: Rebuilding a Nation*. Refer to the Teacher's Resource Book for *The Voyageur Experience in World Geography,* p. 45, and show the sequence that includes the visit to the petroleum storage facility. Follow the suggestions for **Viewing Videos with Language Learners.**

Build Vocabulary Help students understand the key terms in Part A of Activity Sheet 17.2. You can refer to PE p. 140, where the term *free enterprise* is defined, and connect this to the term *capitalism* to come up with a defining paragraph to read to students. Students can complete Part A in pairs. Go over the answers with the class to clarify understanding.

**Step 3
Make Objectives Explicit**

Write these objectives on the overhead or on the board and read them aloud to the class. Have students turn to a partner in the classroom and explain in their own words what they will be learning in the section, based on the objectives. Circulate throughout the class to clarify any misunderstandings. If students' first language is Spanish, have them read the lesson summary in the *Reading Study Guide* (English or Spanish).

- Describe how Russia is changing its economic system.
- Identify obstacles to economic reform in Russia.

**Step 4
Support Student Reading**

Cooperative Work Divide the class into groups of four and have them work together to read the section and fill in the spider diagram in Part B of Activity Sheet 17.2. Go over the answers with the class using a **Numbered Heads Together** activity.

On One's Own Preview the following questions by asking students what they understand them to mean. Then have students search for the answers while reading. Once students have finished, help them answer in complete sentences.

1. Why did the Russian government start issuing vouchers in 1992? (p. 388, par. 4)

2. Why is distance an obstacle to economic reform in Russia? (p. 389, par. 2)

3. How has organized crime caused economic problems in Russia?
   (p. 390, pars. 1–3)

**Step 5
Prepare for Assessment**

Alternative Assessment Pose the question on TE p. 388 under Focus and Motivate and have students discuss the effects in small groups. Share the Standards for Evaluating a Group Discussion on p. 8 of *Integrated Assessments*. Use the guidelines for evaluating students' contributions to group discussions.

Formal Assessment Go over the test-taking strategies for TT55. Then assign the Section Quiz for Chapter 17 Section 2, found on p. 257 of the *Formal Assessment* book.

ACTIVITY SHEET 17.2

Part A. Build Vocabulary

Key Terms Work with a partner to fill in the blanks in the paragraph, using the key terms.

> **capitalism**   **distance decay**   **privatization**

After the collapse of Communism, Russia tried to move quickly toward
1. _____. This meant ending the central government's
tight control over economic activity. The government also began to sell
its businesses in a process called **2.** _____. This policy
has had mixed success because people have had difficulty buying up
the businesses and making them profitable. Another difficulty Russia
has had in building a healthy economy relates to nation's vast area,
which makes transportation and communication difficult. This is
called **3.** _____.

Part B. Cooperative Work

Work with your group to read the section and fill in the spider diagram.
Go over the answers with the class.

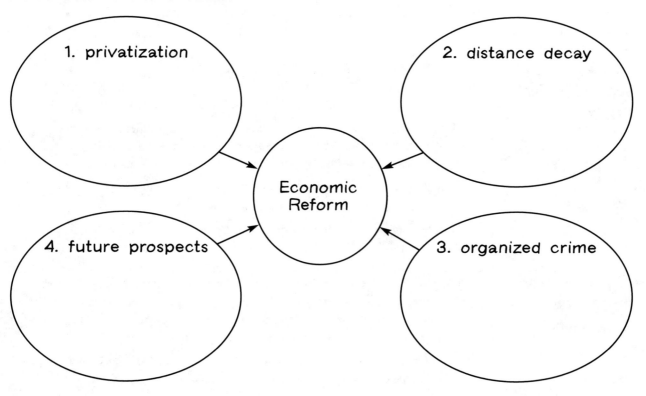

Resources for English Learners
RSG pp. 149–150, 151–152   TE p. 395
FA pp. 258, 259–263, 264–268, 269–273
RSG Audio   TT 56   MLG

The Soviet Union's Nuclear Legacy

Step 1
Activate Prior Knowledge

Do a **K-W-L** activity with the class on nuclear energy and nuclear testing in Russia. Let students take turns telling what they know and what they want to learn about nuclear energy and nuclear weapons in the former Soviet Union. Fill in the L section of the class chart when students complete the section.

Step 2
Preview Main Ideas and Language

Connect Visually Direct students to pair up and turn back to pp. 368–369. Students should look at the illustrations and talk about the kinds of problems a nuclear explosion can cause.

Build Vocabulary Go over the definitions of the terms defined in Part A of Activity Sheet 17.3. Check to see whether students understood the definitions, using any of the **Signals** activities. Have students work in groups of three to complete the graphic organizer on the Activity Sheet.

Step 3
Make Objectives Explicit

Write these objectives on the board and read them to the class. Check students' comprehension using Number of Fingers or another **Signals** Activity. If students' first language is Spanish, have them read the lesson summary in the *Reading Study Guide* (English or Spanish).

- Tell why the world's political leaders are concerned about the fate of Soviet nuclear weapons.

- Discuss political, economic, and environmental consequences related to the Soviet nuclear legacy.

- Analyze primary sources related to the Soviet nuclear legacy.

Step 4
Support Student Reading

Cooperative Work Divide the class into groups of four and direct them to pair up and divide the primary sources so each pair studies two. Student pairs should work together on a **Double-Column Note-Taking** activity on their two primary sources, using Part B of Activity Sheet 17.3. When students are done taking notes on their readings, the pairs should come together to teach one another about the primary sources, sharing their notes and ideas.

On One's Own Preview the following questions by asking students what they understand them to mean. Then have students search for the answers while reading. Once students have finished, help them answer in complete sentences.

1. Why were world leaders concerned about the security of nuclear weapons in Russia and the Republics after 1991? (p. 392, pars. 1–2)

2. What other aspects of the Soviet nuclear legacy concerned them? (p. 392, par. 3)

3. How are the nuclear policies of Russia and the Republics related to their economic problems? (p. 393, pars. 4–5, 7)

Step 5
Prepare for Assessment

Alternative Assessment Have students work in groups of four to complete the Case Study Project. Share the Grading Rubric on TE p. 395 with students.

Formal Assessment Go over the test-taking strategies for TT56. You may want to use *Formal Assessment* Form A, the less-challenging assessment, or administer it as a practice test prior to formal testing with Form B or Form C.

ACTIVITY SHEET 17.3

Part A. Build Vocabulary

Use the graphic organizer to show the relationship among the key terms.
Note that you will need to use plurals of some of the words.

dump: a place where wastes are disposed of

fuel rod: bars of radioactive material used as fuel in a nuclear reactor

missile: a weapon, often cone-shaped, that is fired into the air and that explodes when it reaches its target or otherwise causes damage on impact

nuclear waste: radioactive materials created by or left over from the creation of nuclear energy or nuclear weapons

task force: a group temporarily brought together to accomplish a specific job

warhead: a section of a missile that contains the explosive charge

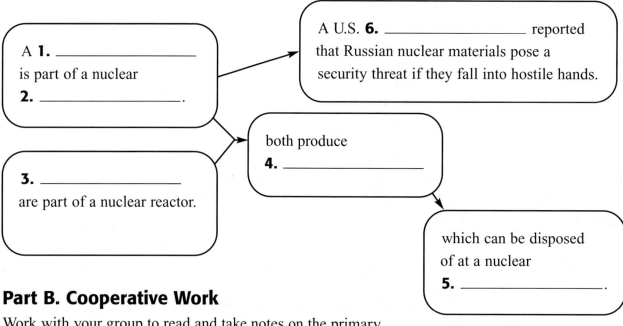

A **1.** _____ is part of a nuclear **2.** _____.

A U.S. **6.** _____ reported that Russian nuclear materials pose a security threat if they fall into hostile hands.

both produce **4.** _____

3. _____ are part of a nuclear reactor.

which can be disposed of at a nuclear **5.** _____.

Part B. Cooperative Work

Work with your group to read and take notes on the primary sources on pp. 394–395. Go over the answers with the class.

Notes on Primary Sources		
Primary Source	Note Taking	Note Making
New York Times editorial		
Newspaper story by U.S. reporter Michael Wines		
Newspaper story by British reporter Christopher Lockwood		

Resources for English Learners
RSG pp. 153–154   RSG Audio
IA p. 8   TT 57
FA p. 274   MLG

Landforms and Resources

Step 1 **Activate Prior Knowledge**	Ask students if they can name any landforms and bodies of water in Africa. Write students' responses on the board. If students have little familiarity with Africa, name some of the more famous landforms, such as the Sahara, and bodies of water, such as the Nile River, and ask students what they know.
Step 2 **Preview Main Ideas and Language**	**Connect Visually** Let students pair up and ask them to turn to the map on p. 403 to find landforms and bodies of water discussed above. Then have students locate these and other landforms and bodies of water on a large wall map.
	Build Vocabulary Go over the definitions of the two boldfaced terms in the chart in Part A of Activity Sheet 18.1. Once you are sure that students understand these terms, ask them to work with a partner to complete the **Semantic Feature Analysis.** Go over the answers with the class.
Step 3 **Make Objectives Explicit**	Write these objectives on the overhead or on the board and read them aloud to the class. Have students identify what they think is the single most important word or phrase in each objective and briefly explain their reasons for their selection. Clarify understanding during this discussion. If students' first language is Spanish, have them read the lesson summary in the *Reading Study Guide* (English or Spanish).

- Identify the main features of Africa's vast plateau.
- Describe Africa's rift valleys, lakes, volcanic mountains, and escarpments.
- Explain how the continent's mineral wealth affects its people.
- Identify Africa's major commodities.

Step 4 **Support Student Reading**	**Cooperative Work** Divide the class into groups of four to complete the chart in Part B of Activity Sheet 18.1. Within each group, students should pair up and each pair of students should fill in half of the chart; pairs can come together to go over the entire chart. Go over the answers with the class.
	On One's Own Preview the following questions by asking students what they understand them to mean. Then have students search for the answers while reading. Once students have finished, help them answer in complete sentences.

1. Why is Africa called the "plateau continent"? (p. 415, par. 3)
2. What are some of Africa's plentiful resources and important commodities? (p. 417, pars. 5–8; p. 418, pars. 2–3)
3. How can Africans take better advantage of their resources? (p. 417, pars. 8–9)

Step 5 **Prepare for Assessment**	**Alternative Assessment** Have students work in pairs to study the map on p. 419. Ask each group to cover up the questions at the bottom of the page and make up three questions about the map. Pairs should get together to swap questions. Share the Standards for Evaluating a Group Discussion on p. 8 of *Integrated Assessment* and use them for evaluating students' participation.
	Formal Assessment Go over the test-taking strategies for TT57. Then assign the Section Quiz for Chapter 18 Section 1, on p. 274 of the *Formal Assessment* book.

ACTIVITY SHEET 18.1

Part A. Build Vocabulary

Work with your partner to complete the Semantic Feature Analysis for the key terms, in boldfaced type.

Type of landform	Is lower than the land around it	Includes features of dramatically different elevations	Is long and thin	Is created by the movement of continental plates	Has steep slopes
plateau					
basin					
rift valley					
escarpment					

Part B. Cooperative Work

Work with your group to fill in the chart to describe Africa's landforms, resources, and products. Review the answers with the class.

Landforms of Africa	
1. Africa's plateau	**2.** basins and rivers
3. rift valleys and lakes	**4.** mountains

	Products/Resources	Whom They Benefit
Mineral Wealth	**5.**	**6.**
Energy Resources	**7.**	**8.**
Commodities	**9.**	**10.**

Chapter 18 Section 2

Resources for English Learners		
TE p. 423	OMA p. 52	RSG pp. 155–156
RSG Audio	IA p. 8	TT 58
FA p. 275	MLG	

Climate and Vegetation

**Step 1
Activate Prior Knowledge**

Ask students to share what they know about the Sahara. Write down their answers on the board. Then have students work with a partner to draw and label the Sahara on an outline map of Africa, such as the one on p. 52 of *Outline Maps with Activities*. Have students keep their maps for the next activity.

**Step 2
Preview Main Ideas and Language**

Connect Visually Remaining in pairs, students should turn to the map on p. 421 and find Africa's desert regions. They should sketch them in on their outline map and then turn to the map on p. 403 to find the names of the desert regions. Students should label the deserts on their outline maps, making corrections to their Sahara label, as necessary. Let students share their maps with the class.

Build Vocabulary Go over the key terms in Part A of Activity Sheet 18.2. Use **Word Imaging** to help students understand the definitions. Then assign students to complete Part A. Let students share their drawings in groups.

**Step 3
Make Objectives Explicit**

Write these objectives on the overhead or on the board and read them aloud to the class. Check students' comprehension using Thumbs Up/Down or another **Signals** Activity. Students who understand the objectives can explain them to students who do not understand them. If students' first language is Spanish, have them read the lesson summary in the *Reading Study Guide* (English or Spanish).

- Discuss the distribution of warm climates in Africa.
- Describe Africa's rainfall patterns.
- Describe Africa's tropical grasslands.
- Describe Africa's rain forests and the threats to them.

**Step 4
Support Student Reading**

Cooperative Work Divide the class into groups of three to complete the chart in Part B of Activity Sheet 18.2. Go over the answers with the class. Then do an **Inside-Outside Circles** activity to review and reinforce the information.

On One's Own Preview the following questions by asking students what they understand them to mean. Then have students search for the answers while reading. Once students have finished, help them answer in complete sentences.

1. What is the Sahara like? (p. 420, pars. 1–4; p. 421, par. 1)
2. Why does most of Africa have high temperatures? (p. 421, par. 2)
3. How does the Serengeti Plain help support huge populations of wildlife? (p. 422, par. 3)
4. Why is Africa's rain forest threatened? (p. 423, par. 1)

**Step 5
Prepare for Assessment**

Alternative Assessment Have students complete the Reteaching Activity on TE p. 423. They should work in small groups to revise their paragraphs. Share the Standards for Evaluating a Group Discussion on p. 8 of *Integrated Assessment* and use it for evaluating student interactions.

Formal Assessment Go over the test-taking strategies for TT58. Then assign the Section Quiz for Chapter 18 Section 2 found on p. 275 of the *Formal Assessment* book.

ACTIVITY SHEET 18.2

Part A. Build Vocabulary

Key Terms Use the spaces below to make a drawing that helps you remember the meaning of each of the key terms.

aquifer	oasis	canopy

Part B. Cooperative Work

Work with your group to fill in the chart. Refer to the map on p. 403, if necessary. Review the answers with the class.

	Location(s)	Characteristics
Deserts	1.	2.
Tropics	3.	4.
Moderate Areas	5.	6.
Tropical Grasslands	7.	8.
Rain Forests	9.	10.

Resources for English Learners
TE p. 429   RSG pp. 157–158, 159–160
RSG Audio   TT 59   MLG
FA pp. 276, 277–280, 281–284, 285–288

Human-Environment Interaction

**Step 1
Activate Prior
Knowledge**

Write the word *desertification* on the board or the overhead and challenge students to try figure out what it means. Use a **Round Robin** approach and write down students' ideas. If necessary, help students focus on the stem of the word, which is *desert,* and to separate out the suffixes *ifi* and *cation.* Write down other similar words that students have had as vocabulary: *acculturation, balkanization, deforestation, privatization.* Guide students to realize that desertification is the process by which a desert expands to areas right next to it.

**Step 2
Preview Main
Ideas and
Language**

Connect Visually Divide students into small groups and tell them to study the illustration on pp. 424–425, which illustrates the process of desertification. Have students read the infographic and work together to make a cause/effect chart that shows how desertification occurs. Let students share their charts.

Build Vocabulary Go over the definitions of the boldfaced terms in Part A of Activity Sheet 18.3. Once you are sure that students understand these terms, ask them to work with a partner to answer the questions.

**Step 3
Make Objectives
Explicit**

Write these objectives on the overhead or on the board and read them aloud to the class. For each objective, have students write a personal goal for studying the section that begins: "I am going to . . ." Students should use their own words to formulate their goal. If students' first language is Spanish, have them read the lesson summary in the *Reading Study Guide* (English or Spanish).

- Describe the process of desertification.
- Explain the harm caused by oil production in Nigeria.
- List the positive and negative effects of the Aswan High Dam.

**Step 4
Support Student
Reading**

Cooperative Work Pair students up for **Peer Tutoring** and have them work together to read the section and complete the chart in Part B of Activity Sheet 18.3. Go over the answers with the class.

On One's Own Preview the following questions by asking students what they understand them to mean. Then have students search for the answers while reading. Once students have finished, help them answer in complete sentences.

1. What are some causes of desertification? (p. 424, par. 3; p. 425, pars. 1–2)

2. How has Nigeria's oil industry affected the nation's environment? (p. 426, par. 1)

3. Why did Egypt build the Aswan High Dam? (p. 426, pars. 4–5)

**Step 5
Prepare for
Assessment**

Alternative Assessment Assign students to work on the Internet Activity on p. 429. Share the grading rubric in the TE note below the activity, and use it for evaluating students' presentations.

Formal Assessment Go over the test-taking strategies for TT59. You may want to use *Formal Assessment* Form A, the less-challenging assessment, or administer it as a practice test prior to formal testing with Form B or Form C.

ACTIVITY SHEET 18.3

Part A. Build Vocabulary

Key Terms Work with a partner to answer the questions. Discuss your answers with the class.

> **Aswan High Dam:** a dam built on the Nile River in Egypt
>
> **desertification:** an expansion or spreading of a desert
>
> **Sahel:** the narrow band of dry grassland on the southern edge of the Sahara
>
> **silt:** loose sediment, often soil, that is deposited by moving water

1. Which key term pairs best with *Sahel?* _____

   Explain your answer: _____

2. Which key term pairs best with *Aswan High Dam?* _____

   Explain your answer: _____

Part B. Cooperative Work

Work with your partner to read the section and fill in the chart. Go over your answers with the class.

	Benefits (actual and potential)	Problems to Solve
Planting Crops and Grazing Animals in the Sahel	1.	2.
Oil in Nigeria	3.	4.
Aswan High Dam	5.	6.

Resources for English Learners
TE p. 434   OMA p. 2   RSG pp. 161–162
RSG Audio   TT 60   IA pp. 30, 31
FA p. 289   MLG

East Africa

**Step 1
Activate Prior Knowledge**

Give students an outline map of the world, such as p. 2 of *Outline Maps with Activities*. Divide the class into groups of four or five and ask them to discuss where peoples meeting in ancient East Africa might have come from. Students should draw arrows on their map to show East Africa as a cultural crossroads. Let students share their maps with the class and keep them for the next activity.

**Step 2
Preview Main Ideas and Language**

Connect Visually List the countries of East Africa on the board or the overhead. Keep students in their groups from the previous activity. Have them work together to identify and label the countries of East Africa, without using their textbook. After a few minutes, display a wall map of Africa. Have students use this map or their textbooks to correct their maps.

Build Vocabulary Before completing Part A of Activity Sheet 19.1, remind students of how to use an **Anticipation Guide.** Allow time after students have read the section to complete the "Textbook" column and to correct answers.

**Step 3
Make Objectives Explicit**

Write these objectives on the overhead or on the board and read them aloud to the class. Have students turn to a partner in the classroom and explain in their own words what they will be learning in the section, based on the objectives. If students' first language is Spanish, have them read the lesson summary in the *Reading Study Guide* (English or Spanish).

- Discuss East Africa's history as a continental crossroads.
- Describe how European colonization disrupted life in East Africa.
- Describe the cultures of two of East Africa's major ethnic groups.
- Discuss major health care problems in East Africa.

**Step 4
Support Student Reading**

Cooperative Work Have students work with a partner to complete the chart in Part B of Activity Sheet 19.1. Go over the answers with the class. Then do a **Carousel Review** to reinforce the information.

On One's Own Preview the following questions by asking students what they understand them to mean. Then have students search for the answers while reading. Once students have finished, help them answer in complete sentences.

1. Why was Aksum an important trading center in East Africa? (p. 431, par. 3)

2. What was the Berlin Conference and how did it affect Africa? (p. 432, pars. 2–4)

3. Why do some East Africans want smaller national parks? (p. 434, par. 2)

4. How might AIDS affect Africa? (p. 435, pars. 3–5)

**Step 5
Prepare for Assessment**

Alternative Assessment Divide the class into two groups and assign the Cooperative Learning Activity on TE p. 434. Share the general criteria for evaluating oral presentations and the specific criteria for debates on pp. 30–31 of *Integrated Assessment* and use them for evaluating students' performances.

Formal Assessment Go over the test-taking strategies for TT60. Then assign the Section Quiz for Chapter 19 Section 1, found on p. 289 of the *Formal Assessment* book.

ACTIVITY SHEET 19.1

Part A. Build Vocabulary

Key Terms Work individually and then with your group to fill in the first two columns of the Anticipation Guide. Fill in the third column after you have read the entire section. Correct any false answers.

You	Group	Textbook	Topic–East Africa
			1. East Africans began to **colonize** Europe in the mid-1800s.
			2. European nations met at the **Berlin Conference** to decide on rules they would follow in dividing up Africa, to help prevent conflict among themselves.
			3. An important **cash crop** in East Africa is coffee, which farmers raise to sell rather than to use themselves.
			4. Excellent health care in Africa has helped prevent AIDS and other diseases from spreading, preventing a **pandemic** across the continent.

Part B. Cooperative Work

Work with your partner to fill in the chart on East Africa. Review the answers with the class.

1. Five places that carried on trade with East Africa before A.D. 1000.	
2. How Europeans set colonial boundaries in Africa, which later caused many conflicts.	
3. How Ethiopia escaped European colonization.	
4. Three cash crops grown in East Africa and one reason relying on cash crops for a country's main income is risky.	
5. Two competing interests related to East African tourism.	
6. Brief description of two major ethnic groups in East Africa.	
7. Critical health care problem in East Africa and its effect on the population.	

Resources for English Learners

RSG pp. 163–164   RSG Audio   FA p. 290

OMA pp. 57–58   IA p. 28   TT 61

MLG

North Africa

Step 1 **Activate Prior Knowledge**	Engage students in a **Think-Pair-Share** activity about shopping. Do they like to shop? How do they shop? at stores? by using catalogs? on the Internet? If they shop at stores, what are their favorite stores and where are they located? Explain that North Africa has distinctive markets, called *souks,* where there are musicians and storytellers as well as items for sale.
Step 2 **Preview Main Ideas and Language**	**Connect Visually** Have students turn to p. 440 and look at the photograph of the Marrakesh market. Encourage them to compare the *souk* in the photo with a U.S. shopping mall or with the places that they most like to shop. Have them list similarities and differences based on this photo. **Build Vocabulary** On the board, make a word web about Islam, based on the one in Part A of Activity Sheet 19.2. Fill out the word web with the class. As students read the section, encourage them to use Part A of the Activity Sheet to take notes on Islam. Then return to the original word web on the board and let students add to or correct it, based on what they learned from the section.
Step 3 **Make Objectives Explicit**	Write these objectives on the board and read them aloud to the class. Check students' comprehension using Number of Fingers or another **Signals** Activity. Students who understand the objectives can explain them to students who do not understand them. If students' first language is Spanish, have them read the lesson summary in the *Reading Study Guide* (English or Spanish). • Describe the roots of civilization in North Africa. • Analyze the impact oil has had on the economies of North African nations. • Describe the cultures of North Africa and the changing roles for women there.
Step 4 **Support Student Reading**	**Cooperative Work** Have students work in groups of three to read the section, using the **SQ3R** method. They should also work together to fill in the chart in Part B of Activity Sheet 19.2. Go over answers in class. **On One's Own** Preview the following questions by asking students what they understand them to mean. Then have students search for the answers while reading. Once students have finished, help them answer in complete sentences. **1.** How did the Nile help make Egyptian civilization possible? (p. 438, pars. 3–5) **2.** What is Islam and why is it important in North Africa? (p. 439, pars. 1–2) **3.** How have the economies of some North African countries changed since oil was discovered there? (p. 439, pars. 3–4) **4.** How have women's roles been changing in Tunisia? (p. 441, pars. 2–4)
Step 5 **Prepare for Assessment**	**Alternative Assessment** Assign students to work in pairs to complete the map activity on pp. 57–58 of *Outline Maps with Activities.* Share the general criteria for information assessing activities and the specific criteria for maps, both on p. 28 of *Integrated Assessment* and use them for evaluating students' maps. **Formal Assessment** Go over the test-taking strategies for TT61. Then assign the Section Quiz for Chapter 19 Section 2, found on p. 290 of the *Formal Assessment* book.

ACTIVITY SHEET 19.2

Part A. Build Vocabulary

Use this word web to take notes about the key term *Islam*.

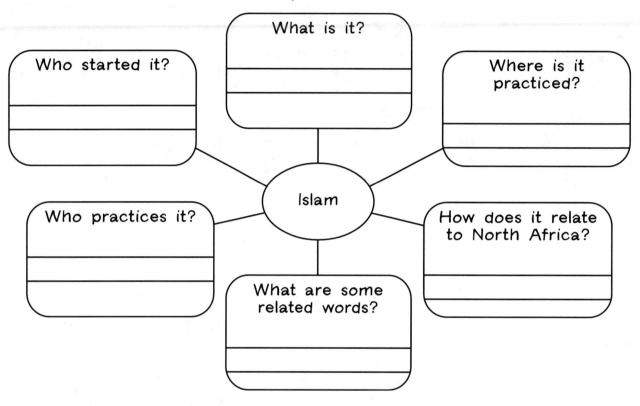

Part B. Cooperative Work

Work with your group to read the section and complete the chart. Go over the answers with the class.

Factors that Have Shaped North Africa		
1. countries of North Africa		
2. the Nile Valley	**3.** Islam	**4.** oil
North African Culture		
5. *souks*	**6.** protest music	**7.** women's roles

Resources for English Learners
TE p. 445   RSG pp. 165–166   RSG Audio
IA p. 8   TT 62   FA p. 291
MLG

West Africa

Step 1
Activate Prior Knowledge

In a **Brainstorming** session, let students share what they know about slavery and the slave trade from Africa. Jot down students' ideas on the board. Explain that many African Americans trace their origins to West Africa.

Step 2
Preview Main Ideas and Language

Connect Visually Explain that the slave trade was not the only kind of commerce that went on in West Africa. This part of Africa has a rich trading history. Have students turn to the map on p. 442. They should work with a partner to trace the different trade routes on the map. They should also note the location of the three West African kingdoms. Students should discuss where these kingdoms were in relation to the trade routes and why. Let students share their ideas in a class discussion and record their answers for revision.

Build Vocabulary Demonstrate how to do a **Think-Aloud** to review the meaning of the key term *cultural hearth*. Once students understand the technique, have them do a Think-Aloud on the key term in Part A of Activity Sheet 19.3, using the textbook and other resources. Then ask students to work in groups of three or four to share what they learned about the key term and to complete Part A. Go over the answers in class.

Step 3
Make Objectives Explicit

Write these objectives on the overhead or on the board and read them aloud to the class. For each objective, ask students to look through the section and identify a map, graph, photograph, or paragraph that might help them learn about that objective. If students' first language is Spanish, have them read the lesson summary in the *Reading Study Guide* (English or Spanish).

• Discuss the history of West Africa, including its empires and government.

• Analyze the economic struggles of West African nations.

• Describe examples of West African art and music.

Step 4
Support Student Reading

Cooperative Work Have students work in groups of three, doing a **Jigsaw Reading** activity to complete the chart in Part B of Activity Sheet 19.3. One student should find the information on history, the second on the economy, and the third on culture. Go over the answers with the class.

On One's Own Preview the following questions by asking students what they understand them to mean. Then have students search for the answers while reading. Once students have finished, help them answer in complete sentences.

1. Which empires flourished because of trade in West Africa? (p. 443, pars. 1–4)

2. Why have some nations in West Africa had economic problems? (p. 444, pars. 2–3)

3. What is West African music like? (p. 445, pars. 2–3)

Step 5
Prepare for Assessment

Alternative Assessment Have students complete the Reteaching Activity on TE p. 445. They should work in small groups to write their lists. Share the Standards for Evaluating a Group Discussion on p. 8 of *Integrated Assessment* and use it for evaluating student interactions.

Formal Assessment Go over the test-taking strategies for TT62. Then assign the Section Quiz for Chapter 19 Section 3, found on p. 291 of the *Formal Assessment* book.

ACTIVITY SHEET 19.3

Part A. Build Vocabulary

Fill in the chart based on your work with your group.

Key Term	stateless society
Defining paragraph in textbook	**1.**
Example	**2.**
My questions or ideas about the word	**3.**

Part B. Cooperative Work

Work with your group to fill in the chart. Correct the chart in class.

West Africa		
History		
1. Names and dates of trading empires:	**2.** What was traded:	**3.** How society was organized (before colonialism):
Economy		
4. Ghana **a.** Basis of economy: **b.** Why stable:	**5.** Sierra Leone **a.** Former basis of economy: **b.** Why unstable:	
Culture		
6. Ashanti crafts	**7.** Benin art	**8.** West African music

Resources for English Learners
TE p. 451   RSG pp. 167–168   RSG Audio
IA pp. 28, 29   TT 63   FA p. 292
MLG

Central Africa

Step 1
Activate Prior Knowledge

Write the word *colonialism* on the board. Have students discuss what they know about colonialism. Encourage them to list related words, as well as facts to answer the *5W* questions (who, what, when, etc.). Then work with students to make a **Cluster Map** from the list. Keep the cluster map for students to revise.

Step 2
Preview Main Ideas and Language

Connect Visually Divide the class into groups of three and have them turn to the historic cartoon on p. 449. Ask students to discuss what they think it shows. Point out that the serpent in the picture is a snake and that some types of large African snakes kill their prey by squeezing. Let students share their interpretations of the cartoon in a class discussion.

Build Vocabulary Explain who the Bantu are and why they are important in Central and Southern Africa. Review what the term *migration* means. Then have students pair up to work on Part A of Activity Sheet 19.4. They should refer to the map on p. 448 as a reference. When students finish tracing the Bantu migrations on the map on the Activity Sheet, let volunteers trace these routes on a wall map.

Step 3
Make Objectives Explicit

Write these objectives on the board. Have students read the objectives and then write a question based on each objective that they will answer after they have studied the section. Have students read their questions aloud and help clarify any misunderstandings. If students' first language is Spanish, have them read the lesson summary in the *Reading Study Guide* (English or Spanish).

- Identify key events in the history of Central Africa.
- Tell how colonialism led to economic problems in Central Africa.
- Note changing themes in Central African art.
- Explain how education is improving in Central Africa.

Step 4
Support Student Reading

Cooperative Work Have students work with a partner to complete the chart in Part B of Activity Sheet 19.4. Students can share their answers in a written **Round Table** activity. Go over the correct answers with the class.

On One's Own Preview the following questions by asking students what they understand them to mean. Then have students search for the answers while reading. Once students have finished, help them answer in complete sentences.

1. Why were the Bantu migrations important in African history? (p. 448, par. 4)
2. Who were the first Europeans to establish the African slave trade? (p. 449, par. 1)
3. What were the effects of colonialism on economy of Central Africa? (p. 450, par. 2)
4. How are countries in Central Africa improving education? (p. 452, pars. 4–5)

Step 5
Prepare for Assessment

Alternative Assessment Have students complete the Internet Activity on TE p. 451. Share the general criteria for information assessing activities and the specific criteria for reports, on p. 28 and p. 29 of *Integrated Assessment* and use them for evaluating students' reports.

Formal Assessment Go over the test-taking strategies for TT63. Then assign the Section Quiz for Chapter 19 Section 4, found on p. 292 of the *Formal Assessment* book.

ACTIVITY SHEET 19.4

Part A. Build Vocabulary

Working with your group, sketch the routes of the **Bantu migrations** on this map; use different colors to indicate migration at different times. Then answer the questions.

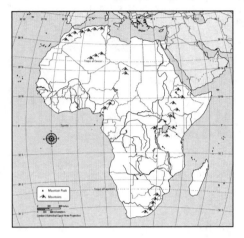

1. In what general direction did Bantu groups migrate?

_____

2. What type of vegetation grew in their original homeland?

_____

3. What very different type of vegetation grew in the region some groups migrated to? _____

4. Over how many years did the Bantu migrations occur?

_____

Part B. Cooperative Work

Work with your group to fill in the chart. Correct the chart in class.

Colonialism in Central Africa		
1. Definition of colonialism:	**2.** Causes of colonialism in Central Africa:	**3.** Effects of colonialism in Central Africa:
		a. On Central Africans under its rule:
		b. On politics/government:
		c. Economic effects:
		d. On art:
		e. On education:

Resources for English Learners
RSG pp. 169–170, 171–172   RSG Audio
IA p. 28   TT 64   MLG
FA pp. 293, 294–297, 298–301, 302–305

Southern Africa

**Step 1
Activate Prior
Knowledge**

Run a **Think-Quickwrite-Pair-Share** activity about racial discrimination. What is it? What is the best way to respond to racial discrimination? Explain that racial discrimination has been a destructive force in Southern African history.

**Step 2
Preview Main
Ideas and
Language**

Connect Visually Students can remain in their pairs and turn to the time line on p. 455. Explain that the time line includes some events related to racial discrimination in Southern Africa. Students should work together to come up with questions about the events on the time line. Let students share their questions in a class discussion.

Build Vocabulary Go over the definition of *apartheid* and use **Word Imaging** to help students better understand the word. Then assign students to complete Part A of Activity Sheet 19.5. Let students share their drawings in small groups.

**Step 3
Make Objectives
Explicit**

Write these objectives on the board and read them aloud to the class. Check students' comprehension using Thumbs Up/Down or another **Signals** Activity. Students who understand the objectives can explain them to students who do not understand them. If students' first language is Spanish, have them read the lesson summary in the *Reading Study Guide* (English or Spanish).

- List some events and issues in Southern African history.
- Describe Southern Africa's economic development.
- Describe modern life in different parts of Southern Africa.

**Step 4
Support Student
Reading**

Cooperative Work Divide the class into groups of three and ask students to work together to complete the time line in Part B of Activity Sheet 19.5. Then make a class time line with input from all of the groups. Let students vote on the events they think are most important in the Southern African history.

On One's Own Preview the following questions by asking students what they understand them to mean. Then have students search for the answers while reading.

1. What was the main economic activity in Great Zimbabwe? (p. 453, par. 4)

2. Who were the three main groups battling for control of Southern Africa in the 1800s? (p. 454, pars. 2–3)

3. How did the policy of apartheid come to an end? (p. 455, top and par. 1)

4. How is AIDS affecting Botswana's economy? (p. 456, par. 3)

5. What are some of the major cultural activities in Southern Africa? (p. 456, pars. 5–6; p. 457, par. 1)

**Step 5
Prepare for
Assessment**

Alternative Assessment Ask students to use a land use and resource map of Africa, such as the one found on p. 93 of McDougal Littell's *Student Atlas of the World* and to work with a partner to list the Southern African countries and their most important economic activities. Share the specific criteria for lists on p. 28 of *Integrated Assessment* and use them for evaluating students' work.

Formal Assessment Go over the test-taking strategies for TT64. You may want to use *Formal Assessment* Form A, the less-challenging assessment, or administer it as a practice test prior to formal testing with Form B or Form C.

ACTIVITY SHEET 19.5

Part A. Build Vocabulary

Use the space below to make a drawing that helps you remember the
meaning the of key term.

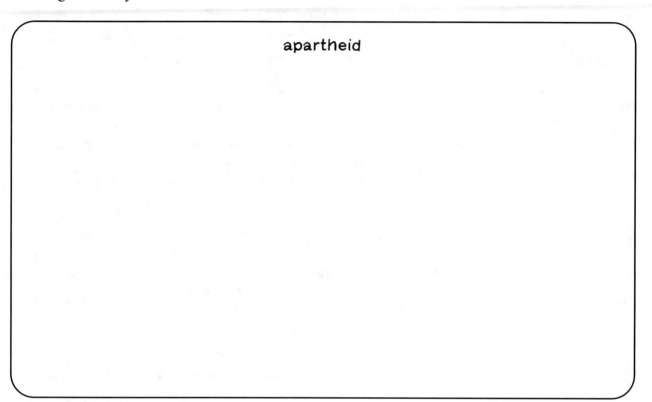

apartheid

Part B. Cooperative Work

As you study the section, work with your group to add eight entries to the
time line, related to important events in Southern African history.

Some Important Events in the History of Southern Africa

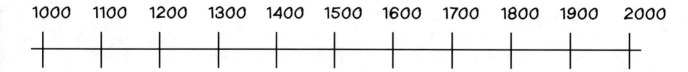

1000   1100   1200   1300   1400   1500   1600   1700   1800   1900   2000

Resources for English Learners
TE p. 463   RSG pp. 173–174   RSG Audio
IA p. 8   TT 65   FA p. 306
MLG

Economic Development

Step 1
Activate Prior Knowledge

Do a **Think-Pair-Share** activity on how students view their economic future in this country. Do they think they will have a higher standard of living than their parents have had? Why or why not? Explain that for many people living in African nations, the standard of living has dropped over the past 30 years.

Step 2
Preview Main Ideas and Language

Connect Visually Have students turn to the photograph on p. 461 and cover the caption. Ask students to describe what the picture shows. Write students' responses on the board. Guide students to realize that a truck stuck in the middle of a muddy road cannot deliver its cargo. Help students understand that if this type of situation is common, it prevents economic growth.

Build Vocabulary Review how to use the **New Word Analysis** strategy for analyzing and decoding vocabulary words, using the example of (economic) *development*. Then have students work in groups of three and use New Word Analysis to understand the key terms in Part A of Activity Sheet 20.1. Note that *infrastructure* is used on p. 462, par. 1; *public debt* is used on p. 462, par. 4. Students should complete Part A on their own. Go over answers with the class.

Step 3
Make Objectives Explicit

Write these objectives on the overhead or on the board and read them aloud to the class. Have students identify what they think is the single most important word or phrase in each objective. Let students explain why they made the choices they did and use the opportunity to clarify understanding. If students' first language is Spanish, have them read the lesson summary in the *Reading Study Guide* (English or Spanish).

- Describe what Africa's economy is like today.
- Identify some ways Africans are working to aid economic development in Africa.
- Explain the role education can play in economic development of a region.

Step 4
Support Student Reading

Cooperative Work Divide the class into groups of five and have students do **Reciprocal Teaching** to study the section. Direct them to work together to fill in the chart in Part B of Activity Sheet 20.1. Go over answers with the class.

On One's Own Preview the following questions by asking students what they understand them to mean. Then have students search for the answers while reading. Once students have finished, help them answer in complete sentences.

1. What are some of the causes of economic problems in Africa? (p. 461, par. 3)
2. How could regional cooperation help Africa improve its economy? (p. 462, par. 5)
3. Why is relying on just one or two principal commodities a problem? (p. 462, par. 6)
4. Why is improving education important to Africa's economy? (p. 463, pars. 2–4)

Step 5
Prepare for Assessment

Alternative Assessment Have students complete the Reteaching Activity on TE p. 463. They should work in small groups to revise their paragraphs. Share the Standards for Evaluating a Group Discussion on p. 8 of *Integrated Assessment* and use it for evaluating student interactions.

Formal Assessment Go over the test-taking strategies for TT65. Assign the Section Quiz for Chapter 20 Section 1, on p. 306 of the *Formal Assessment* book.

ACTIVITY SHEET 20.1

Part A. Build Vocabulary

Key Terms Match each key term with its definition.

_____ **1.** commodity

_____ **2.** diversify

_____ **3.** infrastructure

_____ **4.** public debt

a. the basic support systems needed to keep an economy going, including power, communications, transportation, and water

b. money that a government owes to individuals, institutions, or other governments

c. an agricultural or mining product that can be sold

d. to increase economic variety by promoting manufacturing and developing other industries

Part B. Cooperative Work

Work with your group to complete the chart on the African economy.
Go over the answers with the class.

Africa's Economy		
History of Economic Problems	Possible Solutions	Probable Effects
1.	Eliminate Overwhelming Public Debt	**2.**
	Build Cooperation Among Nations	**3.**
	Diversify Economies	**4.**
	Improve Education	**5.**
	Reverse the Brain Drain	**6.**

Resources for English Learners
RSG pp. 145–146   RSG Audio   IDR6 pp. 34–35
IA pp. 7, 35   TT 66   FA p. 307
MLG

Health Care

Step 1
Activate Prior Knowledge

Pass out blank index cards and ask students to write down what they know about AIDS, putting one fact on each card. Read about 15 cards aloud to the class and work with students to categorize the facts. Once you have headings for your categories, write them on chart paper and post them around the room. Then divide the class into groups of three or four and distribute all of the cards for groups to categorize. Students should tape the categorized cards to the appropriate chart paper, putting duplicate facts on top of one another.

Step 2
Preview Main Ideas and Language

Connect Visually Have students turn to the map on p. 466. In a class discussion, ask which part of Africa has been most affected by AIDS and which has been least affected. Students should name the two countries that have the highest percentage of people living with HIV/AIDS.

Build Vocabulary Use the textbook to describe three other dangerous diseases listed in the chart in Part A of Activity Sheet 20.2. Once you are sure that students understand the descriptions, ask them to work in groups of four to complete the **Semantic Feature Analysis.** Go over the answers with the class.

Step 3
Make Objectives Explicit

Write these objectives on the board and read them aloud to the class. Check students' comprehension using Number of Fingers or another **Signals** Activity. Students who understand the objectives can explain them to students who do not understand them. If students' first language is Spanish, have them read the lesson summary in the *Reading Study Guide* (English or Spanish).

- List major diseases in Africa and describe their effects on the population.
- Describe some strategies to fight the spread of disease in Africa.

Step 4
Support Student Reading

Cooperative Work Have students pair up to read the section and fill out the chart in Part B of Activity Sheet 20.2. Go over the answers with the class.

On One's Own Preview the following questions by asking students what they understand them to mean. Then have students search for the answers while reading. Once students have finished, help them answer in complete sentences.

1. What are some of the serious diseases affecting African countries? (p. 465, par. 3; p. 466, par. 1)
2. How has AIDS caused economic problems in Africa? (p. 468, par. 3)
3. What have Uganda and Senegal done to fight AIDS? (p. 467, par. 2)

Step 5
Prepare for Assessment

Alternative Assessment Assign the case study project on AIDS on pp. 34–35 of Unit 6, *In Depth Resources*. Share the Standards for Evaluating a Cooperative Activity and the guidelines for technology activities and websites on pp. 7 and 35 of *Integrated Assessments*. Use these guidelines for evaluating students' projects.

Formal Assessment Go over the test-taking strategies for TT66. Then assign the Section Quiz for Chapter 20 Section 2, on p. 307 of the *Formal Assessment* book.

ACTIVITY SHEET 20.2

Part A. Build Vocabulary

Key Terms Work with your group to complete the **Semantic Feature Analysis** for the key terms, in **boldfaced** type.

Type of disease	Spread through infection	Carried by mosquitoes	Caused by HIV	Respiratory disease	Spread by unclean water
AIDS					
cholera					
malaria					
tuberculosis					

Part B. Cooperative Work

Work with your partner to fill in the chart. Share your outline with your group and go over your answers with the class.

AIDS and Africa
How many people died of AIDS in 2000?
How many Africans died of AIDS in 2000?
Which part of Africa has the highest infection rates?
How has AIDS affected the general health of people in this part of Africa?
Why does AIDS create economic problems?
What measures are Africans taking to help control AIDS?

Resources for English Learners
TE p. 471   Video: *Kenya: National Identity and Unity*
RSG pp. 177–178, 179–180   **RSG Audio**   TT 67a, TT 67b
FA pp. 308, 309–313, 314–318, 319–323   **MLG**

Effects of Colonialism

Step 1 **Activate Prior Knowledge**	Lead a class discussion on what students think makes for a stable, peaceful country. Let students **brainstorm** and write down their ideas on the chalkboard. Explain that African nations have faced obstacles to achieving stability.
Step 2 **Preview Main Ideas and Language**	**Connect Visually** Show students part of the video *Kenya: National Identity and Unity.* Refer to the Teacher's Resource Book for *The Voyageur Experience in World Geography,* p. 55. Follow the suggestions for **Viewing Videos with Language Learners.** **Build Vocabulary** Review how to use a **Word Square.** Then divide students into groups of four. In each group, every student should choose a different key term from Part A of Activity Sheet 20.3, using the Word Square to define the term. Circulate among the groups to clarify understanding.
Step 3 **Make Objectives Explicit**	Write these objectives on the overhead or on the board and read them aloud to the class. Have students turn to a partner in the classroom and explain in their own words what they will be learning in the section, based on the objectives. If students' first language is Spanish, have them read the lesson summary in the *Reading Study Guide* (English or Spanish). • Describe the effects of European colonialism on Africa. • Examine the challenges independence has posed to African nations. • Analyze primary sources for different views on Africa
Step 4 **Support Student Reading**	**Cooperative Work** Divide the class into groups of three to read the section, using the **SQ3R** method. As they read the primary sources, they should work together to fill in the chart in Part B of Activity Sheet 20.3. Go over answers with the entire class. Then encourage students to find other sources of information as they work on the Case Study Project. **On One's Own** Preview the following questions by asking students what they understand them to mean. Then have students search for the answers while reading. Once students have finished, help them answer in complete sentences. 1. What was one of the main reasons that in the late 1800s, European countries wanted to control Africa? (p. 468, par. 3) 2. Why did European colonization cause so much political and ethnic violence in Africa after African nations gained independence? (p. 468, pars. 4–5; p. 469, top, par. 1)
Step 5 **Prepare for Assessment**	**Alternative Assessment** Have students work in groups of six to eight to complete the Case Study Project. Share the Grading Rubric on TE p. 471 with students and use it to evaluate their project. **Formal Assessment** Go over the test-taking strategies for TT67a and TT67b. You may want to use *Formal Assessment* Form A, the less-challenging assessment, or administer it as a practice test prior to formal testing with Form B or Form C.

ACTIVITY SHEET 20.3

Part A. Build Vocabulary

Key Terms Use the Word Square to help you define one of the terms below. Share your Word Square with your group.

colonize coup hostage unity	Word: Translation:	Symbol or Picture:
	My meaning: Dictionary definition:	Sentence:

Part B. Cooperative Work

Work with your group to read and summarize the primary sources on pp. 470–471. Go over the answers with the class.

Main Idea or Summary of Primary Sources
Eyewitness account of colonialism in the Congo:
Statement of principle by Ghana's leader Kwame Nkrumah:
News analysis by Ron Daniels:
New York Times editorial:
Political cartoon by Canadian Alan King:

Resources for English Learners
OMA p. 4   RSG pp. 181–182   RSG Audio
IA p. 28   TT 68a, T 68b   FA p. 324
MLG

Landforms and Resources

**Step 1
Activate Prior
Knowledge**

Have students pair up. Hand out copies of an outline map of the world, such as the one on p. 4 of *Outline Maps with Activities*. Ask students to label all of the regions they've studied so far. Then ask them to talk about where Southwest Asia would be and label it on their maps. Through class discussion, elicit an explanation of why this region is called Southwest Asia.

**Step 2
Preview Main
Ideas and
Language**

Connect Visually Students should flip through the chapter looking for pictures that they think illustrate the title ("Harsh and Arid Lands"). Have them choose the photo they think best illustrates the title and share their selections with the class. Ask students, based on the title and the photos, what landforms they think are likely to make up a large part of the region.

Build Vocabulary Go over the definition of the boldfaced term in Part A of Activity Sheet 21.1. Check students' understanding with Slates or another **Signals** activity. Once you are sure that students understand the term, ask them to complete Part A. Students can share their drawings with a small group.

**Step 3
Make Objectives
Explicit**

Write these objectives on the overhead or on the board and read them aloud to the class. Have students identify what they think is the single most important word or phrase in each objective and briefly explain their reasons for their selection. Clarify understanding during this discussion. If students' first language is Spanish, have them read the lesson summary in the *Reading Study Guide* (English or Spanish).

• Describe and locate the important landforms of Southwest Asia.

• Name the key resources of Southwest Asia.

**Step 4
Support Student
Reading**

Cooperative Work Divide the class into groups of three to complete the map in Part B of Activity Sheet 21.1. Tell students to refer to the map on p. 479 to locate landforms and bodies of water. When students are finished reading the section, display a wall map for students to use to correct their maps, providing assistance, as necessary.

On One's Own Preview the following questions by asking students what they understand them to mean. Then have students search for the answers while reading. Once students have finished, help them answer in complete sentences.

1. What are the two main peninsulas of Southwest Asia? (p. 487, par. 3)

2. What are the main rivers of the region? (p. 489, pars. 1–3)

3. What is the most abundant resource of Southeast Asia? (p. 489, par. 4)

**Step 5
Prepare for
Assessment**

Alternative Assessment Have students work in pairs to complete the GeoActivity on p. 490. Share the general guidelines for evaluating information assessing activities and for evaluating maps on p. 28 of *Integrated Assessment* and use these for evaluating students' maps.

Formal Assessment Go over the test-taking strategies for TT68a and TT68b. Then assign the Section Quiz for Chapter 21 Section 1, found on p. 324 of the *Formal Assessment* book.

ACTIVITY SHEET 21.1

Part A. Build Vocabulary

Key Term Use the spaces below to make two drawings that help you remember the meaning of the key term, by showing a wadi at different times of year. Label your drawing.

> **wadi:** riverbed that is dry and only becomes full of water during the rainy season.

Part B. Cooperative Work

Work with your group to label the map with the landforms and bodies of water mentioned in the section. You should label at least 16 landforms and bodies of water total. Review your map with the class.

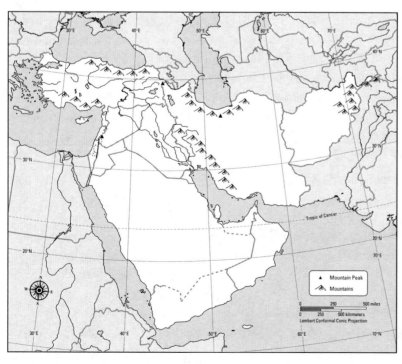

Resources for English Learners
RSG pp. 183–184   RSG Audio
IDR pp. 8, 38   TT 69
FA p. 325   MLG

Climate and Vegetation

**Step 1
Activate Prior
Knowledge**

Hold a class discussion about deserts. Let students who have visited a desert share their experiences. Ask other students to describe what they think deserts are like, what types of animals and plants thrive there, what variations in landform they might find in deserts, and how deserts might affect the economics and transportation of a region. Make a spider diagram on the board or the overhead to record students' ideas. Save it for students to revise after they finish the section.

**Step 2
Preview Main
Ideas and
Language**

Connect Visually Display a wall map of Southwest Asia that names the countries of the region. Have student turn to the map on p. 492 and locate the three different areas of desert. Ask them to name the country that has the largest desert *(Saudi Arabia.)* Ask them what other countries also have significant desert areas *(Jordan, Syria, Israel, Iraq, and Iran.)* Ask them which region has significant highlands *(Afghanistan.)*

Build Vocabulary Use the **Frayer Method** to teach the two key terms in Part A of Activity Sheet 21.2. Then have students work in pairs to complete Part A. Go over the answers with the class to clarify understanding.

**Step 3
Make Objectives
Explicit**

Write these objectives on the overhead or on the board. Have students read the objectives and then write a question based on each objective that they will answer after they have studied the section. Ask students to read their questions aloud and help clarify any misunderstandings. If students' first language is Spanish, have them read the lesson summary in the *Reading Study Guide* (English or Spanish).

• Discuss the variety in arid lands.

• Tell how deserts limit movement.

• Describe the semiarid lands and well-watered coast lands of Southwest Asia.

**Step 4
Support Student
Reading**

Cooperative Work Divide the class into groups of three to complete the spider diagram in Part B of Activity Sheet 21.2. Go over the answers with the class. Then do an **Inside-Outside Circles** activity to review and reinforce the information.

On One's Own Preview the following questions by asking students what they understand them to mean. Then have students search for the answers while reading. Once students have finished, help them answer in complete sentences.

1. What are the types of deserts in Southwest Asia? (p. 491, par. 5; p. 492, top, par. 3)

2. What grows in the semiarid lands and the coast lands? (p. 493, pars. 1–2)

**Step 5
Prepare for
Assessment**

Alternative Assessment Students should work in pairs to create and answer questions about a desert database, on p. 8 of *In-Depth Resources*. Assess their work based on the Answer Key on p. 38.

Formal Assessment Go over the test-taking strategies for TT69. Then assign the Section Quiz for Chapter 21 Section 2, found on p. 325 of the *Formal Assessment* book.

Part A. Build Vocabulary

Key Terms Go over the meaning of each key term in class. Then work with a partner to answer the questions.

(**oasis**   **salt flat**)

1. If you were looking for an oasis in one of the Arabian deserts, what sort of thing would you look for? _____

_____

2. What are two main factors that cause a salt flat desert to form? _____

_____

Part B. Cooperative Work

Work with your group to fill in the spider diagram. Describe the climate, the land, and the vegetation that grows there. Go over the answers and review the information with your class.

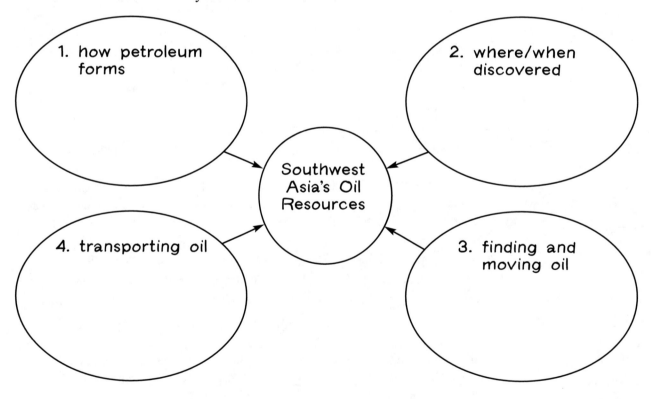

1. how petroleum forms

2. where/when discovered

4. transporting oil

Southwest Asia's Oil Resources

3. finding and moving oil

Resources for English Learners
RSG pp. 185–186, 187–188   RSG Audio
IA p. 25   TT 70a, TT 70b   MLG
FA pp. 326, 327–330, 331–334, 335–338

Human-Environment Interaction

**Step 1
Activate Prior
Knowledge**

Have students share what they know about your local water supply through class discussion. What do they think is your local source of water? Is the water treated in any way, and if so how? Does your area ever have drought or water shortages? What happens during a drought or water shortage? Explain that because Southwest Asia is arid, water is a very precious resource.

**Step 2
Preview Main
Ideas and
Language**

Connect Visually Let students pair up and turn to p. 496 to study the photographs of water systems. One student should read each numbered caption aloud while the other student looks at the photograph. After one students has read all of the captions, students should switch roles. Then they should work together to answer any questions they each have about the pictures.

Build Vocabulary Pair students for **Peer Vocabulary Teaching** to learn the definitions of the key terms in Part A of Activity Sheet 21.3. Students should work on their own to complete Part A. Go over the answers to clarify understanding.

**Step 3
Make Objectives
Explicit**

Write these objectives on the overhead or on the board and read them aloud to the class. Check students' comprehension using Thumbs Up/Thumbs Down or another **Signals** activity. Students who understand the objectives can explain them to students who do not understand them. If students' first language is Spanish, have them read the lesson summary in the *Reading Study Guide* (English or Spanish).

- Discuss how people in Southwest Asia provide themselves with and distribute fresh water.

- Describe the formation, production, and movement of oil in Southwest Asia.

**Step 4
Support Student
Reading**

Cooperative Work Have students work in groups of three to read the section and fill out the chart in Part B of Activity Sheet 21.3. Go over the answers with the class.

On One's Own Preview the following questions by asking students what they understand them to mean. Then have students search for the answers while reading. Once students have finished, help them answer in complete sentences.

1. What are some examples of ways that water is provided to people in Southwest Asia? (p. 495, par. 3, p. 496, illustration, par. 1)

2. Why might water projects in Southwest Asia cause controversy? (p. 495, par. 4)

3. Where are the major oil fields in Southeast Asia? (p. 497, par. 5)

4. What are some dangers in transporting oil? (p. 499, pars. 2–4)

**Step 5
Prepare for
Assessment**

Alternative Assessment Have students work in pairs to make a diagram that shows the steps in the formation of petroleum, using the description on p. 497 as a starting point. Share the guidelines for evaluating diagrams on p. 25 of *Integrated Assessment* and use these for evaluating students' diagrams.

Formal Assessment Go over the test-taking strategies for TT70a and TT70b. You may want to use *Formal Assessment* Form A, the less-challenging assessment, or administer it as a practice test prior to formal testing with Form B or Form C.

ACTIVITY SHEET 21.3

Part A. Build Vocabulary

Key Terms Learn the definitions of these words with your partner. Then write the term in the blank that best completes each sentence.

> **drip irrigation**   **desalination**   **fossil water**
> **crude oil**   **refinery**

1. When oil is first removed from the ground, it is called _____, because it has not yet been processed.

2. In Southwest Asia, water that is pumped up from underground is called _____ because it has been in the aquifer for a very long time and is not likely to be replaced because of the area's low rainfall.

3. One way people in Southwest Asia increase their supply of fresh water is by removing the salt from ocean water at _____ plants.

4. Oil that is pumped from the ground is treated at a _____, where it is converted into useful products.

5. By placing water right near plants' roots, _____ helps prevent waste when farmers water their crops.

Part B. Cooperative Work

Work with your group to fill in the chart. Go over your answers with the class.

Oil in Southwest Asia
How were oil and natural gas deposits formed in Southwest Asia?
How is oil removed from oil deposits?
When was oil discovered in Southwest Asia?
Where was oil discovered in Southwest Asia?
Why is oil important?
How is oil transported from Southwest Asia?
What are risks of transporting oil?

Resources for English Learners
TE p. 504   TPT p. 37, TT 71 IA p. 25
RSG pp. 189–190 RSG Audio   FA p. 339
MLG

The Arabian Peninsula

Step 1 **Activate Prior Knowledge**	Have students make a **Cluster Map** about Islam with the question cards; students can fill in answers as they work on the section. Explain that the Arabian Peninsula was the birthplace of Islam and that it is the main religion there.
Step 2 **Preview Main Ideas and Language**	**Connect Visually** Have students turn to the photograph on p. 503 and read the caption. Working in pairs, they should flip through pp. 503–509, looking at pictures of mosques. Based on these pictures, ask them to figure out what the towers are in the picture on p. 503. Guide them to realize that they are the minarets of mosques. **Build Vocabulary** Have students work in groups of three and use **New Word Analysis** to understand the key terms in Part A of Activity Sheet 22.1. Students should complete Part A on their own. Go over the answers with the class.
Step 3 **Make Objectives Explicit**	Write these objectives on the board and read them aloud to the class. For each objective, ask students to look through the section and identify an illustration or a paragraph that might help them learn about that objective and let them share ideas in a brief class discussion. Clarify understanding during this discussion. If students' first language is Spanish, have them read the lesson summary in the *Reading Study Guide* (English or Spanish). • Discuss the influence of Islam in Southwest Asia. • Describe the rise and fall of Muslim empires and the effects of colonialism on the Arabian Peninsula. • Discuss the importance of oil in the regional economy. • Describe modern life in Arabic countries.
Step 4 **Support Student Reading**	**Cooperative Work** Have students work in groups of four, doing a **Jigsaw Reading** activity to complete the chart in Part B of Activity Sheet 22.1. Each student should answer two questions. Go over the answers with the class. **On One's Own** Preview the following questions by asking students what they understand them to mean. Then have students search for the answers while reading. Once students have finished, help them answer in complete sentences. **1.** How did the teachings of Islam unite the Arabian Peninsula (p. 504, pars. 1–2) **2.** Why is oil important in the economies of the Arabian Peninsula? (p. 505, par. 3) **3.** What changes in daily life have occurred over the past few decades? (p. 505, par. 5; p. 506, pars. 1–3)
Step 5 **Prepare for Assessment**	**Alternative Assessment** Have students work in pairs to complete the Activity on TE p. 504. Share the general guidelines for evaluating art type activities on p. 25 of *Integrated Assessment* and use these for evaluating students' booklets. **Formal Assessment** Go over the test-taking strategies for TT71. Then assign the Section Quiz for Chapter 22 Section 1, found on p. 339 of the *Formal Assessment* book.

ACTIVITY SHEET 22.1

Part A. Build Vocabulary

Key Terms Work with your group to figure out the meaning of the key terms. Then complete the vocabulary exercise on your own by filling in the blanks with the correct key terms.

> **Islam**   **monotheistic**   **mosque**   **theocratic**

The Prophet Muhammad was the founder or the religion
1. _____. Muslims believe in one God, so the religion
is **2.** _____, like Judaism and Christianity. Muslims
pray in a place of worship called a **3.** _____. In
some nations where Islam is the official religion, the government is
4. _____, meaning that religious leaders are also the
political leaders of the country.

Part B. Cooperative Work

Work with your group to fill in the chart. Correct the chart in class.

1. Who were the nomadic desert dwellers of the Arabian Peninsula, and what was their culture based on?	1.
2. Describe the Five Pillars of Islam.	2.
3. Describe the spread of Islam and tell when and how Islamic governments began to decline.	3.
4. How did Saudi Arabia come to be established?	4
5. What is OPEC and how does it help countries of Southwest Asia?	5.
6. How has life changed in the Arabian Peninsula over the past 40 years and why?	6.
7. Why are there many foreign workers in countries on the Arabian Peninsula?	7.
8. What are two Islamic religious duties that shape life in the Arabian Peninsula?	8.

Resources for English Learners
TE p. 513   RSG pp. 191–192   RSG Audio
IA p. 8   TT 72   FA p. 340
MLG

The Eastern Mediterranean

Step 1 Activate Prior Knowledge	In a **Brainstorming** activity, ask students to share what they know about the Arab-Israeli conflict. Write students' responses on the board for students to add to or revise. Explain that the history of this conflict is complex and has affected all aspects of life in the Eastern Mediterranean.
Step 2 Preview Main Ideas and Language	**Connect Visually** Refer students to the map of Religious Groups of Southwest Asia on p. 483. Ask them which part of the region has the most different religions *(the Eastern Mediterranean)*. Have students name the different religions important to the subregion. **Build Vocabulary** Divide the class in groups of four and direct students to each choose one of the key terms in Part A of Activity Sheet 22.2 to teach to their group. Then have students work together to categorize the key terms, using the chart in Part A.
Step 3 Make Objectives Explicit	Write these objectives on the board and read them aloud to the class. Have students turn to a partner in the classroom and explain in their own words what they will be learning in the section, based on the objectives. Circulate through the class, to clarify understanding. If students' first language is Spanish, have them read the lesson summary in the *Reading Study Guide* (English or Spanish). • Describe the holy places important to different religions in the Eastern Mediterranean. • Outline the history of political unrest in the Eastern Mediterranean. • Describe economic problems and potential, and modern life, in the region.
Step 4 Support Student Reading	**Cooperative Work** Dividing the class into groups of three, have students to work together to complete the time line in Part B of Activity Sheet 22.2. Then make a class time line with input from all of the groups. Let students vote on the events they think are most important in the history of the Eastern Mediterranean. Hold a class discussion for student to explain their reasoning. **On One's Own** Preview the following questions by asking students what they understand them to mean. Then have students search for the answers while reading. Once students have finished, help them answer in complete sentences. 1. What are some religious holy places found in the Eastern Mediterranean? (p. 510, pars. 1, 3–5; p. 511, top, par. 1) 2. How did colonial rule lead to tension in the subregion? (p. 511, par. 3) 3. Why has modernization been difficult in parts of the subregion? (p. 513, pars. 3–7) 4. Which ethnic groups live in Lebanon and Israel? (p. 515, pars. 1–3)
Step 5 Prepare for Assessment	**Alternative Assessment** Have students work in pairs to complete the Activity on TE p. 513. Share the Standards for Evaluating a Group Discussion on p. 8 of *Integrated Assessment* and use these for evaluating student interaction. **Formal Assessment** Go over the test-taking strategies for TT72. Then assign the Section Quiz for Chapter 22 Section 2, on p. 340 of the *Formal Assessment* book.

ACTIVITY SHEET 22.2

Part A. Build Vocabulary

Key Terms Work with your group to figure out the meaning of the key terms. Then use the chart to categorize the key terms. Discuss your categorization with the class.

| **Western Wall**   **Dome of the Rock**   **Zionism** |
| **Palestinian Liberation Organization (PLO)** |

Part B. Cooperative Work

As you study the section, work with your group to add eight entries to the time line, related to important events in the history of the Eastern Mediterranean.

Some Important Events in the History of the Eastern Mediterranean

1500–1860   1880   1900   1920   1940   1960   1980   2000

Resources for English Learners
TE p. 501c   RSG pp. 193–194, 195–196   MLG
RSG Audio   IA pp. 7, 35, 36   TT 73
FA pp. 341, 342–345, 346–349, 350–353

The Northeast

Step 1
Activate Prior Knowledge

Use a wall map to point out the countries that make up the Northeast subregion of Southwest Asia and write down the names on the board. Then do a **K-W-L** activity on what students know and want to learn about these countries. Fill in the L section of the class chart when students complete the section.

Step 2
Preview Main Ideas and Language

Connect Visually Ask students to turn to the circle graphs and maps of ethnic groups in Southwest Asia. Have the class divide into groups of five to study these.

Build Vocabulary Pair students for **Peer Vocabulary Teaching** to learn the definitions of the key terms in Part A of Activity Sheet 22.3. Suggest that students make flashcards to aid learning. Then students should work on their own to complete Part A.

Step 3
Make Objectives Explicit

Write these objectives on the board and read them aloud to the class. Check students' comprehension using Number of Fingers or another **Signals** activity. Students who understand the objectives can explain them to students who do not understand them. If students' first language is Spanish, have them read the lesson summary in the *Reading Study Guide* (English or Spanish).

- Describe the blend of cultures in the Northeast subregion of Southwest Asia.

- Tell about different clashes over land that have occurred in this subregion.

- Describe how countries in the Northeast subregion of Southwest Asia have been making progress and are facing problems related to their economies.

- Compare traditional and modern life in the subregion.

Step 4
Support Student Reading

Cooperative Work Have students divide into groups of four to fill out the chart in Part B of Activity Sheet 22.3. Within each group, students should pair up. One pair of students should complete the "Cultures" section of the chart and the other pair should complete the "Clashes" section of the chart. Students should share their answers with their larger groups.

On One's Own Preview the following questions by asking students what they understand them to mean. Then have students search for the answers while reading. Once students have finished, help them answer in complete sentences.

1. How do the languages and ethnic groups of the Northeast subregion of Southwest Asia differ from those found elsewhere in the region? (p. 517, pars. 1–2)

2. Why are there so many refugees in this subregion? (p. 517, pars. 4–5)

3. What do nations in this subregion need to do to develop their economies? (p. 518, pars. 1–4)

Step 5
Prepare for Assessment

Alternative Assessment Assign students to work in groups on the multimedia presentation on TE p. 501c. Share guidelines for evaluating a cooperative activity, technology activities, and multimedia presentations on pp. 7, 35, and 36 of *Integrated Assessment*. Use them for evaluating students' work.

Formal Assessment Go over the test-taking strategy on p. 38 of *Test Practice Transparencies* with TT73. You may want to use *Formal Assessment* Form A or administer it as a practice test prior to formal testing with Form B or Form C.

ACTIVITY SHEET 22.3

Part A. Build Vocabulary

Key Terms Learn the definitions of these words with your partner.
Then match each key term with its definition.

_____ **1.** Kurds

_____ **2.** Mesopotamia

_____ **3.** Shi'ite

_____ **4.** Sunni

_____ **5.** Taliban

a. he land between the Tigris and Euphrates rivers, where several ancient empires arose

b. a fundamentalist Muslim political group in Afghanistan

c. people belonging to an ethnic group living in the Northeast subregion of Southwest Asia

d. the smaller of the two main branches of Islam

e. the larger of the two main branches of Islam, with 83% of Muslims belonging to this group

Part B. Cooperative Work

Work with your group to read the section and complete the chart.
Go over the answers with the class.

Generalizations About the Northeast	
Cultures	**1.** ethnic groups **2.** Sunnis **3.** Shi'ites **4.** Taliban
Clashes over land	**5.** Kurds **6.** Refugees **7.** Control of oil fields

Resources for English Learners
RSG pp. 197–198   RSG Audio
IA p. 29   TT 74
FA p. 354   MLG

Population Relocation

**Step 1
Activate Prior
Knowledge**

Let students divide into groups of four to discuss the term *guest worker.* Have they heard this term before? If so, where? What do they think the term means? Do they think guest workers are welcomed into the places they work? Why or why not? How do they think the term relates to Southwest Asia? Let groups share their responses in a class discussion. Write down their ideas for students to revise or add to when they have completed the section.

**Step 2
Preview Main
Ideas and
Language**

Connect Visually Keep students in their groups. Direct them to turn to p. 526 to look at the circle graphs. Ask students where guest workers in Southwest Asia mainly come from. Have students name the country that has the highest percentage of guest workers and the country that has the lowest percentage of guest workers. Let students talk in their groups about other patterns they see.

Build Vocabulary Review how to use a **Word Square.** Then have students pair up and use the Word Square to each define a different key term in Part A of Activity Sheet 23.1. Circulate among the groups to clarify understanding. Then let students share their Word Squares with the class. Make a class list of stateless nations for students to add to as they read the chapter.

**Step 3
Make Objectives
Explicit**

Write these objectives on the overhead or on the board and read them aloud to the class. Have students identify what they think is the single most important word or phrase in each objective. Let students discuss their reasons for selecting that word or phrase; clarify understanding during this discussion. If students' first language is Spanish, have them read the lesson summary in the *Reading Study Guide* (English or Spanish).

• Discuss reasons for the region's large number of guest workers and the impact they have on the region.

• Name and describe some of the stateless nations in Southwest Asia.

**Step 4
Support Student
Reading**

Cooperative Work Divide the class into groups of three and have students do **Reciprocal Teaching** to read and study the section. Direct them to focus on causes and effects of population relocation and to work together to fill in the chart in Part B of Activity Sheet 23.1. Go over the answers with the class.

On One's Own Preview the following questions by asking students what they understand them to mean. Then have students search for the answers while reading. Once students have finished, help them answer in complete sentences.

1. Why is there a need for guest workers in Southwest Asia? (p. 525, pars. 3–4)

2. How did the Kurds become a stateless nation? (p. 526, pars. 5–6)

3. In which areas are Palestinian refugee camps found? (p. 527, pars. 1–2)

**Step 5
Prepare for
Assessment**

Alternative Assessment Have students work in pairs to complete the GeoActivity on p. 527. Share the guidelines for evaluating a Venn Diagram on p. 29 of *Integrated Assessment* and use these for evaluating students' work.

Formal Assessment Go over the test-taking strategies for TT74. Then assign the Section Quiz for Chapter 23 Section 1, on p. 354 of the *Formal Assessment* book.

ACTIVITY SHEET 23.1

Part A. Build Vocabulary

Key Terms Working with a partner, use the Word Square to help you define
the key terms. Share your completed Word Squares with your class.

guest worker

stateless nation

Word: Translation:	Symbol or Picture:
My meaning: Dictionary definition:	Sentence:

Part B. Cooperative Work

Work with your group to complete the chart on causes and effects of
population relocation in Southwest Asia. Go over the answers with the
class.

Population Relocation in Southwest Asia		
	Causes	Effects
Economic	**1.** In Oil-Rich countries:	**2.** **3.** **4.** **5.** **6.**
Political	**7.** Related to the Kurds:	**8.** **9.**
	10. Related to the Palestinians:	**11.** **12.**

Resources for English Learners
Video: *United Arab Emirates: Oil and Water Resources*
RSG pp. 199–200   RSG Audio   IDR7 pp. 26, 42
TT 75   FA p. 355   MLG

Oil Wealth Fuels Change

**Step 1
Activate Prior
Knowledge**

In a class discussion, make a **T-Chart** to list ways in which an oil boom can both help and hurt a nation's economy. Prompt students to consider what they have learned about how oil wealth has affected Russian and the Republics and Africa, as well as Southwest Asia. Keep the T-Chart for students to revise after they complete the section.

**Step 2
Preview Main
Ideas and
Language**

Connect Visually Show students part of the video *United Arab Emirates: Oil and Water Resources.* Refer to the Teacher's Resource Book for *The Voyageur Experience in World Geography,* p. 65, and show the section on what the UAE is like; point out that the lifestyle people in the UAE enjoy is largely due to the nation's oil wealth. Follow the suggestions for **Viewing Videos with Language Learners.**

Build Vocabulary Use the **Frayer Method** to teach the two key terms in Part A of Activity Sheet 23.2. Then have students work in pairs to complete Part A. Go over the answers with the class to clarify understanding.

**Step 3
Make Objectives
Explicit**

Write these objectives on the overhead or on the board and read them aloud to the class. For each objective, have students write a personal goal for studying the section. Let students discuss their goals with a partner, as you circulate to clarify understanding. If students' first language is Spanish, have them read the lesson summary in the *Reading Study Guide* (English or Spanish).

• Explain the global importance of oil.

• Discuss the importance of using oil wealth to diversify the economies of Southwest Asia.

**Step 4
Support Student
Reading**

Cooperative Work Have students work in a group of three to complete the chart in Part B of Activity Sheet 23.2. Go over the answers with the class. Then do a **Carousel Review** to reinforce the information.

On One's Own Preview the following questions by asking students what they understand them to mean. Then have students search for the answers while reading. Once students have finished, help them answer in complete sentences.

1. What effect have unpredictable oil prices had on Southwest Asia? (p. 529, par. 5)

2. What are some ways Southwest Asian nations have improved their infrastructure? (p. 530, pars. 2–4)

3. Why have women had increased opportunities in Southwest Asia? (p. 531, par. 3)

**Step 5
Prepare for
Assessment**

Alternative Assessment Students should work in pairs on the Skillbuilder Practice on p. 26 of *In-Depth Resources.* Assess their work based their interactions and on the Answer Key on p. 42.

Formal Assessment Go over the test-taking strategies for TT75. Then assign the Section Quiz for Chapter 23 Section 2, on p. 355 of the *Formal Assessment* book.

ACTIVITY SHEET 23.2

Part A. Build Vocabulary

Key Terms Go over the meaning of each key term in class. Then work
with a partner to answer the questions.

> **strategic commodity**   **human resources**

1. a. What do strategic commodities have in common with other
commodities?

_____

b. How do strategic commodities differ from other commodities?

_____

2. a. How are human resources different from natural resources?

_____

_____

b. How are human resources similar to natural resources?

_____

_____

Part B. Cooperative Work

Work with your group to fill in the chart on oil wealth and Southwest
Asian economies. Review the answers with the class.

Oil Wealth and Southwest Asian Economies
1. why oil reserves do not necessarily mean economic growth
2. modernizing the infrastructure
3. developing natural resources
4. developing human resources

Religious Conflict Over Land

Step 1 Activate Prior Knowledge	Do a **K-W-L** activity with the class on the city of Jerusalem. Encourage students to share what they know based on their reading in this class, in world history classes, from reading the newspaper, or listening to media news. Fill in the L section of the class chart when students complete the section.
Step 2 Preview Main Ideas and Language	**Connect Visually** Have students work in groups to study the map of Jerusalem on p. 533. Ask them to discuss how Jerusalem's location has resulted in conflicts. Guide students to see that Jerusalem is on the border between the West Bank and Israel.

Build Vocabulary Go over the definitions of the terms defined in Part A of Activity Sheet 23.3. Check to see whether students understood the definitions, using any of the **Signals** activities, and redefine terms if needed. Have students work in pairs to complete Part A. |
| **Step 3 Make Objectives Explicit** | Write these objectives on the board and read them aloud. Have students turn to a partner and explain in their own words what they will be learning in the section, based on the objectives. Circulate among students to help clarify their understanding. If students' first language is Spanish, have them read the lesson summary in the *Reading Study Guide* (English or Spanish).

• Outline the issues surrounding the control of Jerusalem.

• Examine some of the proposed solutions to the conflict over Jerusalem.

• Analyze different perspectives on Jerusalem and how to resolve the conflicts related to the city. |
| **Step 4 Support Student Reading** | **Cooperative Work** Divide the class into groups of five, so that one student in each group reads one of the primary sources on pp. 532–533. Students should work on a **Double-Column Note-Taking** activity on their primary source, using Part B of Activity Sheet 23.3. When students are done taking notes, the group should come together to teach one another about the primary sources, sharing their notes and their ideas.

On One's Own Preview the following questions by asking students what they understand them to mean. Then have students search for the answers while reading. Once students have finished, help them answer in complete sentences.

1. How did Israel gain control of Jerusalem? (p. 532, par. 2)

2. What is the Palestinian "right of return"? (p. 532, par. 3)

3. What are some proposed solutions to the issue of control of Jerusalem? (p. 533, par. 1) |
| **Step 5 Prepare for Assessment** | **Alternative Assessment** Have students work in groups of five to complete the Case Study Project. Share the Grading Rubric on TE p. 535 with students and use it to evaluate their project.

Formal Assessment Go over the test-taking strategies for TT76a and TT76b. You may want to use *Formal Assessment* Form A, the less-challenging assessment, or administer it as a practice test prior to formal testing with Form B or Form C. |

ACTIVITY SHEET 23.3

Part A. Build Vocabulary

Key Terms Go over the definitions with your class. Then fill in the blanks with the correct key terms. You may need to change the form or one or more words.

> **annex:** to add certain territory to a nation, state, city, or town
>
> **cabinet:** a group of people appointed by the head of a government to act as official advisors
>
> **international:** involving two or more nations

After World War II, the United Nations recommended that Jerusalem become a(n) **1.** _____ city. It would be governed by a group of people from several different countries. However, after the Arab-Israeli war of 1948, Jerusalem was divided between Arabs and Jews; then during the Six-Day War, in 1967, Israelis captured the entire city. In the coming years Israel **2.** _____ Arab lands near Jerusalem, and the city expanded with these Jewish settlements. The official statement of the Palestinian **3.** _____ is that they will not negotiate a peace settlement in which they would give up control of Jerusalem.

Part B. Cooperative Work

Work with your group to read and take notes on the primary sources on pp. 534–535. Go over the answers with the class.

Notes on Primary Sources		
Primary Source	Note Taking	Note Making
UN Resolution 181, adopted in 1947		
Official statement of the Palestinian cabinet, 2000		
Personal observation of Yossi Sarid, peace advocate and head of an Israeli political party		
Editorial comment by Kenneth L. Woodward of *Newsweek* magazine		
Political cartoon by Mark Fiore		

Resources for English Learners
TE p. 554   RSG Audio   FA p. 372
IA pp. 7, 28, 29   TT 77   MLG
RSG pp. 205–206

Landforms and Resources

Step 1 **Activate Prior** **Knowledge**	Lead a **Brainstorming** activity for students to tell what they know about the Himalayas and Mt. Everest. Write what students say on the board and save it for them to add to or revise after they complete the section.
Step 2 **Preview Main** **Ideas and** **Language**	**Connect Visually** With students working in pairs, direct them turn to the diagram on p. 551 to understand the causes of the formation of the Himalayas. Ask students to come up with a demonstration to show how the Himalayas formed. Provide sponges, clay blocks, or other materials for them to use. **Build Vocabulary** Divide students into groups of four and have them learn the meaning of each key term listed in Part A of Activity Sheet 24.1. Students should complete Part A on their own. Go over the answers with the class.
Step 3 **Make Objectives** **Explicit**	Write these objectives on the board and read them aloud to the class. Check students' comprehension using Thumbs Up/Thumbs Down or another **Signals** Activity. Students who understand the objectives can explain them to students who do not understand them. If students' first language is Spanish, have them read the lesson summary in the *Reading Study Guide* (English or Spanish). • Describe the landforms on the subcontinent of South Asia. • Identify major rivers of South Asia and their importance to the people there. • Compare the two island countries that make up part of South Asia. • Describe some of the natural resources of South Asia.
Step 4 **Support Student** **Reading**	**Cooperative Work** Divide the class into groups of three to complete the landforms and resources map in Part B of Activity Sheet 24.1. Refer students to the map on PE p. 543 for help locating landforms and bodies of water. Students should refer to the map on PE p. 554 to help them locate different resources. **On One's Own** Preview the following questions by asking students what they understand them to mean. Then have students search for the answers while reading. Once students have finished, help them answer in complete sentences. **1.** How was the subcontinent of South Asia formed? (p. 551, diagram; p. 552, par. 2) **2.** What are South Asia's three largest rivers, and where are their sources? (p. 552, pars. 6–7) **3.** Describe the two island countries included in South Asia. (p. 553 pars. 3–5) **4.** What are two of South Asia's important mineral resources? (p. 555, pars. 1–3)
Step 5 **Prepare for** **Assessment**	**Alternative Assessment** Students can work in small groups to write a report on South Asia's mineral resources, as described on TE p. 554. Share the guidelines for evaluating cooperative activities, information assessing activities, and reports on pp. 7, 28 and 29 of *Integrated Assessment* and use these for evaluating students' projects. **Formal Assessment** Go over the test-taking strategies for TT77. Then assign the Section Quiz for Chapter 24 Section 1, on p. 372 of the *Formal Assessment* book.

ACTIVITY SHEET 24.1

Part A. Build Vocabulary

Key Terms Learn the meaning of each key term with your group.
Then match each key term with its definition.

_____ **1.** alluvial plain

_____ **2.** archipelago

_____ **3.** atoll

_____ **4.** subcontinent

a. a large group of islands

b. a large landmass that is like a continent, only smaller

c. a broad, level area where soil is dropped by flooding rivers

d. an island that is the top of an underwater volcano surrounded by coral reefs and shallow pools of seawater

Part B. Cooperative Work

Work with your group to label the map with the landforms, bodies of
water, and important mineral resources mentioned in the section. You
should label at least 12 landforms and bodies of water and at least 5
mineral resources. Review your map with the class.

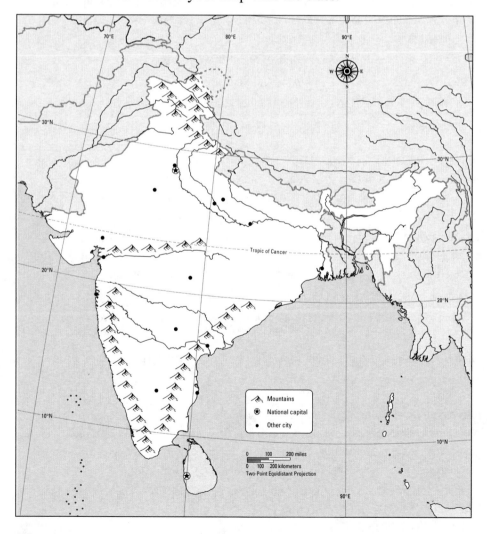

Climate and Vegetation

**Step 1
Activate Prior
Knowledge**

Write the phrase *rainy season/dry season* on the board and ask students to draw what they think of when they read the phrase. Then have students do a **Pair-Share** activity to discuss their drawings. Explain that one of South Asia's climate zones has a dramatic rainy season followed by a scorching dry season.

**Step 2
Preview Main
Ideas and
Language**

Connect Visually Direct students to work in groups of three and study the map on p. 557. Have them locate the tropical wet and dry zone and note the kind of vegetation that generally grows in this climate. Then have students name the five other climate zones and locate them on the map.

Build Vocabulary Go over the definitions of the two boldfaced terms in the chart in Part A of Activity Sheet 24.2. Ask students to work in small groups to complete the **Semantic Feature Analysis.** Go over the answers with the class.

**Step 3
Make Objectives
Explicit**

Write these objectives on the board. Have students read the objectives and then write a question based on each objective that they will answer after they have studied the section. Ask students to read their questions aloud and help clarify understanding. If students' first language is Spanish, have them read the lesson summary in the *Reading Study Guide* (English or Spanish).

- Describe the climate zones and weather patterns that occur in South Asia.
- Identify South Asia's main types of vegetation.

**Step 4
Support Student
Reading**

Cooperative Work Display a wall map of South Asia and have students use it to label the countries on the map in Part B of Activity Sheet 24.2. Then have students work in groups of four to draw in the climate zones, based on reading the section. Ask students to cover up the maps on p. 557 as they read, but encourage them to use the landform maps from Activity Sheet 24.1 or to turn to the map on p. 543 to identify the landforms mentioned. Students should draw in six different climate zones on their maps. Use the wall map to check students' comprehension.

On One's Own Preview the following questions by asking students what they understand them to mean. Then have students search for the answers while reading. Once students have finished, help them answer in complete sentences.

1. How many different climate zones does South Asia have? (p. 556, par. 4)

2. What are cyclones and how do they affect South Asia? (p. 557, par. 3)

3. Where are South Asia's tropical rain forests located? (p. 557, map; p. 558, par. 2)

**Step 5
Prepare for
Assessment**

Alternative Assessment Divide students into groups of three to study the map on p. 559. Ask each group to cover up the questions at the bottom of the page and make up three questions about the map. Groups should get together to swap questions. Share the Standards for Evaluating a Group Discussion on p. 8 of *Integrated Assessment* and use them for evaluating students' interactions.

Formal Assessment Go over the test-taking strategies for TT78. Then assign the Section Quiz for Chapter 24 Section 2, on p. 373 of the *Formal Assessment* book.

ACTIVITY SHEET 24.2

Part A. Build Vocabulary

Key Terms Work with your partner to complete the **Semantic Features Analysis** for the key terms, in **boldfaced** type.

	Type of wind	Type of storm	Occurs seasonally	Comes from the northeast from Oct. to Feb.	Comes from the southwest from June to Sept.	Always brings fierce winds	May or may not bring heavy rains
monsoon							
cyclone							

Part B. Cooperative Work

As you read the section, work with your group to label the map with South Asia's six different climate zones. Keep the maps on p. 557 covered until you have finished your map and are ready to check your answers.

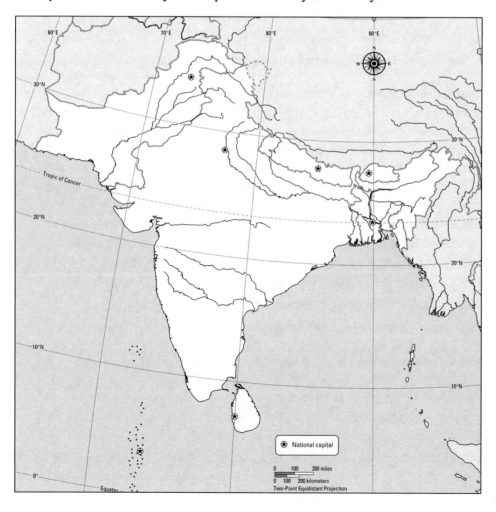

Resources for English Learners
RSG pp. 209–210, 211–212   TE p. 563
RSG Audio   IA p. 8   TT 79
FA pp. 374, 375–378, 379–382, 383–386   MLG

Human-Environment Interaction

**Step 1
Activate Prior
Knowledge**

Do a **K-W-L** activity with the class on Hinduism. Record what students know and what they want to learn on the board. Fill in the L section of the class chart when students complete the section.

**Step 2
Preview Main
Ideas and
Language**

Connect Visually Let students pair up and turn to p. 561 to look at the photograph of the Ganges. They should discuss what they learn about Hinduism from studying the photo. Encourage groups to share their ideas.

Build Vocabulary Go over the key terms in Part A of Activity Sheet 24.3. Use **Word Imaging** to help students understand the definitions. Then assign students to complete Part A. Let students share their drawings in groups.

**Step 3
Make Objectives
Explicit**

Write these objectives on the board and read them aloud to the class. Check students' comprehension using Number of Fingers or another **Signals** activity. Students who understand the objectives can explain them to students who do not understand them. If students' first language is Spanish, have them read the lesson summary in the *Reading Study Guide* (English or Spanish).

• Describe the relationship between Hindus and the Ganges River.

• Explain why and how the people of Bangladesh built a dam across the Feni River.

**Step 4
Support Student
Reading**

Cooperative Work Divide the class in groups of four. Assign students to read the section and to fill in the chart in Part B of Activity Sheet 24.3. Within each group, one pair of students should work together to fill in the top part of the chart; the other pair of students should work together to fill in the bottom part of the chart. The pairs should then come together to teach each other about their part of the section. Go over the answers with the class.

On One's Own Preview the following questions by asking students what they understand them to mean. Then have students search for the answers while reading. Once students have finished, help them answer in complete sentences.

1. Why do Hindu pilgrims visit the Ganges River? (p. 560, pars. 2, 5)

2. Why is the Ganges River so polluted? (p. 561, par. 1)

3. Why does the Feni River cause problems for people in Bangladesh? (p. 562, pars. 2–3)

4. What is the dam that the Bangladeshis built across the Feni like? (p. 562, par. 4; p. 563, pars. 1–4)

**Step 5
Prepare for
Assessment**

Alternative Assessment Assign the Reteaching Activity on TE p. 563 for students to complete in groups of three. Share the Standards for Evaluating a Group Discussion on p. 8 of *Integrated Assessment* and use these for evaluating students' interaction.

Formal Assessment Go over the test-taking strategies for TT79. You may want to use *Formal Assessment* Form A, the less-challenging assessment, or administer it as a practice test prior to formal testing with Form B or Form C.

ACTIVITY SHEET 24.3

Part A. Build Vocabulary

Key Terms Use the spaces below to make a drawing that helps you remember the meaning of each of the key terms, given below in each box.

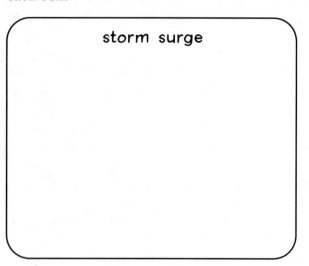

storm surge	estuary

Part B. Cooperative Work

Work with your group to fill in the chart. Go over your answers with the class.

Ganges River	
Reasons Ganges is important	**1.** **2.** **3.**
Reasons Ganges is polluted	**4.** **5.** **6.**
Plans/progress related to cleaning up the Ganges	**7.** Plans: **8.** Progress:
Feni River	
Reasons the Feni floods	**9.** **10.**
Effects on people living nearby	**11.** **12.**
Description of dam project	**13.** Purpose: **14.** How built: **15.** Why built this way: **16.** Who helped: **17.** When completed: **18.** Results:

Resources for English Learners
TE p. 563   RSG pp. 213–214   RSG Audio
IA p. 8   TT 80   FA p. 387
MLG

India

Step 1 **Activate Prior Knowledge**	Bring in recordings of Indian music, such as sitar music, and play them for students. Direct students to do a **Think-Quickwrite-Pair-Share** activity to record their impressions of the music. Explain that India has a rich culture, and its music has influenced and been influenced by music of the Western Hemisphere.
Step 2 **Preview Main Ideas and Language**	**Connect Visually** Ask students to look at the photograph on p. 571, and tell what they notice about the way the two young women are dressed. What is distinctive about this clothing? How is their make up and jewelry different from what students are used to? Have students share their answers. **Build Vocabulary** Tell students to look at Part A of Activity Sheet 25.1. Review how to use an **Anticipation Guide,** with students first filling in their individual (true/false) responses, then discussing each statement with a small group and filling in a second set of responses. Allow time after students have read the section to complete the "Textbook" column and to correct any false answers.
Step 3 **Make Objectives Explicit**	Write these objectives on the board and read them aloud to the class. Check students' comprehension using Thumbs Up/Down or another **Signals** activity. Students who understand the objectives can explain them to students who do not understand them. If students' first language is Spanish, have them read the lesson summary in the *Reading Study Guide* (English or Spanish). • Describe India's history of invasions, empires, and eventual independence. • Describe India's government and list some of the challenges facing it. • Discuss economic challenges in India. • Tell about modern life in India and explain why India's culture is so diverse.
Step 4 **Support Student Reading**	**Cooperative Work** Divide the class into groups of three to read the section, using the **SQ3R** method. Students should also work in their groups to fill in the chart in Part B of Activity Sheet 25.1. Go over answers in class. **On One's Own** Preview the following questions by asking students what they understand them to mean. Then have students search for the answers while reading. Once students have finished, help them answer in complete sentences. **1.** What were the main empires in India before the British arrived? (p. 567, pars. 5–6; p. 568, top) **2.** How did Britain gain control of India's trade? India's government? (p. 568, par. 2) **3.** What is the traditional Indian diet? (p. 570, par. 5) **4.** What are the central beliefs of the Hinduism? (p. 571, par. 4; p. 572, pars. 1, 3)
Step 5 **Prepare for Assessment**	**Alternative Assessment** Divide the class into groups of four and assign the Reteaching Activity on TE p. 563. Share the Standards for Evaluating a Group Discussion on p. 8 of *Integrated Assessment* and use these for evaluating student interaction. **Formal Assessment** Go over the test-taking strategies for TT80. Then assign the Section Quiz for Chapter 25 Section 1, on p. 387 of the *Formal Assessment* book.

ACTIVITY SHEET 25.1

Part A. Build Vocabulary

Key Terms Work individually and then with your group to fill in the first two columns of the Anticipation Guide. Fill in the third column after you have read the entire section. Correct any false answers.

You	Group	Textbook	Topic—India
			1. India gained its independence from Britain through the leadership of Mohandas Gandhi, who used a tactic of armed warfare called **nonviolent resistance.**
			2. India is considering distributing its farmland in a more balanced way through a government program of **land reform.**
			3. One way that India has aided the growth of its iron industry is through the use of the **caste system,** which was developed in the late 1940s.

Part B. Cooperative Work

Work with your group to read the section and complete the chart.
Go over the answers with the class.

Historical Factors that have Influenced India
1. Aryans
2. Mauryan Empire
3. Gupta Empire
4. Mughal Empire
5. Raj
6. Nonviolent resistance

Factors that Affect Life in Modern India	
7. democracy	**8.** agriculture
9. industry	**10.** education
11. multiple languages	**12.** caste system

Resources for English Learners
TE p. 565d   RSG pp. 215–216   RSG Audio
IA p. 8   TT 81   FA p. 388
MLG

Pakistan and Bangladesh

**Step 1
Activate Prior
Knowledge**

Do a written **Roundtable** activity for students to review what they already know about religious and cultural conflict. After groups have shared what they wrote with the class, explain that Pakistan and Bangladesh came into existence because of religious conflicts that occurred when India gained its independence and there is still serious conflict in the region today.

**Step 2
Preview Main
Ideas and
Language**

Connect Visually Keep students in their groups. Direct them to turn to the map on p. 574. Explain that before 1947 all of the mainland regions labeled on the map were united as the colony of British India. Ask them to identify the country that separated West Pakistan from East Pakistan in 1947 *(India)*. Then they should name the territory that was under dispute in 1947 *(Kashmir)*.

Build Vocabulary Have students work in groups of three and use **New Word Analysis** to understand the key terms in Part A of Activity Sheet 25.2. Students should complete Part A on their own. Go over the answers with the class.

**Step 3
Make Objectives
Explicit**

Write these objectives on the board and read them aloud to the class. Have students turn to a partner in the classroom and explain in their own words what they will be learning in the section, based on the objectives. If students' first language is Spanish, have them read the lesson summary in the *Reading Study Guide* (English or Spanish).

- Discuss the ancient and recent history of Pakistan and Bangladesh.
- Compare the economies of Pakistan and Bangladesh.
- Describe the religion and ethnic diversity of the two countries.
- Tell about modern life and culture in Pakistan and Bangladesh.

**Step 4
Support Student
Reading**

Cooperative Work Divide the class into groups of six; within each group students should pair up to read the section and fill in the **Venn Diagram** in Part B of Activity Sheet 25.2. One pair should fill in the oval for Pakistan; one pair should fill in the oval for Bangladesh; the third pair should fill in the overlapping part of the diagram.Then correct the Venn Diagrams with the class.

On One's Own Preview the following questions by asking students what they understand them to mean. Then have students search for the answers while reading. Once students have finished, help them answer in complete sentences.

1. How were Pakistan and Bangladesh formed? (p. 574, pars. 1–2)

2. What role does farming play in the economies of the two countries?
   (p. 574, par. 4; p. 575, top, pars. 1–2)

3. What are some ethnic groups in Pakistan? in Bangladesh? (p. 576, pars. 4–5)

4. What are some popular traditions in the two countries? (p. 577, pars. 1, 3)

**Step 5
Prepare for
Assessment**

Alternative Assessment Have students work in groups of four to do the Technology Activity on TE p. 565d. Share the Standards for Evaluating a Group Discussion on p. 8 of *Integrated Assessment* and use these for evaluating student interaction.

Formal Assessment Go over the test-taking strategies for TT81. Then assign the Section Quiz for Chapter 25 Section 2, on p. 388 of the *Formal Assessment* book.

ACTIVITY SHEET 25.2

Part A. Build Vocabulary

Key Terms Work with your group to figure out the meaning of the key terms. Then complete the vocabulary exercise on your own by filling in each blank to best complete the statement. You may have to make one or more of the words plural.

> **partition**   **microcredit**   **entrepreneur**

1. _____ can help a country economically by starting new businesses that contribute to economic growth.

2. A bank might consider a small business too risky to qualify for a loan. In Bangladesh, such businesses can get _____ and receive small loans from the government and other nonprofit groups.

3. When Britain granted independence to its colony in India, the new nation decided to divide into a Hindu state (India) and a Muslim state (Pakistan). This division was called the _____ of India.

Part B. Cooperative Work

Work with your group to read the section and complete the Venn Diagram. Go over the answers with the class.

PAKISTAN

History: 1. a.

Economy: 2. a.

Religion: 3. a.

Ethnic groups: 4. a.

Modern Life: 5. a.

BOTH

History: 1. c.

Economy: 2. c.

Religion: 3. c.

Modern Life: 5. c.

BANGLADESH

History: 1. b.

Economy: 2. b.

Religion: 3. b.

Ethnic groups: 4. b.

Modern Life: 5. b.

Resources for English Learners
RSG pp. 217–218   RSG Audio   MLG
OMA pp. 83–84, 113   IA p. 28   TT 82
FA p. 389

Nepal and Bhutan

**Step 1
Activate Prior
Knowledge**

Write the phrase the *Forbidden Kingdom* on the board or the overhead and ask students to draw or write what they think about or envision when they read this phrase. Then do a **Pair-Share** activity for students to discuss their ideas. Explain that Bhutan used to be called the Forbidden Kingdom, because outsiders were not allowed to visit.

**Step 2
Preview Main
Ideas and
Language**

Connect Visually Ask students to turn to the diagram on p. 582. While they remain in pairs, direct them to discuss what the diagram shows about the geography of Nepal and Bhutan. Discuss how geography might explain the isolation of these two countries.

Build Vocabulary Review how to do the **Think-Aloud** technique to help students learn new vocabulary words. Then direct students to do a Think-Aloud on the key term in Part A of Activity Sheet 25.3, using the textbook and other resources. Let students work in groups of three or four to share what they learned about the key term and to complete Part A.

**Step 3
Make Objectives
Explicit**

Write these objectives on the board. Have students read the objectives and then write a question based on each objective that they will answer after they have studied the section. If students' first language is Spanish, have them read the lesson summary in the *Reading Study Guide* (English or Spanish).

- Describe the mountain kingdoms of Nepal and Bhutan.
- Compare the economies of the two countries.
- Describe the religion and culture of Nepal and Bhutan.

**Step 4
Support Student
Reading**

Cooperative Work Divide the class into groups of four; within each group students should pair up to read the section and fill in the **Venn Diagram** in Part B of Activity Sheet 25.3. One pair should complete the items related to geography and history and government; the other pair should complete the items related to the economy and ethnic groups and religion. When students have finished, have them come together as a group to discuss their answers.

On One's Own Preview the following questions by asking students what they mean. Then have students search for the answers while reading. Once students have finished, help them answer in complete sentences.

1. How has geography affected Nepal and Bhutan? (p. 580, pars. 2–3)

2. Compare tourism in Nepal and Bhutan. (p. 581, par. 4; p. 582, top, par. 1)

3. What religions are practiced in Nepal and Bhutan? (p. 582, par. 5; p. 583, top, par. 2)

**Step 5
Prepare for
Assessment**

Alternative Assessment Assign students to pair up and complete the activity related to Nepal and Bhutan on pp. 83–84 of *Outline Maps with Activities*. Share the guidelines for evaluating maps on p. 28 of *Integrated Assessment*; use these and the answers to the questions on OMA p. 113 for evaluating students' work.

Formal Assessment Go over the test-taking strategies for TT82. Then assign the Section Quiz for Chapter 25 Section 3, on p. 389 of the *Formal Assessment* book.

ACTIVITY SHEET 25.3

Part A. Build Vocabulary

Key Terms Fill in the chart based on your work with your group.

Key Term	constitutional monarchy
Defining paragraph in textbook	**1.**
Example	**2.**
My questions or ideas about the word	**3.**

Part B. Cooperative Work

Work with your group to read the section and complete the Venn Diagram. Go over the answers with the class.

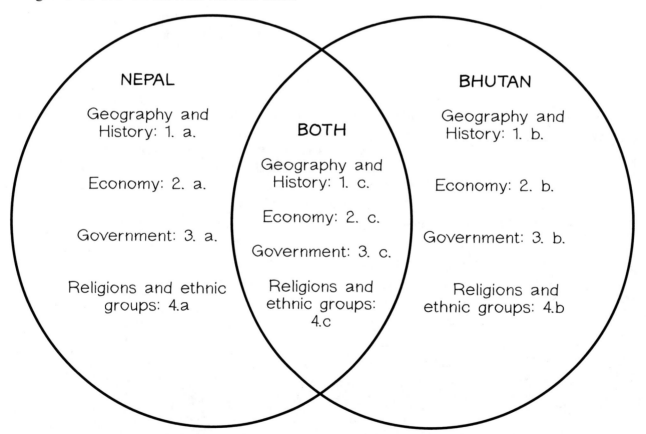

NEPAL

Geography and History: 1. a.

Economy: 2. a.

Government: 3. a.

Religions and ethnic groups: 4.a

BOTH

Geography and History: 1. c.

Economy: 2. c.

Government: 3. c.

Religions and ethnic groups: 4.c

BHUTAN

Geography and History: 1. b.

Economy: 2. b.

Government: 3. b.

Religions and ethnic groups: 4.b

Chapter (25) Section 4

Resources for English Learners
RSG pp. 219–220, 221–222   RSG Audio
IA pp. 7, 25   TT 83a, TT 83b
FA pp. 390, 391–394, 395–398, 399–402   MLG

Sri Lanka and the Maldives

Step 1
Activate Prior Knowledge

Take a class vote on which island nation is bigger, Sri Lanka or the Maldives. Then display a wall map of South Asia and have students locate the two countries. Students should estimate the area of the two countries and decide whether the class was correct or not.

Step 2
Preview Main Ideas and Language

Connect Visually Let students form groups of three and look at the photographs on pp. 585, 586, and 587. Based on the photographs, what do students think might be a main economic activity on these islands. Record students' ideas on the board and keep them for students to revise after they complete the section.

Build Vocabulary Go over the definitions of the two boldfaced terms in the chart in Part A of Activity Sheet 25.4. Use a **Signals** activity such as Slates to check students' comprehension. Then have students work with a partner to complete the **Semantic Feature Analysis.** Go over the answers with the class.

Step 3
Make Objectives Explicit

Write these objectives on the board and read them aloud to the class. For each objective, have students write a personal goal for studying the section. Let students discuss their goals with a partner, as you circulate to clarify understanding. If students' first language is Spanish, have them read the lesson summary in the *Reading Study Guide* (English or Spanish).

- Describe the early settlers of Sri Lanka and of the Maldives.
- Describe the religious, ethnic, and cultural life of Sri Lanka and the Maldives.
- Discuss the economic strengths of and challenges faced by these two nations.

Step 4
Support Student Reading

Cooperative Work Have students pair up to complete the chart in Part B of Activity Sheet 25.4. Go over the answers with the class. Then do an **Inside-Outside Circles** activity to review and reinforce the information.

On One's Own Preview the following questions by asking students what they understand them to mean. Then have students search for the answers while reading. Once students have finished, help them answer in complete sentences.

1. Who were the first create an advanced civilization on Sri Lanka? Who came next? (p. 584, pars. 3–4)

2. Why is there tension between the ethnic groups in Sri Lanka? (p. 584, par. 5)

3. What is cultural life in the Maldives like? (p. 586, par. 1)

4. What are some of the economic strengths of Sri Lanka and the Maldives? (p. 586, par. 3; p. 587, top, par. 1)

Step 5
Prepare for Assessment

Alternative Assessment Divide the class in groups of three and assign the GeoActivity on p. 587. Share the guidelines for evaluating a cooperative activity and the guidelines for evaluating posters on pp. 7 and 25 of *Integrated Assessment* and use them to assess students' work.

Formal Assessment Go over the test-taking strategies for TT83a and TT83b. You may want to use *Formal Assessment* Form A, the less-challenging assessment, or administer it as a practice test prior to formal testing with Form B or Form C.

ACTIVITY SHEET 25.4

Part A. Build Vocabulary

Key Terms Work with your partner to complete the **Semantic Features Analysis** for the key terms, in **boldfaced** type.

	Live on Sri Lanka	Came from India	Arrived around 300 B.C.	Arrived around A.D. 300	Absorbed the ethnic groups already on the island	Practice Buddhism	Practice Hinduism
Sinhalese							
Tamils							

Part B. Cooperative Work

Work with your group to read the section and complete the chart.
Go over the answers and review the information with your class.

	Sri Lanka	**Maldives**
Geography	1.	2.
Populations	3.	4.
Religions	5.	6.
Economies	7.	8.
Challenges	9.	10.

Resources for English Learners

TE p. 595	Video: *India: Population and Resources*	
RSG pp. 223–224	RSG Audio	IA p. 7
TT 84	FA p. 403	MLG

Population Explosion

Step 1 **Activate Prior Knowledge**	Ask students what they think a population explosion is and write the term on the board or the overhead, if necessary. Then make a **T-Chart** to list benefits and problems of a population explosion. Through class discussion, consider the issue from the viewpoint of both an individual and his or her family, as well as society in general. Save the T-Chart for students to add to or revise when they complete the section.
Step 2 **Preview Main Ideas and Language**	**Connect Visually** Show students part of the video *India: Population and Resources.* Refer to the Teacher's Resource Book for *The Voyager Experience in World Geography,* p. 75, and show the section that includes the discussion with Vijay Kumar about the influx of people to Bangalore. If time permits, you can also show the section that includes the interview with Bangalore's city planner. Follow the suggestions for **Viewing Videos with Language Learners.** **Build Vocabulary** Use the **Frayer Method** to teach the two key terms in Part A of Activity Sheet 26.1. Then assign students to complete Part A. Let students share their drawings in small or large groups.
Step 3 **Make Objectives Explicit**	Write these objectives on the overhead or on the board and read them aloud to the class. For each objective, direct students to look through the section and identify a photo, map, or paragraph that might help them learn about that objective. If students' first language is Spanish, have them read the lesson summary in the *Reading Study Guide* (English or Spanish). • Discuss the reasons for and problems created by the population explosion in India and other South Asian nations. • Analyze the difficulties in managing India's population growth.
Step 4 **Support Student Reading**	**Cooperative Work** Pair students up for **Peer Tutoring** and have them work together to read the section and complete the chart in Part B of Activity Sheet 26.1. Go over the answers with the class. **On One's Own** Preview the following questions by asking students what they understand them to mean. Then have students search for the answers while reading. Once students have finished, help them answer in complete sentences. **1.** Why is the size of India's population a problem? (p. 593, par. 2) **2.** How has the government of India tried to address the population explosion? (p. 594, par. 3) **3.** Why has the government program had mixed success? (p. 594, pars. 3–4)
Step 5 **Prepare for Assessment**	**Alternative Assessment** Have students work in pairs to complete the Reteaching Activity on TE p. 595. Share the Standards for Evaluating a Cooperative Activity on p. 7 of *Integrated Assessment* and use these for evaluating student interaction. **Formal Assessment** Go over the test-taking strategies for TT84. Then assign the Section Quiz for Chapter 26 Section 1, on p. 403 of the *Formal Assessment* book.

ACTIVITY SHEET 26.1

Part A. Build Vocabulary

Key Terms Use the spaces below to make a drawing that helps you remember the meaning of each of the key terms, given below in each box.

basic necessities	illiteracy

Part B. Cooperative Work

Work with your partner to read the section and fill in the chart.
Go over your answers with the class.

Problems	Solutions
1. population growth	**2.** smaller families
3. inadequate resources	**4.** education

Living with Extreme Weather

**Step 1
Activate Prior
Knowledge**

Work with the class to define the term *extreme weather.* Then, do a **Round Robin** activity to name different types of extreme weather. Write these down on the board. Once the class has completed the list, read the items one by one. Explain that extreme weather can cause problems anywhere, but because of South India's geography and large population, these problems are particularly severe in South Asia.

**Step 2
Preview Main
Ideas and
Language**

Connect Visually Direct students to turn to p. 579 and look at the photos on this page. Have students discuss the pictures, reviewing what cyclones are, the damage they cause, and how people protect themselves against cyclones.

Build Vocabulary Review the definition of *monsoon* from Chapter 24 Section 2. Then outline the differences between South Asia's summer monsoon and winter monsoon. Once you are sure that students understand these terms, ask them to work in small groups to complete the **Semantic Feature Analysis** in Part A of Activity Sheet 26.2. Go over the answers with the class.

**Step 3
Make Objectives
Explicit**

Write these objectives on the board. Have students read the objectives and then write a question based on each objective that they will answer after they have studied the section. Ask students to read their questions aloud and help clarify any misunderstandings. If students' first language is Spanish, have them read the lesson summary in the *Reading Study Guide* (English or Spanish).

- Describe summer and winter monsoons.
- Explain how the monsoons affect South Asia.

**Step 4
Support Student
Reading**

Cooperative Work Have students divide into groups of three to fill out the spider diagram in Part B of Activity Sheet 26.2. Go over the answers in class using a **Numbered Heads Together** activity.

On One's Own Preview the following questions by asking students what they understand them to mean. Then have students search for the answers while reading. Once students have finished, help them answer in complete sentences.

1. What are South Asia's two monsoon seasons and what physical problems can they cause? (p. 597, pars. 3–4; p. 598, pars. 1–2)

2. What economic impact do monsoons have on South Asia? (p. 598, par. 3; p. 599, top, par. 1)

3. What political tensions have resulted from the effects of extreme weather? (p. 599, par. 2)

**Step 5
Prepare for
Assessment**

Alternative Assessment Have students work in pairs to complete the GeoWorkshop on pp. 37–38 of Unit 8 *In-Depth Resources.* Share the Standards for Evaluating a Cooperative Activity on p. 7 of *Integrated Assessment* and use these and the answers to the questions on *IDR* p. 45 for evaluating students' work.

Formal Assessment Go over the test-taking strategies for TT85. Then assign the Section Quiz for Chapter 26 Section 2, on p. 404 of the *Formal Assessment* book.

ACTIVITY SHEET 26.2

Part A. Build Vocabulary

Key Terms Work with your group to complete the **Semantic Features Analysis** for the key terms in **boldfaced** type.

	Type of wind	Occurs from June to September	Occurs from October to February	Blows from the northeast	Blows from the southwest	Brings rain	Carries little moisture
summer monsoon							
winter monsoon							

Part B. Cooperative Work

Work with your partner to read the section and fill in the spider diagram.
Go over your answers with the class.

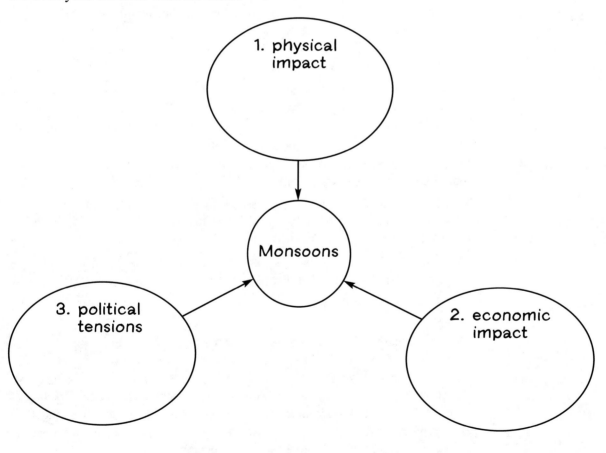

Resources for English Learners

TE p. 603   RSG pp. 227–228, 229–230
RSG Audio   TT 86   MLG
FA pp. 405, 406–410, 411–415, 416–420

Territorial Dispute

Step 1 **Activate Prior Knowledge**	Use a **Carousel Review** to go over what happened when British India gained independence in 1947. What two countries were created from the former colony? Why did two countries form? What kind of relationship do students think these countries had then? Keep student responses for students to correct after they complete the Case Study.
Step 2 **Preview Main Ideas and Language**	**Connect Visually** Have students remain in their groups and direct them to study the time line on p. 600. Students should talk about when the dispute began, whether the dispute involved military action, and what makes the dispute tense. Groups should share their ideas in a brief class discussion. **Build Vocabulary** Go over the definitions of the key terms listed in Part A of Activity Sheet 26.3. Then have students work with a partner to complete the activity.
Step 3 **Make Objectives Explicit**	Write these objectives on the board and read them aloud to the class. Check students' comprehension using Number of Fingers or another **Signals** activity. Students who understand the objectives can explain them to students who do not understand them. If students' first language is Spanish, have them read the lesson summary in the *Reading Study Guide* (English or Spanish). • Describe the dispute between India and Pakistan over Kashmir. • Explain why this dispute could lead to nuclear war. • Analyze primary sources to understand different views related to the conflict.
Step 4 **Support Student Reading**	**Cooperative Work** Divide the class into groups of three to read the section, using the **SQ3R** method. As students read the primary sources, they should work together to fill in the chart in Part B of Activity Sheet 26.3. Go over answers with the entire class. Then encourage students to find other sources of information as they work on the Case Study Project. **On One's Own** Preview the following questions by asking students what they understand them to mean. Then have students search for the answers while reading. Once students have finished, help them answer in complete sentences. 1. Where is Kashmir, when did the dispute over Kashmir begin, and who is involved? (p. 600, pars. 1, 3) 2. What is Pakistan's main economic reason for wanting Kashmir? (p. 601, par. 1) 3. Why are world leaders very concerned about the dispute? (p. 601, par. 2)
Step 5 **Prepare for Assessment**	**Alternative Assessment** Have students work in groups of five to complete the Case Study Project. Share the Grading Rubric on TE p. 603 with students and use it to evaluate their project. **Formal Assessment** Go over the test-taking strategies for TT86. You may want to use *Formal Assessment* Form A, the less-challenging assessment, or administer it as a practice test prior to formal testing with Form B or Form C.

ACTIVITY SHEET 26.3

Part A. Build Vocabulary

Key Terms Working with your partner, fill in the blanks with the correct key terms. You may have to make one or more of the words plural or change the form of one or more verbs.

> **cede:** to give up possession of, especially by signing a treaty
>
> **deterrent:** a way of discouraging an enemy attack that involves the threat of harsh punishment
>
> **strategic:** important, often for military reasons
>
> **territorial:** related to a nation's land

India and Pakistan have a **1.** _____ dispute over which of them should have control of the state of Kashmir. **2.** Kashmir is of _____ importance to both Pakistan and India, because it includes the foothills of the Himalayas and many tributaries of the important river, the Indus. Neither side is willing to **3.** _____ the part of Kashmir that it controls to the other nation. Both sides have nuclear weapons, which they each say are **4.** _____ against the other side stepping up the conflict.

Part B. Cooperative Work

Work with your group to read and summarize the primary sources on pp. 602–603. Go over the answers with the class.

Main Idea or Summary of Primary Sources
Government Document from Pakistan, 1999:
Government Policy Declaration from India, 2000:
Speech by a Kashmiri politician, 1999:
Personal story of a Kashmiri native:
Political cartoon from a U.S. newspaper:

Resources for English Learners
TE p. 610   RSG pp. 231–232   RSG Audio
IA p. 8   TT 87   FA p. 421
MLG

Landforms and Resources

Step 1 **Activate Prior** **Knowledge**	Lead a **Brainstorming** activity for students to tell what they know about the Great Wall of China. If you have any students who have visited China, you can ask them if they would like to share anything about the landscape of China.
Step 2 **Preview Main** **Ideas and** **Language**	**Connect Visually** Have students turn to the photograph of the Great Wall of China on p. 618. Focus students' attention on the terrain near the Great Wall and guide them to realize that this landscape is extremely rugged. Explain that many parts of China have rugged or difficult terrain. **Build Vocabulary** Write the key places from Part A of Activity Sheet 27.1 on the board or the overhead and read the names aloud. Use a wall map to point to the mountains and rivers in the list and have students name what you are pointing to. When the class can identify these landforms and rivers, tell them to label the map on the Activity Sheet. Go over the answers.
Step 3 **Make Objectives** **Explicit**	Write these objectives on the board and read them to the class. Have students turn to a partner in the classroom and explain in their own words what they will be learning in the section. If students' first language is Spanish, have them read the lesson summary in the *Reading Study Guide* (English or Spanish). • Explain how China's rugged mountains and plateaus affected its history and culture. • Identify important peninsulas and islands in East Asia. • Describe China's three major river systems and tell why they are important. • List key natural resources and tell how they influence daily life in China.
Step 4 **Support Student** **Reading**	**Cooperative Work** Let students pair up to complete the chart in Part B of Activity Sheet 27.1. Tell students to look at the map on p. 620 to locate the different landforms and bodies of water. Explain that they will need to use the map to find the names of all the different mountain ranges in the region. Encourage students to describe the location and importance of the different resources listed. **On One's Own** Preview the following questions by asking students what they understand them to mean. Then have students search for the answers while reading. Once students have finished, help them answer in complete sentences. **1.** What effects did East Asia's high mountains have on the development of China? (p. 619, par. 3) **2.** What are some important islands off the coast of China? (p. 621, par. 1) **3.** Why are China's three main river systems so important? (p. 623, par. 4)
Step 5 **Prepare for** **Assessment**	**Alternative Assessment** Have students work in small groups to answer the Making Comparison questions on p. 610. Share the Standards for Evaluating a Group Discussion p. 8 of *Integrated Assessment* and use these and the answers on TE p. 610 for evaluating students' interactions and understanding. **Formal Assessment** Go over the test-taking strategies for TT87. Then assign the Section Quiz for Chapter 27 Section 1, on p. 421 of the *Formal Assessment* book.

ACTIVITY SHEET 27.1

Part A. Build Vocabulary

Key Places Label all of the key places on the map below.

Kunlun Mountains

Qinling Shandi Mountains

Huang He

Chang Jiang

Xi Jiang

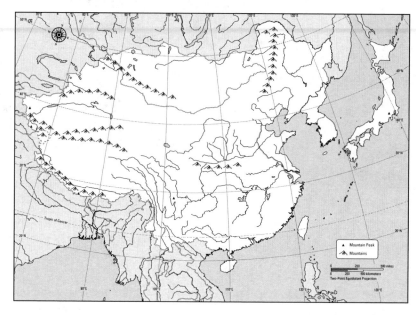

Part B. Cooperative Work

Work with your partner to fill in the chart, listing examples of the different landforms and bodies of water, and noting their general location in parentheses. (The first entry has been started for you as an example.) Use the bottom of the chart to take notes related to the different resources.

Important Landforms and Bodies of Water in East Asia				
Mountain Ranges	Plateaus and Plains	Peninsulas	Islands	River Systems
Kunlun (western China)				
		X	X	
Important Resources				

Land	Forests	Minerals	Energy Resources	Water

Climate and Vegetation

Step 1 Activate Prior Knowledge	Lead a **Round Robin** discussion of what the climate is like in different states, including your state and in other states that students have visited. Explain that China has many of the same climate zones as those in the United States.
Step 2 Preview Main Ideas and Language	**Connect Visually** Have students turn to the climate map on p. 626. They should locate their state or a state with a similar climate on the map and identify the part of China that has a similar climate (southeast, northwest, etc.). Using the map and information from the Round Robin discussion, let students tell what they think different parts of China are like.

Build Vocabulary Use the **Frayer Method** to teach the key term in Part A of Activity Sheet 27.2. Then review the terms *hurricane,* taught in Chapter 3, and *cyclone,* taught in Chapter 24. Have students work in pairs to complete Part A. Go over the answers with the class to clarify understanding. |
| **Step 3 Make Objectives Explicit** | Write these objectives on the overhead or on the board. Have students locate the headings and subheadings that will help them learn about each objective. If students' first language is Spanish, have them read the lesson summary in the *Reading Study Guide* (English or Spanish).

• Describe the high latitude climate zones of East Asia.

• Identify the mid-latitude, dry, and tropical zones of the region. |
| **Step 4 Support Student Reading** | **Cooperative Work** Let students work in groups of three on Part B of Activity Sheet 27.2. Display a wall map students can use to label the countries on the map in the Activity Sheet. Then direct students to read the section and draw in the climate zones on their map. Ask students to cover up the map on p. 626 as they read, but encourage them to use the map on p. 620 to identify the landforms mentioned, as necessary. Students should draw in seven climate zones on their maps. Have them use the map on p. 61 or p. 626 to correct their answers. Check students' comprehension using a wall map and **Slates** or another **Signals** activity.

On One's Own Preview the following questions by asking students what they understand them to mean. Then have students search for the answers while reading. Once students have finished, help them answer in complete sentences.

1. Why is western China sparsely populated? (p. 626, par. 4)

2. What are the two mid-latitude climate zones in East Asia? (p. 6a6, pars. 1–3)

3. What are the two deserts of East Asia? (p. 627, par. 2) |
| **Step 5 Prepare for Assessment** | **Alternative Assessment** Let each student choose a partner who has similar preference about climate and weather; have them work on the GeoActivity on p. 627. Share the general guidelines for art type activities on p. 25 of *Integrated Assessment* and use them for evaluating students' posters.

Formal Assessment Go over the test-taking strategies for TT88. Then assign the Section Quiz for Chapter 27 Section 2, on p. 422 of the *Formal Assessment* book. |

ACTIVITY SHEET 27.2

Part A. Build Vocabulary

Key Term Go over the meaning of the key term in class. Then work with
a partner to answer the questions.

typhoon

1. How are typhoons similar to hurricanes and cyclones? _____

_____

2. How are typhoons different from hurricanes and from cyclones?
   Hurricanes occur in **a.** _____;

   cyclones occur in **b.** _____.

Part B. Cooperative Work

As you read the section, work with your group to label the map with East
Asia's climate zones. Keep the map on p. 626 covered until you have
finished your map and are ready to check your answers.

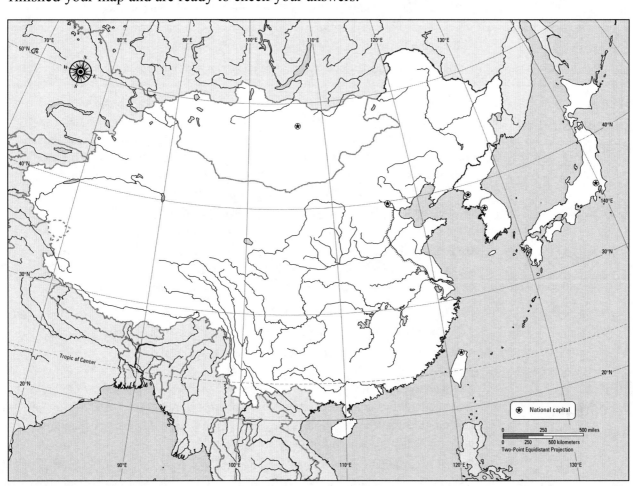

Resources for English Learners
RSG pp. 235–236, 237–238   RSG Audio
IDR9 pp. 8, 40   IA p. 8   TT 89a, TT 89b
FA pp. 423, 424–427, 428–431, 432–435   MLG

Human-Environment Interaction

Step 1 **Activate Prior Knowledge**	Do a **Think-Pair-Share** activity for students to share their experiences related to floods. Have they ever been in a place that became flooded? What was it like? If students haven't had personal experience, encourage them to relate what they know about flooding based on watching news programs, reading newspapers, or from any other source of factual information.
Step 2 **Preview Main Ideas and Language**	**Connect Visually** Students can work in small groups and study the pictures of the floods on pp. 640–641. What words would they use to describe the physical effects of the flood? Let groups share their ideas. **Build Vocabulary** Help students understand the key terms in Part A of Activity Sheet 27.3. Students can complete Part A in pairs. Let students share their sentences while you circulate to clarify understanding.
Step 3 **Make Objectives Explicit**	Write these objectives on the overhead or on the board and read them aloud to the class. Have students identify what they think is the most important word or phrase in each objective. Clarify understanding as students discuss the words and phrases they chose. If students' first language is Spanish, have them read the lesson summary in the *Reading Study Guide* (English or Spanish). • Identify the purpose and the possible positive and negative effects of China's Three Gorges Dam project. • List some ways that the Japanese deal with overcrowding in their cities.
Step 4 **Support Student Reading**	**Cooperative Work** Dividing the class in groups of four, assign students to read the section and to fill in the chart in Part B of Activity Sheet 27.3. Within each group, one pair of students should work together to fill in the top part of the chart; the other pair should work together to fill in the bottom part of the chart. **On One's Own** Preview the following questions by asking students what they understand them to mean. Then have students search for the answers while reading. Once students have finished, help them answer in complete sentences. 1. What are some possible positive effects of building China's Three Gorges Dam? (p. 629, pars. 3–5) 2. What are some possible negative effects of building China's Three Gorges Dam? (p. 630, pars. 2–4) 3. Why are Japanese cities crowded and how have the Japanese adapted to this? (p. 630, pars. 5–7; p. 631, pars. 1–3)
Step 5 **Prepare for Assessment**	**Alternative Assessment** Let students work in groups of four or five to do the Making Decisions activity on p. 8 of Unit 9, *In-Depth Resources*. Share the Standards for Evaluating a Group Discussion on p. 8 of *Integrated Assessment* and use these and the answers on IDR9 p. 40 for evaluating students' interaction and reasoning skills. **Formal Assessment** Go over the test-taking strategies for TT89a and TT89b. You may want to use *Formal Assessment* Form A, the less-challenging assessment, or administer it as a practice test prior to formal testing with Form B or Form C.

ACTIVITY SHEET 27.3

Part A. Build Vocabulary

Key Terms Work with your partner to write one or two sentences related to each term in **boldfaced** print that shows your understanding of the term.

PCBs: _____

_____

_____

landfill: _____

_____

_____

Part B. Cooperative Work

Work with your group to fill in the chart. Go over your answers with the class.

China's Three Gorges Dam	
Benefits	Costs
1.	4.
2.	5.
3.	6. a.
	b.
	c.
Japan's Cities	
Space-related Problems	Solutions
7.	8.
	9.
	10.

Resources for English Learners		
TE p. 639	RSG pp. 239–240	RSG Audio
IA p. 8	TT 90	FA p. 436
MLG		

China

Step 1 **Activate Prior Knowledge**	Do a **K-W-L** activity on China. Use the board or the overhead to record what students know and what they want to learn. Fill in the L section of the class chart when students complete the section.
Step 2 **Preview Main Ideas and Language**	**Connect Visually** Have students pair up and look at the time line on pp. 636–637. Encourage them to notice the different events on the time line that relate to education, art, and political history. Have students jot down three questions related to the time line that they will try to answer as they read. **Build Vocabulary** Go over the descriptions of the three religions/ethical traditions listed in the chart in Part A of Activity Sheet 28.1. Once students have a basic knowledge of these traditions, let them work with a partner to complete the **Semantic Feature Analysis.** Go over the answers with the class.
Step 3 **Make Objectives Explicit**	Write these objectives on the board and read them aloud to the class. Check students' comprehension using Number of Fingers or another **Signals** activity. Students who understand the objectives can explain them to students who do not understand them. If students' first language is Spanish, have them read the lesson summary in the *Reading Study Guide* (English or Spanish). • Discuss China's early history. • Describe China's growth and political and economic changes. • Describe China's culture and achievements.
Step 4 **Support Student Reading**	**Cooperative Work** Divide the class into groups of four and let students work together to complete the time line in Part B of Activity Sheet 28.1. Then make a class time line with input from all of the groups. Let students vote on the events they think are most important in Chinese history. Hold a class discussion for student to explain their reasoning. **On One's Own** Preview the following questions by asking students what they understand them to mean. Then have students search for the answers while reading. Once students have finished, help them answer in complete sentences. 1. What kind of government has China had since 1949? (p. 636, par. 5; p. 637, par. 1) 2. How is China able to feed its huge population? (p. 637, pars. 3, 5) 3. What are the main ideas of Confucianism? (p. 638, par. 6) 4. What is Chinese health care like? (p. 639, pars. 4–5)
Step 5 **Prepare for Assessment**	**Alternative Assessment** Assign the Reteaching Activity on TE p. 639 and share the Standards for Evaluating a Group Discussion on p. 8 of *Integrated Assessment.* Use these for evaluating student interaction. **Formal Assessment** Go over the test-taking strategies for TT90. Then assign the Section Quiz for Chapter 28 Section 1, on p. 436 of the *Formal Assessment* book.

ACTIVITY SHEET 28.1

Part A. Build Vocabulary

Key Terms Work with your partner to complete the **Semantic Features Analysis** for the key terms, in **boldfaced** type.

	Began around 500 B.C.	Started in China	Based on the teachings of Confucius	Based on the teachings of Lao-tzu	Based on the teachings of Buddha	Encourages respect for the past and for an orderly society	Stresses education
Confucianism							
Taoism							
Buddhism							

Part B. Cooperative Work

As you study the section, work with your group to add ten entries to the time line, related to important events in Chinese history.

Some Important Events in Chinese History

- 1700 B.C.
- 1400
- 1100
- 900
- 600
- 300
- A.D. 1
- 300
- 600
- 900
- 1200
- 1500
- 1800
- 2000

Resources for English Learners
RSG pp. 241–242   RSG Audio
IA p. 25   TT 91
FA p. 437   MLG

Mongolia and Taiwan

Step 1 **Activate Prior** **Knowledge**	Do a **Round Robin** activity for students to name different empires they have learned about that have ruled throughout history. Make a class list on the board or the overhead. Then ask students which empire they think was the largest in terms of land area. Explain that the Mongol Empire in East Asia was the world's largest.
Step 2 **Preview Main** **Ideas and** **Language**	**Connect Visually** Divide students in groups of three and direct them to study the map on p. 643. Ask students to gauge the extent of the Mongol Empire, both east to west and north to south. Have them name the regions other than East Asia where people became subject to the Mongols. **Build Vocabulary** Go over the key terms in Part A of Activity Sheet 28.2. Use **Word Imaging** to help students better understand the definitions. Then assign students to complete Part A. Let students share their drawings in small or large groups.
Step 3 **Make Objectives** **Explicit**	Write these objectives on the overhead or on the board and read them aloud to the class. For each objective, have students write a personal goal for studying the section. If students' first language is Spanish, have them read the lesson summary in the *Reading Study Guide* (English or Spanish). • Examine Mongolia's and Taiwan's early history and links to China. • Describe the cultures and economies of Mongolia and Taiwan. • Describe daily life in Mongolia and Taiwan.
Step 4 **Support Student** **Reading**	**Cooperative Work** Have students form groups of three and work together to complete the chart in Part B of Activity Sheet 28.2. Go over the chart with the class using a **Carousel Review** activity. **On One's Own** Preview the following questions by asking students what they understand them to mean. Then have students search for the answers while reading. Once students have finished, help them answer in complete sentences. **1.** How has China influenced both Mongolia and Taiwan? (p. 643, pars. 1, 3) **2.** What is the basis for Mongolia's economy? (p. 644, pars. 5–6) **3.** What is Taiwan's economy based on? (p. 645, par. 3)
Step 5 **Prepare for** **Assessment**	**Alternative Assessment** Assign students to work in pairs to draw a political cartoon comparing the economies of Mongolia and Taiwan. Share the guidelines for art type activities and the specific guidelines for political cartoons on p. 25 of *Integrated Assessment*. Use these for evaluating students' cartoons. **Formal Assessment** Go over the test-taking strategies for TT91. Then assign the Section Quiz for Chapter 28 Section 2, on p. 437 of the *Formal Assessment* book.

ACTIVITY SHEET 28.2

Part A. Build Vocabulary

Key Terms Use the spaces below to make a drawing that helps you remember the meaning of each of the key terms, given below in **boldfaced** print.

economic tiger	Pacific Rim

Part B. Cooperative Work

Read the section and then work with your group to complete the comparison chart. Review and correct your answers in class.

	Mongolia	**Taiwan**
History, related to China		
Culture		
Economy		
Daily Life		

The Koreas: North and South

**Step 1
Activate Prior
Knowledge**

Write the phrase *the hermit kingdom* on the board and lead students in a **Brainstorming** activity about what a "hermit kingdom" might be liked. Write students' ideas on the board and save them for students to revise when they finish the section. Explain that in the 1600s and 1700s, Korea was known as "the hermit kingdom."

**Step 2
Preview Main
Ideas and
Language**

Connect Visually Have the class form groups of four and direct them to study the photograph on p. 647. They should compare this photo to those on pp. 606 and 607. Guide students to realize that the building on p. 647 is similar in style to China's Forbidden City (shown on p. 606) and that this probably indicates that Korea was greatly influenced by Chinese culture.

Build Vocabulary Display a wall map of the Korean Peninsula, pointing out North Korea and South Korea and the two capital cities (which are the key terms in Part A of Activity Sheet 28.3). Pronounce the names of the cities slowly for students. Then check students' comprehension by having them name the city you are pointing to. Tell students to label the map on the Activity Sheet. Go over the answers with the class.

**Step 3
Make Objectives
Explicit**

Write these objectives on the board. Have students read the objectives and then write a question based on each objective that they will answer after they have studied the section. Ask students to read their questions aloud and help clarify any misunderstandings. If students' first language is Spanish, have them read the lesson summary in the *Reading Study Guide* (English or Spanish).

• Summarize the history of North Korea and South Korea.

• Identify different influences on Korean culture.

• Discuss the effects of war and conflict on Korean life.

• Describe the economic and human resources of North and South Korea.

**Step 4
Support Student
Reading**

Cooperative Work Let students pair up to read the section, using the **SQ3R** method. Students should also work in their groups to fill in the chart in Part B of Activity Sheet 28.3. Go over answers in class.

On One's Own Preview the following questions by asking students what they understand them to mean. Then have students search for the answers while reading. Once students have finished, help them answer in complete sentences.

1. Which two countries have tried to control Korea and why? (p. 647, par. 4)

2. What happened in Korea after World War II? (p. 648, pars. 1–2)

3. Why would North and South Korea form an economic powerhouse if they were to unite? (p. 650, pars. 3–4)

**Step 5
Prepare for
Assessment**

Alternative Assessment Have students work in groups of three to complete the GeoActivity on p. 650. Share the guidelines for evaluating a Venn Diagram on p. 29 of *Integrated Assessment* and use these for evaluating students' work.

Formal Assessment Go over the test-taking strategies for TT92. Then assign the Section Quiz for Chapter 28 Section 3, on p. 438 of the *Formal Assessment* book.

ACTIVITY SHEET 28.3

Part A. Build Vocabulary

Key Places Label North Korea and South Korea. Then label the key places on the map below.

> Seoul
>
> Pyongyang

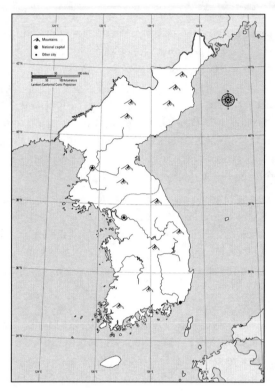

Part B. Cooperative Work

Work with your partner to read the section and complete the chart.
Go over the answers with the class.

	North Korea	**South Korea**
Political influences after 1945	1.	2.
Chinese cultural influences	3.	4.
Other cultural influences	5.	6.
Armaments	7.	8.
Economies	9.	10.
Population Patterns	11.	12.

Resources for English Learners
TE p. 652   RSG pp. 245–246, 247–248
RSG Audio   IA pp. 30–31   TT 93
FA pp. 439, 440–443, 444–447, 448–451   MLG

Japan

Step 1
Activate Prior Knowledge

Do a **Roundtable** activity for students to share what they already know about Japan. Encourage students to come up with questions based on things that they would like to learn about Japan. Write these questions on the board for students to return to after they complete the section.

Step 2
Preview Main Ideas and Language

Connect Visually Divide the class into groups of three and have them turn to the charts in the Regional Data File on pp. 616–617. Direct students to compare the information about Japan and the United States. They should focus on the information related to population and area.

Build Vocabulary Teach the key terms in Part A of Activity Sheet 28.4 by asking students to turn to the picture on p. 651 when you teach the term *samurai* and to the lefthand picture on p. 652 when you teach the word *shogun*. Use **Picture Imaging** to help students notice the samurai's armor and weapons and the shogun's dignified clothes and posture. Let students complete Part A on their own.

Step 3
Make Objectives Explicit

Write these objectives on the board and read them aloud to the class. Show students the questions they wrote in the Activate Prior Knowledge activity. Let students identify the objective that most closely matches the topic of each question. Use this opportunity to clarify students' understanding of the objectives. If students' first language is Spanish, have them read the lesson summary in the *Reading Study Guide* (English or Spanish).

- Describe different stages in Japanese history.
- Discuss Japan's economic development.
- Identify aspects of Japanese culture and modern life.

Step 4
Support Student Reading

Cooperative Work Have students work in groups of four, doing a **Jigsaw Reading** activity to complete the chart in Part B of Activity Sheet 28.4. Each student should answer two questions. Go over the answers with the class.

On One's Own Preview the following questions by asking students what they understand them to mean. Then have students search for the answers while reading. Once students have finished, help them answer in complete sentences.

1. What happened to Japan during World War II? (p. 652, pars. 3–4)

2. What are at the heart of Japan's economy? (p. 653, par. 2)

3. What are some examples of traditional Japanese culture? (p. 655, pars. 4–7)

4. Why is education important in Japan? (p. 655, par. 1)

Step 5
Prepare for Assessment

Alternative Assessment Let students pick a partner and work on the art activity described on TE p. 652. Share the general guidelines for evaluating oral presentations and the specific guidelines for evaluating oral reports on pp. 30–31 of *Integrated Assessment* and use these for evaluating students' presentations.

Formal Assessment Go over the test-taking strategies for TT93. You may want to use *Formal Assessment* Form A, the less-challenging assessment, or administer it as a practice test prior to formal testing with Form B or Form C.

ACTIVITY SHEET 28.4

Part A. Build Vocabulary

Key Terms Learn the meaning of the key terms. Then work with your partner to answer the questions.

> **samurai   shogun**

1. Which of these people would you expect to make decisions about how to repel Mongolian invaders sailing toward Japan? _____

2. Which of these people would you call on to protect you if you were a clan chief going to visit another clan chief? _____

Part B. Cooperative Work

Work with your group to fill in the chart. Correct the chart in class.

1. Between 400 and about 1900, which two different types of rulers headed the government, each at different times?	**1.**
2. When did Japan become a major military power?	**2.**
3. a. When did Japan become a very strong economic power? **b.** What activities are at the heart of Japan's economy?	**3. a.** **b.**
4. a. Which culture had a big influence on Japan? **b.** How does this influence show?	**4. a.** **b.**
5. What does Kyoto show about Japanese culture?	**5.**
6. What influences have Western nations had on Japanese culture?	**6.**
7. What is Japanese education like?	**7.**
8. How is Japanese society beginning to change?	**8.**

Resources for English Learners
RSG pp. 249–250   RSG Audio
IA p. 8   TT 94
FA p. 452   MLG

The Ring of Fire

Step 1
Activate Prior Knowledge

Do a **Round Robin** activity to have students name all the places they can think of that have earthquakes and/or volcanoes. Write students' answers on the board or the overhead. Then display a wall map and have students locate some or all of the different places on the map. Guide students to realize that many volcanoes and earthquake zones are located along the Pacific coasts of America and Asia.

Step 2
Preview Main Ideas and Language

Connect Visually Direct students to turn to the map of the Ring of Fire on p. 662 and ask them what the map shows and why the region has this title. Then have students form groups of three and locate some of the places from the Round Robin activity on this map. Students can also turn to the map on p. 37 to see the direction of plate movement in this region of the earth. Remind students that the movement of the earth's tectonic plates causes earthquakes and volcanoes.

Build Vocabulary Review or reteach the key term in Part A of Activity Sheet 29.1. Then let students work with a partner to complete Part A. Go over the answers in class.

Step 3
Make Objectives Explicit

Write these objectives on the overhead or on the board and read them aloud to the class. Have students turn to a partner in the classroom and explain in their own words what they will be learning in the section, based on the objectives. If students' first language is Spanish, have them read the lesson summary in the *Reading Study Guide* (English or Spanish).

- Describe the physical forces that have caused the formation of the Ring of Fire.

- Describe the geology of Japan.

- Discuss issues related to disaster preparedness.

Step 4
Support Student Reading

Cooperative Work Have students form groups of three to read the section and complete the chart in Part B of Activity Sheet 29.1. Go over the answers with the class. Then use an **Inside-Outside Circles** activity to reinforce the information.

On One's Own Preview the following questions by asking students what they understand them to mean. Then have students search for the answers while reading. Once students have finished, help them answer in complete sentences.

1. What causes earthquakes? (p. 661, pars. 3–5)

2. Why do the Japanese islands exist and why are they under geologic threat? (p. 662, par. 1)

3. How do people in Japan prepare for disasters? (p. 663, par. 4)

Step 5
Prepare for Assessment

Alternative Assessment Have students pair up and study the map on p. 664. Direct them to cover up the questions at the bottom of the page and make up three questions about the map. Pairs should get together to swap questions. Share the Standards for Evaluating a Group Discussion on p. 8 of *Integrated Assessment* and use them for evaluating students' interactions.

Formal Assessment Go over the test-taking strategies for TT94. Then assign the Section Quiz for Chapter 29 Section 1, on p. 452 of the *Formal Assessment* book.

ACTIVITY SHEET 29.1

Part A. Build Vocabulary

Key Terms Work with your partner to fill in the **Sunshine Outline.**
Go over your answers with the class.

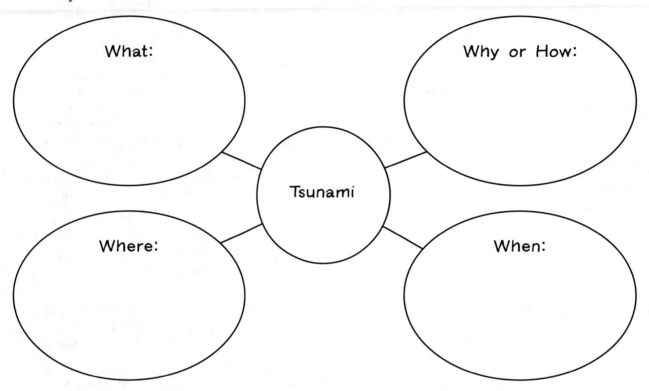

What:

Why or How:

Tsunami

Where:

When:

Part B. Cooperative Work

Work with your group to read the section and fill in the chart. Go over
your answers with the class.

Cause	Effects (in Japan)	Solutions to resulting problems
The Pacific oceanic plate is colliding with the Eurasian continental plate; stress builds up at plate boundaries.	1.	4.
	2.	5.
	3.	6.

Resources for English Learners
RSG pp. 251–252   RSG Audio
IDR9 pp. 26–27, 44   TT 95a, TT 95b
FA p. 453   MLG

Trade and Prosperity

Step 1 **Activate Prior Knowledge**	Write the phrase *Jakota Triangle* on the board and let students guess what this means. Write down their answers. Point out that the name contains the first two letters of three different East Asian countries. Give students time to figure out what the countries are. Explain that these countries have strong economies and are prosperous.
Step 2 **Preview Main Ideas and Language**	**Connect Visually** Have students form small groups and turn to the graphs on p. 666. Encourage students to use the graphs to make two generalizations about the trading partners of the Jakota Triangle countries. Ask students to share their generalizations in a class discussion. **Build Vocabulary** Divide students into groups of five and have them learn the meaning of each key term listed in Part A of Activity Sheet 29.2, using the textbook section for context. Students should complete Part A on their own. Go over the answers with the class to clarify understanding.
Step 3 **Make Objectives Explicit**	Write these objectives on the board and read them aloud to the class. Check students' comprehension using Thumbs Up/Down or another **Signals** activity. Students who understand the objectives can explain them to students who do not understand them. If students' first language is Spanish, have them read the lesson summary in the *Reading Study Guide* (English or Spanish). • Describe how East Asian economies have grown since they opened their markets to the West. • Discuss the some of the problems East Asian nations have experienced related to their economic growth.
Step 4 **Support Student Reading**	**Cooperative Work** Divide the class in groups of four and have students do a **Jigsaw Reading** activity to complete the chart in Part B of Activity Sheet 29.2. Go over the answers with the class. **On One's Own** Preview the following questions by asking students what they understand them to mean. Then have students search for the answers while reading. Once students have finished, help them answer in complete sentences. **1.** Why did trade between the East and the West increase after World War II? (p. 666, par. 1) **2.** How does Japan's economy show how the global economy works? (p. 666, par. 2) **3.** What are some problems with East Asian economies that arose or became apparent in the 1990s? (p. 667, pars. 1–4)
Step 5 **Prepare for Assessment**	**Alternative Assessment** Assign students to work in groups of three on the map activity on pp. 26–27 of Unit 9 *In-Depth Resources*. Assess their work based their interactions and on their answers, given on IDR p. 44. **Formal Assessment** Go over the test-taking strategies for TT95a and TT95b. Then assign the Section Quiz for Chapter 29 Section 2, found on p. 453 of the *Formal Assessment* book.

ACTIVITY SHEET 29.2

Part A. Build Vocabulary

Key Terms Learn the meaning of each key term with your group. Then match each key term with its definition.

_____ **1.** currency

_____ **2.** global economy

_____ **3.** recession

_____ **4.** stocks

_____ **5.** sweatshop

a. an extended slowdown or decline in general business activity

b. an economic system in which nations are dependent on each other for goods and services

c. paper money in circulation (that people use for business transactions)

d. a workplace in which people work long hours under poor conditions and are paid very little

e. shares in a business that can be bought and sold

Part B. Cooperative Work

Work with your group to read the section and fill in the chart. Go over your answers with the class.

Cause	Effect
1.	opening of the East to the West
2.	economic recession
3.	prevention of global economic turndown
4.	workplace reform in East Asia

Resources for English Learners	
TE p. 669	RSG pp. 253–254, 255–256
RSG Audio	TT 96 MLG
FA pp. 454, 455–458, 459–462, 463–466	

Population and the Quality of Life

Step 1 Activate Prior Knowledge	Write the title of the Case Study on the board, posing it as a question for the class in a **Brainstorming** activity. Write students' answers on the board and save them for students to revise or add to when they complete the section.
Step 2 Preview Main Ideas and Language	**Connect Visually** Direct students to form groups of three to compare the population density map of East Asia on p. 615 with the population density map of the United States and Canada on p. 107. What do students notice when they make this comparison? Then have students look at the photo at the bottom of p. 609. Encourage students to share their experiences being in dense crowds.

Build Vocabulary Present the definitions of the terms listed in Part A of Activity Sheet 29.3 and check students' comprehension. Have students work in pairs to complete Part A. Go over the answers to clarify understanding. |
| **Step 3 Make Objectives Explicit** | Write these objectives on the overhead or on the board and read them aloud to the class. For each objective, have students write a personal goal for studying the section. If students' first language is Spanish, have them read the lesson summary in the *Reading Study Guide* (English or Spanish).

• Examine the patterns, problems, and solutions related to population growth in East Asia.

• Describe how the quality of life has changed in East Asia since the 1950s.

• Analyze different perspectives on population and quality of life in East Asia. |
| **Step 4 Support Student Reading** | **Cooperative Work** Divide the class into groups of five, so that one student in each group reads one of the primary sources on pp. 670–671. Students should work on a **Double-Column Note-Taking** activity on their primary source, using Part B of Activity Sheet 29.3. Ask one student in each group to be the peer tutor, to help students understand difficult vocabulary. The group should come together to teach one another about the primary sources, sharing their notes and their ideas.

On One's Own Preview the following questions by asking students what they understand them to mean. Then have students search for the answers while reading. Once students have finished, help them answer in complete sentences.

1. How developed was East Asia in the middle of the 20th century? (p. 668, par. 3)

2. How had East Asia changed between the 1950s and the 1990s? (p. 669, par. 2)

3. What are some environmental stresses that occur with unrestricted or even modest population growth? (p. 668, par. 5; p. 669, par. 4–5) |
| **Step 5 Prepare for Assessment** | **Alternative Assessment** Have students work in groups of five to complete the Case Study Project. Share the Grading Rubric on TE p. 669 with students and use it to evaluate their project.

Formal Assessment Go over the test-taking strategies for TT96. You may want to use *Formal Assessment* Form A, the less-challenging assessment, or administer it as a practice test prior to formal testing with Form B or Form C. |

ACTIVITY SHEET 29.3

Part A. Build Vocabulary

Key Terms Go over the definitions with your class. Then work with your partner to answer the questions.

> **family planning:** a program to regulate the number and spacing of children in a family through the use of one or more methods of birth control
>
> **fertility rate:** the average number of children a woman in a particular group or nation would have during her lifetime
>
> **life expectancy:** the average length of time the person in a group or a nation is expected to live
>
> **sanitation:** safe disposal of sewage

1. When this is high, a country's population may grow very, very rapidly. What is it? _____
2. The Chinese government developed a program for this to help slow its population growth. What is it? _____
3. When a city or region is overcrowded, there may be problems with this, because treatment facilities cannot handle all the human wastes. What is this? _____
4. When there is widespread poverty, this may be low, because people are not able to get the medical care that they need? What is this? _____

Part B. Cooperative Work

Work with your group to read and take notes on the primary sources on pp. 670–671. Go over the answers with the class.

Notes on Primary Sources		
Primary Source	Note Taking	Note Making
Bar graph on projected population growth		
Policy statement by President Clinton, 1998		
News analysis from online source about Asia		
Fact sheet from an organization that advocates family planning in East Asia, 1997		

Resources for English Learners
RSG pp. 257–258   TE p. 703   RSG Audio
IA pp. 7, 28, 29   TT 97a, TT 97b   FA p. 467
MLG

Landforms and Resources

**Step 1
Activate Prior Knowledge**

Display a wall map that shows Southeast Asia, Oceania, and Australia, and lead students in a **Round Robin** activity to discuss what they notice about the region. Write students' responses on the board and save them for students to add to or revise after they complete the section. Point out that this region includes many islands, some of which are in the center of the Pacific Ocean.

**Step 2
Preview Main Ideas and Language**

Connect Visually Direct students to work in groups of three to study the diagram on p. 690 and the photo on p. 691. Students should take turns explaining the process by which the two different types of islands form and asking and answering questions about these processes.

Build Vocabulary Review the **Frayer Method** and then have students pair up to use this method to learn the key terms in Part A of Activity Sheet 30.1. Students can work together to complete Part A.

**Step 3
Make Objectives Explicit**

Write these objectives on the overhead or on the board and read them aloud to the class. For each objective, ask students to look through the section and identify a map, a paragraph, or a set of paragraphs that might help them learn about that objective. If students' first language is Spanish, have them read the lesson summary in the *Reading Study Guide* (English or Spanish).

- Describe the landforms and resources of Southeast Asia.
- Describe the landforms and resources of the Pacific islands, New Zealand, Australia, and Antarctica.

**Step 4
Support Student Reading**

Cooperative Work Divide the class into groups of four to complete the landforms in Part B of Activity Sheet 30.1. Refer students to the maps on pp. 678–679 and p. 689 if they need help locating countries, landforms, and islands. Go over the answers with the class and then do a **Carousel Review** to consolidate students' understanding of the physical geography of these regions.

On One's Own Preview the following questions by asking students what they understand them to mean. Then have students search for the answers while reading. Once students have finished, help them answer in complete sentences.

1. What are the two peninsulas that make up Southeast Asia? (p. 689, par. 3)

2. Why does Southeast Asia have fertile soil? (p. 690, par. 4)

3. How do the two types of islands in Oceania differ? (p. 691, par. 2)

4. In terms of landforms, how do New Zealand and Australia differ? (p. 692, pars. 2–3)

**Step 5
Prepare for Assessment**

Alternative Assessment Have students work in small groups to do the Internet Activity on p. 703. Share the grading rubric on TE p. 703 and the guidelines for evaluating cooperative activities, information assessing activities, and reports on pp. 7, 28, and 29 of *Integrated Assessment* and use these for evaluating students' projects.

Formal Assessment Go over the test-taking strategies for TT97a and TT97b. Then assign the Section Quiz for Chapter 30 Section 1, on p. 467 of the *Formal Assessment* book.

ACTIVITY SHEET 30.1

Part A. Build Vocabulary

Key Terms Learn the meaning the key terms with your partner. Then work together to answer the questions.

> **archipelago**   **high island**   **low island**

1. Why is a high island high? _____

2. Why are low islands low? _____

3. Do you think it would be possible to have an archipelago of low islands? Explain.

_____

4. Do you think it would be possible to have an archipelago of high islands? Explain.

_____

Part B. Cooperative Work

Work with your group to label the map with 18 of the countries, landforms, and islands mentioned in the section. Review your map with the class.

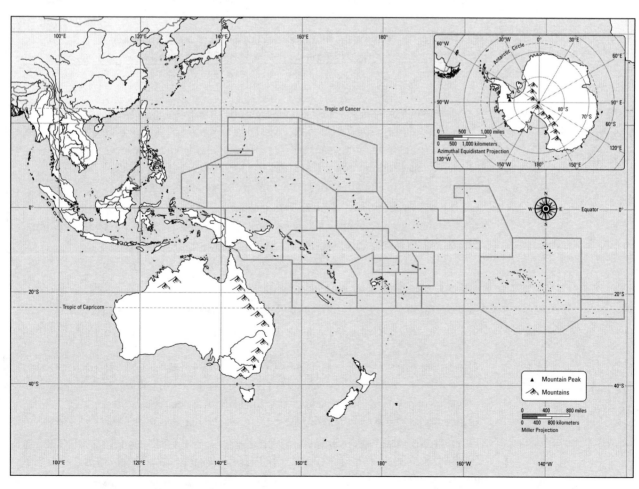

Resources for English Learners
TE p. 697   RSG pp. 259–260   RSG Audio
IA p. 32   TT 98a, TT 98b   FA p. 468
MLG

Climate and Vegetation

**Step 1
Activate Prior
Knowledge**

Write the phrase *white desert* on the board or the overhead and ask students to explain what they think of when they hear the phrase. Record all answers and then let the class vote on what they think is most likely. Explain that Antarctica is sometimes called a white desert, because although it is covered with snow, it is also very dry. Point out that Antarctica is one of two continents that they will study in this unit, which includes regions of great climatic variety.

**Step 2
Preview Main
Ideas and
Language**

Connect Visually Have students form groups of four or five and compare the photos in the middle of p. 674 and at the top of p. 695. Have them make a list of descriptive words related to the two pictures and the differences they show. Let the groups share their lists with the class.

Build Vocabulary Review how to use a **Word Square.** Then direct students to use the Word Square to define the key term in Part A of Activity Sheet 30.2. Let students share their Word Squares in small groups. Circulate among the groups to clarify understanding.

**Step 3
Make Objectives
Explicit**

Write these objectives on the board. Have students read the objectives and then write a question based on each objective that they will answer after they have studied the section. Ask students to read their questions aloud and help clarify understanding. If students' first language is Spanish, have them read the lesson summary in the *Reading Study Guide* (English or Spanish).

- Describe the tropical climate zones and vegetation of Southeast Asia and Oceania.
- Compare the moderate climates of Australia and New Zealand.
- Compare the deserts of Australia and Antarctic.

**Step 4
Support Student
Reading**

Cooperative Work Pair students up for **Peer Tutoring** and have them work together to read the section and complete the chart in Part B of Activity Sheet 30.2. You may wish to display one or more wall maps of the regions for students to use as reference as they read. When students have finished the chart, go over the answers with the class.

On One's Own Preview the following questions by asking students what they understand them to mean. Then have students search for the answers while reading. Once students have finished, help them answer in complete sentences.

1. What type of climates cover most of Southeast Asia and Oceania? (p. 694, par. 3)

2. Why don't low islands generally have diverse vegetation? (p. 695, par. 3)

3. Of the places mentioned, where are the deserts located? (p. 697, par. 1)

**Step 5
Prepare for
Assessment**

Alternative Assessment Have students pair up to do the Reteaching Activity on TE p. 697. Share the guidelines for writing activities and written answers on p. 32 of *Integrated Assessment* and use them for evaluating students' paragraphs.

Formal Assessment Go over the test-taking strategies for TT98a and TT98b. Then assign the Section Quiz for Chapter 30 Section 2, on p. 468 of the *Formal Assessment* book.

ACTIVITY SHEET 30.2

Part A. Build Vocabulary

Key Terms Use the Word Square to help you define the key term. Share your completed Word Squares in a small group.

Word: outback Translation:	Symbol or Picture:
My meaning: Dictionary definition:	Sentence:

Part B. Cooperative Work

Work with your partner to complete the chart. Go over the answers with the class.

Location	Climate	Vegetation
Coastal Myanmar, Thailand, Vietnam, Oceania, and most of Malaysia, Indonesia, and the Philippines		
The more northern and inland parts of Myanmar, Thailand, Laos, Cambodia, Vietnam, Oceania, and northern Australia		
The northern part of Australia's east coast and the northernmost parts of Vietnam, Laos, Thailand, and Myanmar		
New Zealand and the southern part of Australia's east coast		
Central Australia		
Antarctica		

Resources for English Learners
RSG pp. 261–262, 263–264   RSG Audio
IA pp. 7, 28   TT 99   MLG
FA pp. 469, 470–473, 474–477, 478–481

Human-Environment Interaction

**Step 1
Activate Prior
Knowledge**

Display a map that shows Southeast Asia and Oceania. Explain to students that the islands of Oceania were probably first settled by people who came from Southeast Asia. Lead a **Brainstorming** activity about how people might have reached these far-flung islands. Write down students' ideas and keep them for the class to revise in the next activity.

**Step 2
Preview Main
Ideas and
Language**

Connect Visually Ask students to form groups of four and to turn to the illustration on p. 699. Was this the form of transportation they envisioned Pacific Islanders using? How is it similar to their ideas? How is it different? Let the groups share their ideas with the class, revising the list they made.

Build Vocabulary Go over the definitions of the two boldfaced terms in the chart in Part A of Activity Sheet 30.3. Ask students to work with a partner to complete the **Semantic Feature Analysis.** Go over the answers with the class.

**Step 3
Make Objectives
Explicit**

Write these objectives on the board and read them aloud to the class. Check students' comprehension using Number of Fingers or another **Signals** activity. Students who understand the objectives can explain them to students who do not understand them. If students' first language is Spanish, have them read the lesson summary in the *Reading Study Guide* (English or Spanish).

• Explain how ancient islanders traveled the Pacific.

• Discuss the invasion of rabbits in Australia and methods of controlling them.

• Describe the nuclear tests done in the Pacific and the effects they had on people and the environment.

**Step 4
Support Student
Reading**

Cooperative Work Divide the class into groups of three and have students do **Reciprocal Teaching** to study the section. Direct them to work together to fill in the chart in Part B of Activity Sheet 30.3. Go over the answers with the class.

On One's Own Preview the following questions by asking students what they understand them to mean. Then have students search for the answers while reading. Once students have finished, help them answer in complete sentences.

1. How did Pacific Islanders navigate the ocean? (p. 698, pars. 3–4)

2. How have Australians tried to control their rabbit problem? (p. 700, pars. 1–3)

3. Why are the Bikini Islands uninhabitable now? (p. 700, pars. 7–8; p. 701, top, par. 2)

**Step 5
Prepare for
Assessment**

Alternative Assessment Assign the GeoActivity on p. 703 for students to complete in small groups. Share the guidelines for cooperative activities, the guidelines for information assessing activities, and the guidelines for maps on pp. 7 and 28 of *Integrated Assessment*s. Use these guidelines to evaluate students' interactions and their maps.

Formal Assessment Go over the test-taking strategies for TT99. You may want to use *Formal Assessment* Form A, the less-challenging assessment, or administer it as a practice test prior to formal testing with Form B or Form C.

ACTIVITY SHEET 30.3

Part A. Build Vocabulary

Key Terms Work with your partner to complete the **Semantic Features Analysis** for the key terms, in **boldfaced** type.

	Type of boat	Used close to shore	Used for traveling on the open sea	Has two hulls	Has sails	Could have a cabin	Has a frame with an attached float to one side
voyaging canoe							
outrigger canoe							

Part B. Cooperative Work

Work with your group to complete the chart on human-environment interactions in Oceania and Australia. Go over the answers with the class.

Person or People	How they interacted with the environment	Effects on the environment	Effects on people
Ancient Pacific Islanders			
Australian Thomas Austin			
U.S. government officials			

Resources for English Learners
OMA pp. 4, 104   RSG pp. 265–266
RSG Audio   TT 100a, TT 100b
FA p. 482   MLG   IA pp. 7, 28

Southeast Asia

Step 1 **Activate Prior Knowledge**	Hand out copies of an outline map of the world, such as the one on p. 4 of *Outline Maps with Activities*. Ask students to locate Southeast Asia, label it on their maps, and check their maps against the map on p. 704.
Step 2 **Preview Main Ideas and Language**	**Connect Visually** Write the names of the ten countries that make up Southeast Asia on the board. Hand out to pairs of students copies of a map of Southeast Asia, such as the one on p. 104 of *Outline Maps and Activities*. Ask students to work together to label as many of the countries as they can. **Build Vocabulary** Introduce the term *mandala* and define it for students. Point out that this word is a homonym, a word that has the same sound and the same spelling as another word—one that they learned when they studied South Asia. Have students tell you the definition of the term they previously learned, using the textbook, if necessary. Then have students work in groups of three and use **Word Imaging** to contrast the two meanings of *mandala*. Direct them to use the space in Part A of Activity Sheet 31.1 to draw a picture that helps them remember the meaning the homonyms.
Step 3 **Make Objectives Explicit**	Write these objectives on the overhead or on the board and read them aloud to the class. Have students identify what they think is the most important word or phrase in each objective. If students' first language is Spanish, have them read the lesson summary in the *Reading Study Guide* (English or Spanish). • Summarize Southeast Asian precolonial history. • Discuss the effects of European colonialism. • Compare the economies of different countries in Southeast Asia. • Describe the diverse cultures and lifestyles in Southeast Asia.
Step 4 **Support Student Reading**	**Cooperative Work** Have students divide into groups of four to fill out the spider diagram in Part B of Activity Sheet 31.1. Go over the answers and use **Slates** or another **Signals** activity to check students' comprehension. **On One's Own** Preview the following questions by asking students what they understand them to mean. Then have students search for the answers while reading. **1.** What were *mandalas?* (p. 705, par. 6) **2.** How did European colonialism affect Southeast Asia? (p. 706, pars. 4–6) **3.** How did the Vietnam War affect the economy of Southeast Asia? (p. 707, par. 6) **4.** What arts are important in different parts of Southeast Asia? (p. 708, pars. 4–5)
Step 5 **Prepare for Assessment**	**Alternative Assessment** Divide the class in groups of four to do the GeoActivity on p. 709. Share the guidelines for evaluating cooperative activities, information assessing activities, and charts on pp. 7 and 28 of *Integrated Assessment* and use these for evaluating students' projects. **Formal Assessment** Go over the test-taking strategies for TT100a and TT100b. Then assign the Section Quiz for Chapter 31 Section 1, found on p. 482 of the *Formal Assessment* book.

ACTIVITY SHEET 31.1

Part A. Build Vocabulary

Key Terms Use the spaces below to make drawings that help you
remember the difference between the homonyms.

mandala, as related to Buddhism	mandala, as related to Southeast Asian political history

Part B. Cooperative Work

Work with your group to read the section and fill in the spider diagram.
Go over your answers with the class.

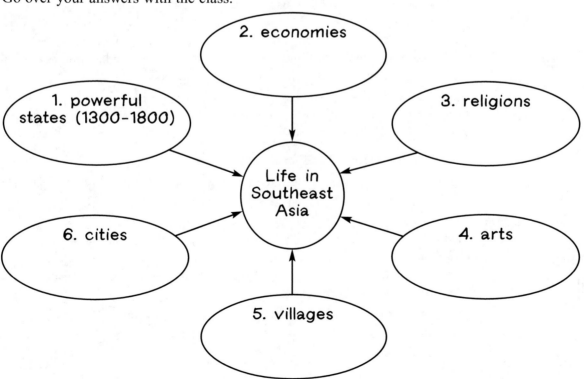

2. economies

1. powerful states (1300–1800)

3. religions

Life in Southeast Asia

6. cities

4. arts

5. villages

Resources for English Learners
RSG pp. 267–268   RSG Audio   OMA p. 106
TT 101a, TT 101b   IA p. 28   FA p. 483
MLG

Oceania

Step 1 **Activate Prior Knowledge**	Lead a **Brainstorming** activity about what the name *Oceania* tells about the subregion by that name. Record students' answers on the board. Ask students to discuss how the physical setting of the region might have affected the lives of the people living in the region. When students are done brainstorming, work with the class to categorize the answers and make a **Cluster Map** based on them.
Step 2 **Preview Main Ideas and Language**	**Connect Visually** Ask students to turn to the map on p. 713 and continue the class discussion. Ask students how many miles Oceania spans, both north to south and east to west. Direct students to read out the names of some of the different islands, island nations, and island groups. **Build Vocabulary** Go over the definitions of the terms defined in Part A of Activity Sheet 31.2. Check to see whether students understood the definitions, using any of the **Signals** activities, and redefine terms if needed. Have students work in pairs to complete the Part A.
Step 3 **Make Objectives Explicit**	Write these objectives on the overhead or on the board and read them aloud to the class. For each objective, have students write a personal goal for studying the section. If students' first language is Spanish, have them read the lesson summary in the *Reading Study Guide* (English or Spanish). • Discuss different stages in the history of Oceania. • Describe the economy of different Pacific Islands in Oceania. • Describe the cultures and lifestyles of Oceania.
Step 4 **Support Student Reading**	**Cooperative Work** Divide the class into groups of three to read the section, using the **SQ3R** method. As students read, they should work together to fill in the chart in Part B of Activity Sheet 31.2. Go over answers with the class. **On One's Own** Preview the following questions by asking students what they understand them to mean. Then have students search for the answers while reading. Once students have finished, help them answer in complete sentences. **1.** How were the Pacific Islands of Oceania first settled? (p. 712, par. 4) **2.** Beginning in the 1800s, what caused many island societies to decline? (p. 713, pars. 3–4) **3.** What are some main crops of Oceania? (p. 714, par. 2; p. 715, pars. 3–4) **4.** What are some recent changes in Oceania? (p. 715, pars. 6–7)
Step 5 **Prepare for Assessment**	**Alternative Assessment** Have students pair up and turn to the chart on p. 686. Using copies of the outline map of Oceania on p. 106 of *Outline Maps and Activities,* students should locate and label the territories listed in the chart. They can use a wall map or the map on pp. 680–681 as a reference. Share the guidelines for evaluating maps on p. 28 of *Integrated Activities* and use them for evaluating students' work. **Formal Assessment** Go over the test-taking strategies for TT101a and TT1010b. Then assign the Section Quiz for Chapter 31 Section 2, found on p. 483 of the *Formal Assessment* book.

ACTIVITY SHEET 31.2

Part A. Build Vocabulary

Key Terms Go over the definitions with your class. Then work with your partner to fill in the blanks with the terms that best complete the sentences. You may need to make one or more of the nouns plural.

hunter-gatherer: a person who lives by hunting, fishing, and collecting wild food to feed himself or herself and other family or group members

missionary: a person sent from a foreign country who comes to try to convert local people to a particular religion

shantytown: a section of town that is made up mainly of small, crudely built dwellings

subsistence activities: activities that allow a family to produce only the food, clothing, and shelter that they themselves need

taro: a plant with a starchy root used for food

1. People who support themselves by growing and making what they need engage in _____.

2. _____ are people who feed themselves on wild foods that they get from their environment.

3. One crop that is common in Oceania is _____, which has a starchy root that people boil or grind to make flour for bread.

4. European _____ who came to Oceania tried to convince Pacific Islanders to adopt Christianity.

5. When a city grows rapidly, there may be a shortage of housing; people use anything they can find to build shelters on vacant land in or at the edge of the city. Such areas are called _____.

Part B. Cooperative Work

Work with your group to read the section and fill in the chart. Go over your answers with the class.

History of Oceania	
How Oceania came to be settled in prehistoric times	
Contact with peoples from Europe, 1500s	
Contact with peoples from Europe, 1800s and 1900s	
Recent history	

Australia, New Zealand, and Antarctica

Step 1
Activate Prior
Knowledge

Do a **K-W-L** activity with the class on Australia, New Zealand, and Antarctica. Record what students know and what they want to learn about each. Then fill in the L section of the class charts after the next activity and when students complete the section.

Step 2
Preview Main
Ideas and
Language

Connect Visually Have students survey the section, looking at the illustrations and skimming the section heads and subheads. Then return to the K-W-L charts and ask students if there is anything else they want to add to the three columns.

Build Vocabulary Go over the definitions of the boldfaced terms in the chart in Part A of Activity Sheet 31.3. Use one of the **Signals** activities to check comprehension. Have students pair up to complete the **Semantic Feature Analysis.**

Step 3
Make Objectives
Explicit

Write these objectives on the board. Have students turn to a partner and explain in their own words what they will be learning. If students' first language is Spanish, have them read the lesson summary in the *Reading Study Guide* (English or Spanish).

- Explain how Australia and New Zealand became European outposts.
- Identify important national issues in modern Australia and New Zealand.
- Describe the economies of Australia and New Zealand.
- Compare cultures and lifestyles of Australia and New Zealand.

Step 4
Support Student
Reading

Cooperative Work Have students divide into groups of four to fill out the chart in Part B of Activity Sheet 31.3. Two students should work together to fill in the Australia column and two students should work together to fill in the New Zealand column. The pairs should come together to share answers. Go over the answers with the entire class, using a **Numbered Heads Together** activity.

On One's Own Preview the following questions by asking students what they understand them to mean. Then have students search for the answers while reading. Once students have finished, help them answer in complete sentences.

1. Who were the original inhabitants of Australia and New Zealand? (p. 718, par. 5; p. 719, par. 1)

2. What mineral lured Europeans to Australian and New Zealand in the 1800s? (p. 719, par. 6)

3. Who owns Antarctica? (p. 720, par. 5; map)

Step 5
Prepare for
Assessment

Alternative Assessment Have students form groups of four or five to do the Antarctica activity on TE p. 720. Share the guidelines for evaluating cooperative activities, writing activities, and proposals on pp. 7, 32, and 34 of *Integrated Assessment* and use these for evaluating students' projects.

Formal Assessment Go over the test-taking strategies for TT102. You may want to use *Formal Assessment* Form A, the less-challenging assessment, or administer it as a practice test prior to formal testing with Form B or Form C.

ACTIVITY SHEET 31.3

Part A. Build Vocabulary

Key Terms Work with your partner to complete the **Semantic Feature Analysis** for the key terms, in **boldfaced** type.

	Native to Australia	Native to New Zealand	Lived in their homeland for more than 40,000 years	Originally came from mainland Asia	Originally came from Polynesia	Originally lived solely by hunting and gathering	Originally lived by farming as well as by fishing and hunting
Aboriginal people							
Maori							

Part B. Cooperative Work

Work with your group to read the section and to complete the chart.
Go over your answers with the class.

	Australia	**New Zealand**
Original Inhabitants	1.	2.
European Settlement	3.	4.
Rights and Issues	5.	6.
Economy	7.	8.
Cultures	9.	10.
Modern Life	11.	12.

Resources for English Learners
RSG pp. 273–274   RSG Audio   MLG
IA pp. 7, 30, 31   TT 103   FA p. 497
IDR10 pp. 28–29

Aboriginal Land Claims

Step 1
Activate Prior Knowledge

Have students do a **Think-Pair-Share** activity to discuss the benefits and drawbacks of being a member of a minority group. Point out that the Aboriginal people, a minority group in Australia, have some of the same concerns as many groups of Native Americans in this country.

Step 2
Preview Main Ideas and Language

Connect Visually Explain that one of the concerns Aboriginals of Australia share with Native Americans relates to the status of the land their ancestors used to live on. Direct students to turn to the map on p. 728. Ask students where Aboriginal peoples currently have been given rights to land. Direct them to turn to the climate map on p. 683 to determine what most of this land is like.

Build Vocabulary Have students work in small groups using **Peer Vocabulary Teaching** to learn the definitions of the terms given in Part A of Activity Sheet 32.1. Circulate among groups to clarify understanding. Then ask students to work individually to complete Part A. Let students share their answers.

Step 3
Make Objectives Explicit

Write these objectives on the board and read them aloud to the class. Check students' comprehension using Thumbs Up/Thumbs Down or another **Signals** Activity. Students who understand the objectives can explain them to students who do not understand them. If students' first language is Spanish, have them read the lesson summary in the *Reading Study Guide* (English or Spanish).

- Describe the process by which Aboriginal people lost their land and suffered from forced assimilation.
- Discuss the issues related to land claims in Australia.
- Outline the steps by which Aboriginals have regained rights to some land.

Step 4
Support Student Reading

Cooperative Work Let students work in groups of three or four to read the section and complete the chart in Part B of Activity Sheet 32.1. Go over the answers with the class. Then organize a **Carousel Review** to reinforce the information.

On One's Own Preview the following questions by asking students what they understand them to mean. Then have students search for the answers while reading. Once students have finished, help them answer in complete sentences.

1. What was the doctrine of *Terra Nullius* and how did it affect the Aboriginal peoples? (p. 727, par. 4)
2. What happened in the *Mabo* Case? (p. 728, par. 6)
3. Why did the Australian government amend the *Wik* decision? (p. 729, pars. 3–4)

Step 5
Prepare for Assessment

Alternative Assessment Assign the case study project on Aboriginal land claims on pp. 28–29 of Unit 10, *In Depth Resources*. Share the Standards for Evaluating a Cooperative Activity and the guidelines for oral presentations on pp. 7, 30, and 31 of *Integrated Assessment*s. Use these guidelines for evaluating students' presentations.

Formal Assessment Go over the test-taking strategies for TT103. Then assign the Section Quiz for Chapter 32 Section 1, on p. 497 of the *Formal Assessment* book.

ACTIVITY SHEET 32.1

Part A. Build Vocabulary

Key Terms Go over the definitions of the key terms with your group.
Then write sentences that include each key term, as directed below.

> **assimilation:** the process by which a minority group gives up its
> culture and adopts the culture of the majority group
>
> **claim:** a demand for something; the right to demand something
>
> **lawsuit:** a court proceeding to recover a right or to bring a claim

1. Use the word *claim* in a sentence that shows what Aboriginal peoples were
fighting for.

_____

2. Use the word *lawsuit* in a sentence that relates to how people define and
redefine their rights through legal action.

_____

3. Use the word *assimilation* in a sentence that explains your own ideas about the process.

_____

Part B. Cooperative Work

Work with your group to read the section and fill in the chart. (The first
item has been done as an example.) Go over your answers with the class.

Year	Event related to the law or government action	Effect on Aboriginal peoples
1788	British declared Australia *Terra Nullius*	Aboriginal people had no rights to the land, based on British law
1909–1969		
1967		
1972		
1976		
1985		
1992		
1996		

Resources for English Learners
Video: *Singapore: Industrialization and Migration*   MLG
RSG pp. 275–276   RSG Audio   IA p. 32
TE p. 732   TT 104   FA p. 498

Industrialization Sparks Change

Step 1
Activate Prior Knowledge

In a class discussion, let students share what they know about rapid industrialization and its effects. Make a cause-effects chart on the board and let students come up with as many effects as they can, through **Brainstorming.** Encourage students to think about both positive and negative effects.

Step 2
Preview Main Ideas and Language

Connect Visually Show students part of the video *Singapore: Industrialization and Migration.* Refer to the Teacher's Resource Book for *The Voyageur Experience in World Geography,* p. 93, and show the sequence that includes the discussion of immigration with Kenneth Lim.

Build Vocabulary Review how to use an **Anticipation Guide,** which forms Part A of Activity Sheet 32.2. Students should first fill in their individual (true/false) responses. Next they should discuss each statement with a small group and fill in a second set of responses. Allow time after students have read the section to complete the "Textbook" column and to correct any false answers.

Step 3
Make Objectives Explicit

Write these objectives on the board. Have students read the objectives and then write a question based on each objective that they will answer after they have studied the section. Ask students to read their questions aloud and help clarify any misunderstandings. If students' first language is Spanish, have them read the lesson summary in the *Reading Study Guide* (English or Spanish).

- Identify reasons for urban growth in Southeast Asia and discuss effects of this growth.
- Analyze effects of industrialization on Southeast Asian economies and on the environment.

Step 4
Support Student Reading

Cooperative Work Direct students to survey the graphic organizer in Part B of Activity Sheet 32.2 to help them focus on the kind of information they should look for after they begin reading. Then have students form groups of four to read the section and complete Part B. Go over the answers with the class.

On One's Own Preview the following questions by asking students what they understand them to mean. Then have students search for the answers while reading. Once students have finished, help them answer in complete sentences.

1. What factors push people out of rural areas? (p. 730, pars. 4–5; p. 731, pars. 1–2)

2. How does industrialization affect cities? (p. 731, pars. 6–8)

3. What are some economic and environmental effects of industrialization? (p. 732, pars. 1–5)

Step 5
Prepare for Assessment

Alternative Assessment Have students work in pairs to do the Reteaching Activity on TE p. 732. Students can brainstorm ideas together, but then they should each write their own letter. Share the guidelines for writing activities and for letters on p. 32 of *Integrated Assessment.* Use these for evaluating students' letters.

Formal Assessment Go over the test-taking strategies for TT104. Then assign the Section Quiz for Chapter 32 Section 2, on p. 498 of the *Formal Assessment* book.

ACTIVITY SHEET 32.2

Part A. Build Vocabulary

Key Terms Work individually and then with your group to fill in the first two columns of the Anticipation Guide. Fill in the third column after you have read the entire section. Correct any false answers.

You	Group	Textbook	Topic—Changes in Southeast Asia Due to Industrialization
			1. Factories are often located out in the country, where there is a lot of space for big buildings. For this reason, **industrialization** often goes along with cities losing population and becoming smaller and smaller.
			2. People usually do not leave their homes without strong reasons to do so. Such reasons can be categorized as **push-pull factors:** push factors drive people away from one place while pull factors draw them toward another place.

Part B. Cooperative Work

Work with your group to read the section and fill in the graphic organizer. Go over your answers with the class.

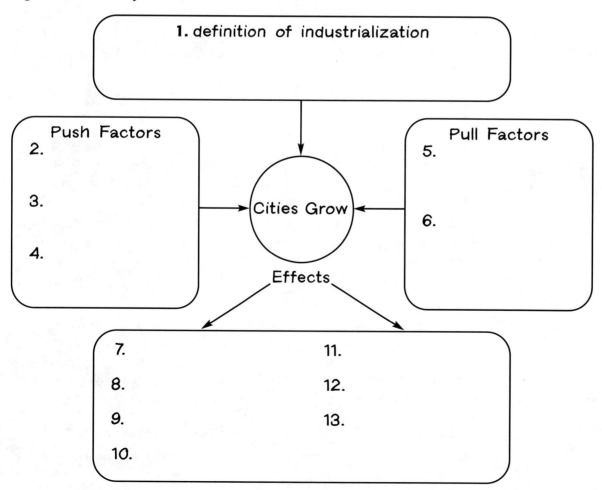

1. definition of industrialization

Push Factors
2.
3.
4.

Cities Grow

Pull Factors
5.
6.

Effects

7.   11.
8.   12.
9.   13.
10.

Resources for English Learners	
TE p. 737	RSG pp. 277–278, 279–280
RSG Audio	TT 105	MLG
FA pp. 499, 500–503, 504–507, 508–511	

Global Environmental Change

**Step 1
Activate Prior
Knowledge**

Do a **Roundtable** activity for students to list all the environmental problems they can think of. Let groups share their lists and record students' answers on the board or the overhead. Save these answers for students to add to and revise.

**Step 2
Preview Main
Ideas and
Language**

Connect Visually Direct students remain in their groups and have them study the graph on p. 737. Students should look at the graph title and at the horizontal and vertical scales to figure out the subject of the graph. Explain that the line at 0.0 represents the number that is the average annual temperature for the period of the graph, 1880–2000.

Build Vocabulary Go over the definitions of the key terms listed in Part A of Activity Sheet 32.3. Have students work with a partner to complete the activity.

**Step 3
Make Objectives
Explicit**

Write these objectives on the board and read them aloud to the class. Check students' comprehension using Number of Fingers or another **Signals** Activity. Students who understand the objectives can explain them to students who do not understand them. If students' first language is Spanish, have them read the lesson summary in the *Reading Study Guide* (English or Spanish).

- Identify issues related to global environmental damage.

- Describe possible future effects of environmental change and talk about international efforts to take action.

- Analyze primary sources to understand different views and data related to environmental change.

**Step 4
Support Student
Reading**

Cooperative Work Divide the class into groups of five to read the section. Have students fill in the chart in Part B of Activity Sheet 32.3 using a **Jigsaw Reading** activity. Go over answers with the entire class. Then encourage students to find other sources of information as they work on the Case Study Project.

On One's Own Preview the following questions by asking students what they understand them to mean. Then have students search for the answers while reading. Once students have finished, help them answer in complete sentences.

1. What are greenhouse gases and why are they important? (p. 734, pars. 3–4)

2. If global warming is taking place, what problems could occur? (p. 734, par. 7; p. 735, par. 1)

3. What is the ozone hole? (p. 734, par. 5)

4. What problems could occur due to current changes in the ozone layer? (p. 735, par. 2)

**Step 5
Prepare for
Assessment**

Alternative Assessment Have students work in groups of five to complete the Case Study Project. Share the Grading Rubric on TE p. 737 with students and use it to evaluate their project.

Formal Assessment Go over the test-taking strategies for TT105. You may want to use *Formal Assessment* Form A, the less-challenging assessment, or administer it as a practice test prior to formal testing with Form B or Form C.

ACTIVITY SHEET 32.3

Part A. Build Vocabulary

Key Terms Working with your partner, fill in the blanks with the correct key terms.

> **emissions:** a substance given off into the air, especially from automobile engines or other types of fossil-fuel burning engines
>
> **fossil fuels:** oil, natural gas, and coal, all of which are fuels that formed beneath the earth's surface millions of years ago from the remains of microscopic plants and animals
>
> **global warming:** the buildup of carbon dioxide and other greenhouse gases in the atmosphere, preventing heat from escaping into space and causing rising temperatures and shifting weather patterns
>
> **ozone:** a form of oxygen, which makes a layer in the upper atmosphere of the earth that protects the earth from ultraviolet rays
>
> **ultraviolet rays:** a type of light that people cannot see, which the sun gives off and which causes sunburn, sun tanning, and skin changes that lead to skin cancer

In the past century, there has been a great increase in the burning of
1. _____. This has increased **2.** _____
of greenhouse gases—gases that trap heat near the earth. For this reason,
many scientists think that these gases have built up to such a point that
average temperatures around the world are increasing. This temperature
change is called **3.** _____. Another global environmental
change humans have caused is a thinning of the **4.** _____
layer. This blanket of gas high in the atmosphere protects the earth from
harmful **5.** _____ from the sun, which are linked to crop
damage, eye problems, and skin cancer.

Part B. Cooperative Work

Work with your group to read and summarize the primary sources on
pp. 736–737. Go over the answers with the class.

Main Idea or Summary of Primary Sources
Educational pamphlet from the UN:
Political commentary from the American Policy Center:
Graph of data from the National Climate Data Center:
New York Times science article about the ozone hole:
Satellite images showing the ozone layer over Antarctica:

Answer Key

CHAPTER 1, SECTION 1

Part A. Build Vocabulary

1. equator
2. relative location
3. longitude
4. latitude
5. absolute location

Part B. Cooperative Work

Complete the chart by working with your group to define each term and list examples.

Theme	Definition/description	Examples
Location: Absolute Location (p. 6, pars. 1–4)	Answers the question "Where is it?"; tells exactly where a place is on earth; employs a grid system of latitude and longitude lines	Melbourne, Australia, is 37° South latitude, 145° East longitude
Location: Relative Location (p. 6, pars. 1, 5)	Answers the question "Where is it?"; tells where a place is in comparison to other places around it.	Cairo, Egypt, is near the mouth of the Nile River in Africa
Place (p. 7, par. 1 and photograph)	Answers the question "What is it like?"; includes the physical features and cultural characteristics of a location	Place features of Rio de Janeiro, Brazil include Sugarloaf Mountain; the harbor and shipyard at Botafogo Bay.
Region (p. 7, pars. 2–3; p. 8, pars. 1–2)	Answers the question "How are areas similar or different?"; there are formal regions, functional regions, and perceptual regions.	Latin America, Europe, and Africa are examples of formal regions; Chicagoland (including the city and suburbs) is a functional region; the Midwest is a perceptual region.
Human-Environment Interaction (p. 8, pars. 3–4)	Answers the question "How do people relate to the physical world?"; people shape the environment and the environment shapes people.	People build irrigation ditches; people plant crops.
Movement (p. 9)	Answers the question "How do people, ideas, and products move from one location to another?"; geographers analyze movement by looking at linear distance, time distance, and psychological distance.	People move from one city or country to another; ideas travel through phone conversations and e-mail correspondence.

CHAPTER 1, SECTION 2

Part A. Build Vocabulary

1. cartographers
2. databases or satellites (either is correct)
3. satellites or databases (the term NOT used in question 2)
4. maps or globes (either is correct)
5. globes or maps (the term NOT used in question 4)

Part B. Cooperative Work

1. List 2 advantages a globe has over a map. (p. 10, pars. 3–4)	It shows the earth's true shape, in three dimensions. It does not distort the earth's features.
2. List 2 advantages a map has over a globe. (p. 10, par. 4)	It is more easily portable than a globe. It can be drawn to any scale and show selected parts of the earth's surface.
3. Name 3 basic types of maps and tell the purpose of each. (p. 11, par. 1)	Topographic maps: used for general reference; shows natural and human-made features on the earth. Thematic maps: emphasize specific information, such as climate. Navigation maps: used by pilots and sailors.
4. What is the first step in making a map? What are 2 ways this can be done? (p. 11, par. 3; p. 12, par. 1)	Complete a survey, by either making measurements in the field or by gathering data through remote sensing (aerial photography or satellite).
5. What is Geographic Information Systems (GIS) and how is it used? (p. 12 diagram, p. 13 pars. 1 and 2)	GIS is a digital database of geographic data. Geographers use it to layer information that can be used to create a composite map helpful in solving problems.
6. How do geographers use Global Positioning System (GPS)? (p. 13, pars. 3)	For tracking the location of animals and moving objects to aid in solving problems related to land or resource use.

CHAPTER 2, SECTION 1

Part A. Build Vocabulary

Earth in outer Space	Earth's landmasses	Structure of Earth	
solar system	continent continental drift	(Inside the Earth) core mantle crust magma	(At or above the Earth's surface) atmosphere hydrosphere lithosphere biosphere

Part B. Cooperative Work

1. sun, planets, other celestial bodies that orbit the sun, comets, asteroids
2. 9
3. third planet from the sun
4. core
5. mantle
6. crust
7. atmosphere
8. lithosphere
9. hydrosphere
10. biosphere

CHAPTER 2, SECTION 2

Part A. Build Vocabulary

1. hydrologic cycle
2. drainage basin
3. ground water
4. water table

Part B. Cooperative Work

In the square labeled "Oceans", students' drawings should indicate the size of the world's ocean and the four main parts; they should illustrate how currents, waves, and tides move ocean water and how ocean water helps distribute heat on the earth.

In the square labeled "Hydrologic Cycle", students should draw and label the steps in the cycle, showing how one step leads to another.

In the square labeled Lakes, Rivers, and Ground Water", students' drawings should explain the origin of both freshwater and saltwater lakes; their drawings should show how water drains throughout a drainage basin; they should show what ground water is and label the water table in their drawings.

In the square labeled "Landforms", students should show some different kinds of landforms that appear on land and under the ocean; they should label the continental shelf in a drawing and show two ways islands form; they should define the term relief and the term topography through drawings.

CHAPTER 2, SECTION 3

Part A. Build Vocabulary

1. volcano
2. tectonic plates
3. Earthquakes
4. fault
5. tsunamis

Part B. Cooperative Work

1. Magma (melted rock) beneath the earth's crust circulates (moves in circles) like a conveyor belt. This movement causes the tectonic plates to move.
2. The tectonic plates in this area moved apart; this is an example of a divergent boundary.
3. The plate that includes Asia and the plate that includes India are crashing into each other, with one plate riding over the other; this is an example of a convergent boundary.
4. Plates grind or slip past each other at a fault—a crack in the earth's crust.
5. Earthquakes can cause tsunamis—giant, fast-moving waves in the ocean.

CHAPTER 2, SECTION 4

Part A. Build Vocabulary

Textbook column

1. F; Weathering refers to physical and chemical processes that change the rock on or near the earth's surface.
2. T
3. T
4. T
5. F; Humus is the organic material (material from living things) that is included in the soil.

Part B. Cooperative Work

1. Mechanical weathering breaks down rock into smaller pieces; chemical weathering causes rock to decompose into smaller pieces; these sediments can become part of the soil and can also be subject to erosion.
2. Water erosion causes sediments from one part of the stream to move downstream; it causes stream- and riverbeds to become deeper and wider; it causes delta formation; it changes the size of beaches and islands.
3. Wind erosion causes sediments from one place to move to another place; it creates sand dunes and soil deposits and sculpts rock.
4. Glacial erosion causes the formation of soil, of U-shaped valleys, moraines (rocky ridges or hills) eskers, and kettles.
5. Soil formation determines the kinds of plants that can grow in a region.

CHAPTER 3, SECTION 1

Part A. Build Vocabulary

solstice: pictures might show sunset, a tree with no leaves, and a clock with an early time for winter solstice and sunset, a tree with leaves, and a clock with a late time for summer solstice

equinox: pictures might be divided in half with one half showing the sun and indicate 12 hours of sunlight and the other half showing a dark sky and indicate 12 hours of night

climate: pictures might show a warm place or a cold place and indicate that the place has been this way for a long time

weather: pictures might indicate how weather changes over a few days

precipitation: pictures might show a cloud with rain or snow falling

Part B. Cooperative Work

Cause of the seasons: The earth is tilted. As the earth revolves around the sun, one half of the earth and then the other half of the earth is tilted toward the sun. When the northern half of the earth is tilted toward the sun, this part of the earth receives direct rays of the sun for more hours of the day; then it is summer there; when the northern half of the earth is tilted away from the sun, this part of the earth receives indirect rays of the sun for fewer hours of the day; then it is winter there.

Causes of weather patterns:

water vapor in the earth: determines whether there will be precipitation

cloud cover: determines how much sunshine reaches the area

landforms/water bodies: determines how quickly or slowly the area warms up or cools off elevation: the higher the elevation the cooler and drier the area will be

air movement: wind distributes solar energy and moisture, causing the weather to change

Precipitation forms when warm air rises and then cools; cooler air cannot hold as much water vapor as warm air can, so the water vapor condenses into clouds. When a cloud cannot hold more moisture, rain or snow falls from it.

Convectional precipitation forms in hot, moist places; the hot air rises in the morning, forming clouds in the afternoon; the rain falls late in the day.

Orographic precipitation forms when warm, moist air rises when it hits a mountain range, causing the air to rise and cool and the water vapor to condense, forming clouds. Rain tends to fall before the clouds cross the mountain peaks, causing that side of the mountain to be rainy and the other side to be dry.

Frontal precipitation forms when air masses of different temperatures meet; when warm air is pushed upward by colder air, the rising air cools, water vapor condenses, and rain falls.

Causes and effects of hurricanes: Hurricanes form when warm moist air flows into a low-pressure core of swirling clouds, high winds, and drenching rains; hurricanes cause great wind damage and can cause floods from heavy rains and/or from storm surges.

Causes and effects of tornadoes: Tornadoes result from strong thunderstorms; they cause wind damage and death.

Causes and effects of blizzards: Blizzards are heavy snowstorms with winds of more than 35 miles per hour. They cause traffic problems, endanger livestock, and trap and sometimes endanger travelers.

Effects of droughts: A drought is a long period of time without rain or with minimal rainfall. Droughts can cause crop failure, loss of topsoil, and loss of water in lakes, reservoirs, and wells.

Effects of floods: Floods occur when water spreads over land not normally covered with water. Floods can cause water damage and kill people and livestock.

CHAPTER 3, SECTION 2

Part A. Build Vocabulary

1. topography
2. elevation
3. convection
4. the greenhouse effect

Part B. Cooperative Work

Wind currents: Convection circulates air, causing hot air to flow toward the poles and cold air to flow toward the equator.

Ocean currents: These currents can be warm or cold. Wind blowing over these currents picks up or loses heat, depending on the temperature difference between the air and the water; these winds affect the temperature of the land they blow over. They also affect the amount of precipitation that falls on the land: cold currents flowing near land chill and dry the air.

Latitude: The higher the latitude, the colder the climate.

Elevation: The higher the elevation, the colder the climate.

Topography: Mountains affect climate; often one side of a mountain receives much more precipitation than the other side of a mountain.

El Niño: This is a periodic switch in the wind direction over the central Pacific, causing flooding in the Americas and drought in Australia and Asia.

The Greenhouse Effect: This increase in temperature, due to an increase in certain heat-trapping gases in the atmosphere, may be causing the earth's climate to warm up.

CHAPTER 3, SECTION 3

Part A. Build Vocabulary

1. Temperature doesn't belong. Tundra and permafrost both relate to cold climates; permafrost is the frozen subsoil of the tundra.
2. Temperature doesn't belong. Humid and semiarid both relate to the amount of moisture in the air; humid refers to moistness; semiarid refers to dryness.

Part B. Cooperative Work

Students' maps do not need to be as detailed as the map on pp. 60–61, but they should show the general locations of all of the climate regions, labeling the smaller regions, such as Marine west coast and Mediterranean.

CHAPTER 3, SECTION 4

Part A. Build Vocabulary

1. Biomes
2. Forests

Coniferous and Deciduous appear in the Forests category

3. Grasslands

Savanna and Steppe appear in the Grasslands category

Note: 2. and 3. can be in switched order in the chart

Part B. Cooperative Work

Biome			
Rain Forest	trees	hot	wet
Deciduous Forest	trees	temperate	wet
Coniferous Forest	trees	temperate	semi-arid
Savanna	grass	hot	semi-arid
Steppes/pampas	grass	temperate	semi-arid
Desert	cacti or shrubs	hot	dry
Tundras	moss	polar	dry

CHAPTER 4, SECTION 1

Part A. Build Vocabulary

1. culture
2. acculturation
3. diffusion
4. innovation

Part B. Cooperative Work

1. innovation, diffusion
2. acculturation
3. helps build group identity and sense of unity
4. language that reflects social class, region, education, etc.
5. monotheistic; polytheistic; animistic
6. Judaism; Christianity: Islam; Hinduism; Buddhism.
7. Performing arts; visual arts; literature.

CHAPTER 4, SECTION 2

Part A. Build Vocabulary

1. mortality rate
2. population
3. carrying capacity
4. population density

Part B. Cooperative Work

1. Birthrate is the number of live births per thousand; a high birthrate is one indication of rapid world population growth.
2. fertility rate: shows the average number of children a woman of childbearing years would have in her lifetime; a fertility rate above 2.1 indicates a growing population.
3. mortality rate: also called the death rate, this is the number of deaths per thousand people; this can give some indication of the health of a population.
4. infant mortality rate: gives the number of deaths among infants under age one per thousand live births; this can give some indication of the health of a population.
5. rate of natural increase: this is the difference between the mortality rate and the birthrate; it gives the rate at which the population is growing.
6. population pyramid: this graphic device that shows gender and age distribution in a population; it can show the effect that wars, famine, epidemics, and other specific events have on the population of a country or of the world.
7. population distribution: where people live. Most of the world's population lives in habitable lands, between 20 degrees and 60 degrees North latitude; the population distribution between urban and rural areas is shifting toward urban areas; large-scale migration affects population distribution.
8. population density: the average number of people who live in a measurable area; this may be affected by the land's carrying capacity or by the economics of a region; it also may vary greatly from one part of a nation to another during different periods of history.

9. carrying capacity: the number of people a piece of land can support; carrying capacity can affect population density, because a region with fertile land may be able to support far more people than a region with little fertile land; it can also affect population distribution, because a region with a low carrying capacity may force people to migrate to survive as the population of the region grows.

CHAPTER 4, SECTION 3

Part A. Build Vocabulary

1. democracy
2. monarchy
3. dictatorship
4. communism

Part B. Cooperative Work

1. state: an independent unit that occupies a specific territory and has full control of its internal and external affairs; country
2. nation: a group of people with a common culture living in a territory and having a strong sense of unity
3. nation-state: a nation and a state that occupy the same territory

4–7. can appear in any order

4. democracy: citizens hold power either directly or through elected representatives
5. monarchy: a ruling family headed by a king or queen holds political power, which it may or may not share with citizens
6. dictatorship: an individual or group holds complete political power
7. communism: a governmental and economic system in which nearly all political power and means of production (economic resources) are held by the government in the name of all the people

8–10. can appear in any order

8. size: a larger country might have more economic resources and people to build economic and military power than a smaller country might have
9. shape: shape can influence how easy it is to govern a country or to transport goods from one part to another or to the rest of the world
10. location: location can affect transportation, trade, and security

11–12. can appear in either order

11. a natural boundary is based on a physical feature of the land; examples include rivers, lakes, mountain ranges
12. an artificial boundary is a fixed line that generally follows either latitude or longitude lines; the Great Wall of China, a humanmade boundary, is another example of an artificial boundary
13. regional political units smaller than a state might include cities, towns, villages, school districts, provinces, what we call states in the United States, functional units such as the Tennessee Valley Authority; students might come up with other examples

14. regional political units larger than a state includes the European Union and the United Nations; students might come up with other examples

CHAPTER 4, SECTION 4

Part A. Build Vocabulary

Following are glossary definitions for the key terms.

suburb: political unit or community touching the borders of the central city or bordering other suburbs that border the city

metropolitan area: a functional area including a city and its surrounding suburbs and exurbs that are all linked together economically

urbanization: a sharp rise in the number of cities and the changes in lifestyle that result

Part B. Cooperative Work

1. The central city should have suburbs touching it on at least one side.
2. There should be open land between the smaller cities and towns and the urban area drawn in 1.
3. These might include a lake, river, harbor on the ocean, a particular natural resource, or an important political function.
4. Students should show residential, industrial, and commercial land use, each in a separate color; these may be broken down further into particular categories.
5. Such functions might include shopping districts, entertainment, government services, educational institutions, museums or symphonic halls, etc. The map should include some roads, a freeway system, and public transportation of some sort.

CHAPTER 4, SECTION 5

Part A. Build Vocabulary

1. economy
2. per capital income
3. infrastructure

Part B. Cooperative Work

Types of Economic Systems

	Production of goods and services is determined by a central government	Production of goods and services is determined by consumer demand
command economy	+	-
market economy	-	+
mixed economy	+	+

Sample charts:

Levels of Economic Activity

	gathering materials for immediate use	changing the form of materials to add value	providing business or professional services	providing information, management, or research services
Primary	+	-	-	-
Secondary	-	+	-	-
Tertiary	-	-	+	-
Quaternary	-	-	-	+

Basic Types of Natural Resources

	Can be replaced through natural processes people can control	Can be replaced through solar or planetary processes	Includes sources of energy	Are limited in supply
Renewable	+	-	-	-
Non-renewable	-	+	-	-
Inexhaustible	-	-	+	-

Statistics to Measure the Economy

	includes goods	Includes services	All produced during a set time period	All produced inside the country	All produced by the country
Gross National Product (GNP)	+	+	+	-	+
Gross Domestic Product (GDP)	+	+	+	+	+

Levels of Economic Development

	High GDP	Varied economic activity	Much secondary economic activity	Much tertiary economic activity	Much quaternary economic activity
Developing nations	+	+	+	-	+
Developed nations	+	+	+	+	+

CHAPTER 5, SECTION 1

Part A. Build Vocabulary

Possible methods of categorization:

1. Mountains (Appalachian, Rocky); Flat Areas (Great Plains, Canadian Shield); Bodies of Water (Great Lakes, Mackenzie River)
2. East (Appalachian Mountains, Canadian Shield); Central (Canadian Shield, Great Plains, Great Lakes); West (Rocky Mountains; Mackenzie River)
3. Canada only (Mackenzie River); United States only (no entries); Canada and the United States (Appalachian and Rocky Mountains, Great Lakes, Great Plains, Canadian Shield)

Part B. Cooperative Work

Possible answers:

Canadian and U.S. Landforms	Eastern Lowlands	Appalachian Mountains	Great Plains	Canadian Shield	Rocky Mountains	Canadian Islands
Description	flat coastal plain	eastern mountain chain	mostly treeless area	rocky, flat region	western mountain chain	Canada's northern-most lands
General location/size	along the Atlantic and Gulf coasts	1600 miles from New-foundland to Alabama	extend from Texas to southern Canada	encircles Hudson Bay and extends into northern U.S.; covers 18 million square miles	extend from Alaska to New Mexico	in the Arctic Ocean
Variety	Between the plains and the Appalachian Mountains is the piedmont.	include Green, Catskill, Blue Ridge, and Smokey Mountains	2,000 to 4,000 feet above sea level	1,500 to 5,000 feet above sea level	up to 12,000 feet high; Continental Divide comes through here	Ellesmere, Victoria, and Baffin Islands are North America's largest after Greenland
Age/other	———	400 million years old	———	formed by the glaciers	young, 80 million years old	———
Way shapes life	Excellent harbors encourage commerce.	coal-producing region	oil- and coal-producing areas; some very fertile soil	deposits of iron ore, nickel, copper, gold, and uranium	silver, gold, copper, and uranium	———

CHAPTER 5, SECTION 2

Part A. Build Vocabulary

Drawings will vary. For permafrost, students' drawing should indicate that the ground below the surface is permanently frozen; for prevailing westerlies, students' drawings should indicate through drawings and perhaps symbols that the wind usually comes from the west.

Part B. Cooperative Work

Climate Zones of the United States and Canada

Climate zones of the United States (only): humid subtropical climate, desert climate, Mediterranean climate, tropical climate

Climate zones of Canada (only): (none)

Climate zones of both the United States and Canada: tundra, subarctic climate, highland climate, humid continental climate, Marine west coast, semiarid climate

Vegetation of the United States and Canada

Vegetation of the United States (only): desert, Mediterranean shrub, tropical forest, tropical grassland

Vegetation of Canada (only): (none)

Vegetation of both the United States and Canada: tundra, coniferous forest, mixed deciduous and coniferous forest, temperate grasslands

CHAPTER 5, SECTION 3

Part A. Build Vocabulary

1. nomads
2. urban sprawl
3. transcontinental
4. locks
5. highway

Part B. Cooperative Work

Building agricultural settlements (p. 127, par. 4–5)	Purpose: to raise food. Changes: trees cut down; soil plowed; natural vegetation replaced; ditches dug.
Building Montreal (p. 128, par. 2)	Purpose: to increase trade. Changes: built homes, spreading around the mountain there; built underground shelters, networks, and stores.
Building Los Angeles (p. 128, par. 3–4)	Purpose: to expand a settlement in a pleasant climate. Changes: urban sprawl into foothills and valleys; building on earthquake-threatened land; air pollution; decreased amounts of freshwater.
Building trails and inland waterways (p. 129, par. 1–3)	Purpose: to overcome vast distances and promote trade. Changes: some loss of natural vegetation; the connecting of waterways not previously connected.
Building transcontinental railroads (p. 130, par. 1–2)	Purpose: to overcome vast distances, promote trade and national unity. Changes: forests cut down; bridges built; tunnels blasted through mountains.
Building national highway systems (p. 120, par. 2–3)	Purpose: to overcome vast distances, promote trade, and ease travel. Changes: cities and towns connected; same kinds of changes as transcontinental railroads.

CHAPTER 6, SECTION 1

Part A. Build Vocabulary

1. immigration
2. a representative democracy
3. the frontier
4. migration

Part B. Cooperative Work

Students could include any six of the following on their time lines:

11,000 B.C. to A.D. 1500 Hundreds of different cultures develop in what is today the United States

1500 Europeans begin to arrive in what is today the United States

1565 Founding of St. Augustine

1600s French settle along the northern Atlantic coast

1607 English settlers found Jamestown

1691 First Africans arrive in North America

1763 British gain control of all of North America east of the Mississippi River

1775–1783 American Revolution: the United States is formed

1803 The Louisiana Purchase doubles the size of the United States

1804–1806 Lewis and Clark expedition explores the Louisiana Purchase

Early 1800s Many immigrants arrive from Western Europe

1840s Wagon trains begin moving pioneers to the West

1861–1864 Civil War

1869 Completion of the first transcontinental railroad

1890 Closing of the frontier

1860–1900 About 14 million immigrants arrive from Eastern and Western Europe

1898 The United States annexes Hawaii

1913 Use of assembly line in Ford auto plant

1920 First regular radio broadcasting begins

1945 End of World War II; U. S. has become a world power

1945–1991 Cold War between the U.S. and the Soviet Union

1947 first mass television audience for the World Series

1955–1975 Vietnam War

1959 Development of integrated circuit leads to computer development

1960–1970 Social unrest including the civil rights movement, the feminist movement

1961 U.S. crewed exploration of space starts

1969 Development of computer network that leads to the Internet

2000 Mapping of human DNA

CHAPTER 6, SECTION 2

Part A. Build Vocabulary

1. exports
2. multinational
3. services
4. postindustrial
5. free enterprise

Part B. Cooperative Work

1. available natural resources, skilled labor, stable political system that encouraged business through the free enterprise system
2. The U.S. feeds itself and supplies 40% of the world's corn, 20% of its cotton, and 10% of its wheat, cattle, and hogs.
3. information processing, finance, medicine, transportation, and education

4. Christians about 85%, with 56% Protestant and 38% Roman Catholic; Jews about 2%; Muslims about 2%. Statistics are of the religious population, not the population as a whole.
5. Jazz, blues, gospel, rock 'n' roll have African-American origins; country and bluegrass were developed by Southern whites whose background was British.
6. in cities or surrounding suburbs

CHAPTER 6, SECTION 3

Part A. Build Vocabulary

Venn Diagrams should have a large circle that is labeled BosWash (megalopolis); inside this circle should be 8 smaller circles labeled with the names of the metropolitan areas in the chart; labels or a color key should indicate that these smaller circles are all metropolitan areas.

Part B. Cooperative Work

Possible Answers:

1. Maine, Vermont, New Hampshire, Massachusetts, Rhode Island, Connecticut, Pennsylvania, New York, New Jersey
2. fishing and farming; international trade centers; coal, iron ore, oil; electronics, communications, chemicals, medical research, finance, tourism
3. highly urbanized megalopolis
4. 12 states of the north-central United States
5. nation's breadbasket; meat-packing, food processing, farm equipment, grain milling, and automaking; trade, transportation, and distribution center
6. farming declining in employment; urban areas expanding; people leaving for the South and the West
7. 16 states, covering one-fourth of the land area of the United States
8. cotton, tobacco, fruits, peanuts, and rice; livestock production; oil, coal, natural gas, steel, chemicals, food processing, electronics, textiles, tourism
9. has attracted many industries fleeing the harsher weather of the Northeast and the Midwest; attracts many tourists and retirees
10. 13 states and about one-half of the U.S. land area
11. varied economic activity including farming, ranching, food processing, logging, fishing, mining, oil refining, tourism, filmmaking, computers, foreign trade with Asia
12. most rapidly growing region in the United States

CHAPTER 7, SECTION 1

Part A. Build Vocabulary

1. confederation
2. Both relate to the units of a government.
3. prime minister
4. Both are important parts of a parliamentary government.

Part B. Cooperative Work

1. Asians who crossed the land bridge were the first settlers of Canada; some groups gave rise to the Inuit; other groups gave rise to North American Indian peoples.
2. Both British and French colonists came; the British defeated the French in the French and Indian War in 1763; but the French settlers remained in Canada.
3. The Dominion was a step toward the unification of Canada, creating a loose political union of Upper Canada, Lower Canada, Nova Scotia, and New Brunswick.
4. The transcontinental railroad, discovery of gold and silver, and the mining of other minerals led to settlement of the West.
5. Urban and industrial growth, concentrated within 100 miles of the U.S.-Canadian border, helped Canada become a major economic power in the 20th century.

CHAPTER 7, SECTION 2

Part A. Build Vocabulary

Drawings will vary. For First Nations students' drawing might show people who look like Inuit or Native Americans; for métis, students' drawings should indicate a combination of French and native cultures, perhaps through use of symbols, as well as drawings; for reserves, students' drawings should indicate that this is land set aside for native peoples.

Part B. Cooperative Work

1. Fishing: Canada exports more fish than any other country.
2. Forestry: Canada's biggest export trade is in forest products; no other country exports as much wood pulp and paper products as Canada does.
3. Services: Account for more than 60% of Canada's GDP; include finance, utilities, transportation, tourism, communication, insurance, and real estate.
4. First Nations: include people of different cultures with different languages; many live on reserves
5. English: Protestant; English-speaking; dominate Canadian society
6. French: Roman Catholic; French-speaking; mainly live in Quebec
7. métis: people of mixed French and native heritage

CHAPTER 7, SECTION 3

Part A. Build Vocabulary

When students have completed their map, all six of the places listed will be correctly labeled on the map. Refer to the map on p. 154 for the correct labeling of the subregions.

Part B. Cooperative Work

Possible Answers:

1. Prince Edward Island, New Brunswick, Nova Scotia, Newfoundland
2. logging, fishing, mining, shipbuilding, hydroelectric power
3. small population due to rugged terrain and severe weather
4. Quebec, Ontario
5. agriculture, mining, manufacturing, banking and finance
6. center of economic and political activity in Canada; Quebec is the heart of French Canadian life, Ontario is the most populated province, is English-speaking, and has the national capital
7. Manitoba, Saskatchewan, Alberta
8. center of agriculture; mining including coal, oil, natural gas
9. cultural mix of diverse groups, ranging from Ukranian and Polish to the métis; to Lebanese and Vietnamese
10. British Columbia and the Yukon, Northwest, and Nunavut territories
11. logging, mining, hydroelectric power production, foreign trade, and fishing; northern regions are sparsely populated and climate is severe
12. Vancouver and Victoria are large prosperous cities in British Columbia; the territories are too sparsely populated to become provinces

CHAPTER 8, SECTION 1

Part A. Build Vocabulary

1. terrorism
2. biological weapons
3. coalition
4. global network

Part B. Cooperative Work

Possible answers:

1. Planes crashed into the World Trade Center (twin towers) and the Pentagon; in New York, the twin towers and nearby buildings were destroyed; the Pentagon suffered major damage to one of its wings. In all, about 3,000 people died.
2. People afraid of further attacks both in the U.S. and other places throughout the world; fear of use of biological, nuclear, and chemical weapons.
3. The September 11 attacks were probably carried out by al-Qaeda, a global network of extremist Islamic terrorists.
4. The United States needs to figure out ways to secure its citizens and fight terrorism while, at the same time, safeguarding individual rights for people in this country.

5. The United States and other countries joined together to form a coalition against terrorism. They pledged to share information, arrest terrorists, and freeze terrorists' financial assets. The coalition also carried out military action in Afghanistan, where al-Qaeda's main leaders had been based, and brought down the Taliban government, which had sheltered al-Qaeda.

6. Airport security measures were strengthened as were security measures at large, public gatherings; expanded security was put in place at nuclear power plants and water-supply facilities; Canada took similar anti-terrorist measures and signed a border security pact with the U.S.

CHAPTER 8, SECTION 2

Part A. Build Vocabulary

Following are glossary definitions for the key terms:

infrastructure: basic facilities, services, and installations needed for a community to function

smart growth: efficient use and conservation of land and other resources in growing cities

sustainable community: community where residents can live and work

Part B. Cooperative Work

Possible answers:

1. Urban sprawl is the spread of a city's population over a wider and wider area

2. Urban sprawl occurs when there is unrestricted growth and no plans to contain such growth; the widespread use of automobiles and the building of expressways also helps cause urban sprawl.

3. Effects of urban sprawl include strains on infrastructure, such as roads and bridges, causing need for more frequent repair; increased air pollution; depletion of water supplies; high cost of city services; separation of different classes of people from one another.

4. Portland drew a growth boundary line in 1971, stopping building beyond a certain point. The surrounding undeveloped green spaces have remained.

5. Vancouver created sustainable communities out of suburbs, so that residents could live and work in close proximity; downtown Vancouver also has large residential areas nearby, so that many people walk to work. This has helped cut down on commuting and the problems it causes.

6. Citizens in some areas have organized to try to prevent urban sprawl either locally or nationally, through political activism and education.

CHAPTER 8, CASE STUDY

Part A. Build Vocabulary

1. mosaic
2. multicultural
3. ethnic
4. assimilation

Part B. Cooperative Work

Main Idea or Summary of Primary Sources

Possible answers:

Newspaper article by William Booth: Historians believe that people today are more interested in maintaining their ethnic identity than people used to be.

Social commentary by Michelle Young: The concept of America as a melting pot is not realistic; instead people need to take pride in their own roots, which will help them become interested in and respectful of the cultures of people of different backgrounds.

Political commentary by Patrick Buchanan: Assimilation is important for the U.S. to survive as one nation; the country needs to halt illegal immigration, reduce legal immigration, and emphasize the English language.

Excerpt from the Canadian Multiculturalism Act: This law promotes full participation of Canadians of all different backgrounds in shaping Canadian society.

Excerpt from the U.S. 2000 census: The form offers 14 choices for race and a write-in line for "other"; Native Americans can name their tribe.

CHAPTER 9, SECTION 1

Part A. Build Vocabulary

1. b
2. c, e
3. a, d

Part B. Cooperative Work

1. Andes on the Pacific coast of South America are a barrier to movement

2. Guiana Highlands in northern South America and the Brazilian Highlands in eastern South America

3. large, grassy treeless plains for farming and grazing in Colombia and Venezuela

4. savannas of Brazil whose flat terrain and moderate rainfall make them suitable for farming

5. plains of Argentina and Uruguay covered with rich soil; used for raising wheat and raising cattle

6. located in northern South America, one of the world's greatest rivers, fed by more than 1,000 tributaries; carries more water than any other river in the world

7. the Orinoco, draining areas of Venezuela and Colombia; the Paraná, originating in the Brazilian Highlands, flowing through Paraguay and Argentina and forming the border between Argentina and Uruguay

8. island groups are the Bahamas, the Greater Antilles (including Cuba, Jamaica, Hispaniola, and Puerto Rico) and the Lesser Antilles

9. many abundant minerals, including gold, silver, iron, copper, bauxite, tin, lead, nickel, gems, titanium, and tungsten

10. Venezuela and Mexico have major oil reserves; Brazil is rich in hydroelectric power, oil, and gas; Trinidad has large reserves of natural gas; coal and uranium are also plentiful in Latin America

CHAPTER 9, SECTION 2

Part A. Build Vocabulary

1. Possible answers: set to subset; whole to part; category to subcategory; accept other answers that indicate a similar relationship.
2. **a.** Answers could include any subregion of or country in Latin America
   b. Possible answers: Andes Mountains, Guiana Highlands, or Brazilian Highlands
   c. Possible answers include any of the tributaries of the Amazon, such as the Negro River, the Madeira River, the Araguaía River; these are shown on the map on p. 191 or p. 193
   d. Possible answers include gold, silver, iron, copper, bauxite, tin, lead, nickel, zinc, or other minerals.

Part B. Cooperative Work

1. tropical wet
2. Central America, Caribbean, and Brazil
3. hot and rainy year round
4. tropical wet and dry
5. Brazil, Colombia, Argentina
6. hot with seasonal rain
7. semiarid
8. Mexico, Brazil, Uruguay, and Argentina
9. dry, with some rain
10. desert
11. Mexico, Peru, Chile, Argentina
12. dry—very little rain
13. humid subtropical
14. Paraguay, Uruguay, Brazil, Bolivia, Argentina
15. rainy winters and hot, humid summers
16. Mediterranean
17. Chile
18. hot, dry summers and cool, moist winters
19. marine west coast
20. Chile, Argentina
21. cool, rainy winters and mild, rainy summers
22. highlands
23. mountains of Mexico and South America
24. temperature depends on elevation

CHAPTER 9, SECTION 3

Part A. Build Vocabulary

Two Agricultural Methods Used in Latin America

	Ancient technique	Used in tropical, humid areas	Used in mountainous areas	Requires farmers to move frequently to new land	Reduces soil erosion
Slash-and-burn	+	+	-	+	-
Terraced farming	+	-	+	-	+

Part B. Cooperative Work

Urbanization in Latin America

Pros

Possible answers:

1. gives people the possibility for better-paying jobs
2. gives people the possibility for better medical care
3. gives people the possibility for better education

Cons

Possible answers:

4. growing slums
5. high unemployment
6. high crime rates
7. high levels of air pollution
8. shortages of drinkable water
9. inadequate infrastructure, including sewers, transportation, electricity and housing

Tourism in Latin America

Pros

Possible answers:

10. brings in money to the region
11. creates jobs in the region
12. can help reduce the income gap between area residents
13. give residents a stake in the local economy

Cons

Possible answers:

14. development of undeveloped land causes congestion
15. development of undeveloped land causes pollution
16. puts a strain on local communities
17. highlights income gap between rich tourists and less well-off local residents, possibly leading to hostility
18. raises local public debt for infrastructure necessary to support tourist economy
19. absentee owners of tourist facilities send profits from tourism back to their own home cities or countries
20. absentee owners often make decisions that do not benefit the local community
21. absentee owners influence local political and business decisions

CHAPTER 10, SECTION 1

Part A. Build Vocabulary

1. a. People of mixed Spanish and Native American heritage
   b. mes-TEE-so
   c. Possible question: Are mestizos always Mexican, or are people from the American Southwest or from South America called mestizos, too?
2. a. Factory in Mexico that assembles imported materials into finished products that are then exported, mostly to the United States.
   b. mah-KEY-la-DOE-rah
   c. Possible question: I wonder what conditions are like in the maquiladoras.

3. a. an abbreviation that stands for the North
American Free Trade Agreement
   b. NAF-tuh
   c. Possible question: How is NAFTA affecting
emigration patterns from Mexico?

Part B. Cooperative Work

1. native way of life destroyed; Mexico became a part
of the Spanish Empire
2. First Mexico was ruled by its own emperor; then
Juárez reformed the government, increased
educational opportunities, and aided distribution of
land to poorer Mexicans; harsh rule by dictator Díaz
led to political revolution in the early 1900s
3. introduced democracy; country became politically
stable; government was corrupt, undermining
democracy
4. Aztec ruins present in many cities; Indian heritage
strong; beautiful native sites; mural painters blend
European and native influences
5. Spanish language and Spanish Catholicism
dominate modern Mexico; Spanish missions and
cathedrals are part of architectural heritage
6. People moving to Mexico's cities to find better
economic opportunities.
7. Profits from oil industry have helped finance
manufacturing industries.
8. Many new factories have been built along the
Mexican-U.S. border. These include factories
assembling electronic equipment, clothing, and
furniture. NAFTA is increasing trade with the U.S.
and Canada and may help create many jobs for
Mexicans.

CHAPTER 10, SECTION 2

Part A. Build Vocabulary

Drawings will vary. For cultural hearth, students'
drawing might show a fireplace or a symbol of Mayan
civilization with arrows leading out from it; for informal
economy, drawings might show street vendors of any
kind, street musicians, or people shining shoes or
carrying luggage in an airport.

Part B. Cooperative Work

1. the Maya
2. Spain, Great Britain
3. native groups, Spanish conquerors and settlers
4. Catholicism is the dominant religion; Protestant
missionaries are active in the region
5. Spanish
6. Tainos
7. Spain, France, Great Britain, Denmark, Netherlands
8. Tainos, Africans, Spanish, French, British, Danish,
and Dutch
9. Catholicism, Protestant Christian, Santeria, Voodoo,
Rastafarianism
10. Spanish, French, English, some Dutch and Danish

CHAPTER 10, SECTION 3

Part A. Build Vocabulary

1. b
2. c
3. a

Part B. Cooperative Work

1. T
2. F
3. F; Portuguese, French, Dutch, and Quechua and
other native languages are still spoken; Catholicism
is the main religion, but not the only religion.
4. F Most countries fought for independence from
Spain during this time.
5. T
6. T
7. T
8. T

CHAPTER 10, SECTION 4

Part A. Build Vocabulary

Possible categorization:

Relates to Brazilian History	Relates to Brazilian Culture
Treaty of Tordesillas	Carnival
	capoeira
	samba

Part B. Cooperative Work

1. native tribes, Portuguese, Africans, immigrants
2. Portuguese
3. mostly Catholic; Protestant minority; religions that
combine African beliefs with Catholicism
4. nation's capital, Brasília was built in 1960 and has a
very modern design
5. Carnival
6. Brazil's cultural center; slums called favelas

CHAPTER 11, SECTION 1

Part A. Build Vocabulary

1. debt
2. global warming
3. biodiversity
4. deforestation

Part B. Cooperative Work

1. rain forest
2. ranch

(3, 4, and 5 in any order)

3. lumber
4. crops
5. beef
6. erodes

(7 and 8 in either order)

7. plant

8. animal

9. global warming

10. medicines

CHAPTER 11, SECTION 2

Part A. Build Vocabulary

Supported by Latin America's wealthy: caudillo, junta, oligarchy

To spread wealth in Latin America more fairly: land reform

Part B. Cooperative Work

1. freely and fairly elected government

2. government's respect for the law

3. majority rule with minority rights

4. guaranteed freedoms

5. educated public

6. economic security and stability, possibly accomplished through land reform

7. participation of all citizens, including women, in political affairs

CHAPTER 11, SECTION 3

Part A. Build Vocabulary

1. d

2. c

3. e

4. a

5. b

Part B. Cooperative Work

Sample answers:

Primary Source	Note Taking	Note Making
Income Distribution Graph	The poorest 40% of Latin Americans have only 8% of the income; the wealthiest 20% of Latin Americans have 62% of the income.	The poor have so little; this could easily cause social unrest.
Cable News story by Marina Marabella	In 1996, three Brazilian police officers were put on trial for murdering street children in Rio. About 500 homeless children murdered in Brazil per year.	This sounded terrible to me, but human rights activists consider it a victory, because people who murder homeless children have not been put on trial before.
Newspaper story by Steven Gutkin	Describes the big contrasts between rich shopping mall in Caracas, Venezuela, and the filthy slums nearby; blames Latin American governments for failing to offer good education, failing to collect taxes, and tolerating corruption for the lack of opportunities for poor people; also blames Latin America's culture of elitism, which considers poor people unworthy . . .	What are poor people unworthy of, according to these people? respect? help to better their lives?
Magazine article from *The Economist*	Describes a successful program in Pôrto Alegre, Brazil, in which street children are given dormitories to sleep in, school classes, and counseling.	It's strange that Brazil's homeless children don't all migrate to Pôrto Alegre!

CHAPTER 12, SECTION 1

Part A. Build Vocabulary

Following are glossary definitions for the key terms:

fjords: steep U-shaped valleys that connect to the sea and that filled with seawater after the glaciers melted

uplands: hills or low mountains that may also contain mesas or high plateaus

peat: partially decayed plant matter found in bogs; it can be burned as fuel

Part B. Cooperative Work

How Landforms Shape Life in Europe		
Landform	**Location**	**How Shapes Life**
fjords	Norway	provide excellent harbors
Alps	France, Italy, Germany, Switzerland, Austria, Slovenia (northern Balkans)	cut Italy off from the rest of Europe
Pyrenees Mountains	on the border between France and Spain	restrict movement between Spain and Portugal and the rest of Europe
Apennines Mountains	runs north-south down the Italian Peninsula	divide eastern Italy from western Italy
Balkan Mountains	on the border between Bulgaria and Romania; run throughout the lower (southern) Balkans	separates the Balkans from the rest of Europe and isolates ethnic groups from one another
Danube River	cuts through the heart of Europe; 1771 miles long	trade route; links Europe to the Black Sea
Rhine River	flows from the interior of Europe to the North Sea	trade route; connection between Europe and the rest of the world
Northern European Plain	France, Belgium, the Netherlands, Denmark, Germany, and Poland	agricultural land, producing vast quantities of food; easy route for invading armies

CHAPTER 12, SECTION 2

Part A. Build Vocabulary

mistral: blows from the north, cold, dry

sirocco: blows from the south, hot, dry, may bring rain, may bring desert sand or dust

Part B. Cooperative Work

1. marine west coast: warm summers, cool winters; adequate moisture

2. North Atlantic Drift; prevailing westerly winds

3. mixed forests cleared for farms; crops include grains, livestock feed, sugar beets, and root crops

4. humid continental; cold winters, warm or hot summers; adequate rainfall

5. coniferous forests and grasslands; most cleared for farms; crops include wheat, rye, barley, potatoes, and sugar beets

6. Mediterranean climate: hot, dry summers; moderate, wet winters

7. most of this area is shielded by mountain ranges that block cold north winds; mistral, on the coast of France, is a cold, dry winter wind; sirocco, occurs in most Mediterranean countries is a hot, steady wind from the south

8. evergreen shrubs and short trees; crops include citrus fruits, olives, grapes, and wheat

9. tundra climate; subarctic climate: cool most of the time with very cold winters

10. tundra has permafrost, in which mosses and lichens grow, but no trees; subarctic has stunted trees; no agriculture

CHAPTER 12, SECTION 3

Part A. Build Vocabulary

1. reclaim
2. dikes
3. polder
4. terpens

Part B. Cooperative Work

Who: the Dutch

Where: in the Netherlands (Holland)

What: drained areas of low seawater to gain farmland

Why: to provide farmland for their growing population

How: They made polders by building dikes around shallow areas of the sea, draining the water, letting the salt wash away, planting alfalfa, and eventually planting any suitable crop. They built dikes to keep the seawater from flooding the low land. They build terpens (high earthen platforms) for their own safety during floods. They transformed the Zuider Zee into a freshwater lake by diking off its outlet to the North Sea; they drained the land around it to make hundreds of square miles of land.

Who: the Venetians

Where: on islands in a lagoon at the north end of the Adriatic Sea

What: built a city

Why: originally to escape enemies; eventually as a port/commercial center

When: Students can infer before the 1800s; actually by 840 it was a city-state

How: They sunk wooden pilings in the swampy land to support buildings; forests were leveled in northern Italy and Slovenia to make the building of Venice possible. Today there are problems with the city sinking and with pollution destroying buildings and making life unpleasant or unhealthful.

Who: Europeans in general

Where: throughout the continent

What: destroyed forests

Why: for building material, firewood, and to make charcoal; as a result of industrial pollution

When: from ancient times to the present

How: individuals and groups exploiting the forest resources and clearing land; acid rain formed as a result of industrial pollution, especially sulfur dioxide and nitrogen oxide kills trees

CHAPTER 13, SECTION 1

Part A. Build Vocabulary

1. a republic
2. a city-state
3. classical
4. a democracy

Part B. Cooperative Work

Students should pick 8 of the following and locate them correctly on their time line.

753 B.C. Founding of the city of Rome

400 B.C. Conflict among Greek city-states weakens Greece

338 B.C. Macedonia conquers Greece

336 B.C. Alexander the Great makes conquests, spreading Greek culture

275 B.C. Rome had become a republic

A.D. 100 Rome had conquered a huge empire

A.D. 300s Christianity becomes Rome's official religion

395 Roman Empire split into eastern and western parts

476 Western Roman Empire falls to invaders

700 Muslims from North Africa conquer Iberian Peninsula (Spain and Portugal)

1096 European Christians launch the Crusades

1300 Italian Renaissance begins

1347 Bubonic plague devastates Europe

1400 Portugal and Spain launch the Age of Exploration

1492 Ferdinand and Isabella retake Spain from the Muslims; send Columbus on his first voyage

CHAPTER 13, SECTION 2

Part A. Build Vocabulary

1. feudalism: a political system in which powerful lords owned most of the land.
2. nationalism: the belief that people should be loyal to their nation, the people with whom they share land, culture, and history.

Part B. Cooperative Work

1. a. France and Germany
   b. France
   c. Germany
2. a. the Reformation
   b. France
   c. the Netherlands, Switzerland, Germany
3. feudalism
4. Strong kings gained power over feudal lords; the kings represented a larger region—a nation.
5. 1789; French kings had absolute power and ignored the needs of their people.
6. nationalistic rivalries and competition for colonies among European nations
7. German resentment over surrender terms of World War I

8. It was split into non-Communist West Germany and Communist East Germany.

9. The two halves of Germany reunited under a democratic government.

10. Belgium, France, the Netherlands, and Switzerland

11. France, Germany, the Netherlands

12. It has varied scenery, a mild climate, and many historic sites.

CHAPTER 13, SECTION 3

Part A. Build Vocabulary

Textbook column

1. T

2. F; Representative government, such of that of Britain, is any democratic system of government in which people elect officials who represent them in the making and enforcing of laws.

3. T

4. F; The euro is the common currency of the European Union.

Part B. Cooperative Work

1. Denmark, Finland, Iceland, Norway, Sweden

2. United Kingdom; Ireland

3. the Sami, the Celts

4. the Celts, the Romans, Germanic invaders

5. no Nordic country ever became a major empire

6. the British Empire, which included lands throughout the world

7. Germanic languages predominate; Sami language spoken in the far north; Protestant Christianity

8. Celtic languages; Germanic language (English) predominates; Ireland is Catholic; the rest of Britain is predominantly Protestant

9. Henrik Ibsen; Ingmar Bergman

10. William Shakespeare, William Wordsworth, Charlotte Brontë, James Joyce

11. smorgasbord (buffet style food); saunas; cross-country skiing, ski-jumping

12. afternoon tea, horseback riding, horse jumping, fox hunting, rugby, cricket

13. child-care allowance, national health insurance

14. national health insurance

CHAPTER 13, SECTION 4

Part A. Build Vocabulary

1. cultural crossroads

2. balkanization

3. satellite nations

4. anti-Semitism

Part B. Cooperative Work

1. Fall of Communism has meant a return to strong ethnic loyalties and civil war in Serbia; lack of democratic tradition has made it difficult for countries to be successful in adopting this form of government.

2. Many different languages are spoken in the region, some of which are very different from languages spoken nearby; this makes it difficult to unify the region. Also, there are a number of different religions important in the region, including Catholicism, Eastern Orthodoxy, Protestantism, Judaism, and Islam. This has sometimes made it difficult for Eastern Europeans to be unified.

3. Conflicts between Eastern European ethnic groups have led to civil war in Yugoslavia; discrimination against minority populations, including Jews and Gypsies, has also been a problem in the region.

4. The shift to a market economy has been difficult because of outdated factory equipment from the Soviet era; there has been inflation, unemployment, lack of investment money, lack of educated workers, and workers fleeing and destruction of industries due to war.

CHAPTER 14, SECTION 1

Part A. Build Vocabulary

1. a. 1

  b. The paragraph we read lists the names of six republics; if Bosnia and Herzegovina were separate republics, there would have been seven listed.

  c. 1

  d. There is no border indicated to show a separation between Bosnia and Herzegovina; the entire region is shown in a single color; it is labeled Bosnia & Herzegovina.

2. a. (2)

  b. Both deal with violence against a group of people in order to eliminate them.

  c. The word *cleansing* is related to cleaning; it does not suggest something negative and violent, but rather something helpful that has a positive effect.

Part B. Cooperative Work

Possible answers:

Cause	Effect
Different Slavic groups migrate from Poland and Russia to the Balkans; they came to be called the South Slavs.	**1.** Each group of South Slavs set up its own kingdom—Croatia, Slovenia, and Serbia.
2. The Ottoman Empire, which was Muslim, conquered much of the Balkans. Austria gained control of Slovenia. Hungary ruled Croatia.	Foreign rule led to the development of cultural differences among the South Slavs.
3. South Slavs united under a king and then under the Communists (led by dictator Josip Tito) in a country called Yugoslavia.	Ethnic rivalries of different Balkan groups remained submerged for many decades.
Tito died in 1981; presidency rotated among Yugoslavia's six republics and two provinces.	**4.** No one person or group ran the country.
5. Serbia blocked a Croat from becoming president.	Slovenia and Croatia declared independence.
Slovenia and Croatia declared independence.	**6.** Serbia invaded Slovenia and Croatia.
Thousands of people died.	**7.** UN cease-fire ended the war; Slovenia and Croatia remained independent.
Bosnia and Herzegovina declared independence.	**8.** Serbia invaded the republic; started campaign of ethnic cleansing.

CHAPTER 14, SECTION 2

Part A. Build Vocabulary

1. b
2. c
3. a

Part B. Cooperative Work

1. discharge chemicals into streams and rivers; bury solid wastes, so poisons seep into the ground, contaminating wells and rivers; air pollution released by coal-burning industries causes acid rain, which pollutes water and kills organisms
2. Some cities do not have sewage treatment plants; releasing untreated sewage can cause serious water pollution.
3. Rain washes fertilizers from agriculture into bodies of water; the fertilizers cause too much algae to grow; the rotting algae use up oxygen in the water, causing fish and other organisms to suffocate.
4. Oil spills pollute the water and kill shore animals.
5. Burning fossil fuels causes the formation of smog and leads to the formation of ozone.
6. Fires release smoke and particulates into the air.
7. Dry cleaning, refrigeration, air conditioning, and pesticide use all release harmful chemicals into the air.
8. Factories discharge sulfur and other harmful gases into the air.
9. Countries cooperating with one another to recommend programs to prevent water pollution, such as sewage treatment; the EU passing environmental laws; establishment of the European Environmental Agency to provide information about the environment.

10. Individual countries passing laws to reduce air pollution, such as requiring improved insulation to prevent wasting fuel heating buildings. Countries cooperating on passing clean-air laws, such as reducing emissions allowable from motor vehicles.

CHAPTER 14, SECTION 3

Part A. Build Vocabulary

1. unification
2. stability
3. alliance
4. currency

Part B. Cooperative Work

Political commentary from Global Britain: Some people in Britain are reluctant to adopt the euro as their currency, because they could no longer make national decisions about interest rates and other aspects of monetary policy. They also fear that unemployment would rise steeply.

Speech by Günter Veheugen: Verheugen thinks that unification of Europe helps ensure political stability and democracy and will increase human rights and freedoms in Europe.

Data related to EU Support levels: This poll indicates that EU members are most in favor of Norway and Switzerland joining the EU and least in favor of Slovenia and Turkey joining the alliance.

Political analysis by Edmund C. Andrews: Andrews points out the adjustments the EU will have to make if they admit Central (Eastern) European countries to the alliance, including a building of trust between Central (Eastern) Europeans and Germans. Western Europeans will have to get over their antagonism toward immigrants; Eastern Europeans will have to get over their fears of Westerners buying up their land.

Political cartoon by Pat Oliphant: This cartoon shows that, having adopted the euro, it is difficult for EU members to agree on how to steer their alliance.

CHAPTER 15, SECTION 1

Part A. Build Vocabulary

1. Eurasia
2. chernozem
3. Transcaucasia

Part B. Cooperative Work

Maps should be labeled with landforms, rivers, and lakes as shown on the map on pp. 336–337. Possible facts are given below.

Northern European Plain: includes one of the world's most fertile soils—chernozem; most of the region's population lives on this plain

West Siberian Plain: this plain tilts northward, causing its rivers to flow into the Arctic Ocean

Ural Mountains: separate Europe from Asia

Central Siberian Plateau: plateaus are between 1,000 and 2,000 feet in elevation

Russian Far East: Volcanic mountain ranges, with many active volcanoes; islands in the Pacific, some of which Japan disputes Russian ownership of

Yenisey River: one of three huge river basins; western border of the Central Siberian Plateau

Lena River: one of three huge river basins; western border of the Russian Far East

Ob River: one of three huge river basins

Volga River: longest river in Europe; drains into the Caspian Sea; carries 60% of Russia's river traffic

Caucasus Mountains: border between Russia and Transcaucasia

Transcaucasia: includes the republics of Armenia, Azerbaijan, and Georgia

Tian Shan: mountain range that borders between China and Kyrgyzstan; 1,500 miles long

Central Asia: includes the republics of Kazakhstan, Kyrgyzstan, Tajikistan, Turkmenistan, and Uzbekistan; bordered by mountains to the south that prevent moist air from entering the subregion, causing the climate to be quite arid.

Turan Plain: includes two major rivers, the Syr Darya and the Amu Darya, and two large deserts, the Kara Kum and the Kyzyl Kum.

Caspian Sea: a saltwater lake, the world's largest inland sea

Aral Sea: saltwater lake that has been shrinking due to irrigation

Lake Baikal: world's deepest lake; in places, a mile deep; very clean with thousands of plant and animal species; world's only freshwater seals live here

CHAPTER 15, SECTION 2

Part A. Build Vocabulary

Students' maps might have the label continentality in the middle of the map with arrows pointing outward to indicate vast distance from the sea; the taiga should be labeled in the subarctic area; the steppe should be labeled in the southwestern part of the map, from the western border to the eastern border of the Central Asian republics.

Part B. Cooperative Work

1. Mostly in the Arctic climate zone; only small plants, including mosses, small herbs, and low shrubs and lichens grow here; the rivers and lakes stay frozen for much of the year and are used as roads.
2. The taiga; the largest forest on earth, composed mainly of coniferous trees; deciduous trees are found farther south; many fur-bearing animals live here.

3. Fertile, temperate grassland extending from southern Ukraine through northern Kazakhstan to the Altay Mountains; major farming area of the region.
4. Located in the western and central areas of Central Asia; the two main deserts are the Kara Kum and the Kyzyl Kum.

CHAPTER 15, SECTION 3

Part A. Build Vocabulary

1. Pesticides and fertilizer used by cotton growers are picked up by rainwater that flows over the land (runoff) and is carried by rivers into the Aral Sea.
2. killed 24 native species of fish
3. Fertilizer and pesticide particles (in the form of dust) picked up in windstorms, which dump them on people living nearby.
4. Increased diseases and infant mortality.

Part B. Cooperative Work

	Obstacles for inhabitants	Benefits for inhabitants
Winter	1. Extremely low temperatures make outdoor work very difficult. 2. It is difficult to build on permafrost, because heat from the buildings thaws the land and makes the buildings unstable.	3. Makes invasion of the country very difficult.
Huge Distances	4. Traveling was very time consuming. 5. Building the Trans-Siberian Railroad took decades.s	6. Much land was available for settlers once the railroad was built. 7. The resources of Siberia, including coal and iron ore, became available to Russia.

CHAPTER 16, SECTION 1

Part A. Build Vocabulary

1. F; Collective farms were huge farms organized by the Soviet government, on which large groups of people worked.
2. T
3. F; In a command economy, the central government makes all important economic decisions.
4. F; The Cold War was the name people gave the tension between the United States and the Soviet Union; open warfare between these two countries did not occur during the Cold War.

Part B. Cooperative Work

Possible answers

1. Name two different groups who invaded the region between the Baltic and Black seas and took control of this area.	1. Vikings from Scandinavia came in the 800s, established trade, and took up customs of the local Slavs; the Tartars who were Mongol warriors took over in the 1200s.
2. Who put an end to the rule of the second group?	2. Ivan the Great ended Mongol rule in the 1500s.
3. Why did Peter the Great move his capital to St. Petersburg?	3. to have more contact with Western Europe
4. When and why did the Russian Revolution occur?	4. Industrialization in Russia resulted in harsh working conditions, low wages, and other hardships, which Russians rebelled against; the Russian Revolution began in 1917, during World War I.
5. What happened during the Cold War and why did it end?	5. The Cold War referred to the tensions between the U.S. and the Soviet Union between the late 1940s and 1991, when the Communist government of the Soviet Union collapsed.
6. What was the ideal behind communism?	6. that all citizens of a nation would own property together and everyone would share the wealth
7. What were two goals of the Soviet command economy?	7. to move toward communism; to industrialize
8. What are three ways in which this economy failed?	8. Millions of people starved to death in famines; only a small number of people benefited from the command economy; people who rebelled against the system were punished very harshly
9. Why do Russia and the Western Republics have many different ethnic groups and religions?	9. Many different groups of people were absorbed during the centuries of Russian expansion.
10. Who are some famous Russian writers and composers?	10. Writers: Pushkin, Dostoyevsky; composers: Tchaikovsky; Stravinsky

CHAPTER 16, SECTION 2

Part A. Build Vocabulary

Drawings will vary, but may be quite literal. For *gateway,* students might show a gateway in a fence or an arch as a gateway; for *Red Army,* students might show soldiers marching together with one carrying the Soviet flag; for *supra,* students might show a table filled with fresh fruits, salads, and other produce and people seated around the table eating or giving toasts.

Part B. Cooperative Work

Possible answers

1. more than 50 different peoples (ethnic groups); a great variety of languages from three different families: Indo-European, Caucasian, and Altaic
2. Most people are Christians or Muslims
3. In the 1700s, the Russian czar's army invaded; it took more than 100 years for Russia to gain complete control of the region; this occurred in the late 1870s.
4. For a few years after the Russian Revolution, the Transcaucasian republics were independent; by the early 1920s, the Soviet military had gained control of the subregion.

5. The mild climate makes farming very profitable in the subregion's lowlands and foothills; fruit, grapes, and tea are among the most profitable crops. Industrial centers built by the Soviet Union produce iron, steel, chemicals, and consumer goods.
6. Currently the region's most important industry is the oil industry. Some areas are rich in oil; some areas are important because an oil pipeline may be built across them; oil deposits beneath the Caspian Sea are under dispute, related to how they will be distributed among bordering nations. The distribution depends on whether the Caspian Sea is considered a sea or an inland lake.

CHAPTER 16, SECTION 3

Part A. Build Vocabulary

Following are glossary or dictionary definitions for the key terms:

Silk Road: caravan trade routes that connected China and the Mediterranean Sea

border: the line separating political divisions

nomad: a person who has no permanent home and who moves from place to place according to the seasons, in search of food, water, and grazing land

yurt: a portable tent of felt, stretched around a wooden frame

Part B. Cooperative Work

Possible answers

1. **Silk Road:** trade route between China and the Mediterranean Sea; a channel for trade goods, ideas, technology, and religion
2. **Great Game:** the struggle between the British Empire and the Russian Empire in the 1800s for control of Central Asia; Russia had "won" by the end of the 1800s
3. **Soviet rule:** lasted from 1920 to 1991 and involved drawing borders of the Central Asian republics so as to mix very different ethnic groups in a single nation, so that the groups would be less likely to be able 4o unite and rebel against Soviet rule.
4. **nuclear testing:** went on under Soviet rule from 1949–1989; above ground and underground testing went on in a large region called "the Polygon"; more than a million people in the area, including people in a city called Semey, were exposed to nuclear fallout (dangerous levels of radiation); this has caused dramatic increases in certain types of cancers, birth defects, and mental illness; the effects will continue for many more years.
5. **petroleum:** huge oil fields lie in Kazahkstan and Turkmenistan; nations are competing to make profits from drilling these oil fields; with the establishment of political stability and legal institutions, the profits from these resources could benefit the people of Central Asia

6. forming nations: Soviet border drawing means that the five Central Asian nations have very mixed populations, ethnically, especially in the larger cities.

7. language/religion: Most Central Asians speak languages related to Turkish and many also speak Russian; most are Muslims.

8. traditions: Some groups of people in Central Asia are nomads; they move from place to place with their animals in search of food, water, and grazing land; they live in tents called yurts and generally have few but beautiful furnishings, including reed mats, carpets, and woven storage bags.

CHAPTER 17, SECTION 1

Part A. Build Vocabulary

1. Caucasus
2. Chechnya
3. Nagorno-Karabakh
4. Transcaucasia

Part B. Cooperative Work

Possible answers

Regional Conflict in Russia and the Republics		
	Causes	Effects
General conflict in former Soviet Union	Power vacuum left by collapse of Soviet Union inspired different ethnic and religious groups to try to take control of their own affairs.	Difficulty preserving both law and order and democratic rule.
Chechnya	Chechens' demands for independence brought two Russian invasions of the region.	More than 100,000 casualties; bomb attacks in Russian cities, said to have been carried out by Chechen terrorists; destruction of buildings and infrastructure; economic losses.
Georgia	Ossetians of central Georgia want to unite with Ossetians in Russia; Abkhazians in Georgia declared independence and forced 250,000 Georgians to leave the region.	2,000 deaths and 40,000 refugees before truce ended the Ossetian conflict; many Georgian refugees died in mountain crossings; Abkhazia, which was once a popular resort, is in ruins.
Armenia and Azerbaijan	Armed conflict over which nation should control Nagorno-Karabakh.	Armenia won control of the territory; tens of thousands of people died; almost a million people became refugees.

CHAPTER 17, SECTION 2

Part A. Build Vocabulary

1. capitalism
2. privatization
3. distance decay

Part B. Cooperative Work

Possible answers

1. **privatization:** The Russian government offered vouchers, which were like government loans, in the early 1990s for people to buy businesses that formerly were government-owned; many of the businesses were unsuccessful and the new owners were unable to repay their loans, contributing to Russia's economic collapse in 1998. Nevertheless, private businesses have been growing in Russia.

2. **distance decay:** Long distances in Russia reduce interactions among people, can limit cooperation, and so cause difficulty with the implementation of government economic reforms; this may be counteracted somewhat by the federal districts put in place in 2000 to help carry out economic reforms.

3. **organized crime:** Has infiltrated both private and state-owned businesses; slows economic reform by reducing the amount of taxes the government receives from business activity and by rewarding illegal activity over honest business.

4. **future prospects:** Increases in tax revenue and customs revenue collected is a sign that the Russian economy is growing; government crackdown on organized crime is also important for Russia's economic future.

CHAPTER 17, CASE STUDY

Part A. Build Vocabulary

1. warhead
2. missile
3. fuel rods
4. nuclear wastes
5. dump
6. task force

Part B. Cooperative Work

Sample answers:

Primary Source	Note Taking	Note Making
New York Times editorial	Russia has stocks of nuclear bombs, nuclear ingredients, and biological and chemical agents of warfare that are not well secured or well guarded; people who guard these materials are not well paid; neither are nuclear scientists; the dangerous materials are open to theft or illegal sale; the people who guard or have knowledge of these materials could be bribed, etc. It would only take about $10 billion to eliminate these risks, in comparison with the trillions spent on nuclear weapons during the Cold War.	I wonder if the money was spent in this way or if the security risks still exist.
Newspaper story by U.S. reporter Michael Wines	The shutdown of Chernobyl will cause power shortages in Ukraine and increase that nation's debt to Russia for fuel; it will also cause the loss of jobs; finally it will be very expensive to cover the disaster site with a protective dome and otherwise treat the dangerous wastes.	I wonder why it took so long to get Chernobyl shut down and whether other countries are giving aid to Ukraine for taking this step. I wonder how many other potential Chernobyls there are in the region.
Newspaper story by British reporter Christopher Lockwood	A ship with hazardous nuclear wastes is moored off the northern coast of Russia. Since 1991, Norway and Finland have been negotiating with Russia about the nuclear wastes on board; the Norwegian Defense Minister said that an accident with them could affect Europe's climate for hundreds of years.	I wonder what happened to the ship or whether it is still sitting there with its wastes. I wonder why the Norwegian Defense Minister was worried about the climate, when thousands of people could die from the release of radioactivity.

CHAPTER 18, SECTION 1

Part A. Build Vocabulary

Type of landform	Is lower than the land around it	Includes features of dramatically different elevations	is long and thin	is created by the movement of continental plates	has steep slopes
plateau	-	-	-	-	-
basin	+	-	-	-	-
rift valley	+	+	+	+	+
escarpment	-	+	+	+	+

Part B. Cooperative Work

1. Africa's most prominent feature; covers most of Africa; generally is at least 1,000 feet in elevation
2. five huge basins, each more than 625 miles across; world's longest river—the Nile; many waterfalls, rapids and gorges that inhibit use of rivers for transportation; the meandering courses of many of the rivers also makes river transportation difficult.
3. long, thin valleys in East Africa, that stretch 4,000 miles, from Mozambique to Jordan in Southwest Asia; deep lakes formed at the bottom of some, including the world's longest lake—Lake Tanganyika, with a depth of more than 4,700 feet.

4. volcanic mountains including Mt. Kenya and Mt. Kilimanjaro; the Ethiopian Highlands and the Tibesti Mountains in the Sahara are also of volcanic origins
5. large amounts of gold, platinum, chromium cobalt, copper, phosphates, diamonds
6. have benefited European colonial powers in the past; Africa currently lacks the infrastructure and industries to benefit more fully from these resources
7. petroleum and untapped oil reserves
8. Angola's revenue from drilling offshore oil (for example) recently has gone into fighting a civil war, rather than for education, health care, infrastructure or other more useful purposes.
9. coffee, lumber, sugar, palm oil, cocoa
10. Agricultural resources are very important to many Africans; 66% of Africans earn their living from farming.

CHAPTER 18, SECTION 2

Part A. Build Vocabulary

Student drawing will vary, but might be quite literal, with **aquifer** showing water flowing or pooled underground, **oasis** showing a desert area that has palm trees, grasses, birds, and other animals, and **canopy** showing the upper part of a forest, thick with leaves, and with animals among the branches. Accept any drawings, literal or abstract, that convey the meaning of the word.

Part B. Cooperative Work

1. The Sahara, in northern Africa, stretches about 3,000 miles across the continent, from the Atlantic Ocean to the Red Sea, and also runs 1,200 miles from north to south; the Kalahari is in the middle of southern Africa; the Namib desert is on the west coast of southern Africa.
2. The Sahara: 20% is sand; towering mountains, rock formations, and gravelly plains make up the rest; includes mountains; the temperatures can rise to 136 degrees during the day but drop below freezing at night
3. Africa has the largest tropical area of any continent.
4. Temperatures are high most of the year; the biggest differences in yearly temperature are not seasonal differences but occur between daytime and nighttime temperature
5. The northern and southern tips of Africa have a Mediterranean climate.
6. There is generally rainfall only in winter (December and January in North Africa; June and July in Southern Africa); the rest of the time, there are clear, blue skies and moderate temperatures.
7. Cover most of the continent; the Serengeti Plain in Tanzania is a National Park
8. Dry climate and hard soil prevent the growth of trees; abundant grasses support huge herds of animals, for example, in the Serengeti.
9. on the equator in the Congo Basin
10. They are shady, hot, and humid; many animals live in the canopy, 150 feet above the forest floor; the rain forest is home to a huge variety of plants and animals; farmers have destroyed some parts of the rain forest, especially in Madagascar.

Part A. Build Vocabulary

Possible answers:

1. desertification; the Sahel borders the Sahara, which is a desert in Africa; the desert may be spreading to the Sahel through desertification.
2. silt; the Nile River probably carries silt, which is deposited by moving water; the building of the Aswan High Dam, on the Nile River, may affect how much and where the Nile's silt is deposited.

Part B. Cooperative Work

1. makes it possible for people to make their livelihood in the Sahel, following traditional lifestyles
2. If the land is not tended to carefully, it can easily become subject to erosion through overgazing or from tilling during farming; with increased erosion, the grasses die and are replaced by plants that do not cover or hold the soil as well as grass does; with less vegetation, rain runs off the land or evaporates quickly, making the land drier, and eventually causing it to become desert.
3. accounts for 80 to 90 percent of Nigeria's income; this income has a huge potential to benefit the country
4. Mismanagement of oil revenues and loans based on these revenues has caused economic problems for Nigeria. Spills and fires have harmed the land and people and caused pollution and increases in respiratory diseases; bandits and corrupt government officials have stolen the oil, damaged the pipelines, and caused deadly explosions.
5. provides farmers with a regular supply of water for irrigation, increasing the number of harvests per year from one to two or three; has increased Egypt's farmable land by 50 percent and has helped Egypt avoid floods and drought
6. Construction caused relocation of many people and changed their way of life; it caused the loss of archaeological treasures. The dam decreased the fertility of the soil, because the silt the river carries is not deposited on farmland anymore; farmers must use more fertilizer, which is expensive; increased irrigation has made the soil more salty and less fertile; expensive field drains have to be installed to flush out the salt; because there is more standing water, in irrigation ditches and in Lake Nasser, there is increased evaporation of fresh water; there has also been an increase in mosquitoes, which lay their eggs in the ditches or along the lake shore, and an increase in mosquito-born diseases.

Part A. Build Vocabulary

1. F; Europeans began to colonize East Africa in the mid-1800s.
2. T
3. T
4. F; AIDS has become a pandemic in Africa and may cause serious declines in the population of some African nations.

Part B. Cooperative Work

1. Five places that carried on trade with East Africa before A.D. 1000.	Egypt, the eastern Roman Empire, Arabia, Persia, and India
2. How Europeans set colonial boundaries in Africa, which later caused many conflicts.	They set boundaries that combined ethnic groups who were traditional enemies and divided single ethnic groups across national boundaries.
3. How Ethiopia escaped European colonization.	The Ethiopian emperor bought modern weapons from Russian and France to fight against the similarly armed Italians; Ethiopian military leaders used their knowledge of the country to defeat the Italians.
4. Three cash crops grown in East Africa and one reason relying on cash crops for a country's main income is risky.	Coffee, tea, and sugar; the price (value) of cash crops can vary greatly from year to year.
5. wo competing interests related to East African national parks.	People who live off of tourism who want the parks to remain large; farmers who want to use some or all of the land for farming.
6. Brief description of two major ethnic groups in East Africa.	Masai: herders and farmers who live in the rift valleys of Kenya and Tanzania; make intricate beadwork and jewelry; Kikuyu: herders who traditionally lived near Mt. Kenya, now live throughout Kenya; during colonial times, organized to fight the British.
7. Critical health care problem in East Africa and its effect on the population.	AIDS pandemic; may cause populations in some countries to decline by 10 to 20 percent.

Part A. Build Vocabulary

What is it?: a monotheistic religion

Who started it?: the prophet Muhammad

Who practices it?: Muslims

Where is it practiced?: People all over the world; the map shows that it is practiced throughout North Africa and along Africa's east coast

How does it relate to North Africa?: It is the major cultural and religious influence in North Africa

What are some related words?: Islamic, Islamicist, Muslim, mosque, Koran, Nation of Islam, Black Muslim

Part B. Cooperative Work

1. Algeria, Egypt, Libya, Morocco, Sudan, and Tunisia
2. A great civilization grew up here in ancient times; ancient Egyptians pioneered the use of geometry to set boundaries and had advanced medical practices; trade and travel was extensive, spreading Egyptian civilization
3. the largest cultural and religious influence in North Africa, from the 750 on
4. Oil has transformed the economies of Algeria, Libya, and Tunisia; but many North Africans do not have the training to work in the oil industry; so unemployment remains a problem and many North Africans migrate to Europe to look for work.
5. Marketplaces where many different items are sold through bargaining and storytellers and musicians entertain crowds; often in the old section of a North African town or city.
6. Called rai, started in the 1920s as music for youth; became protest music during the independence movement of the mid-1900s, and has continued as protest music against Islamic fundamentalism.
7. Women traditionally have centered their lives on home; but a growing number of women in North Africa hold professional jobs; women hold 7% of the seats in Tunisia's parliament; they own 9% of the businesses in the Tunisian capital of Tunis.

CHAPTER 19, SECTION 3

Part A. Build Vocabulary

1. A stateless society is one in which people rely on family lineages to govern themselves, rather than on an elected government or a monarch. A lineage is a family group that has descended from a common ancestor. Members of a stateless society work through their differences to cooperate and share power.
2. the Igbo of southeast Nigeria
3. How did people in a stateless society settle disputes that arose? Is life in a stateless society more peaceful than life in a country with a democratic government?

Part B. Cooperative Work

West Africa		
History		
1. Names and dates of trading empires: Ghana 800–1000 Mali 1235–1400 Songhai 1400–1591	2. What was traded: mainly gold and salt	3. How society was organized (before colonialism): stateless societies based on family lineages, in which power was shared
Economy		
4. Ghana a. Basis of economy: export of gold, diamonds, magnesium, and bauxite b. Why stable: free and fair elections since 1992; relatively good transportation system		5. Sierra Leone a. Former basis of economy: high quality diamonds b. Why unstable: political instability, civil wars, relatively uneducated population, lack of roads and good transportation systems
Culture		
6. Ashanti crafts: colorful kente cloth, wooden masks and stools	7. Benin art: from the 1200s, in an area near Nigeria; statues, masks, and jewelry made from brass, but called Benin bronzes	8. West African music: blend of traditional African music and jazz, blues, and reggae, from the Americas; sometimes sung in French or English; sometimes played on traditional West African instruments, such as the kora

CHAPTER 19, SECTION 4

Part A. Build Vocabulary

1. southward
2. rain forest
3. desert
4. 3,000 years

Part B. Cooperative Work

Colonialism in Central Africa		
1. Definition of colonialism:	**2. Causes of colonialism in Central Africa**	**3. Effects of colonialism in Central Africa**
the policy of one nation extending its control over one or more other nations, peoples, or regions	King Leopold II of Belgium wanted to open the interior of Africa, along the Congo River, to European trade and to gather Africa's resources, including rubber, palm oil, and ivory for European use or commerce.	a. On Central Africans under its rule: King Leopold used forced labor, which was akin to enslaving Africans to work for him.
		b. politics/government: Europeans disrupted long-standing systems of government (stateless societies); their borders brought together some groups that were traditional enemies, making government difficult; the legacy of dictatorial leadership from colonial powers has been carried on by inexperienced African leaders, and so few Africans have benefited from independence.
		c. Economic effects: little infrastructure was developed by colonial leaders, so growth of diverse economies has been very slow.
		d. On art: has been a way that Africans have promoted their culture since independence; in some places Western influences on the arts have been banned.
		e. On education: no educational system was put in place by colonial rulers; it has taken decades for African nations to be able to build their schools and universities.

CHAPTER 19, SECTION 5

Part A. Build Vocabulary

Student drawings will vary, but might be quite literal, showing people separated by race, with the white group smaller by having more resources or obviously wealthier and the blacks and Asians in a larger group, but having less resources; drawings might also show all the institutions in which mixing among the races was not allowed, including schools, hospitals, social settings, and neighborhoods; accept all drawings that indicate a clear understanding of apartheid.

Part B. Cooperative Work

Students should pick 8 of the following and locate them correctly on their time line.

1000 the Shona established a city called Great Zimbabwe

1200–1400 Great Zimbabwe was an important gold-trading area

1450 the Shona abandoned Great Zimbabwe

1440 Mutota founded a new state north of Great Zimbabwe

late 1400s Mutapa Empire founded based on Mutota's state

1700s-1800s Europeans migrated to Southern Africa

1819 the Zulu established their supremacy in Southern Africa

1836 Boers came into conflict with native groups in Southern Africa

late 1800s the British defeated the Zulu and took over their land

1891 DeBeers gained 80% of African diamond industry

1890s Boer War fought between the British and the Dutch in what is now South Africa

around 1900 Johannesburg began as a small mining town

1902 British formed the Union of South Africa

1905 the world's largest diamond was cut in South Africa

1912 African National Congress (ANC) was founded

1948 White minority government in South Africa instituted policy of apartheid

1949 Nelson Mandela emerged as a leader of the ANC

1966 Botswana gained independence from Britain

1973 Swaziland banned political parties and its king assumed absolute power

1980 British colonial rule ended in Zimbabwe

1980s Many nations pressured South Africa to end apartheid

1989 F.W. de Klerk became president of South Africa and his government ended apartheid

1994 Nelson Mandela became the first black to become president in South Africa in the first multiracial elections

1996 South Africa adopted a new, democratic constitution that guarantees the rights of all citizens

1999 Southern Africa countries were the most severely affected by AIDS of all African regions

CHAPTER 20, SECTION 1

Part A. Build Vocabulary

1. c
2. d
3. a
4. b

Part B. Cooperative Work

Africa's Economy		
History of Economic Problems	**Possible Solutions**	**Probable Effects**
1. Exploitation of Africa's resources by colonizing countries and Africa's people by both slave traders and colonizers has limited Africa's economic growth; it has fostered political instability, which further limits economic growth.	Forgive Overwhelming Public Debt	2. This would provide African nations money they need to help build their infrastructure and economies.
	Build Cooperation Among African Nations	3. This would improve trade and make it easier for countries to improve their infrastructure.
	Diversify Economies	4. This would help promote economic growth and stability.
	Improve Education	5. This would help provide skilled workers, who are needed to improve and diversify the economy.
	Reverse the Brain Drain	6. This would also help provide skilled workers, who are needed to improve and diversify the economy.

CHAPTER 20, SECTION 2

Part A. Build Vocabulary

Type of disease	Spread through infection	Carried by mosquitoes	Caused by HIV	Respiratory disease	Spread by unclean water
AIDS	+	-	+	-	-
cholera	+	-	-	-	+
malaria	+	+	-	-	-
tuberculosis	+	-	-	+	-

Part B. Cooperative Work

AIDS and Africa

How many people died of AIDS in 2000? 3 million people

How many Africans died of AIDS in 2000? More than 2.4 million

Which part of Africa has the highest infection rates?
Sub-Saharan Africa

(Southern Africa is also correct.)

How has AIDS affected the general health of people in this part of Africa? Millions of people have died; life expectancies have dropped.

Why does AIDS create economic problems? Sick people work less and earn less; people and nations become poorer; treating the disease is expensive, adding to a nation's economic costs.

What measures are Africans taking to help control AIDS? Improving health care, funding AIDS education programs, funding HIV testing programs

CHAPTER 20, CASE STUDY

Part A. Build Vocabulary

Following are glossary or dictionary definitions for the key terms:

colonize: to establish permanent settlements in a new territory; to establish one or more colonies in, with the running of the colonies being controlled by people from a distant country

coup: the violent overthrow of an existing government by a small group; short for "coup d'etat" which is French for "strike at the state"

hostage: a person held by an enemy as a pledge that certain promises or agreements will be carried out or that certain payments will be made

unity: quality of being united or of working together harmoniously

Part B. Cooperative Work

Main Idea or Summary of Primary Sources

Possible answers:

Eyewitness account of colonialism in the Congo:
Explains how in the late 1900s, Belgian King Leopold II would send soldiers to loot villages, attack Africans, and take women as hostage in order to get the Africans to give them a certain amount of rubber; then they would sell back the women for livestock.

Statement of principle by Ghana's leader Kwame
Nkrumah: Written in 1961, outlines the hope that African nations will be given independence, that these nations will unite and find solutions to the problems brought about by colonialism.

News analysis by Ron Daniels: Written in 2000, points out the irony that impoverished and underdeveloped African nations must turn to their former colonizers and slave traders (whose actions caused Africa's problems) for a financial bail-out.

New York Times editorial: Written in 2000, discusses Ghana's success in establishing a democratic, civilian government that is instituting economic reforms, after being run for decades by military dictatorship.

Political cartoon by Canadian Alan King: Comments on the lack of help the former African nation of Zaire (the Democratic Republic of the Congo) received from the international community in 1996 and the ambivalence of Western nations toward this country and presumably toward Africa as a whole.

CHAPTER 21, SECTION 1

Part A. Build Vocabulary

Students' drawings should show a riverbed that is completely dry and a riverbed that is full of water. Both should be labeled wadi, but the one that is full of water should be labeled rainy season; and the other one should be labeled dry season. Accept variations in labeling and drawings as long as these basic ideas are correct.

Part B. Cooperative Work

When students have completed their map, they should have at least 16 landforms and bodies of water labeled correctly on it. Refer to the map on p. 479 for the correct labeling of landforms and bodies of water.

CHAPTER 21, SECTION 2

Part A. Build Vocabulary

1. Possible answers include vegetation, trees, palm trees, plants, or any combination or similar ideas.
2. dry climate and wind evaporating moisture in the soil

Part B. Cooperative Work

1. **sandy deserts:** The largest one, the Rub al-Khali, is in Saudi Aradia; it is one of the largest sandy deserts in the world; some of its sand dunes are 800 feet tall; the sand at the surface can get as hot as 186°F. Other sandy deserts in the region are the An-Nafud Desert in Saudi Arabia, the Syrian Desert, and the Negev in Israel. Parts of the Negev are irrigated for farming.
2. **salt deserts:** In Iran, there are two salt flat deserts, one in central Iran and one in eastern Iran; the lands are salt crusted, hot, surrounded by quicksand-like salt marshes, and are almost completely uninhabited.
3. **semiarid lands:** These are located along the edges of deserts; they have warm to hot summers and enough rainfall for grasses and some shrubs to grow; cotton and wheat can be grown in this climate; the land is good pasturage for animals.
4. **coast lands:** The area along the Mediterranean coast and most of Turkey has a Mediterranean climate, with hot summers and rainy winters. Citrus fruits, olives, and vegetables can be grown year-round, if the land is irrigated in the summer; the region is heavily populated.

CHAPTER 21, SECTION 3

Part A. Build Vocabulary

1. crude oil
2. fossil water
3. desalination
4. refinery
5. drip irrigation

Part B. Cooperative Work

Oil in Southwest Asia

How were oil and natural gas deposits formed in Southwest Asia? They were formed millions of years ago, when an ancient sea covered the region; remains of microscopic sea plants became transformed by heat and pressure, eventually forming oil and natural gas.

How is oil removed from oil deposits? Engineers use sophisticated equipment to take oil out of microscopic pores in rocks.

When and where was oil discovered in Southwest Asia? 1908, Persia; 1938, Arabian Peninsula and the Persian Gulf; 1948, more oil fields in Saudi Arabia (Rub al-Khali).

Why is oil important? It is used to make gasoline, heating oil, fertilizers, and plastics.

How is oil transported from Southwest Asia? Oil is transported by pipelines to refineries or to ports, where tankers load the oil and transport it elsewhere for processing.

What are risks of transporting oil? Oil pipeline leaks or spills can cause pollution on land; oil spills from tankers cause pollution of both the water and the land where the oil washes ashore.

CHAPTER 22, SECTION 1

Part A. Build Vocabulary

1. Islam
2. monotheistic
3. mosque
4. theocratic

Part B. Cooperative Work

1. Who were the nomadic desert dwellers of the Arabian Peninsula, and what was their culture based on?	1. The Bedouin were livestock herders whose culture was based on strong family ties.
2. Describe the Five Pillars of Islam.	2. Faith: Belief in Allah as the only God and Muhammad as God's messenger. Prayer: Five times daily, wherever Muslims are at prayer time. Charity: To support people who are less fortunate. Fasting: During the holy month of Ramadan, fasting during the day is required. Pilgrimage: to Mecca at least once in a lifetime.
3. Describe the spread of Islam and tell when and how Islamic governments began to decline.	3. From 632, after the death of Muhammad, Islam spread throughout the Arabian Peninsula and to many lands in Asia, Africa, and Europe. Islamic governments began to decline in the 1600s, as European colonial powers grew stronger.
4. How did Saudi Arabia come to be established?	4. Abdul al-Aziz Ibn Saud consolidated power in the name of the Saud family and by the 1920s had control of much of the Arabian Peninsula.
5. What is OPEC and how does it help countries of Southwest Asia?	5. OPEC stands for the Organization of Oil Exporting Countries; its members set oil prices and production quotas, aiding the economies of member nations, including Saudi Arabia, Kuwait, Qatar, United Arab Emirates, Iran, and Iraq.
6. How has life changed in the Arabian Peninsula over the past 40 years and why?	6. It has become more urban and many Western technologies have been introduced.
7. Why are there many foreign workers in countries on the Arabian Peninsula?	7. The technology of producing and exporting oil requires educated workers; foreign workers with advanced education have taken these jobs because there are not enough people in the local areas to fill them.
8. What are two Islamic religious duties that shape life in the Arabian Peninsula?	8. Possible answers include: praying five times daily; so work and traffic may stop during prayer times; fasting during Ramadan and the festival at the end of Ramadan

CHAPTER 22, SECTION 2

Part A. Build Vocabulary

Possible categorizations include:

Places related to religion: Western Wall; Dome of the Rock

Political groups or movements: Zionism; Palestinian Liberation Organization

Terms related to Jewish culture: Western Wall; Zionism

Terms related to Arab/Muslim culture: Dome of the Rock; Palestinian Liberation Organization

Part B. Cooperative Work

Students should pick 8 of the following and locate them correctly on their time line.

1520–1922 The Eastern Mediterranean was ruled by the Ottoman Empire

1800s Jewish settlers started buying land and moving to Palestine (today called Israel)

1922 France took control of what is now Lebanon and Syria

1922 Britain gook control of what is now Israel and Jordan

1943 Lebanon became an independent nation

1946 Syria became an independent nation

1939 Britain closed immigration of Jews to Palestine

1947 UN developed a plan to divide Palestine into a Jewish state and an Arab state

1948 Jewish state of Israel established; Arab nations invaded Israel

1949 UN authorized the creation of 53 Palestinian refugee camps

1950s Nation of Israel became firmly established

1960 Cyprus became an independent nation

1960s Palestinian Liberation Organization was formed

1975–6 Civil war in Lebanon

1982 Israel invaded Lebanon

2000 Last Israeli troops left Lebanon

CHAPTER 22, SECTION 3

Part A. Build Vocabulary

1. c
2. a
3. d
4. e
5. b

Part B. Cooperative Work

1. Turks, Kurds, Persians, Assyrians; most do not speak Arabic, which is the dominant language of the rest of the region; their cultures reflect influences of the earlier civilizations (Babylonia, Assyrian, Hittite, Persian, and others)
2. The majority of all Muslims are Sunni; they predominate in Turkey, Iraq, and Afghanistan.
3. Shi'ites are the minority group of Islam; however, most of Iran is Shi'ite; there are also Shi'ite populations in Iraq and Afghanistan
4. This political group was in power in Afghanistan for a time; they imposed strict rules on people's behavior. For example, people had to wear certain types of clothing, had restricted access to television and radio, and women were not allowed to appear in certain public places; similar groups exist in Turkey, Iran, and Iraq, but have not gained strong political control.

5. a stateless nation; attacked with chemical weapons by Iraq in 1988; claim a homeland in parts of Turkey, Iran, and Iraq; after World War I, they were promised a homeland but never received it.
6. Iran has the largest refugee population of any nation in the world; people fleeing oppressive governments and war in Iraq (to the west) and in Afghanistan (to the east) have come here.
7. The British and the Russians clashed over control of Iran's oil fields in the early 1900s; Iran and Iraq went to war over control of oil fields in the 1980s; Iraq invaded Kuwait in 1990 to control Kuwaiti oil fields, leading to the Persian Gulf War.

CHAPTER 23, SECTION 1

Part A. Build Vocabulary

Following are glossary or dictionary definitions for the key terms:

guest worker: a largely unskilled laborer; guest workers come to wealthier countries to fill jobs that go unfilled by the people who live in that country

stateless nation: a nation of people without a land that they legally occupy

Part B. Cooperative Work

1. Oil boom leaves many jobs in oil-rich countries unfilled.
2. A large proportion of the country's population is made up of foreigners.
3. Misunderstandings occur between people of different cultures.
4. People of different countries may be subject to abuse by their employers and have no one to turn to.
5. The country's own workforce may be slow to develop because there are so many guest workers working there.
6. The country may suffer or be afraid it will suffer a weakened national identity or culture.
7. Kurds were promised a homeland after World War I, but it never was granted; this has led to conflict between Kurds and the governments of the countries where they live (Turkey, Syria, and Iraq); some countries have attacked them or forcibly removed the Kurds to relocation camps.
8. Some Kurds have fled to other countries, nearby or in Europe.
9. They live in crowded conditions.
10. The Palestinians were promised a homeland at the same time that the state of Israel was created; wars in the region caused them to flee or forced them to leave the region; many now live in refugee camps.
11. They live in crowded conditions.
12. What happens with the Palestinians is a source of not just local but also international concern and conflict.

CHAPTER 23, SECTION 2

Part A. Build Vocabulary

1. a. Both include agricultural or mining products that can be sold.
   b. Nations will go to war over them to ensure they have a steady supply.
2. a. Natural resources are materials from the earth that have economic value; human resources are talents that people have.
   b. Both natural resources and human resources have economic value.

Part B. Cooperative Work

1. Oil prices can rise and fall unpredictably; this makes economic planning difficult; when the price of oil is low, the economies grow only slowly.
2. Oil revenues allow countries to build new roads, irrigation networks, agricultural storage facilities, desalination plants, airports, shopping malls, port facilities, and technology systems.
3. Oil revenue can be used to help a nation become develop its land and water resources to become agriculturally self-sufficient. Oil revenue can be used to develop other mineral resources, reducing a country's dependence on money from oil.
4. Oil wealth can also be used to develop the skills and talents of the citizens of a nation through education and technology training. This helps the nation's economy expand.

CHAPTER 23, CASE STUDY

Part A. Build Vocabulary

1. international
2. annexed
3. cabinet

Part B. Cooperative Work

Sample answers:

Primary Source	Note Taking	Note Making
UN Resolution 181, adopted in 1947	Explains the UN plan for governing Jerusalem, to protect and preserve the city for people of all religions, to ensure peace, and to promote cooperation among the groups living in the region.	Seems like a beautiful plan; idealistic, yet sensible.
Official statement of the Palestinian cabinet, 2000	The Palestinian cabinet stated that they want Palestinian refugees who wish to to be able to return to lands their families held in Israel; this is supported by a UN resolution signed in 1948. The Palestinian cabinet also stated that they would not give up any control of the city of Jerusalem.	The Palestinians are taking a strong bargaining position; if they stick to this position, it doesn't leave much room for making peace.
Personal observation of Yossi Sarid, peace advocate and head of an Israeli political party	This Israeli politician said that if all Palestinians were allowed to return to Israel, there would no longer be an Israel, meaning a Jewish state.	This is a bind for Israelis. I wonder how many Palestinians Israel could absorb.
Editorial comment by Kenneth L. Woodward of Newsweek magazine	Jerusalem has an important symbolic and spiritual meaning to billions of people who do not live there.	I wonder what Woodward thinks is the best solution to the problem of who should control Jerusalem.
Political cartoon by Mark Fiore	The main point of the cartoon is that peace would be complete, if the conflict over Jerusalem could be solved; but both sides won't or can't put in the last piece.	I don't think this is really the last piece, given that the right of return is another difficult problem.

CHAPTER 24, SECTION 1

Part A. Build Vocabulary

1. c
2. a
3. d
4. b

Part B. Cooperative Work

When students have completed their map, they should have at least 12 landforms and bodies of water labeled correctly on it and the locations of at least 5 mineral resources. Refer to the map on p. 542 for the correct labeling of landforms and bodies of water and to the map on p. 554 for the correct labeling of mineral resources.

CHAPTER 24, SECTION 2

Part A. Build Vocabulary

	Type of		Occurs seasonally	Comes from the northeast from Oct. to Feb.	Comes from the southwest from June to Sept.	Always brings fierce winds	May or may not bring heavy rains
	wind	storm					
monsoon	+	-	+	+	+	-	+
cyclone	-	+	+	-	-	+	-

Part B. Cooperative Work

When students have completed their map, they should have all seven South Asian countries labeled and the six climate zones sketched roughly to resemble those on the Climate map on p. 557; they may also have labeled some of the landforms mentioned in the section, although this is not essential. Make sure students realize that their maps do not have to look exactly like the map on p. 557.

CHAPTER 24, SECTION 3

Part A. Build Vocabulary

Student drawings will vary, but might be quite literal. For **storm surge,** students might show a wall of water sweeping over a beach or an inhabited coast line; for **estuary,** they might show a maplike drawing of an area at the mouth of a river, which empties into an ocean, or they might show a marshlike river with different plants growing, sandy areas, and wide open water as a coast.

Part B. Cooperative Work

Ganges River	
Reasons Ganges is important	1. water for drinking and for irrigation 2. transportation route 3. spiritual significance for Hindus
Reasons Ganges is polluted	4. raw sewage 5. industrial wastes 6. dead bodies of animals and people
Plans/progress related to the Ganges	7. **Plans:** network of sewage treatment plants; laws against industrial pollution 8. **Progress:** slow; few plants built; anti-pollution laws not in place or enforced
Feni River	
Reasons the Feni floods	9. monsoons cause the river to overflow its banks 10. cyclones cause storm surges that flood low-lying areas
Floods effects on people living nearby	11. destroys fields and villages 12. can kill people and livestock
Description of dam projects	13. **Purpose:** to prevent flooding on the Feni River 14. **How built:** Using cheap materials, such as bamboo mats, boulders, and bags of clay; using thousands of workers, contributing manual labor 15. **Why built this way:** Bangladesh has many people available to work on the construction of the dam, but not much money for dam-building equipment 16. **Who helped:** Dutch engineers, who have much experience with flood control 17. **When completed:** around 1985 18. **Results:** largest estuary dam in South Asia; thus far, the dam has held against storm surges

CHAPTER 25, SECTION 1

Part A. Build Vocabulary

1. F; nonviolent resistance is a type of unarmed protest movement; no violence is employed.
2. T
3. F; the caste system is the Hindu system of social classes; it has nothing to do with iron-making or manufacturing.

Part B. Cooperative Work

1. Aryans: first invaders; established small kingdoms on the Ganges plain, pushing the original inhabitants called Dravidians, southward
2. Mauryan Empire: around 321 B.C.; united most of India; helped spread Buddhism throughout Asia
3. Gupta Empire: around A.D. 400; ruled northern India, promoting peace and prosperity
4. Mughal Empire: established around 1500; introduced Muslim practices into India; sometimes led to conflict with the Hindu majority of India
5. raj: period of direct British control; began in 1857 and lasted for 90 years
6. nonviolent resistance: form of peaceful protest used by the Indian opposition movement to British rule, led by Mohandas Gandhi, that eventually caused Britain to grant India independence, in 1947
7. democracy: India is the world's largest democracy; has a prime minister and a parliament; must accommodate Muslim, Sikh, Tamil, and other minorities
8. agriculture: two-thirds of all Indians make their livelihood by farming; most farms are small and crop yields are low; land reform might aid small farmers; use of irrigation, chemical fertilizers, and high-yield crops has helped farmers who own larger plots of land
9. industry: industry has modernized in western India; there, the metal, chemical, and electronic industries thrive; the city of Bangalore is India's high-tech center; other industries include iron, steel, machinery, and food products
10. education: literacy has been rising since the 1950s; but people in slums and rural areas have not made as strong gains as India needs to have an educated workforce
11. multiple languages: India's constitution recognizes 18 major language groups, but more than 1,000 languages and dialects are spoken in India; Hindi is the official language; English is also widely spoke; southern India has Dravidian rather than Indo-European languages
12. caste system: system of social classes that is a cornerstone of Hinduism; untouchables were officially eliminated as a caste in the Indian constitution; however, the caste system still can lead to discrimination and limit people's ability to improve their lives

Part A. Build Vocabulary

1. Entrepreneurs
2. microcredit
3. partition

Part B. Cooperative Work

1. a. Indus Valley civilization
1. b. Was established as East Pakistan in 1947; civil war in 1971 led to independence as the nation of Bangladesh
1. c. Ruled by Mauryan, Gupta, Mughal, and British emperors
2. a. Aridity causes agricultural difficulties; irrigation in the Indus Valle9 allows for export crops of rice an cotton; wool carpets and leather goods are exported.
2. b. One of the poorest countries in the world; seasonal monsoons and cyclones cause agricultural difficulties; jute is an important export crop; fishing is also important.
2. c. Dependent on agriculture; most farmers work small plots and struggle to grow enough food for their families; government has tried to help modernize farming methods without much success; rice is a principal crop; not highly industrialized; growing textile industries; cotton clothes are exported; microcredit has helped some small businesses
3. a. Stricter adherence to Islamic law; purdah (seclusion of women)
3. b. Less strict religiously
3. c. Islam helps unify the country; large, impressive mosques
4. a. 5 main ethnic groups, each with its own language and regional origins; Urdu is the national language
4. b. Most are Bengalis; speak Bengali; small population of Muslims who speak Urdu; 10% Hindus
5. a. Many memorize long poems; poetry readings draw thousands
5. b. Poet Rabindranath Tagore won Nobel Prize for lit in 1913; folk dances in which Bengali myths enacted
5. c. Life revolves around the family; arranged marriages and large families are common; most people live in simple homes in small villages; soccer, cricket, and movies are popular; poetry is very popular; music similar to that of India; folk music and quawwali

CHAPTER 25, SECTION 3

Part A. Build Vocabulary

Key Term	constitutional monarchy
Defining paragraph in textbook	1. Constitutional monarchies are kingdoms in which the ruler's powers are limited by a constitution.
Example	2. In Bhutan, the king is still the supreme ruler, while in Nepal, the king shares power with an elected parliament.
My questions or ideas about the word	3. Why is Bhutan considered a constitutional monarchy if the king is still the supreme ruler? What does it mean that the king is the supreme ruler? Does the king share power with any governing body in Bhutan?

Part B. Cooperative Work

1. a. Hindu kings used to rule small religious kingdoms until a hereditary monarch emerged
1. b. Controlled by China briefly in the 1700s; otherwise ruled by Buddhist priests, until a hereditary monarch emerged
1. c. Isolated by high mountain ranges; landlocked; government influenced by Britain in the 1800s
2. a. The king shares power with an elected parliament.
2. b. The king is still the supreme ruler.
2. c. constitutional monarchies
3. a. Forests are being cut down at a rate of 1% per year; tourism related to mountain-climbing; it has caused environmental damage.
3. b. Government has promoted growing fruit for export; tourism is restricted by the government to limit numbers and places that can be visited.
3. c. Poor countries with economies based on agriculture; limited land suitable for cultivation; terraced farming is practiced; products include rice, corn, potatoes, wheat; livestock include cattle, sheep, and yaks; timber important; problem with deforestation; industries include wood products, food processing, and cement; main trade is with India. Tourism is one of the fastest growing industries.
4. a. Hindu majority; Buddhism has deep roots there and has influenced Hindu religion in Nepal; main language is Nepali; Tibetan minorities, including the Sherpas
4. b. Buddhism is the official religion; Nepalese minority; fortress monasteries and shrines
4. c. Religion is very important in both countries.

CHAPTER 25, SECTION 4

Part A. Build Vocabulary

	Live on Sri Lanka	Came from India	Arrived around		Absorbed the ethnic groups already on the island	Practice Buddhism	Practice Hinduism
			300 B.C.	A.D. 300			
Sinhalese	+	+	+	-	+	+	-
Tamils	-	+	-	+	-	-	-

Part B. Cooperative Work

1. one large island very close to India
2. an archipelago of about 1,200 very small islands, stretching about 500 miles
3. Multi-ethnic: Sinhalese, Tamils, Muslims, and Christians
4. Multi-ethnic: Sinhalese, Dravidians, and Sinhalese or Dravidians who who mixed with Arab, Southeast Asian, and Chinese traders who came to the islands
5. Buddhist majority, with Hindu, Muslim, and Christian minorities
6. Islam is the state religion; no other religions are allowed.

7. agriculture, including rice farming; plantations that produce tea, rubber, and coconuts for export; some manufacturing; gem mining
8. fishing and tourism
9. Civil war threatens the economy and has damaged the nation's infrastructure.
10. Global warming could submerge the islands under rising seas.

CHAPTER 26, SECTION 1

Part A. Build Vocabulary

For *basic necessities,* students might draw items to represent food, clothing, and/or shelter, or show a person procuring such items to meet basic needs; for *illiteracy,* students might draw a person with an open book and a question mark; accept all other drawings that get the main concept of each word across clearly.

Part B. Cooperative Work

1. India will become the most populous nation in the world in forty years, if its population growth does not slow down. South Asia is home to 22% of the world's population, but has less than 3% of the world's land area.
2. A government campaign in India urges people to have smaller families, but this runs counter to general Indian culture.
3. Lack of sanitation and health education have caused people in South Asia to suffer from outbreaks of disease; South Asian nations find it difficult to provide enough food and housing for their people; the governments of populous South Asian nations do not have the resources to build enough schools and employ enough teachers to provide education for all the children born there.
4. Education can break the cycle of poverty and help improve the status of women, who gain the ability to have jobs outside the home; health education can reduce infant mortality rates and reduce the need for people to have large families to ensure some children will survive to adulthood.

CHAPTER 26, SECTION 2

Part A. Build Vocabulary

	Type of wind	Occurs from June to September	Occurs from October to February	Blows from the northeast	Blows from the southwest
summer monsoon	+	-	+	-	-
winter monsoon	+	-	-	-	+

Part B. Cooperative Work

1. can nourish the rain forests, irrigate crops, replenish the soil; cause land damage and death; destroy farmland and homes; cause drought
2. can cause crop failures and famine; can cause poverty; South Asian nations receive international aid in the form of loans, but this causes debt burden
3. Solving problems related to flood control and irrigation, such as building dams, can lead to political tensions between the different nations the rivers run through.

CHAPTER 26, CASE STUDY

Part A. Build Vocabulary

1. territorial
2. strategic
3. cede
4. deterrents

Part B. Cooperative Work

Main Idea or Summary of Primary Sources

Government Document from Pakistan, 1999: Pakistan wishes to have the dispute resolved peacefully and welcomes the mediation of other countries in the dispute; however, Pakistan supports the Kashmiris who are struggling against Indian rule (this is implied) and wants India to stop working against them.

Government Policy Declaration from India, 2000: India pledges that it will not be the first to use nuclear weapons in the Kashmiri dispute; India would like nuclear weapons abolished, if other nations with nuclear weapons would give them up.

Speech by a Kashmiri politician, 1999: The dispute over Kashmir has caused the physical destruction of Kashmir's infrastructure and educational system; the politician hopes peace will ultimately come to Kashmir and that Kashmir can serve as a bridge between India and Pakistan.

Personal story of a Kashmiri native: Describes the fear people in Kashmir live under because of the shelling (bombs) and destruction of cities that once were thriving and drew tourists; he explains that educational system and the health care system are no longer functioning.

Political cartoon from a U.S. newspaper: Shows both Indian and Pakistani poor people struggling under the weight of nuclear weapons, meaning that these weapons are expensive and have increased the suffering of many people in both countries.

CHAPTER 27, SECTION 1

Part A. Build Vocabulary

When students have completed their map, all five the places listed will be correctly labeled on the map. Refer to the map on p. 620 for the locations of the mountain ranges and river systems.

Part B. Cooperative Work

Important Landforms and Bodies of Water in East Asia				
mountain ranges	**Plateaus and Plains**	**Peninsulas**	**Islands**	**River Systems**
Kunlun (western China)	Plateau of Tibet (China)	Shandong Peninsula (east coast of China)	Hainan (China)	Huang He (central China)
Quinling Shandi (southeastern and east central China)	Tarim Pendi Basin (western China)	Leizhou Peninsula (east coast of China)	Hong Kong (China)	Chang Jiang (central China)
Altai (Mongolia)	Mongolian Plateau (Mongolia)	Macao Peninsula (east coast of China)	Japan (island nation)	Xi Jiang (southern China)
Himalayas (China)	Manchurian Plain (northeastern China)	Korean Peninsula (North and South Korea)	Taiwan (island nation disputed by China)	Yula Jiang (Korean border)
Tian Shan (China)	North China Plain (north central China)			Tarin He (western China)

Important Resources				
Land	**Forests**	**Minerals**	**Energy Resources**	**Water**
Land in the river valleys of eastern China is highly productive for farming	abundant in China, Korea, Japan, and Taiwan	China has iron ore, tungsten, manganese and others; Korea has gold, silver, and tungsten; Japan has lead and silver	China has petroleum, coal, and natural gas; Korea and Japan have coal	China's rivers provide irrigation, electric power, transportation; China, Japan, and the other island nations have developed fishing industries

CHAPTER 27, SECTION 2

Part A. Build Vocabulary

1. They are all severe tropical storms.
2. **a.** the Atlantic Ocean
   b. the Indian Ocean

Part B. Cooperative Work

When students have completed their map, they should have all six East Asian countries labeled and the seven climate zones sketched roughly to resemble those on the Climate map on p. 61; they may also have labeled some of the landforms mentioned in the section, although this is not essential. Make sure students realize that their maps do not have to look exactly like the map on p. 61 or the map on p. 626.

CHAPTER 27, SECTION 3

Part A. Build Vocabulary

Student sentences will vary, but should show clear understanding of the meaning of the term.

Sentences related to the word PCBs should indicate that PCBs are dangerous pollutants that have caused health problems in Japan's polluted cities.

Sentences related to the word *landfill* should indicate that landfills are places where garbage is disposed of and that they can be used to create new land.

Part B. Cooperative Work

China's Three Gorges Dam	
Benefits	**Costs**
1. flood control, preventing land damage and loss of life	4. One to two million people will have to move, because their current homes will be flooded by the reservoir.
2. generation of more electric power for China, and increase in reliability of the power system	5. Project has cost much more than expected
3. increased navigation up the rivers at decreased cost	6. **a.** reduced habitat for many animals **b.** water pollution from submerged cities and factories **c.** climate changes may contribute to the extinction of some species

Japan's Cities	
Space-related Problem	**Solutions**
7. Because of the barrier of mountain ranges, large cities have no more space to expand.	8. Houses are small; people live in less space than Americans tend to. 9. Many people live in apartments. 10. Make new land by using landfill to fill in low areas for use by industries and ports.

CHAPTER 28, SECTION 1

Part A. Build Vocabulary

	Began around 500 B.C.	Started in China	Based on the teachings of			Encourages respect for past and for orderly society	Stresses education
			Confucius	**Lao-Tzu**	**Buddha**		
Confucianism	+	+	+	-	-	+	+
Taoism	+	+	-	+	-	-	-
Buddhism	-	-	-	-	+	-	-

Part B. Cooperative Work

Students should pick 10 of the following and locate them correctly on their time line.

1700 B.C. Shang Dynasty arose

1100 B.C. Zhou Dynasty arose

551 B.C. Confucius was born

500 B.C. Taoism developed by Lao-tzu

479 B.C. Confucius died

356 B.C. The first section of the Great Wall was built

221 B.C. Qin Dynasty arose

220 B.C. Emperor Shi Huangdi started the project of building the Great Wall

300 Buddhism was introduced to China

1300 European Marco Polo visited China

1368 Mongol Dynasty was overthrown

1368–1644 Ming Dynasty

1557 Portuguese established a colony on Macao Peninsula

1627 Manchu armies overrun northern Korea

1644 Manchus invaded China and began the Qing Dynasty

1661 Chinese emperor Shunzhi, who came to the throne as a child, died of smallpox

1839 War broke out between Britain and China

1900 Boxer Rebellion occurred when the Chinese tried to throw out Europeans who controlled their country through spheres of influence; the Boxers were defeated

1911 China's last dynasty fell

1912 Chinese republic established by Sun Yat-sen; civil war raged throughout China

1925 Sun Yat-sen died; leadership of the Nationalist Party went to general Chiang Kai-shek

1920s/30s Power of the Communist Party grew in China

1949 The Communists, under Mao Zedong, gained control of the government of China

1950 Chinese government started providing health care for all citizens

1976 Mao Zedong died; Deng Xiaoping became China's leader

1979 China developed the one-child policy to control population growth

1980s China's government exerted less influence in the economy; China's economy became one of the fastest growing in the world

1989 Chinese troops fired on student demonstrations in Tiananmen Square in Beijing

1993 Jiang Zemin became China's leader

2000 1.3 billion people lived in China

CHAPTER 28, SECTION 2

Part A. Build Vocabulary

Student drawings will vary. For **economic tiger,** students might show a snarling beast with dollar signs around it or on it; for **Pacific Rim,** students might show a map-like drawing of countries bordering the Pacific, with the coastal areas or countries labeled "Pacific Rim." Accept other answers that indicate students understand the meaning of each term.

Part B. Cooperative Work

Possible answers:

	Mongolia	**Taiwan**
History, related to China	During the Mongolian Empire, the Mongols ruled China; China gained control of Mongolia from the 1600s to 1911, when the country became independent.	Throughout history many different groups of Chinese settled on Taiwan. The Chinese Nationalists took control of Taiwan after World War II and have remained in control of the island, with an independent government, the Republic of China. Mainland China claims the island as part of its territory.
Culture	The centuries-long rule by the Chinese had a great influence on Mongolian culture; but Mongolia has its own culture based on herding, horsemanship, and warrior skills.	The culture is Chinese because most people who live there are Chinese. People follow a blend of Buddhism, Confucianism, and Taoism and speak Mandarin.
Economy	Based on nomadic herding; cashmere goat-raising a main export industry; Mongolia has large deposits of coal, oil, copper, gold and iron.	Taiwan has a very successful economy based on trade. It has a highly trained and motivated workforce; it manufactures advanced electronic equipment; other important industries are machinery, steel, textiles, plastics, and chemicals.
Daily Life	Related to herding; homes might be yurts; some people keep their animals on large ranches that might have towns at the center of them; few Western influences.	Many Western influences, including baseball.

CHAPTER 28, SECTION 3

Part A. Build Vocabulary

When students have completed Part A correctly, North Korea will be labeled correctly and the capital, Pyongyang will be labeled; South Korea will be labeled correctly and the capital, Seoul will be labeled.

Part B. Cooperative Work

Possible answers:

1. the Soviet Union
2. the United States
3. Confucianism, Buddhism
4. Confucianism, Buddhism
5. Communism from China and the Soviet Union
6. Western culture
7. huge army
8. huge army
9. industry has gained in importance, including the development of natural resources and raw materials
10. industry has gained in importance; South Korea has the world's largest shipbuilding industry and large auto, steel, and chemical industries
11. Most people live on the plains along the coasts, in river valleys.
12. Most people live on the plains along the coasts, in river valleys; South Korea is more densely populated than North Korea.

Part A. Build Vocabulary

1. the shogun
2. a samurai

Part B. Cooperative Work

Possible answers:

1. Between 400 and about 1900, which two different types of rulers headed the government, each at different times?	1. emperors and shoguns
2. When did Japan become a major military power?	2. in the early 1900s
3. a. When did Japan become a very strong economic power? b. What activities are at the heart of Japan's economy?	3. a. after World War II b. manufacturing and trade
4. a. Which culture had a big influence on Japan? b. How does this influence show?	4. a. China b. in the language, religion, art, music, and government of Japan
5. What does Kyoto show about Japanese culture?	5. It shows Japanese respect for traditions and their ideas of beauty, which relate to how buildings harmonize with their natural surroundings.
6. What influences have Western nations had on Japanese culture?	6. Western culture has influenced the sports, clothing, and music of Japan.
7. What is Japanese education like?	7. It is highly structured and more intense than education in the U.S. Students go to school 6 days a week and get only 6 weeks off in the summer; the good colleges are extremely difficult to get in to.
8. How is Japanese society beginning to change?	8. People are asking for shorter workdays and more vacation; they are demanding less pollution and crowding.

CHAPTER 29, SECTION 1

Part A. Build Vocabulary

Tsunami

What: A tsunami is a huge wave of great destructive power

Why or How: Develops as a result of an underwater disturbance, such as an earthquake, a volcanic eruption, or a coastal landslide

When: Develops right after the underwater disturbance

Where (also see p. 40): Can travel quickly and come to shore hundreds of miles from the site of the underwater disturbance

Part B. Cooperative Work

Cause	Effects (in Japan)	Solutions to resulting problems
The Pacific oceanic plate is colliding with the Eurasian continental plate; stress builds up at plate boundaries.	1. earthquakes (1,000 per year) 2. volcanoes (60 active) 3. tsunamis	4. strict building codes to help prevent damage and death 5. studies of earthquake damage to improve building codes to better prevent damage 6. disaster preparedness education for children and adults

CHAPTER 29, SECTION 2

Part A. Build Vocabulary

1. c
2. b
3. a
4. e
5. d

Part B. Cooperative Work

1. European threats, use of violence, and treaties to create spheres of influence—areas where they could control trade without interference from other Western nations—in East Asia; Commodore Perry's display of power toward Japan
2. Through mismanagement, a series of East Asian banks and other companies went bankrupt, sparking panic among foreign investors, who began selling their Asian stocks and currencies.
3. The World Bank and the International Monetary fund lent money to East Asian companies that promised to make reforms in the ways they did business.
4. The economic crisis led to an awareness that serious reform in how workers were treated was necessary in East Asia.

CHAPTER 29, CASE STUDY

Part A. Build Vocabulary

1. fertility rate
2. family planning
3. sanitation
4. life expectancy

Part B. Cooperative Work

Sample answers:

Primary Source	Note Taking	Note Making
Bar graph on projected population growth	This bar graph shows that Asia's population rate is expected to soar above 5 billion by the year 2050; Africa's population, however, is growing at the fastest rate.	It looks like Europe's population is in decline; and Asia's population must include all of the regions, not just East Asia.
Policy statement by President Clinton, 1998	Clinton thinks China should take strong measures to control and prevent air pollution and water pollution; he notes that there is so much air pollution over some Chinese cities that they do not show up in satellite photos.	Even though our population isn't growing as fast as Asia's, we too, need to reduce air pollution.
News analysis from online source about Asia	Stresses that inadequate supplies of clean water will cause catastrophe in Asia if people do not prevent pollution as well as conserve water.	I wonder if China has any planning policy for water use as it has had for population growth.
Fact sheet from an organization that advocates family planning in East Asia, 1997	Indicates that by having smaller families, East Asians have been able to save more money and that government expenditures went down, as well. Indicates that an enterprising business sector, wise public investment, and a good education system were also important.	I wonder what families have done with their savings that improves their lives and the lives of their children.

CHAPTER 30, SECTION 1

Part A. Build Vocabulary

1. It formed from an active volcano that spews lava, making the island become larger or taller.
2. It formed over long periods of time from coral reefs building up under the water; the high part of the island eroded over the length of time it takes for the corals to build up.
3. Yes. A chain of islands could form from coral reefs forming around underwater mountains.
4. Yes. A chain of islands could form from a chain of volcanoes near one another.

Part B. Cooperative Work

When students have completed their map, they should have at least 18 countries, landforms, and islands labeled correctly on it. Refer to the maps on pp. 678–679 and p. 689 for the correct labeling of these items.

CHAPTER 30, SECTION 2

Part A. Build Vocabulary

Following is the glossary definition for the key term:

outback: sparsely populated and inland region of Australia

Part B. Cooperative Work

Location	Climate	Vegetation
Coastal Myanmar, Thailand, Vietnam, Oceania, and most of Malaysia, Indonesia, and the Philippines	Tropical wet climate with high temperatures and rainfall year-round; temperatures drop with elevation.	Tropical evergreen forests; Oceania generally has fewer plants because of poor soil.
The more northern and inland parts of Myanmar, Thailand, Laos, Cambodia, Vietnam, Oceania, and northern Australia	Tropical wet and dry climate shaped by monsoons; high temperatures; great variation in rainfall; precipitation can vary with relative location to mountains.	Deciduous forests with a wide variety of plants; Oceania generally has fewer plants and less variety because of poor soil.
The northern part of Australia's east coast and the northernmost parts of Vietnam, Laos, Thailand, and Myanmar	Humid subtropical with hot summers, mild winters, and heavy rainfall	Australia has trees more than 300 feet tall.
New Zealand and the southern part of Australia's east coast	Marine west coast climate with mild temperatures year-round; mountains can influence temperature and rainfall	Evergreen trees and tree ferns; trees 300 feet tall in Australia
Central Australia	Desert, with less than 10 inches of rain per year, or semiarid, with less than 20 inches of rain per year; hot year-round	Desert; crops can be grown in semiarid areas with irrigation.
Antarctica	Icecap climate with very cold temperatures and very little precipitation	Lichens and mosses

CHAPTER 30, SECTION 3

Part A. Build Vocabulary

	Type of boat	Used close to shore	Used for traveling on the open sea	Has two hulls	Has sails	Could have a cabin	Has a frame with an attached float to one side
voyaging canoe	+	-	+	+	+	+	-
outrigger canoe	+	+	-	-	-	-	+

Part B. Cooperative Work

Person or People	How they interacted with the environment	Effects on the environment	Effects on people
Ancient Pacific Islanders	Traveled long distances on the Pacific Ocean to settle on uninhabited islands	Pacific Islanders brought nonnative plants to the different Pacific islands they settled on.	Pacific Islanders were able to expand their territory and improve their sailing and navigational skills
Australian Thomas Austin	Released 24 rabbits in Australia in 1859s	By 1900, rabbits had wiped out native plants, destroyed crops, and ruined pastures, causing erosion, economic decline, and decline of native animals.	Economic decline of farming and ranching
U.S. government officials	Tested more than 60 atomic weapons in the Bikini Atoll in the Pacific	Several islands vaporized; the area became contaminated with high levels of radiation	Bikini islanders were displaced from their homes several times; when they returned, they got sick from radiation and had to move again.

CHAPTER 31, SECTION 1

Part A. Build Vocabulary

Student drawings will vary. For the Buddhist **mandala,** students might make some kind of abstract drawing with geometric shapes, or they might show a person meditating with such a drawing in the background; for the political **mandala,** students might draw a map of Southeast Asia that shows overlapping kingdoms labeled mandalas. Accept other drawings that indicate students know the meaning of each term.

Part B. Cooperative Work

1. Five powerful states became established in what are now Myanmar, Vietnam, Thailand, Java, and the Malay Peninsula; people in these groups began to form their national identities and some important cities were established.
2. Cambodia, Myanmar, Laos, and Vietnam base their economy mainly on agriculture, especially rice; Brunei, Indonesia, Malaysia, the Philippines, Singapore, and Thailand have more industry and finance.
3. Buddhism is widespread in the region; the Philippines is mostly Catholic; Indonesia and Brunei are mostly Muslim; Hinduism and regional traditional beliefs are also practiced.
4. Buddhist and Hindu sculpture and architecture; performing arts, literature, Thai and Indonesian traditional dance; poetry in Vietnam
5. Many have wooden houses built on stilts with thatch or metal roofs; in Laos, Myanmar, and Thailand most villages have a Buddhist temple that is the center of social life; in Indonesia, most villages have a group of leaders who govern together.

6. Kuala Lumpur, Malaysia, and Singapore are bustling cities with skyscrapers; in most Southeast Asian cities, most people live in apartment buildings; there are housing shortages and dangerous, unstable shantytowns.

CHAPTER 31, SECTION 2

Part A. Build Vocabulary

1. subsistence activities
2. Hunter-gatherers
3. taro
4. missionaries
5. shantytowns

Part B. Cooperative Work

History of Oceania	
How Oceania came to be settled in prehistoric times	People used small rafts, canoes, and land bridges to travel from Southeast Asia to islands near the coasts; over time, they developed voyaging canoes that allowed them to sail longer distances across the open ocean to islands farther away.
Contact with peoples from Europe, 1500s	European explorers visited many Pacific Islands
Contact with peoples from Europe, 1800s and 1900s	Christian missionaries from Europe came to try to convert Pacific Islanders; traders and whalers came; some Europeans settled on the island to start plantations for growing coconuts, coffee, pineapples, and sugar. They brought diseases that killed many Pacific Islanders; they took control of the islands, turning them into territories or possessions.
Recent history	Fighting on many of the islands during World War II; after WWII, some islands were used for nuclear testing, leading to radioactive contamination. Since 1962, 12 nations have gained independence and are now self-governing.

CHAPTER 31, SECTION 3

Part A. Build Vocabulary

	Native to Australia	Native to New Zealand	Lived in their homeland for more than 40,000 years	Originally came from mainland Asia	Originally came from Polynesia	Originally lived solely by hunting and gathering	Originally lived by farming as well as fishing and hunting
Aboriginal people	+	-	+	+	-	+	-
outrigger canoe	-	+	-	-	+	-	+

Part B. Cooperative Work

1. Aboriginal people
2. Maori
3. colonized by Britain as a penal colony
4. colonized by hunters and whalers from Europe, America, and Australia; became a British colony in 1840
5. Aboriginal people have made claims for their former lands; movement to leave the British Commonwealth

6. the first country to grant women the right to vote; one of the first countries to provide old-age pensions for citizens; the Maoris have made claims for their former lands

7. major exporter of farm products; sheep ranching; mining; few industries—food processing is the largest

8. major exporter of farm products; world's largest exporter of kiwi fruit; ranching; logging; few industries—food processing is the largest; also paper products

9. most people of British descent; high rates of immigration; one percent of people are Aboriginals

10. most people of European, mainly British, descent; Maori make up 15% of population

11. About 85% of the population lives in cities; cities tend to be crowded and have pollution

12. About 85% of the population lives in cities; cities are smaller, quiet, and uncrowded

CHAPTER 32, SECTION 1

Part A. Build Vocabulary

1. Sentences should indicate that Aboriginal people wanted to be able to live on or use the land that they had lived on for thousands of years, before Europeans arrived.

2. Sentences should indicate that a lawsuit can clarify what rights a government grants people or groups in certain situations.

3. Sentences should explain students' own viewpoints on assimilation.

Part B. Cooperative Work

Year	Event related to the law or government action	Effect on Aboriginal peoples
1788	British declared Australia Terra Nullius	Aboriginal people had no rights to the land, based on British law
1909–1969	Australian government took 100,000 mixed race children and had them raised in white families to force assimilation.	Aboriginals feel great loss, call the children the Stolen Generation; they are fighting assimilation by determinedly passing their culture to their children and increasing their efforts to regain their land.
1967	Aboriginal peoples recognized as full citizens	They gained special Aboriginal rights.
1972	Australian government denied claim of some Aboriginal people trying to regain ancestral land.	Aboriginal protesters set up the Aboriginal Tent Embassy to publicize their plight of having no permanent right to the land they claimed.
1976	Land Rights Act passed	Aboriginal peoples gained the right to claim land in the Northern Territory, including the reserves they lived on and other land.
1985	The Australian government granted ownership of Uluru to the Anangu people (an Aboriginal group)	The Anangu let the outcropping be part of a national park.
1992	Court decision in the Mabo Case overturned the doctrine of Terra Nullius.	Aboriginals granted title to land that they had worked for generations.
1996	Court decision in the Wik Case indicated and Aboriginal people can claim land held under pastoral lease (rent by farmers or ranchers); amendment to the Wik Case wiped out many Aboriginal land claims	Issue unresolved; additional lawsuits possible

CHAPTER 32, SECTION 2

Part A. Build Vocabulary

1. F; factories are often located in or near cities, because of good transportation networks and a large workforce. For this reason, industrialization often goes along with increased urbanization—cities gaining population and growing in size.

2. T

Part B. Cooperative Work

1. the growth of industry

2. loss of important resources, such as loss of soil due to erosion, loss of lumber due to deforestation, shortage of water due to overuse

3. scarcity of land

4. population growth, causing land shortages to worsen

5. opportunity to find factory jobs

6. access to other services, such as education or government benefits

7. increased pollution

8. increased traffic

9. problems with sanitation

10. an increase in trade and exports

11. higher incomes for some citizens

12. growth of the middle class

13. depletion of resources, such as water and trees

CHAPTER 32, CASE STUDY

Part A. Build Vocabulary

1. fossil fuels

2. emissions

3. global warming

4. ozone

5. ultraviolet rays

Part B. Cooperative Work

Main Idea or Summary of Primary Sources

Educational pamphlet from the UN: Explains how we are changing the balance of gases in the atmosphere, thickening the layer of greenhouse gases. This will likely cause global warming, an increase in average temperatures of 1.5 to 4.5°C over the next 100 years.

Political commentary from the American Policy Center: This commentary denies that global warming is occurring and denies that there is any evidence for it and that any scientists think it is occurring. It says that U.S. government temperature measurements from satellites and (weather) balloons indicate that the temperature is actually cooling slightly. The writer cites temperature readings taken during three scattered years (between 1936 and 1997) for the Midwest related to number of days above 90 degrees.

Graph of data from the National Climate Data Center: The graph uses a line to indicate the average surface temperature of the earth from 1880 to 2000; bars above and below the line indicate whether the surface temperature was above or below average for a particular year. These data indicate that between 1880 and 1940, the surface temperature for most years was below the average; from 1940 to 2000, the surface temperature for most years was above the average. This graph seems to indicate that in the 1900s, the earth was experiencing a general warming trend of at least 0.5°F.

New York Times science article about the ozone hole: The article reports an increase in the size of the ozone hole; the writer reports that some scientists think the increase in size of the ozone layer may relate to global warming. (The chemical reactions that break down ozone take place more rapidly under warmer conditions.) Others think the increased size could relate to natural variations in Antarctic weather.

Satellite images showing the ozone layer over Antarctica: Shows changes in ozone concentration over Antarctica from 1980–1988; during this time the region of low concentration of ozone grew, while the region of high concentration got smaller.